John Milton: Introductions

THE CAMBRIDGE MILTON FOR
SCHOOLS AND COLLEGES

GENERAL EDITOR: J. B. BROADBENT

Frontispiece Detail of the 'Onslow' portrait of Milton aged 21, by an unknown artist. From the National Portrait Gallery, London.

John Milton:
Introductions

ROY DANIELLS
JOHN DIXON HUNT
WINIFRED MAYNARD
W. REAVLEY GAIR

ISABEL RIVERS
LORNA SAGE
ELIZABETH SEWELL SIRIGNANO
J. B. TRAPP

Edited by
JOHN BROADBENT
University of East Anglia, Norwich

Then Milton fell through Albion's heart, travelling outside of
humanity
Beyond the stars in chaos, in caverns of the mundane shell...
Then they lamented that they had in wrath & fury & fire
Driven Milton into the Ulro; for now they knew too late
That it was Milton the Awakener
WILLIAM BLAKE *Milton* 1804–8

Cambridge at the University Press 1973

52842

Published by the Syndics of the Cambridge University Press
Bentley House, 200 Euston Road, London NWI 2DB
American Branch: 32 East 57th Street, New York, N.Y. 10022

© Cambridge University Press 1973

Library of Congress Catalogue Card Number: 72–93144

ISBNS: 0 521 20172 1 hard covers
0 521 09799 1 paperback

Printed in Great Britain
at the University Printing House, Cambridge
(Brooke Crutchley, University Printer)

Contents

The items between chapters indicate excerpts for
private consideration (see Foreword, p. 2).

Editor's Foreword *p.* 1

Philip Wheelwright *The burning fountain*

ELIZABETH SEWELL SIRIGNANO
To be a true poem p. 4

Kierkegaard on the religious poet

ISABEL RIVERS
Milton's life and times: aids to study p. 21

Note on biographical material – Chronology – Milton's friends, and the
chief persons named in his works – England in the early 17th century –
Milton as a student *c.* 1620–37 – Milton's travels 1638–9 – Milton as a
teacher: early 1640s and after – Milton's marriages and attitudes to
divorce – The civil war: a summary of the issues 1640–9 – Milton and
church reform 1641–4, 1659 – Milton as a public servant 1649–60 –
Milton at the Restoration 1660–74 – Milton's character, appearance
and blindness – Milton's religious opinions – Milton's reputation in his
lifetime

Peter Laslett *The world we have lost*
Jeremy Taylor *XX sermons*
John Donne *Epithalamion*
William Austin *Haec homo*
William Habington *Dialogue between Araphil and Castara*
John Donne *The anniversary*

Robert Filmer *Patriarcha*
Norman O. Brown *Love's body*
Charles I *Eikon basilike*
Edmund Waller *A panegyric to the Lord Protector* and *To the king upon His Majesty's happy return*
Milton *Second defence* and *Of reformation*
Ben Jonson *Bartholomew Fair*
John Donne *Satire III*
George Herbert *The British Church* and *To all angels and saints*
Matthew Stevenson *Occasion's offspring*
Anon *Beauty in worship*

Carlo Dati on Milton

Milton's education – Poetic theory – The problem of the poet's role – The question of style: metaphysical poetry – Religious poetry: the baroque tradition – The problem of religious style – Religious poetry: the didactic tradition – Poetic developments in the Interregnum and Restoration – The development of Milton – Suggestions for further reading

An interdisciplinary topic: Carew

Family – Imagery and language – Friendship – Love – Marriage – Repairs – Middle age – Conclusion

The Richardsons, father and son, on Milton

Changes in knowledge – Scholasticism and empiricism: Milton and Bacon – Hobbes and materialism – Browne: science and faith – Elements and humours – Body and soul – Melancholy – Astronomy – The cosmos – Providence and astrology – Alchemy – Technology – Scientific education – Science and morality – Further reading

Samuel Butler *The elephant in the moon*

earth – Milton and Henry Lawes – Some later settings of Milton –
Further reading

LORNA SAGE

Milton's early poems: a general introduction p. 258

An adjustment of perspective – Idealism – Community – Allegory –
Lycidas – Resources for further study

LORNA SAGE

Milton in literary history p. 298

The late 17th century: Milton without a role – The early 18th century:
epic mock epic – Mid to late 18th century: pastiche and pastoral – The
19th century: 1 The romantic rewriting of *PL* – 2 The emergence of
the Victorian Milton – Milton now

Illustrations

The cover shows a photograph of *Dream anvil* (1953–8) by Eduardo Chillida. Bronze on wooden base. Height 20 inches. Collection Bo Bonstedt, Kungälv, Sweden. By permission of Thames and Hudson Ltd.

Detail of the 'Onslow' portrait of Milton aged 21, by an unknown artist. From the National Portrait Gallery, London *frontispiece*

xi

The contributors

JOHN BROADBENT MA (Edinburgh) PHD (Cambridge) professor of English, University of East Anglia, Norwich. Brought up partly in an extreme dissenting environment, partly otherwise. Research at St Catharine's College, Cambridge; senior tutor of King's College. *Some graver subject: an essay on PL*; *Milton: Comus and Samson* (Studies in Literature); *Poetic love*; programmes on art history for BBC Schools TV in the 1960s; ed. Smart's *Song to David* and now editing a two-volume anthology of 17th-century poetry.

ROY DANIELLS Companion of the Order of Canada PHD LLD (Toronto) professor of English, University of British Columbia, Vancouver. Born in London, taken to British Columbia as a child, brought up among Plymouth Brethren (hence interest in Milton), worked as bank clerk and farmhand, then academic career, teaching at various other Canadian universities. *Milton, Mannerism and Baroque*; *Alexander Mackenzie and the North West*; co-editor of *Literary history of Canada*, writing a book on Mannerism.

JOHN DIXON HUNT MA (Cambridge) PHD (Bristol) lecturer in English, University of York. Bristol Grammar School and King's College, Cambridge. Taught for three years in the United States. Author of *The Pre-Raphaelite imagination* and a commentary on *The tempest*; editor of *Encounters: essays on literature and the visual arts* and 'casebooks' on *The rape of the lock* and *In memoriam*. At present studying relationships between literature and garden design.

WINIFRED MAYNARD BA DIPED (Durham) BLITT (Oxford) senior lecturer in English, University of Edinburgh. Whitley Bay Grammar School, Northumberland, then Durham and St Hilda's College, Oxford, where she studied English song; now writing on relations between English lyric poetry and music. Musician, and regular visitor to Greek islands.

WILLIAM REAVLEY GAIR PHD (Cambridge) associate professor of English, University of New Brunswick, Fredericton, Canada. Tynemouth School, national service in Royal Navy, Cambridge. Farms Christmas trees on 150 acres. A-level edition of Marston's *Antonio's revenge*, now working on Elizabethan clubs.

ISABEL RIVERS MA (Cambridge) PHD (Columbia) research fellow of Girton College, Cambridge. Co-director with her husband of the Rivers Press. Spent a year teaching at East Anglia. Author of *The poetry of conservatism 1600–1745*.

LORNA SAGE BA (Durham) MA (Birmingham) lecturer in English, University of East Anglia. Husband also lecturer in English. Writing a book on Platonism; has recorded a critical conversation about Milton with the editor for Sussex Tapes.

ELIZABETH SEWELL SIRIGNANO PHD (Cambridge) professor of English, Hunter College of the City University of New York. Took her BA and research degree at Cambridge in modern languages, then from about 1949 spent part of her time teaching in a wide variety of institutions in the United States, and writing in England. More recently, has taught in colleges for black students in the South, and been active in experimental education in America at various levels. Now a permanent resident in the United States. Her books include fiction, volumes of poetry, *The field of nonsense* on Edward Lear and Lewis Carroll, *Paul Valéry, the mind in the mirror* and *The Orphic voice: poetry and natural history*.

J. B. TRAPP MA (New Zealand) Librarian of the Warburg Institute, University of London. Born in 1925 and educated in New Zealand; has taught at Wellington, Toronto, Reading and London; at the Warburg since 1953.

Acknowledgements

We are grateful to the following for permission to reproduce illustrations: the National Portrait Gallery for frontispiece; Private Collection, U.S.A., for 1; the Trustees of the British Museum for 3, 4, 7, 15, 16 and 17; the British and Foreign Bible Society for 5 and 6; the Mansell Collection for 8 and 12; Bibliothèque des Arts Décoratifs for 9; Fratelli Alinari for 11; Service de Documentation Photographique de la Réunion des Musées Nationaux for 13; the Trustees of the Wallace Collection for 14; the Tate Gallery for 18 and 19; the Walker Gallery, Liverpool, for 20: Thames and Hudson Ltd. for 21.

Extracts reprinted from *Collected Shorter Poems 1927–1957* by W. H. Auden, copyright 1945 by W. H Auden, quoted by permission of Faber and Faber Ltd., and Random House Inc.; and from *The Collected Poems of Wallace Stevens* by Wallace Stevens, copyright 1936 by Wallace Stevens, renewed 1964 by Elsie Stevens and Holly Stevens, quoted by permission of Faber and Faber Ltd. and Alfred A. Knopf Inc.

Foreword

To grammarians and critics, who are principally occupied in editing the works of others, or in correcting the errors of copyists, we willingly concede the palm of industry and erudition; but we never bestow on them the surname of great. He alone is worthy of that appellation who either does great things, or teaches how they may be done, or describes them with a suitable majesty when they have been done; but those only are great things which tend to render life more happy, which increase the innocent enjoyments and comforts of existence, or which pave the way to a state of future bliss more permanent and more pure.

Second defence of the English people

This volume is part of the Cambridge Milton series. The series supersedes A. W. Verity's Pitt Press edition of Milton's poetry published from Cambridge 1891 *et seq.* It is designed for use by the individual student, and the class and the teacher in schools and colleges, from about the beginning of the sixth form to the end of the BA course in England. This volume can be used independently but we assume that you refer as appropriate to others in the series, especially:

Paradise lost: introduction J. B. Broadbent. General introduction to the poem as a whole with chapters on myth and ritual; epic; history of publication; ideology; structures; allusion; language; and other stylistic features. Also contains a list of resources (books, art, music, speech etc.) designed for the launching of projects; and a chronology of the Bible, biblical writings, epic, and other versions of Miltonic material.

Comus, pastorals, early religious poems An editorial team. This will print, with annotation and individual introductions, most of the poems that Lorna Sage deals with in her general introduction to the early poems in *John Milton: introductions*, as well as much of the material referred to in other chapters here, especially Winifred

I

Maynard's on music, and Isabel Rivers's on Milton's life and development as a poet.

Those and the other volumes also contain a general preface on the aims of the series, and ways of reading Milton.

The best rivals to this book are:

LOIS POTTER *A preface to Milton* (Longmans preface books, an excellent series, 1971) with many illustrations; particularly good on geography and other concrete details; includes critical analyses of some poems and excerpts.

J. H. HANFORD and J. G. TAAFE *A Milton handbook* 5th revised ed 1969; largely concerned with backgrounds to, and contents of, the poems.

C. V. WEDGWOOD *Milton and his world* 1969 with many illustrations; concentrates on biography and history.

For other suggestions see the footnotes and reading lists provided with each chapter here and in other volumes of the series. In the reading lists in this volume, the place of publication is London or New York, unless otherwise stated.

Of course another volume could be put together introducing other aspects of Milton. I should like to see essays on him by a linguistician and a semiologist; his treatment of mythology needs to be reconsidered, by an anthropologist; I should like to have found someone to write a serious psychological analysis of his symbolism and obsessions. In this volume he appears very much as a poet of the 17th century but he needs placing against the renaissance – or what the renaissance means in England needs defining in terms of Milton; as with much literature and history, we need local reconstruction – what exactly was it like in Bread Street?

No doubt the reader will be starting to write that extra volume. For this reason I have included at the end of the chapters, following the double lines, some additional material. This is entirely my responsibility and is meant to be used as a springboard for private working. Sometimes it implies a view different from the adjacent contributor's and is intended to initiate discussion. I am also responsible for any textual errors or omissions in the chapters, which I edited for the press, and for the choice and titling of the illustrations. I am grateful to my colleagues for their contributions, and for their patience while the volume was put together.

July 1973   J. B. B.

Consider such a passage as this one from Eliot's *Ash Wednesday*:

> Redeem
> The unread vision in the higher dream
> While jewelled unicorns draw by the gilded hearse.

In his Dante essay Eliot says of the pageantry of the *Paradiso* that it 'belongs to the world of what I call the *high dream*, and the modern world seems capable only of the *low dream*'. We dream whether we like it or not, and all knowledge, whether in poetry or out of it, involves suspension of disbelief. In our low dreams, our everyday states of consciousness, such suspension takes the form of simple credulity...In the low dream we wear a mask without realising it, in the high dream we put on a mask with stylised grace. The virtue of a poem consists in expressing, promoting, and communicating some phase of the high dream...A poetic utterance invites our imaginative assent...Even though a certain statement in a poem would be false if taken out of context (as is surely the case with Eliot's 'jewelled unicorns'), the relevant question is, How true is it within that context? And let us not delude ourselves with the hope that there are truths independent of any context whatever. When we think that, and act on it, we become blind to the contextual limitations that condition every judgement and every insight; we fall, so to speak, into a dream within a dream. The poet stakes out his context, the 'world' of his poem, with his imagination audaciously alive and responsive; that is the route, if any, toward the regaining of Terrestial Paradise. Most of us most of the time, with imaginations either stale or running riot, slip into some form of the lower dream, thereby constantly reënacting Adam's fall. The ground-bass of poetic truth is the truth, contextual but real, of man's possible redemption through the fullest imaginative response.

PHILIP WHEELWRIGHT from *The burning fountain: a study in the language of symbolism* rev ed 1968

3

ELIZABETH SEWELL SIRIGNANO

To be a true poem

And long it was not after, when I was confirmed in this opinion, that he who would not be frustrate of his hope to write well hereafter in laudable things, ought himself to be a true poem... *Apology for Smectymnuus*

A poet writes for people. He does not write for professors, English classes, textbooks, examination papers. If any of these lead to a better understanding and friendship between poet and ourselves, they may serve their turn. Mostly, something else happens: they come between the living man who writes poems and the living beings he writes for, with an icy, sterilizing, or just plain wearisome apparatus of technicality and 'scholarship'. The whole approach of the formal education we receive at school and college tends that way. It is a method; *a* method, no more. There is, also, another method. It has its importance because it is the one which the poets pursue, and people can and will agree to it if anyone gives them encouragement. It is another way of learning. As people, we do want to learn, and delight and instruction are what older poets have said poetry is for. This way of learning involves living; living poet and living people; live and learn.

John Milton, that towering phenomenon in English literature in general and the 17th century in particular, may seem an unlikely companion for living with and learning from. Is there not too much learning about him already? He is, in my experience, always presented within the academic method mentioned above as a learned, difficult poet, needing comment and elucidation by experts if the modern reader is even to understand, let alone respond to, what he wrote. In some sense this is what this present Cambridge Milton is all about. Milton *is* learned, no doubt about it, and we are not. Just the same, we in this other method are living people, those for whom, as much as for any others, this poet wrote; or rather, those to whom this poet spoke. One does not write if one is blind, as he was for his three last and greatest works. It takes some of the bookishness out of

4

it too. There is, none the less, work to be done. Milton himself was not unduly sanguine about the people who would want to listen, asking only that he might 'fit audience find, though few' for *Paradise lost*. So let us get to work, in that other, poetic, method, and deal if we can with this formidable learning of his. (We shall have to do the same thing shortly for another major barrier, also much brought to the fore by criticism – his theology.)

A good way to come at this will be to gather up the scattered autobiographical passages in his prose and poetry where he speaks of his studies. Languages and philosophy were the beginning, he tells us in *The second defence of the people of England*, letting us glimpse there also the schoolboy of twelve so avid to read that he sat up every night till midnight, struggling with the headaches which were already the shadow of that darkening to come upon him in his middle years. He records, in his Latin poem to his father, the languages he studied: Latin, Greek, French, Italian, Hebrew – all this before he went to Cambridge. Other facts can be gathered from the account he gives of himself in his pamphlet, *An apology for Smectymnuus*,[1] from which I have taken the title, epigraph and theme of this chapter. He speaks again of his passion for reading, mentioning orators, historians, poets, no doubt in all the languages at his command; we hear of Dante and Petrarch, of the fables and romances of knighthood, then Plato and Xenophon; and training in the precepts of the Christian religion. Back now to the *Second defence*, where he describes his post-university years as entirely devoted to the Greek and Latin classics; in 1698 one of his biographers, John Toland, said that Milton could almost repeat Homer's two poems 'without book', and again one thinks of a blind man, and a prodigious memory. Then came his travels, and the meetings with distinguished men of learning in Europe, Grotius the jurist, Diodati the theologian, Galileo; then the beginnings of the civil war in England and his return home, marking effectively the end of his formal studies and the start of his active years in politics and controversy. And as a last self-statement on learning one could perhaps look at his treatise *On education* and see what he prescribes for young and more standard minds.

[1]

'bless us! what a word on
A title page is this!'

One cherishes Milton's rare flashes of humour. He speaks here of his own *Tetrachordon*, a mouthful no less. Smectymnuus is an acronym of the initials of the five Presbyterian divines who wrote the original pamphlet Milton is here defending.

5

Where does all this leave us? At a gross disadvantage, we may feel, most of us not even having received what used to be called 'a good classical education', but a strange hybrid of no clear character. The only thing to do is to remember that a poet, learned as he may be, writes for people, not in the first place literati. He will impart his learning – after all, it is a part of his life, and if we take it that way we shall escape being daunted, estranged, or, curiously, resentful of it. We too are looking for 'delight and instruction', and, as part of both, great men are generous with their learning; it is a part of magnanimity. Once we can take that learning as an archway, not a barrier, we can walk through and into it. Anyone can.

The other Milton largely focused upon by academic and critical studies, it seems to me, perhaps out of all proportion in so great a poet, is Milton the theologian, the Puritan, the dogmatic if idiosyncratic Christian. This may seem reasonable enough in regard to one who in his epic declares his intention of justifying the ways of God to man, chooses biblical subjects for his three major works, writes a great tractate on Christian doctrine, and so on. Yet in a poet speaking to people, within the poetic method, these concerns are really not important. For one thing, such an approach cannot touch people in our time, and it is to them that the poetic method is rightly directed. Arguments on dogma or on ecclesiastical institutions are dead, as far as Christianity is concerned, here and now. People's needs in religion, which is another thing, our needs of the spirit, are deep and desperate, and Milton the poet may begin to speak to them, but not Milton the Christian polemicist as presented in so many academic studies. Once he is out of the way as theologian or Puritan (puritan – this man who says poetry should be 'simple, sensuous and passionate', who married three times and wrestles with the erotic so long and painfully?), the poet may begin to speak to our real needs.

Let me quickly get out of the way too one other distortion we visit upon poets, before we start to listen, as people, to poet as poet, and what is more, to respond, for we need, in whatever sense you may take this, to talk to poets, living or dead. I mean the presentation of Milton, or any other comparable figure, whether tacitly or explicitly, as 'the great man', largely or wholly unapproachable. Instead of vital beings with whom we can converse, poets in our tradition seem to have become Great Masters of English Literature, set like statues on marble pedestals in some cold Pantheon, as unhelpful as unreal. (Is this due to our cult of 'success' – as if most poets, John Milton

6

among them, had ever been successes in a worldly sense?[1] Is it our miscomprehension of the nature of genius, or the dead educational processing we undergo instead of a living poetic tradition?) Anyway, nothing could be more unpoetic or un-Miltonic. The more you read of this man, the more he emerges as a struggling, anguished human being, as we are, dealing with question after question with which we too are caught up, but also mysteriously endowed from time to time with a great voice which tells us things we desperately need to know.

He himself, in the *Second defence*, speaks of the underlying theme, or dynamic, of his prose writing as he saw it: 'three species of liberty which are essential to the happiness of social life – religious, domestic, and civil'. The first he characterizes as combat with 'slavery and superstition'. The second includes his work, *The doctrine and discipline of divorce*, and, he says, interestingly, his brief essay *On education*. Under the third, civil liberty, come the attacks on monarchy become tyranny, and the condemnation of censorship of printed matter, *Areopagitica*. Already this, with a little translation, should catch our minds: marriage and divorce, education, the nature of revolution, the life of the spirit released from dead forms, institutional or devotional – these are all matters which a late 20th-century mind must find itself thinking long and hard over, if it thinks at all. Yet beyond this it is possible and, I think, desirable, to tease them out a little further. Look at it this way: freedom – what is it? (Milton says, in this same place, that real and substantial freedom is to come from within ourselves and depends on integrity of life.) How are we to be governed and to govern ourselves? And slavery, what is it to be a slave or enslaved? And where is true authority?

Then there is rebellion, some of which is right and some wrong, so that obedience has to be thought about too; and love, erotic love and sex and marriage and divorce, the central mystery of man and woman, and what religion and society do to regulate and perhaps prison it. And how much of life is to be action, with words and language and the mind's activity moving into deeds, and how much is to be quiet and strong patience? ('Silence and sufferance, and speaking deeds against faltering words', as Milton says of himself in the *Apology*.) How can despair be balanced by hope?

And so it could go on. But already we are moving into another

---

[1] Not for nothing are the heroes of his two greatest works, *Paradise lost* and *Samson agonistes*, in a profound sense failures. One cannot read his pamphlet of 1660, *The ready and easy way to establish a free commonwealth*, without hearing in it the note of desperation at what might be about to happen, the ruin of all he had stood for in politics and religion. It did happen, too.

dimension, through the prose and its preoccupations, to the poetry and the life, although I want also to emphasize at this point that some knowledge of his prose in its full range is essential if we are ever to get to know Milton as man and poet. This is not a matter of working doggedly through *Areopagitica* as a 'set book'. It has far more to do with poking about in secondhand bookshops for old copies of Milton's prose works, and discovering for oneself the man of argument and sudden surprising self-exposé, of nobility, insight and pig-headedness, in works like *Divorce* and the *Apology* and the two *Defences of the people of England*. With such acquaintance goes the right, of course, to disagree violently with him, time and again, as one does with a friend. This also is part of the conversation I spoke of earlier.

I have so far dwelt, rather insistently, on a conversation, two-way, which goes on between poet and hearers, Milton and ourselves, aware as I do so of an odd mixture of passion and hopelessness in myself, because I am sure that some such approach to great work is a matter of life and death for poet and people both, and because I am also sure that no-one in today's educational setting is likely to take so simple an approach seriously. There has been all the time, however, another conversation going on, which we listen in to rather than listen to, of a more hidden, subtle, perhaps essential nature. A poet, in his poetry, speaks to himself; or, rather, initiates and pursues a relationship where the living self and the work being done converse each with each. Not just conversation either, and perhaps I should shift my metaphor, for this is much more like a mutual constructing, a fusion, a marriage. Life = poem; poem = life. It is here that the quotation from the *Apology* belongs: Milton saying of himself that the man who desires 'to write well hereafter in laudable things ought himself to be a true poem'. Not a true poet, you notice – a true poem.

We are not accustomed to thinking in this fashion, and perhaps I had better pause and comment a little on what is going on here. The life–poem equation does not mean that the works need be directly autobiographical, nor that they consist of introspection. It does mean, however, as Coleridge says (and he too as a poet works in this manner) that John Milton is in every line of *Paradise lost*; indeed, that in every one of Milton's poems it is Milton himself whom we see, that his Satan, his Adam, his Raphael, even – almost – his Eve, are all John Milton; and Coleridge adds at this point, 'The egotism of such a man is a revelation of spirit'. So there is self-study of a sort, but again Coleridge comments: 'In the *Paradise lost* the sublimest

8

parts are the revelations of Milton's own mind, producing and evolving its own greatness.'[1]

A mind, a life, an organism producing and evolving itself – is this a way of looking at what a man is? And in this case doing it in and through a poem. Then what a poem is had better be asked about too.

Suppose we begin by thinking of life – and ourselves, our own life – as something we make; each one of us astonishing human organisms daily and hourly making, unmaking and remaking the self.[2] How thinly we think of ourselves ordinarily, it seems to me, the self an unclear form drudging along a line in time, both the form and the line more or less fixed and given! And when we look at it squarely, our idea of a poem is about as meagre, a blob of words affixed to a page. But a poem too is a process, endlessly constructed:

> With everything five wits contain,
> Poem is something that is made,

and this may let us see that poem = life is a feasible metaphor, for that of course is what it is. The metaphor is not simply between poet's life and poet's product. If it be true that 'the mind knows its constructive faculty in the act of constructing, and contemplates the act in the product',[3] this does not, in the case of poem and poet, affect poets alone. Otherwise this interchange would be of interest only to

---

[1] The last remark is from *Coleridge's miscellaneous criticism* ed Raysor 1936, p. 164; the rest is from his *Table talk*. It is good to be reminded that in our pursuit of this other method the guides will be not professional literary critics, but other poets, and what they say about Milton. I would suggest a good look at Blake, who thought of himself, at times at least, as Milton's reincarnation, and who in his prophetic books, especially *Milton*, as well as in *The marriage of heaven and hell*, works hard at assimilating and interpreting Milton, as also in the illustrations he made for Milton's poetical works. Wordsworth provides crucial insight in his lines beginning 'On man, on nature and on human life', part of *The recluse* fragment, where he makes plain that he in *The prelude* is taking on where Milton left off, and that the task of both, in their differing ways, has been and is the exploration of the cosmic deeps and spaces of the human mind. Then there is Keats, in his letters and poems, especially the second of the two *Hyperions*. I have written something on the Milton–Keats connection, and their common task, in *The human metaphor* Notre Dame 1964.

[2] *Quisque sui faber* – each man the artificer of himself, as Coleridge says in his Notebook for 1804. He is full of information about what he calls the rudiments (in a letter of September 1817) and in *Biographia literaria* the process of self-construction. He speaks too of thought as self-observation, of self-intuition, of self-knowledge. I. A. Richards, in *Coleridge on the imagination*, says of him that he postulates an 'activity of the mind in which knowing and doing and making and being are least to be distinguished'.

[3] Coleridge, *Aids to reflection*, Moral and Religious Aphorisms, Aphorism XIV.

9

that (rather unsatisfactory) piece of psychology which may deal with 'creativity'. But poems always have to be constructed, by reader or hearer, warmed into activity if they are not to be just blobs, and by that act we, the non-poets as it may seem to us, construct and reconstruct our own minds, lives, acts. This is not a literary technique nor a whimsy. It is a way of learning, a great system of education, almost wholly forgotten or ignored now, to our dire peril. One could call it imagination.

If it is not done through direct shifting-over of the life into the poem, how is it done? Part of the answer to that question is that it is done by *figures*. Images, myths, legends, historical personages, ordinary people, objects, stories – all these we can choose from if we are writing our own poem and trying in this way to understand our own story or life or poem. Equally, we can for the understanding process accept those which the poets offer to us, and make them our own. In either case we lend our lives to the figure we are contemplating, learning about ourselves by identifying with them, no matter how wildly different from our own usually rather dull circumstances the story or figure we are contemplating may be. Drama effects this in a particularly concentrated way, but all poetry works by it, except perhaps satire. The identification of self and figure is not total (this is important because total identification is called madness in our society); but it has to be deep and passionate if it is to be, as it is meant to be, an organ of learning. I think of it as 'I-am-and-am-not', hyphened like that and damn the contradiction which is a concept pertaining to logic but not imagination. I-am-and-am-not Dido and the Ancient Mariner and Raskolnikov. Milton is-and-is-not Comus and Samson and Adam, and we with him. In this way, mysterious, human, and – make no mistake – as yet very little understood or used in what we call our education, we produce and evolve ourselves. Produce and e-volve – Coleridge has given us a beautiful pair of prefixes and verbs, for thinking and feeling and forward-living creatures.

We may be ready now to turn to Milton and to look at some of the figures he lends his life to. Let it be clear that I am not cataloguing his use of particular myths. Indexes of this sort exist, and very useful they are. All we are doing is noticing some of the recurrent figures which we also may want to identify ourselves with.[1]

[1] The first time I worked in this way with Milton I was following the figure of Orpheus (in *The Orphic voice* 1960). I do not mean to repeat that here; but do not miss Orpheus in Milton, for that myth gave him a vision of the poet's task and fate, and runs all through his poems, from early to late. See *PL: introduction* in this series, p. 81, for a student view.

We shall work here with three figures: Hercules, Achilles, and
Samson. And at once a certain difficulty arises, for these three bring
with them a number of other figures and characters in the poet's life
and work. Lines of connection and relationship run from each to
other, cross-references, fusions, shared themes and questions. So
what I am going to do, if you will excuse this, is to set them out
schematically for the moment, together with three groups of themes
(and I mean life-themes, not literary ones) which these figures conjure
up and comment on; this is how the themes fall in my mind and I set
them down this way, not quite sure in what order we will deal with
them, but knowing all are equally important. Imagine on the page an
as yet invisible network of imaginative and interpretative connections
between the figures and the themes here set out, and you will get some
idea of what we are after. For this is how a poem works, or a life.

Hercules
Achilles
Samson

Adam − − − Christ⎫
Satan ⎬
Eve − − − − − − − the Lady in *Comus*
Circe (who is Comus's mother)
Dalila

1	2
freedom	despair
slavery	hope
tyranny	failure
authority	glory
rebellion	action
obedience	suffering and quiet
	patience and passivity

3
chastity, i.e. truth and integrity in love
falsehood in love
woman

Hercules and Achilles are minor figures in Milton's imagination,
and for that reason make good starting points. What, I wonder, can
we conjure up in our non-classical minds by way of information about
them? I hope something even as minimal as what follows: *Hercules* − a
demigod with Jove to his father, a being of superhuman strength, who
undertook twelve Labours (which we certainly could not name in
full), these Labours taking the form either of huge trials of strength,
as we say, or ordeals full of danger, from which he had to emerge

triumphant, only then to take on the next Labour. *Achilles* – a Greek hero, or rather *the* Greek hero in the *Iliad*, also of partly supernatural parentage, a matchless and ruthless warrior who fights and wins the great duel with Hector, champion of the Trojans; and just possibly we may know of him that his fate is ordained to be as tragic as that of his dead and defiled victim, for he was offered by the Oracle short life with great glory or long life with little glory, and chose the former.

(If you will cast your eye back over that paragraph, already certain words – ideas? happenings? – stand out. Labour, trial, ordeal, duel: a sense of struggle is embedded even in these preliminary figures, and then one reminds oneself that every single one of Milton's dramatic and epic poems, *Comus, Paradise lost, Paradise regained, Samson agonistes* or Samson the wrestler, has struggle at its heart. It almost makes one feel exhausted straight away, and if this is how the poems are, how about the life? Back to our two pagans for the moment.)

Hercules He appears once as Milton himself, in a rather fretful jest at the end of *Colasterion*, where the author compares his task in combating the misunderstanding and insult his work on divorce had brought him, to Hercules' cleansing of the Augean stables. Calling his opponent's work dung is fairly characteristic; he was never mealy-mouthed. To give the figure its full implications is to see a Milton in middle life, the time of his revolutionary involvement and fighting prose, calling up his strength time and again for Labour after Labour such as this. But Hercules also appears, three times over, as Christ. Two of the references are early, and passing, as it were. The first is from the *Nativity ode*:

> Nor all the gods beside,
> Longer dare abide,
>   Not Typhon huge ending in snaky twine:
> Our Babe to show his Godhead true,
> Can in his swaddling bands control the damnèd crew.

Here Christ routs the pagan gods as, so the legend goes, the baby Hercules strangled a couple of venomous snakes in his cradle, one in each hand. The second early reference comes from that fragmentary poem on Christ's *Passion* at the end of which Milton notes, movingly, that he found the subject more than he could handle at his age:

> Most perfect hero, tried in heaviest plight
> Of labours huge and hard, too hard for human wight.

The image of Christ as hero, and of the hero as subject to trial and struggle, is interesting as early as 1629–30, the mythic Labours transposed now into some higher setting. A full forty years later this identification will return, and at the supreme testing point, when Satan in a last desperate bout in his struggle to overcome Christ catches him up bodily, as the biblical story tells, except that Milton has shifted the order of events, and poises him breathlessly in high mid-air on Jerusalem's temple-top. *Paradise regained* is so little known, and the passage is so marvellous, that it seems worth quoting at some length:

> There on the highest pinnacle he set
> The Son of God; and added thus in scorn:
>   There stand, if thou wilt stand; to stand upright
> Will ask thee skill; I to thy Father's house
> Have brought thee, and highest placed, highest is best;
> Now shew thy progeny; if not to stand,
> Cast thyself down; safely if Son of God...
>   To whom thus Jesus: Also it is written,
> Tempt not the Lord thy God; he said, and stood.
> But Satan smitten with amazement fell.
> As when Earth's son Antaeus (to compare
> Small things with greatest) in Irassa strove
> With Jove's Alcides, and oft foiled still rose,
> Receiving from his mother Earth new strength,
> Fresh from his fall, and fiercer grapple joined,
> Throttled at length in the air, expired and fell;
> So after many a foil the tempter proud,
> Renewing fresh assaults, amid his pride
> Fell whence he stood to see his victor fall.

The Tempter is the one who attempts, who tries – the struggle again; and we may notice the almost formal element of duel here, the bitter taunting at the beginning, the reversal and drama of 'he said, and stood', the final plunge of the Adversary, now worsted once for all. Alcides is Hercules' Greek name, and this is another piece of his story, his combat with the earth-giant Antaeus, who every time he touched the ground regained his full strength and so could be killed only by being strangled in mid-air while his feet were off the ground. We shall meet Hercules once more, but joined up with Samson and Adam and Eve, and we are not ready for that yet.

Now *Achilles*, and, first, what Milton does with him in the *Second defence*. Both the *Defences* deal with the action, and the right, of Englishmen in their recent revolution, of contesting and eventually executing their monarch in the name of freedom and of that law of

13

the land which King Charles I had maintained did not apply to him, as monarch. So now enter history and politics, accompanying the figure of Achilles who is, for Milton as for tradition, the very embodiment of the epic, and also tragic, hero. Milton concludes the *Second defence* by seeing himself in the character of epic poet, ascribing to his fighting fellow-countrymen in their more active role the part of Achilles. Here is combat and struggle, but a little earlier in this work Milton brings in the other aspect of Achilles also, the hero of the tragic and glorious choice of fame and early death, and it is this with which he identifies himself. It is not his own death the poet is contemplating, but the deliberate ruining of his eyesight if he was to finish his task of political controversy and publication, and here he moves on to something else, some kind of revelation or glory – I am not quite sure what to call it – which he glimpses as lying beyond heroism of the more active and martial kind, to be attained only through weakness and suffering. It is an inner quiet, 'a treasured store of tranquillity and delight', he says, yet no mere passivity or withdrawal, for it is 'a way to strength through weakness', and the 'feebleness' will, as he says, 'invigorate the energies of my rational and immortal spirit'. We should connect this immediately with that other crucial passage early in *Paradise lost* IX where again the epic hero and his nature come into question, and again the poet sees some transformation that must take place at this point, a struggling towards a vision of 'a better fortitude', in his figures, his heroes, his own life, something which in *Paradise regained*, where so many of his themes come to climax and are resolved, he calls by the rather marvellous name of 'strong sufferance' (I 160). This is, in the main, the second group of themes we charted earlier.

And so to *Samson*: doer of great deeds of strength like Hercules, national hero destined to a premature and violent death like Achilles, but bringing with him the Old Testament lore which underlies Milton's Christianity, the struggle in the spirit. There can be little doubt that, of all the figures Milton uses, this one comes closest to home: the blinded giant, the impotence, the threat from political foes, the loneliness, the utter collapse of all hope for great things in public life, not to mention the experience in marriage, where much must remain conjecture for us in Milton's regard, but where the raw nerve is evident. Yet the figure, such being a figure's power and function, is much more than a mirroring of the poet's circumstances. Theme after theme comes now into play. Despair and hope make their entrance, but despair principally, which Samson shares, though

14

as mortal to immortal, with Satan.[1] So does failure and its consequences, which he shares with Adam and Eve. And now the third group of subjects mentioned earlier, woman, love, sex, marriage, is focused upon, centrally, for in the old story which Milton follows it was to his wife, Dalila, that Samson blabbed the secret of his God-given strength, whereupon she in turn betrays him to his political enemies who blind and enslave him. The political and the erotic in the struggle for freedom are strangely interwoven, as are all the figures and themes henceforward. If, however, we are to hold by the poetic method, we have to resist the temptation to pull them apart again, i.e. to use analysis, almost the only tool our present-day education puts at our disposal. We have to hold all together, struggle as it may be, letting the living filaments run from centre to centre as they do in mind and organism and life, Milton's or our own.

By the time he wrote *Samson*, Milton, although politics are an aspect of that play, was not working directly on political themes any more. For that reason it may be good to watch him using the figure of Samson to express active political thought, in one of his polemical works, *The reason of church government urged against prelaty*, 1641–2:

I cannot better liken the state and person of a king than to that mighty Nazarite Samson; who being disciplined from his birth in the precepts and the practice of temperance and sobriety, without the strong drink of injurious and excessive desires, grows up to a noble strength and perfection with those his illustrious and sunny locks, the laws, waving and curling about his god-like shoulders. And while he keeps them about him undiminished and un-shorn, he may with the jawbone of an ass, that is, with the word of his meanest officer, suppress and put to confusion thousands of those that rise against his just power. But laying down his head among the strumpet flatteries of prelates, while he sleeps and thinks no harm, they wickedly shaving off all those bright and weighty tresses of his laws, and just prerogatives, which were his ornament and strength, deliver him over to indirect and violent counsels, which, as those Philistines, put out the fair and far-sighted eyes of his natural discerning, and make him grind in the prison-house of their sinister ends and practices upon him: till he, knowing

---

[1] The great self-statement of Satanic despair in *PL* is at the beginning of iv. But Satan has a fiercer and more concentrated cry at *PR* iii 204:

> all hope is lost
> Of my reception into grace; what worse?
> For where no hope is left, is left no fear...
> I would be at the worst; worst is my port,
> My harbour and my ultimate repose,
> The end I would attain, my final good.

So an archangel may speak. Mortals had better remember the warning in Edgar's speech in *Lear* (iv i), 'O gods! Who is't can say, "I am at the worst?" I am worse than e'er I was.'

this prelatical razor to have bereft him of his wonted might, nourish again his puissant hair, the golden beams of law and right; and they sternly shook, thunder with ruin upon the heads of those his evil counsellors, but not without great affliction to himself.

Simply by his choice of this figure, Milton typifies political, i.e. intellectual seduction by sexual seduction. But from this passage we learn also how little of an anti-royalist, or a bigot, Milton is. Samson, Milton's chosen figure for himself, is here a king. This is part of the inner freedom he commends to us as to himself. Perhaps only truly free poetic and revolutionary genius would have dared to do what Milton does in *Paradise lost* – describe a revolt which leads straight to hell, against the authority of a supreme monarch; a parliament, one is tempted to say a Long Parliament, of devils in Pandemonium; and a kind of privy council, of the powers of darkness, in *Paradise regained*. Trustworthy and committed revolutionary as Milton was, coming near to paying for his convictions with his life, he was not against authority as such; laws in the state, conscience in the individual, would constitute for him the due authorities, I suppose.

Thus, to return to kingship for a moment, it is not, for him, anathema but a quality inherent in man himself, the authority within, as he expounds in a nobly Shakespearean passage, spoken by Christ, in *Paradise regained*:

> For therein stands the office of a king,
> His honour, virtue, merit and chief praise,
> That for the public all this weight he bears.
> Yet he who reigns within himself, and rules
> Passions, desires and fears, is more a king;
> Which every wise and virtuous man attains:
> And who aspires not, ill aspires to rule
> Cities of men, or headstrong multitudes,
> Subject himself to anarchy within
> Or lawless passions in him which he serves.   II 463

The passage, along with much of Milton's thought, fits our present situation almost frighteningly well. Cities and multitudes and anarchy – these we know, and if you will look at his description of physical chaos in the universe of space, across which Satan has to make his vast flight in *Paradise lost*, you may find an even closer shadowing of our present revolutionary world, not of atoms but of men, 'eternal anarchy amidst the noise of endless wars', where 'atoms...around the flag Of each his faction, in their several clans... Swarm populous...To whom these most adhere He rules a moment' (II 896). In conditions such as these, our outer and inner living condi-

16

tions, it is reassuring to find a revolutionary who scorns any one-track anti-establishment stuff, of which we have our bellyful today. For this poet, neither authority nor revolution is good in itself. Freedom is the good, in either case, and because he grasps this and lives by it, his views in our present crisis of authority can be helpful.[1] Above all, he reminds us that freedom starts within. So, it follows, does slavery also.

If, as Milton warns us, politics in its widest sense is one area where we may most easily lose our freedom, must struggle to hold on to it or, if lost, to regain it, he warns equally emphatically that sex, love, the erotic relationship between man and woman, is another such. It is here that Samson, and also Adam, fall into slavery, through over-weening love for a woman. Samson admits repeatedly that his enslavement began at the moment when he revealed his divine secret to Dalila, and that the actual bondage he later incurred, manacles, prison-house and treadmill, is only a shadow of that far more real inner servitude. Adam meets a similar fate at the moment of his fall. Eve is deluded into her act of disobedience to God by the serpent's tales of marvels that will accrue to humanity after they have eaten of the Tree of Knowledge. Not so Adam. He chooses deliberately to share Eve's guilt because she is already fallen and he cannot bear to be separated from her:

> he scrupled not to eat
> Against his better knowledge, not deceived
> But fondly overcome with female charm.   *PL* IX 997

At once the innocence of both, their freedom in sexual enjoyment, 'emparadised in one another's arms', is gone, and at this very point in the narrative Milton compares them to 'Herculean Samson' rising shorn and humiliated from his wife's lap, already in slavery. Again the figures coalesce.

Were we dealing with some meagre moralizer we could expect at this point a sermon on illicit love as slavery and moral love as freedom. Not at all. Milton does distinguish falsehood and that integrity in love which he could still, as we cannot, call chastity; but he uses one image for both, a cup of wine, beautiful whether it be the magic cup which Comus (who is the son of Circe and Bacchus) offers the Lady in Milton's masque, or whether it be the image of free and honest love in the *Apology*, where Milton is speaking, from his own experience, of the rejection of sexual licence:

[1] Cf. for instance his phrase, 'authority, which is the life of teaching', in *Areopagitica*.

if I should tell ye what I learnt of chastity and love, I mean that which is truly so, whose charming cup is only virtue, which she bears in her hand to those who are worthy (the rest are cheated with a thick intoxicating potion, which a certain sorceress, the abuser of love's name, carries about).

The false cup, Circe's, turns men to beasts, but even the true cup is 'charming', that is to say, magic also. It is significant that in *Comus*, although the Lady rejects the intoxicant, she is nevertheless held temporarily a prisoner in Comus's chair, as if even with integrity preserved there is, through the magic, some involuntary loss of freedom at this juncture. And again it can be solid legal marriage that is the prison for Milton, as we see in one last tiny heart-chilling Samson reference, from *The doctrine and discipline of divorce*: 'O perverseness!...that to grind in the mill of an undelighted and servile copulation, must be the only forced work of a Christian marriage.' That needs no comment; but the opposite of undelighted and servile is delighted and free, and the note of freedom, the quest for it in matters of love and sex, runs all through this poet's work, from the early *Comus* where it is the centre of attention, through the figures of Adam and Samson as we have seen, in a diminuendo of importance yet never wholly dying out, for even in *Paradise regained* Belial proposes to tempt Christ with women, only to be scoffed at by Satan, who has a firmer grip on reality in such a context.

That our era needs to learn about freedom here no less than in the world of politics and public life, goes without saying. If Milton's answers do not seem to fit our needs, that is no reason for not following out his questioning at this point. (Curiously it is his view of the politics between man and woman – and much is political in that small society of two – which fails him and us, the one area where we find him counselling 'despotic power' – *Samson* 1054.) Yet he has much to tell if we will ask; as, for instance, 'We know it is not the joining of another body that will remove loneliness' in his work on divorce, when, alas, we no longer know any such thing, and all is to be relearned. We have no better answers than Milton had. The questioning is all.

Freedom and questions – this is what we end up with. In this vision, freedom, whether it be political, sexual or spiritual, is no free gift, not since loss of Eden. It has to be laboured for as if we were Hercules, and it demands courage in taking action and making choices as if we were Achilles. The one thing not to do is to acquiesce permanently in our own enslavement, inner or outer – outer because inner,

> to love bondage more than Liberty,
> Bondage with ease than strenuous Liberty.

Samson 270

Here the questioning comes in. The figures in Milton's poetry are not just vehicles for the asking of questions, even the deepest ones about our dark and perplexing world. Those figures are themselves subject to question, by life itself. So are we. One almost wants to use the fierce 17th-century phrase 'put to the question', which means being tortured, so great is the effort and suffering involved.

'When God gave him [Adam] reason, he gave him freedom to choose, for reason is but choosing' (*Areopagitica*). Choice and action imply, if we are truly free, possible wrong choice and wrongdoing. If we make the wrong choice (the right one may lie in taking action as with Milton and the revolution of his day, or in refraining from action, the latter being the harder one, to judge by Adam and Eve's failure, and Samson's, in such case) we are at once enslaved by the consequences of our choice, and fall into suffering. The marvellous thing about Milton is that he takes this almost for granted, as a part of being human, and tells us, in the person of Adam and of Samson, that this suffering can lead to fresh vision and a transformed and undreamed-of glory. This is perfected, and most beautifully spoken, by Christ, as mortal man, in *Paradise regained*:

> What if he hath decreed that I shall first
> Be tried in humble state, and things adverse,
> By tribulations, injuries, insults,
> Contempts and scorns and snares and violence,
> Suffering, abstaining, quietly expecting
> Without distrust or doubt, that he may know
> What I can suffer, how obey? who best
> Can suffer, best can do; best reign, who first
> Well hath obeyed; just trial...

III 188

Yet for all the seraphic quiet which, beyond this transformation-point, falls over the struggling figures – Adam and Eve walking slowly out into the world, the almost dream-like peace after Samson's end, Christ going home to his mother's house after ordeal in the wilderness – we never lose the fighting Milton[1] and the note of challenge and duel, heroic deeds, great achievements, mortal combat reaching its peak of intensity between those two who, in *Paradise lost*,

---

[1] 'Nor, though very thin, was I ever deficient in courage or in strength; and I was wont constantly to exercise myself in the use of the broadsword, as long as it comported with my habit and my years. Armed with this weapon, as I usually was, I should have thought myself quite a match for anyone' (*Second defence*).

2-2

volunteered, each as champion of his side, and who meet and settle the issue in *Paradise regained* – Christ and Satan. For all of Milton's rejection of traditional chivalry as heroism in his epic, we find him saying, in the context of his own life, 'Only this my mind gave me, that every free and gentle spirit...ought to be born a knight.' This, from the *Apology* where Milton sees life as 'a true poem', may be inconsistency or paradox; or it may be that twofold vision which Blake claims for the poet. To alter Milton's own words slightly, it is this, the duel not of arms, which justly gives heroic name to person and to poem. The life that is true poem is epic after all, but epic transfigured.

If our own lives seem to us to lack any such dimensions, we could remember that our place is not alongside giants of old, of classical or religious legend, or even the great and dear poet who challenges us in this way. We have, as he gives it to us, an even older heritage, alongside Adam, crestfallen all-father. 'By small,' Milton's Adam says, 'accomplishing great things.' True poems may be small as well as great.

A religious poet is in a peculiar position. Such a poet will seek to establish a relation to the religious through the imagination; but for this very reason he succeeds only in establishing an aesthetic relationship to something aesthetic. To hymn a hero of faith is quite as definitely an aesthetic task as it is to eulogize a war hero. If the religious is in truth the religious, if it has submitted itself to the discipline of the ethical and preserves it within itself, it cannot forget that religious pathos does not consist in singing and hymning and composing verses, but in existing; so that the poetic productivity, if it does not cease entirely, or if it flows as richly as before, comes to be regarded by the individual himself as something accidental, which goes to prove that he understand himself religiously. Aesthetically it is the poetic productivity which is essential, and the poet's mode of existence is accidental.

SØREN KIERKEGAARD 1813–55

ISABEL RIVERS

Milton's life and times: aids to study

These notes are not meant to provide a narrative of Milton's life. They are for use as reference, as a brief anthology illustrating Milton's prose writings, his position among his contemporaries, and important issues of the time, and as a guide to further reading. The student wanting to go further should begin with Milton's autobiographical accounts in *The reason of church government*, *Apology for Smectymnuus*, and *Second defence*. The complete prose writings are in the Columbia edition (18 vols New York 1931–40), but they are not annotated; the Yale edition of the prose is in progress (New Haven 1953–), with detailed introductions and notes. Those editions are for the specialist. The best one-volume edition, with helpful introductions, is by J. Max Patrick 1967.

Biographies of Milton appeared quite soon after his death. John Aubrey the antiquarian and gossip made notes in 1681 for Anthony à Wood, historian of Oxford, who published his life in 1691; it is critical of Milton's politics. Edward Phillips, Milton's nephew, published his life in 1694, partly to scotch hostile rumours; there is too an anonymous life, also used by Wood, possibly by Cyriack Skinner who acted as one of Milton's scribes. In 1698 John Toland the deist published an admiring life together with a collected edition of the prose; in his life of 1734 Jonathan Richardson included information obtained from Milton's descendants. These lives are all collected by Helen Darbishire in *The early lives of Milton* 1932. Samuel Johnson's eccentric account in the *Lives of the poets* 1779 shows dislike for the man and his ideas and grudging admiration for the poetry. The fullest biography ever likely to be written is by David Masson (6 vols 1858–80). It is an enthusiastic and ambitious work, providing a detailed history of the time, with an emphasis on religion.

Though it contains errors, and the historical interpretations are sometimes out of date, it remains invaluable for scholars. The most detailed recent life is by W. R. Parker (2 vols Oxford 1968); but it is much narrower in scope. The factual material available for the modern biographer is collected by J. M. French in *The life records of JM* (5 vols New Brunswick 1949–58). There are several recent introductory accounts; the most useful for the student is by J. H. Hanford *JM Englishman* 1950.

Chronology

DATE	PRIVATE EVENTS	WRITING AND PUBLICATIONS	PUBLIC EVENTS
1608	Born in apartment called the Spread Eagle in house called the White Bear in Bread St, near St Paul's London, 9 Dec. Father a well-to-do scrivener (lawyer, money-lender, accountant, investor). Elder sister Anne.		
1609		Shakespeare's *Sonnets* pub.	
1611		Authorized version of Bible. Donne *Anatomy of the world* pub. Tourneur *Atheist's tragedy* pub.	
1614		Raleigh *History of the world* pub. Jonson *Bartholomew fair* acted.	
1615	Brother Christopher b. (became lawyer and royalist). M perhaps enters St Paul's School (or 1620). Diodati also pupil.		
1616			Shakespeare d.
c. 1618	Also tutored privately by Thomas Young.		Raleigh executed. Beginning of Thirty Years' War on continent. England keeps out.
1619	Portrait painted.		
1620			Voyage of *Mayflower* to New England.
1623	Sister Anne m. Edward Phillips, a lawyer.		
1624		Paraphrases *Psalms* 114 and 136.	

DATE	PRIVATE EVENTS	WRITING AND PUBLICATIONS	PUBLIC EVENTS
1625	Admitted to Christ's College, Cambridge, under Chappell.	Writes *Death of fair infant* (or perhaps 1628 on niece Anne Phillips).	Death of James I. Accession of Charles I and marriage to Henrietta Maria.
1626	Perhaps rusticated. Changes tutor at Christ's.	*Elegy I* to Diodati. *In quintum Novembris.*	Bacon d.
1627		*Elegy IV* to Thomas Young.	
1628	*Prolusions* delivered *c.* 1628–32.	*Vacation exercise.*	Petition of Right. Murder of Buckingham. Laud bishop of London.
1629	Takes BA. Portrait painted.	*Elegy V. Elegy VI* to Diodati. *Nativity ode* (winter).	Charles I rules without parliament till 1640.
1630	Edward King has fellowship at Christ's. M's nephew Edward Phillips b.	*Arcades* (?). *Passion. On Shakespeare.* Quarles *Divine poems* pub.	Charles II born. Much emigration to New England. Harvey d. Kepler d.
1631	Nephew John Phillips b.	Quarles *Samson* pub. *L'allegro* and *Il penseroso* (?). *Epitaph on Marchioness of Winchester. Sonnet VII: How soon hath time.*	Donne d. Dryden b.
1632	Father retires to Hammersmith. Takes MA; retires to parents' house for programme of study.	'Letter to a friend' written (?). Shakespeare 2nd Folio pub. with M's epitaph. *Ad patrem* (?).	
1633			Laud archbishop of Canterbury, enforces church policy.
1634		*Comus* performed at Ludlow Castle 29 Sept.	
1635	Moves with parents to Horton, Bucks; continues studies.	Quarles *Emblems* pub.	Ship money levied.
1637	Mother d. (April). Edward King drowned (Aug.). Brother Christopher marries (?).	*Comus* pub. *Lycidas* written.	Punishment of Prynne, Burton and Bastwick (Puritans). Prayer book introduced in Scotland. Ben Jonson d.
1638	Leaves England (May?). Meets Grotius in Paris. To Italy. Diodati d. (Aug.). Well received in Florentine academies. Meets Galileo. To Rome, Naples. Meets Manso.	*Lycidas* pub. in *Justa Edouardo King naufrago.*	Scottish National Covenant signed (against episcopacy). Hampden loses challenge against ship money.

23

DATE	PRIVATE EVENTS	WRITING AND PUBLICATIONS	PUBLIC EVENTS
1639	Decides to return via Rome, Florence, Geneva, France. In England *c.* July. Thinking about epic.	*Mansus* (?). *Epitaphium Damonis.*	1st Bishops' war (March–June) against Scotland, over church government.
1640	Takes lodgings in London, then house in Aldersgate teaches Phillips' nephews, and sons of gentry. Keeps common-place book; makes notes on tragedies (subjects from scripture and British history); begins study of Christian doctrine.	J. Hall *Episcopacy by divine right* pub. *Epitaphium Damonis* pub. (?).	Short parliament (Apr.). 2nd Bishops' war (June–Sept.); Scots invade England. Beginning of Long Parliament (Nov.). Strafford and Laud impeached. Root and Branch petition, against bishops. Rubens d.
1641		Pamphlets about bishops: Hall *Humble Remonstrance*; Smectymnuus *Answer*; Hall *Defence*; Smectymnuus *Vindication*. *Of reformation* pub. (May); *Of prelatical episcopacy* pub. (June?), answer to Usher. *Animadversions* pub. (July?), answer to Hall.	Laud in tower. Strafford executed. Several reform statutes passed (June–Aug.). Grand Remonstrance (Nov.). Irish rebellion. Effective end of bishops' power in church and state. Van Dyck d.
1642	Marries 1st wife Mary Powell (summer); wife returns to mother near Oxford; M tries to get her back.	Hall's (?) *Confutation... of animadversions. Reason of church government* pub. (Feb?); *Apology for Smectymnuus* pub. (May?). Browne *Religio medici* (unauthorized pub.).	Charles fails to arrest 5 members; leaves London. Act excluding bishops from Lords. King and commons fall out over control of militia. 1st Civil War begins (Aug.). Oxford royal HQ. Theatres closed.
1643	Christopher M and brother-in-law Richard Powell royalists. Father comes to Aldersgate.	*Doctrine and discipline of divorce* pub. (Aug.).	Ordinance for licensing press. Westminster Assembly meets. Solemn league and covenant signed with Scots.
1644	Divorce books attacked. Begins to notice failure of sight.	2nd ed. *Doctrine and discipline* (Feb.); *Of education* pub. (June); *Judgement of Martin Bucer* pub. (Aug.); *Areopagitica* pub. (Nov.).	Scottish army in England. Marston Moor won by parliament and Scots.
1645	Wife Mary returns. Moves to larger house in Barbican to accommodate pupils.	*Tetrachordon* and *Colasterion* pub. (March); *Poems* registered (Oct.).	Book of Common Prayer abolished. Laud executed. Self-denying ordinance; Cromwell exempted. Naseby won by New Model Army.

| --- | --- | --- | --- |
1646	Powell family at M's house. 1st daughter Anne b. (July). Father-in-law d.	*Poems 1645* pub. (Jan.). Sonnet *On the new forcers of conscience.*	Charles goes over to Scots. Oxford surrenders; end of 1st Civil War. Bishops finally abolished.
1647	Father d. Moves to smaller house in Holborn. Late 1640s working on *History of Britain* and reading theology. Some authorities suggest writing *Samson agonistes* about now.		Scots hand Charles to parliament; kidnapped by army; escapes to Isle of Wight; back in parliamentary control. Treats with all parties; makes agreement with Scots. Leveller agitation.
1648	2nd daughter Mary b. (Oct.).	Translates *Psalms* 80–8. Sonnet *To Fairfax.* *Character of Long Parliament* written (?). Herrick *Hesperides* pub.	2nd Civil War; Fairfax defeats royalists, Cromwell defeats Scots. Pride's Purge (Presbyterians excluded from parliament). Thirty Years' War ends.
1649	Appointed secretary for foreign tongues to Council of State (March), salary £288 pa. Asked to answer *Eikon basilike.* Official lodgings in Whitehall.	*Eikon basilike* pub. (Charles I ghosted by John Gauden). *Tenure of kings and magistrates* pub. (Feb.). *Observations upon the articles of peace* pub. (May). Salmasius *Defensio regia* appears in England (May). *Eikonoklastes* pub. (Oct.).	Trial and execution of Charles (Jan.). Monarchy and house of Lords abolished; government by Council and Rump of Long Parliament. Levellers crushed. Cromwell campaigning in Ireland till 1650. Westminster Assembly ceases to sit. Engagement Act replaces Covenant in England. Charles II, recognized by Scots, accepts Covenant; Scots defeated by Cromwell at Dunbar.
1650	Ordered to answer Salmasius (Jan). In ill health; almost blind.	2nd editions of *Eikonoklastes* and *Tenure.* Marvell writes *Horatian ode.*	
1651	Only son John born (March). Acts as licenser to *Mercurius politicus* government newspaper. *1st defence* widely read in Holland and Sweden, condemned and burned in France. Moves from Whitehall to Petty France, Westminster.	*Defensio pro populo Anglicano* pub. (Feb.), i.e. *1st defence.* John Phillips' *Responsio* to Rowland's *Apologia*, attack on M.	Charles II crowned in Scotland, defeated at Worcester, escapes to France.
1652	Becomes totally blind. 3rd daughter Deborah born, 2 May, 1st wife Mary dies *c.* 5 May. Son John dies (June). Ordered to reply to	Filmer's *Observations* attacks M. Sonnet XVI *When I consider* (?). Sonnets *To Cromwell* and *Vane.* Pierre du Moulin *Regii sanguinis clamor*	Committee considering state church. Disagreement between army leaders and parliament. Dutch war.

DATE	PRIVATE EVENTS	WRITING AND PUBLICATIONS	PUBLIC EVENTS
	Clamor. ?Helps Davenant get freedom.	pub. (Aug.), answer to *1st defence.*	
1653	Recommends Marvell for employment. Salmasius dies (Sept.).	Translates *Psalms* 1–8.	Cromwell dissolves Rump. Military rule. Barebones parliament (July–Dec.). Cromwell Protector under Instrument of Government (Dec.). Republican opposition.
1654		*Defensio secunda* pub. (May). More's *Fides publica* answers.	Peace with Dutch. Commission of triers (to examine clergy). 1st protectorate parliament.
1655	Working on *History of Britain,* Latin dictionary, and *Christian doctrine* (late 1650s). Salary reduced but to be paid for life.	Sonnet *On massacre in Piedmont.* ?Sonnets *To Cyriack Skinner.* More *Supplement* to *Fides publica* pub. *Defensio pro se* pub. (Aug.), i.e. *3rd defence.* Waller *Panegyric to Protector,* Marvell *1st anniversary* pub.	Rule of major-generals in counties. Fifth monarchist agitation. Royalist risings. Piedmontese massacre. War with Spain.
1656	Marries 2nd wife Katherine Woodcock (Nov.).		2nd protectorate parliament (to 1658); Protector excludes many members.
1657	?Helps Spenser's grandson recover estate. Marvell appointed assistant secretary. Daughter Katherine born (Oct.).		Cromwell asked to take crown by parliament; refuses because of army opposition. Now has power to nominate successor. Creation of upper house.
1658	Begins *Paradise lost* about now. 2nd wife Katherine dies (Feb.); daughter Katherine dies (March). In Cromwell's funeral procession.	Sonnet *XIX* on deceased wife (?). Publishes Raleigh's *Cabinet council.* Revised ed of *1st defence* (Oct.).	Cromwell dies (Sept.). Succeeded by son Richard.
1659	No record of official work after Oct.	*Treatise of civil power* pub. (Feb.). *Considerations touching hirelings* pub. (Aug.). *Letter to a friend* pub. (Oct.).	Richard abdicates. Army and Rump rule. Royalist rising. Uncertainty about future of government. Poussin died 1665.
1660	Dismissed from secretaryship (*c.* Feb.). Loses money at Restoration. Goes into hiding (?May). Parliament move to get *1st defence* and *Eikonoklastes* burned, and M arrested; books burned	*Ready and easy way* pub. (March), 2nd edition (April?). Attacked in *The censure of the Rota* and *The dignity of kingship.* M answers in *Brief notes upon a late sermon* (April). L'Estrange attacks in	Monk in London (Feb.); restores excluded members of Long Parliament. Strong royalist feeling. Declaration of Breda; king's restoration voted by Convention parliament (April). Charles II in

26

DATE	PRIVATE EVENTS	WRITING AND PUBLICATIONS	PUBLIC EVENTS
	(June); royal proclamation against his books (Aug.). Not excluded from Act of Indemnity; helped by Davenant? Arrested (Oct.); released (Dec.); Marvell protests in parliament about jail fees.	*No blind guides.* Salmasius' posthumous *Responsio* pub. (Dec.).	England (May). Act of Indemnity (Aug.). Punishment of regicides (Oct.).
1661	Moves to Jewin Street.		Cavalier parliament (to 1679). Coronation of Charles II. Rising of Fifth monarchists.
1662	Meets and begins teaching Thomas Ellwood.	Sonnet *To Vane* pub. in Sikes' *Life and death of Sir Henry Vane.* Butler *Hudibras* I.	Act of Uniformity; nonconforming clergy lose livings. Several more acts against nonconformists early 1660s. Charles marries Catherine of Braganza.
1663	Marries 3rd wife Elizabeth Minshull (Feb.). Moves to Artillery Walk, Bunhill Fields (perhaps later).		
1664		Poem on Shakespeare repr. in 3rd Folio.	
1665	Ellwood hires house for M at Chalfont St Giles, Bucks, because of plague. Ellwood reads *PL* in MS.		2nd Dutch war (to 1667); badly managed. Plague. Poussin d.
1666	Returns to London.	Bunyan *Grace abounding.*	Fire of London.
1667		*Paradise lost* pub. (Aug.). Dryden *Annus mirabilis* pub. Sprat *History of Royal Society* pub.	Disillusionment with government. Clarendon exiled, as scapegoat.
1669		*Accidence commenced grammar* pub.	
1670	Consulted about divorce proceedings for Lord Roos. Du Moulin identifies himself as author of *Clamor.*	*History of Britain* pub. Pascal *Pensées.*	Secret treaty of Dover between Charles II and Louis XIV.
1671		*Paradise regained* and *Samson agonistes* pub. (date of writing latter unknown).	
1672		*Art of logic* pub.	Declaration of indulgence (freedom of worship for Catholics and nonconforming Protestants). 3rd Dutch war.

DATE	PRIVATE EVENTS	WRITING AND PUBLICATIONS	PUBLIC EVENTS
1673	Dryden visits M about now, intending to turn *PL* into opera.	Marvell defends M in *The rehearsal transprosed* II against attacks by Samuel Parker and Richard Leigh. *Of true religion* pub. (May?). 2nd ed *Poems* pub., with some additions and *Of education* (Nov?).	Charles withdraws declaration. Test act. Anti-Catholic agitation. Shaftesbury in opposition.
1674	Dies of gout in Bunhill about Nov. 9. Buried in St Giles, Cripplegate (now part of the Barbican pedestrian precinct).	*Familiar letters* and *Prolusions* pub. (May). 2nd ed revised *Paradise lost* (July).	Traherne and Herrick d.

Posthumous publications:

1676	*Letters of state.*
1677	Dryden's *State of innocence* based on *PL*.
1681	*Character of Long Parliament.*
1682	*History of Muscovia.*
1698	Toland's edition of English prose writings.
1825	*Christian doctrine.*

Milton's friends, and the chief persons named in his works

Those of Milton's works which were written for these people or with which they were directly connected are given in parentheses.

Oliver Cromwell 1599–1658 (*To the Lord General Cromwell, Second defence*) Successively MP, parliamentary general, commander-in-chief, Lord Protector. M's acquaintance probably began in 1649, when Cromwell became one of his employers.

Carlo Dati 1619–76 (mentioned in *Epitaphium Damonis*) An Italian, secretary to one of the Florentine academies that M visited in 1638. Wrote admiring Latin tribute which M printed in front of his Latin poems. Corresponded with M in late 1640s.

Charles Diodati c. 1609–38 (*Elegy I, Elegy VI, Epitaphium Damonis*) An Englishman of Italian ancestry. Educated at St Paul's with M, and at Oxford. Died while M was on Italian tour. M's closest early friend, with whom he exchanged letters, poems, and ideas. M visited his theologian uncle in Geneva.

Thomas Ellwood 1639–1713 Quaker student and friend of M after Restoration. Briefly imprisoned for his religion. Found M house in Buckinghamshire during plague 1665. First known reader of complete *PL*; claimed to have suggested idea of *PR*.

The Egerton family Alice Spencer, Dowager Countess of Derby 1559–1637 (*Arcades*). Previously celebrated by Spenser. Her stepson and son-in-law John Egerton, Earl of Bridgewater, Lord President of Wales 1579–1649 (*Comus*). His children Lady Alice Egerton 1619–89, John Viscount Brackley 1623–86, Thomas Egerton 1625–*c*.48 (*Comus*). They were taught music by Henry Lawes.

Sir Thomas Fairfax 1612–71 (*On the Lord General Fairfax*, praised in *Second defence*) Parliamentary commander-in-chief. Refused to associate himself with king's execution. Resigned 1650 because he did not want to invade Scotland. His place taken by Cromwell. Retired to Yorkshire estates, where Marvell tutored his daughter. No office under Protectorate. Sympathetic to Restoration.

Samuel Hartlib c. 1600–62 (*Of education*) Prussian-born merchant and social reformer, disciple of the educationalist Comenius (from whose views M dissociated himself). Encouraged M to write out his educational theories and perhaps to extend his teaching practice.

Edward King c. 1612–37 (*Lycidas*) Contemporary of M at Cambridge, fellow of Christ's 1630, intended for holy orders, drowned at sea. Not close friend of M.

Henry Lawes 1596–1662 (*Comus, Sonnet XIII*) Musician, friend of poets, courtier, royalist. Taught music to Egerton family and introduced M to them. May have written music for *Arcades* as well as for *Comus* (in which he acted the Attendant Spirit).

Edward Lawrence c. 1633–57 (*Sonnet XVII* 'Lawrence of virtuous father virtuous son') Father Henry President of Council of State under Cromwell. Edward close friend of M in 1650s, perhaps student earlier.

Lady Margaret Ley dates unsure (*Sonnet X*) Little is known about her. A neighbour of M in London; she and her husband John Hobson were close friends of M during his first wife's absence. Her father held office under James I and Charles I.

Giovanni Battista Manso, Marquis of Villa 1561–*c.* 1647 (*Mansus,* mentioned in *Epitaphium Damonis*) Italian nobleman, former patron of Tasso and Marini. M visited him in Naples in 1638.

Andrew Marvell 1621–78 Lyric poet, tutor, MP, satirist, pamphleteer. It is not known when his friendship with M began. M recommended him to the Council of State for employment in 1653 without success, but Marvell joined him as secretary in 1657. After the Restoration they seem to have met less frequently, but Marvell defended M in *The rehearsal transprosed* against the slurs of Samuel Parker, and wrote a commendatory poem for the second edition of *PL*.

John Milton c. 1562–1647 (*Ad patrem*) M's father. Well-to-do scrivener (i.e. lawyer and moneylender), and amateur musician. Brought up a Catholic but became an Anglican, Puritan in his sympathies. Gave M his early educational opportunities, planned a church career for him, and supported his private studies until 1638.

Jane Paulet, Marchioness of Winchester 1607–31 (*Epitaph on the Marchioness of Winchester*) Died of an infected abscess on her face, after having a still-born son. She and her husband came from ancient Catholic families. The Marquess was a royalist in the Civil War. Jonson also wrote mourning verses.

Edward Phillips 1630–*c.* 96 M's nephew (son of his sister Anne), student, friend, biographer, and editor of his *Letters of state* (1694). Made living as translator, editor, and literary journalist. Claimed to have read Satan's speech to the sun (*PL* IV) in early 1640s (when M was planning Christian tragedy). A sister of his may have been the subject of *On the death of a fair infant*.

John Phillips 1631–*c.* 1706 Edward's brother, also M's student, a prolific journalist, satirist, and hack writer. His *Responsio* (1651) is a virulent attack on one of M's opponents in the controversy with Salmasius. His *Satire against hypocrites* (1655) is anti-Puritan. Has been suggested as author of the anonymous biography.

FIG I *Milton et ses filles* painted by Eugène Delacroix after his visit to London in 1825. The eldest daughter, Anne, is on the left. The girl next to Milton is Mary, the most like her mother. From the original in a private collection in America.

Cyriack Skinner 1627–1700 (*Sonnet XVIII* 'Cyriack, whose grandsire'; *To Mr Cyriack Skinner upon his blindness*) Student and close friend of M (also of Marvell), lawyer by profession. Has also been suggested (more convincingly) as author of the anonymous biography. His grandfather was the famous lawyer and opponent of James I, Sir Edward Coke.

George Thomason c. 1602–66 (*Sonnet XIV* is on the death of T's wife) Bookseller and friend of M in 1640s, whose huge collection of civil war literature survives in the British Museum. M gave him several signed copies of his books.

Sir Henry Vane 1613–62 (*To Sir Henry Vane the Younger*) Governor of Massachusetts as a young man, member of the Council of State early 1650s. A tolerationist who, like M, wanted the church disestablished. As a firm republican he disliked the Protectorate. Executed after the Restoration, though not a regicide.

Katherine Woodcock 1628–58 (*Sonnet XIX* 'Methought I saw my late espoused saint') M's second wife, who died four months after giving birth to a daughter. (M's first wife Mary Powell, who died in childbirth, has been suggested as the poem's subject.)

Thomas Young c. 1587–1655 (*Elegy* IV, antiprelatical tracts) A Scottish Presbyterian, M's private tutor. One of the Smectymnuans, to whose defence M came in his pamphlets on the bishops. Member of the Westminster Assembly. Their friendship probably ended after 1644, when M broke with the Presbyterians.

Milton's daughters. Though M had five children only the three daughters of his first wife survived to adulthood – Anne (1646–*c.* 77), Mary (1648–?), and Deborah (1652–1727). They were not sent to school but taught by a private governess. M was disappointed in them. The eldest, Anne, was crippled and had difficulty with her speech; she never learned to write. The others were unable to share M's intellectual interests. They regularly read aloud to their blind father in several languages, but without understanding what they read. They disliked their stepmother, M's third wife Elizabeth Minshull, and seem to have rebelled against their father. M had them taught trades, lacemaking and embroidery, in order that they might support themselves. All three left home before M's death, Deborah moving to Ireland; after M's death they disputed his will. Anne and Mary died obscurely. Deborah married Abraham Clarke, a Dublin weaver, had several children, and returned to England; she lived in poverty most of her life, supporting herself at one point by teaching. She was interviewed by admirers of M like Addison, and given some financial help as a result of a public appeal. Her daughter Elizabeth Foster, M's last known direct descendant, also lived in obscure poverty; Samuel Johnson took an interest in her case. She died in 1754.

England in the early 17th century

The population of England in Milton's youth was roughly $4\frac{1}{2}$ million, mostly living in the country; that of London was about 300,000. Contemporaries sometimes divided the population into the 'three estates' of clergy, nobility, and commons. The commons included both what we would call the middle class, the gentry, the various professions, merchants, and yeomen (prosperous farmers); and artisans and agricultural labourers – the 'meaner sort'. This last group, who formed the bulk of the population, had no say in the government of the country; when contemporaries talked about the people they rarely meant to include these. The attitude to the poor was theoretically paternalistic; they were supposed to be provided for, but in practice lived appallingly hard lives.

The central government was in two parts: the executive comprised the king and his privy council, and the legislative the king in parliament (consisting of lords and commons). Only men of a certain property had the right to elect members of parliament. Local government was in the hands of the gentry, who as justices of the peace, aided by the parish officers, kept the countryside in order. The great gulf between rich and poor was controlled by an authoritarian system. A prosperous Londoner like Milton might remain ignorant of how most of his countrymen lived.

Nevertheless in comparison with European countries, which were constantly engaged in religious wars, England in the early part of the century could seem to contemporaries, and to those who looked back in nostalgia after the experience of the civil war, a haven of peace and prosperity.

Some views of England in the early 17th century

I may not deny but that this nation of ours...is a most noble, a most flourishing kingdom, by common consent of all geographers, historians, politicians,...a blessed, a rich country, and one of the Fortunate Isles: and for some things preferred before other countries, for expert seamen, our laborious discoveries, art of navigation, true merchants...We have besides many particular blessings, which our neighbours want, the gospel truly preached, church discipline established, long peace and quietness, free from exactions, foreign fears, invasions, domestical seditions, well manured, fortified by art and nature...But in which we excel all others, a wise, learned, religious king [James I]...most worthy senators, a learned clergy, an obedient commonalty, etc. Yet amongst many roses some thistles grow...

ROBERT BURTON *The anatomy of melancholy* 1621–40

The happiness of the times I mentioned [the 1630s] was enviously set off by this, that every other kingdom, every other province were engaged, many entangled, and some almost destroyed, by the rage and fury of arms;... whilst alone the kingdoms we now lament were looked upon as the garden of the world...England was generally thought secure, with the advantages of its own climate; the court in great plenty, or rather (which is the discredit of plenty) excess and luxury; the country rich, and, which is more, fully enjoying the pleasure of its own wealth, and so the easier corrupted with the pride and wantonness of it; the church flourishing with learned and extra-ordinary men...; trade increased to that degree, that we were the exchange of Christendom...But all these blessings could but enable, not compel, us to be happy; we wanted that sense, acknowledgement, and value of our own happiness, which all but we had; and took pains to make, when we could not find, ourselves miserable.

EDWARD HYDE, EARL OF CLARENDON *History of the rebellion*
first pub. 1702–4

The land was then at peace [at the end of James I's reign]...if that quietness may be called a peace, which was rather like the calm and smooth surface of the sea, whose dark womb is already impregnated with a horrid tempest.

Life of Mrs Hutchinson by herself first pub. 1806

Further reading W. Notestein *The English people on the eve of colonisation* New York 1954 is an introductory account with valuable examples. See also D. Mathew *The Jacobean age* 1938 and *The social structure in Caroline England* Oxford 1948. L. Stone's anthology *Social change and revolution in England 1540–1640* 1965 is an excellent introduction to the vexed question of the social causes of the civil war; it has a valuable bibliography. One of the best introductions to 17th-century life is through contemporary letters and biographies. See the anthology by D. Nichol Smith *Characters from the histories and memoirs of the 17th century* Oxford 1918; John Aubrey *Brief lives*, John Earle *Microcosmography*, Dorothy Osborne *Letters*, Henry Peacham *The complete gentleman*, Izaac Walton *Lives of Donne, Hooker, Herbert*.

Milton as a student c. 1620–37

Milton was educated at St Paul's School, London, from about 1620 or earlier, to 1624; and at Christ's College, Cambridge 1625–32. On leaving Cambridge he did not enter the church as expected, nor take up a profession, but spent the years from 1632 to early 1638 pursuing his education in private. It was in the period 1625 to 1637 that he wrote the best of his minor poems. Important influences on his childhood were his private tutor Thomas Young, a Presbyterian and later one of the Smectymnuans, and his schoolfriend Charles Diodati, who died in 1638; Milton wrote Latin letters and poems to both. Like other famous contemporaries Milton was critical of the universities, and he seems to have quarrelled with his first college tutor Chappell. His objections were to the narrowness of the curriculum; his private study ranged far beyond it, hence his indignation with adversaries who in later life slighted his learning.

When he went to school, when he was very young he studied very hard and sat up very late, commonly till twelve or one o'clock at night, and his father ordered the maid to sit up for him...And was a very hard student in the university, and performed all his exercises there with very good applause.

JOHN AUBREY, using information from
Christopher Milton 1681

Further reading Those interested in Milton's work at Cambridge should look at the *Prolusions*, his academic exercises. The following are good accounts of 17th-century education (the last two are detailed and scholarly): D. L. Clark *JM at St Paul's School* 1948; H. F. Fletcher *The intellectual development of JM* 2 vols 1956–; M. Curtis *Oxford and Cambridge in transition* 1959.

Milton's travels 1638–9

Milton left England in the spring of 1638 for a European tour (the usual way of completing a gentleman's education), and was away for about fifteen months. He travelled through France, via Paris and Nice, to Italy. Here he visited Genoa, Pisa, Florence, Sienna, Rome, and Naples, returning home through Rome and Florence to Lucca, Venice, Verona, and Milan, thence to Geneva, and through France back to England. He made extended stays in Florence and Rome and was warmly received by scholars and academicians, patrons of the arts, and princes of the church. The notable men he met on this tour included the lawyer and writer Grotius, the scientist Galileo, and the patron Manso. Milton's travels had the most important effect on his self-esteem; he emerged from obscurity to be received as an equal by European scholars. After his return to England Milton kept up a correspondence with his Italian friends, and printed their commendations in front of his *Poems* of 1645. He was always to be concerned with his European reputation; his Latin *Defences* of the 1650s were aimed at a European audience.

35

Having departed from Rome to Naples, he was introduced by his fellow traveller to Giovanni Battista Manso, Marquis of Villa, a person most nobly descended, of great authority, renowned for his military achievements, and a patron of learned men. To him the famous Tasso inscribed his poem of friendship, and makes honourable mention of him among the princes of Campania in the twentieth book of his *Gerusalemme conquistata*. He went himself to show him all the remarkable places of that city, visited him often at his lodging, and made this distich in his commendation, which he addresses to himself:

Ut mens, forma, decor, facies, mos, si pietas sic,
Non Anglus, verum hercle Angelus ipse fores.
[If your religion matched your mind, shape, grace, bearing, and manners, you would truly be not an Angle but an angel.]

This exception of his piety relates to his being a Protestant; and the Marquis told him, he would have done him several good offices, had he been more reserved in matters of religion. But our author out of gratitude for all these singular favours from one of his high quality, presented him at his departure with an incomparable Latin eclogue, entitled *Mansus*...And that I may mention it by the way, I don't question but it was from Manso's conversation and their discourses about Tasso, that he first formed his design of writing an epic poem. JOHN TOLAND 1698

As I was preparing to pass over also into Sicily and Greece, I was restrained by the melancholy tidings from England of the civil war [the first Bishops' war]: for I thought it base, that I should be travelling at my ease, even for the improvement of my mind abroad, while my fellow-citizens were fighting for their liberty at home. As I was about to return to Rome, the merchants gave me an intimation, that they had learned from their letters, that, in case of my revisiting Rome, the English Jesuits had laid a plot for me, because I had spoken too freely on the subject of religion...I...returned notwithstanding to Rome; I concealed from no one, who asked the question, what I was; if any one attacked me, I defended in the most open manner, as before, the orthodox faith, for nearly two months more, in the city even of the sovereign pontiff himself. *Second defence* 1654

In the private academies of Italy, whither I was favoured to resort, perceiving that some trifles which I had in memory...met with acceptance above what was looked for, and other things which I had shifted in scarcity of books and conveniences to patch up amongst them, were received with written encomiums, which the Italian is not forward to bestow on men of this side the Alps, I begun thus far to assent both to them and divers of my friends here at home, and not less to an inward prompting which now grew daily upon me, that by labour and intent study (which I take to be my portion in this life), joined with the strong propensity of nature, I might perhaps leave something so written to aftertimes, as they should not willingly let it die. *Reason of church government* 1642

36

Milton as a teacher: early 1640s and after

On his return from the continent Milton set up house in London and began to make his living teaching his nephews and sons of friends. The intensive and ambitious training he provided was meant to be in complete contrast to his own experience at Cambridge. Edward Phillips has left a detailed account of the rigorous curriculum. Drawing on his practical experience Milton wrote in 1644 a small tract *Of education* for the educational reformer Samuel Hartlib. Much criticism of the universities in the 17th century was political in origin; they were regarded as hotbeds of puritanism, republicanism, or royalism (depending on who was doing the criticizing), and political changes were usually followed by purges of college fellows. But Milton's attacks were non-political and in some ways old-fashioned. Though he criticized the university curriculum and advocated a practical and ethical rather than a logical and metaphysical training, he made it clear that he was out of sympathy with the democratic and utilitarian programme of the contemporary Bohemian reformer Comenius. He was however obviously influenced by Bacon's plea for an extension of the fields and methods of study in *The advancement of learning* 1605. Milton's imaginary academy (comprising both school and university) is for the gentry. They are to proceed quickly from the learning of language to practical sciences and then to ethics, politics, history, etc., finally reaching logic and poetics. Music and military exercise are essential. Milton restated his aristocratic view of education in a later political work, the *Ready and easy way* 1660.

He continued to act as a teacher in later life; the Quaker Thomas Ellwood, who read to him after his blindness, benefited from his severity. A blot on Milton's record is his treatment of his daughters, who received only a rudimentary education, though he ensured that they learned trades.

Possibly his proceeding thus far in the education of youth may have been the occasion of some of his adversaries calling him pedagogue and schoolmaster; whereas it is well known he never set up for a public school to teach all the young fry of a parish, but only was willing to impart his learning and knowledge to relations, and the sons of some gentlemen that were his intimate friends; besides, that neither his converse, nor his writings, nor his manner of teaching ever savoured in the least anything of pedantry; and probably he might have some prospect of putting in practice his academical institution, according to the model laid down in his sheet of education. The progress of which design was afterwards diverted by a series of alteration in the affairs of state.   EDWARD PHILLIPS 1694

Now persons so far manducted into the highest paths of literature both divine and human, had they received his documents with the same acuteness of wit and apprehension, the same industry, alacrity, and thirst after knowledge, as the instructor was indued with, what prodigies of wit and learning might they have proved!   *Ibid.*

As he was severe on one hand, so he was most familiar and free in his conversation to those to whom most severe in his way of education.
                                        JOHN AUBREY 1681

Let not our veneration for Milton forbid us to look with some degree of merriment on great promises and small performance – on the man who hastens home because his countrymen are contending for their liberty, and, when he reaches the scene of action, vapours away his patriotism in a private boarding-school...He did not sell literature to all comers at an open shop; he was a chamber-milliner, and measured his commodities to his friends.
                                        SAMUEL JOHNSON *Life of Milton* 1779

We do amiss to spend seven or eight years merely in scraping together so much miserable Latin and Greek, as might be learned otherwise easily and delightfully in one year.   *Of education* 1644

And for the usual method of teaching arts, I deem it to be an old error of universities not yet well recovered from the scholastic grossness of barbarous ages, that instead of beginning with arts most easy, and those be such as are most obvious to the sense, they present their young unmatriculated novices at first coming with the most intellective abstractions of logic and metaphysics: so that they having but newly left those grammatic flats and shallows where they stuck unreasonably to learn a few words with lamentable construction, and now on the sudden transported under another climate to be tossed and turmoiled with their unballasted wits in fathomless and unquiet deeps of controversy, do for the most part grow into hatred and contempt of learning, mocked and deluded all this while with ragged notions and babblements, while they expected worthy and delightful knowledge.   *Ibid.*

[The gentry in each county] should have here also schools and academies at their own choice, wherein their children may be bred up in their own sight to all learning and noble education not in grammar only, but in all liberal arts and exercises. This would soon spread much more knowledge and civility, yea religion through all parts of the land, by communicating the natural heat of government and culture more distributively to all extreme parts.
                                        Ready and easy way 1660

[Deborah] informed me, that she and her sisters used to read to their father in eight languages; which by practice they were capable of doing with great readiness and accuracy, though they understood what they read in no other

38

language but English; and their father used often to say in their hearing, 'one tongue was enough for a woman'. None of them were ever sent to school, but all taught at home by a mistress kept for that purpose.

JOHN WARD to Thomas Birch 1738

Milton's marriages and attitudes to divorce

Milton was married three times. He married his first wife Mary Powell in 1642; she bore him three daughters, Anne, Mary, and Deborah, and a son John who died in infancy; she herself died after the birth of Deborah in 1652. Milton married his second wife Katherine Woodcock in 1656; she bore him a daughter Katherine, but both mother and child died in 1658 a few months after the birth. In 1663 Milton married his third wife Elizabeth Minshull, who survived him, living until 1727.

Milton's domestic life has been the subject of a good deal of comment, because of the behaviour of his first wife, his writings on marriage and divorce, and his treatment of his children. Mary Powell was the daughter of a royalist country gentleman, a client of Milton's father. Milton met and married her in a great hurry, and the marriage seems to have been immediately unhappy. She soon left him and went home to her mother, ostensibly for a visit, and did not return for three years. After trying unsuccessfully to get her back, Milton set down his views on marriage and the grounds permissible for divorce in four tracts published between 1643 and 1645: *The doctrine and discipline of divorce, The judgement of Martin Bucer, Tetrachordon* and *Colasterion*. Before his marriage Milton had idealized chastity; now he set forward his view of marriage as a spiritual as well as a physical union which depended for its validity on mutual love and respect, and which could be dissolved by mutual consent. The status of marriage had been elevated by the Protestant reformers, who welcomed a married priesthood, but Milton's views on divorce were shocking to his contemporaries. He achieved his first notoriety as author of the divorce tracts; attacks on him by Presbyterian divines led him to abandon his support for Presbyterianism and to turn to the question of religious liberty. In spite of his idealization of marriage he shared the contemporary view that a woman was a man's intellectual inferior; but it is inaccurate to accuse him of having, as Samuel Johnson says, 'something like a Turkish contempt for females'.

Having had the doctrine of holy scripture unfolding those chaste and high mysteries with timeliest care infused, that 'the body is for the Lord and the

Lord for the body', thus also I argued to myself; that if unchastity in a woman whom St Paul terms the glory of man, be such a scandal and dishonour, then certainly in a man who is both the image and glory of God, it must, though commonly not so thought, be much more deflowering and dishonourable. In that he sins both against his own body which is the perfecter sex, and his own glory which is in the woman, and that which is worst, against the image and glory of God which is in himself.

Apology for Smectymnuus 1642

His manner of settlement fitting him for the reception of a wife, he in a month's time (according to his practice of not wasting that precious talent) courted, married, and brought home from Forest Hill near Oxford a daughter of Mr Powell. But she, that was very young, and had been bred in a family of plenty and freedom, being not well pleased with his reserved manner of life, within a few days left him, and went back into the country with her mother. Nor though he sent several pressing invitations could he prevail with her to return, till about four years after, when Oxford was surrendered...she of her own accord came, and submitted to him; pleading that her mother had been the inciter of her to that frowardness.   Anonymous biographer

About Whitsuntide it was, or a little after, that he took a journey into the country; nobody about him certainly knowing the reason, or that it was any more than a journey of recreation. After a month's stay, home he returns a married man, that went out a bachelor.   EDWARD PHILLIPS 1694

I have so much charity for her that she might not wrong his bed but what man (especially contemplative) would like to have a young wife environed and stormed by the sons of Mars and those of the enemy party.

JOHN AUBREY 1681

That indisposition, unfitness, or contrariety of mind, arising from a cause in nature unchangeable, hindering and ever likely to hinder the main benefits of conjugal society, which are solace and peace, is a greater reason of divorce than natural frigidity, especially if there be no children, and that there be mutual consent.   *Doctrine and discipline of divorce* 1643

In God's intention a meet and happy conversation is the chiefest and the noblest end of marriage...And with all generous persons married thus it is, that where the mind and the person pleases aptly, there some unaccomplishment of the body's delight may be better borne with, than when the mind hangs off in an unclosing disproportion, though the body be as it ought; for there all corporal delight will soon become unsavoury and contemptible.

Ibid.

Love in marriage cannot live nor subsist, unless it be mutual; and where love cannot be, there can be left of wedlock nothing, but the empty husk of an outside matrimony; as undelightful and unpleasing to God, as any other kind of hypocrisy.   *Ibid.*

With regard to marriage, inasmuch as it is not an institution peculiar to Christian nations, but common to them all by the universal law of man-kind...it is not even a religious ceremony, still less a sacrament, but a compact purely civil; nor does its celebration belong in any manner to the ministers of the church.   *Christian doctrine* late 1650s

Either...polygamy is a true marriage, or all children born in that state are spurious; which would include the whole race of Jacob, the twelve holy tribes chosen by God...It appears to me, that, so far from the question respecting the lawfulness of polygamy being trivial, it is of the highest importance that it should be decided...   *Ibid.*

If divorce were suffered...it would be an occasion to the corrupt heart of man without any just cause at all, merely for to satisfy his lust, to pretend causes of divorce when there is none...Who sees not, how many thousands of lustful and libidinous men would be parting from their wives every week and marrying others,...with a hundred more the like inconveniences, even to the overturning and overthrowing of all human society, which would inevitably follow if this loose doctrine of divorce were once established by law.   *An answer to ' The doctrine and discipline of divorce'* 1644

But that solace and peace which is contrary to discord and variance...is not the main end of marriage or conjugal society, is very plain and apparent: nor yet the solace and content in the gifts of the mind of one another only, for then would it have been every ways as much, yea more content and solace to Adam, and so consequently to every man, to have had another man made to him of his rib instead of Eve: this is apparent by experience, which shows, that man ordinarily exceeds woman in natural gifts of mind, and in delect-ableness of converse.   *Ibid.*

I must seriously profess that, when I first did cast my eyes upon the front of the book, I supposed some great wit meant to try his skill in the maintenance of this so wild and improbable a paradox; but ere I could run over some of those too well-penned pages, I found the author was in earnest...I cannot but blush for our age.   JOSEPH HALL *Cases of conscience* 1649

The civil war: a summary of the issues 1640–9

There is perpetual disagreement among historians as to what exactly the civil war was about. This is partly because some of the issues only emerged during the course of events, and people took a long time to recognize them. The opponents of Charles I in the early 1640s did not foresee the outcome; no one set out with a programme to abolish the monarchy and establish a commonwealth; there was no long-term solution for the problems of the church. Individuals fought the king for a variety of reasons. However we can distinguish three main areas of conflict – political, religious, social. Nineteenth-century historians (such as Macaulay and Gardiner) concentrated on the first two; partly as a reaction, 20th-century historians (such as Tawney, Trevor-Roper and Hill) have concentrated on the last. There was similar disagreement among contemporaries about the causes of the conflict (though the social division was not clearly observed until the end of the first civil war). The religious conflict is summarized in the section on church reform below. Milton was not interested in, and indeed largely ignorant of, the social and economic conflicts of the protagonists, so they are hardly touched on here. This does not mean that the socio-economic issues were unimportant, but this section deals only with the political.

The political conflict was chiefly over the question of sovereignty, over where the power of the state was to reside, though it was not originally seen in these terms. The most widely held political theory was that of the balanced constitution, or mixed monarchy, in which sovereignty was shared between king and parliament, with a balance between 'prerogative' and 'privilege'. At the beginning of the Long Parliament Charles and his advisers were attacked for overstepping the limits of prerogative; appeal was made to the traditional constitution and fundamental laws. Much of this opposition to the crown was conservative. Conversely, as parliament asserted itself Charles counterattacked by accusing parliament (quite accurately) of attempting to encroach on his prerogative.

Constitutional royalism proved an inadequate theory in a period of conflict. On one side it was challenged by the theory of the divine right of kings. Though put forward by James I, that was a minority view held chiefly by high Anglican clergymen. Divine right theory did not come into its own until the reign of James II (although one important aspect of it, the idea that the ruler makes law and is not bound by it, is an essential element of the thought of Hobbes, who asserted the need for absolute sovereignty). There was however a widespread emotional reverence for monarchy. On the other side some of the king's opponents began to abandon their appeal to tradition, and switch to revolutionary opinions: that parliament could make law by itself; that government was based on a contract between ruler and ruled, so that the king was answerable to his subjects; and that rights were more important than custom.

The conflict was originally between two parties, king and parliament; in the course of the first civil war (1642–6) the army became a third party. The Presbyterians in parliament had limited objectives and wanted reconciliation with the king. The army Independents under Cromwell wanted religious toleration and more extreme constitutional changes, though still under monarchy. Only a minority group like the Diggers wanted social equality, though the army, particularly after it had been new-modelled, was regarded as a social threat and a haven for upstarts. The Levellers, army radicals opposed by Cromwell, wanted the abolition of the monarchy, an extension of the franchise, and other political reforms. The king tried to play the rival groups against each other; then he allied with the Scots. Cromwell ceased to trust him, and after the royalist defeat in the second civil war (1648) the king's execution became inevitable.

Whereas a majority of the people may have supported the Long Parliament's initial reforms, the victors of the second civil war and the establishers of the commonwealth were a tiny minority. This paradox, the fact that their appeal to a theory of popular sovereignty was combined with dependence on army support for survival, was to plague the attempts of the Cromwellians for the next ten years to arrive at a satisfactory constitutional settlement.

Some views of the balanced constitution

The law is the boundary, the measure between the king's prerogative and the people's liberty. Whilst these move in their own orbs they are a support and a security to one another...If the prerogative of the king overwhelm the liberty of the people it will be turned into tyranny; if liberty undermine the prerogative, it will grow into anarchy.

> JOHN PYM's reply to Strafford at the latter's trial 1641. Both sides used the same argument.

[The king's advisers] were averse to absolute monarchy, as also to absolute democracy, or aristocracy, all which governments they esteemed tyranny; and were in love with *mixarchy* which they used to praise by the name of mixed monarchy, though it were indeed nothing else but pure anarchy.   THOMAS HOBBES *Behemoth* 1679

Some views of divine right

That which concerns the mystery of the king's power, is not lawful to be disputed; for that is to wade into the weakness of princes, and to take away the mystical reverence, that belongs unto them that sit in the throne of God.

                    JAMES I *Speech in Star Chamber* 1616

The most high and sacred order of kings is of divine right, being the ordinance of God himself, founded in the prime laws of nature, and clearly established by express texts both of the old and new testaments.

                    Constitutions and canons ecclesiastical 1640

43

For subjects to bear arms against their kings, offensive or defensive, upon any pretence whatsoever, is at the least to resist the powers which are ordained of God; and though they do not invade, but only resist, St Paul tells them plainly, 'they shall receive to themselves damnation'. *Ibid.*

The need for absolute sovereignty

There can be no laws without a supreme power to command or make them... In a monarchy the king must of necessity be above the laws. There can be no sovereign majesty in him that is under them.

SIR ROBERT FILMER *Patriarcha c.* 1635–40

The virtue of a subject is comprehended wholly in obedience to the laws of the commonwealth. To obey the laws is justice and equity, which is the law of nature; and, consequently, is civil law in all nations of the world; and nothing is injustice or iniquity otherwise than it is against the law.   HOBBES *Behemoth*

Leveller arguments

This power of commons in parliament [to make laws on behalf of the people] is the thing against which the king hath contended, and the people have defended with their lives, and therefore ought now be demanded as the price of their blood.   JOHN WILDMAN *The case of the army truly stated* 1647

Really I think that the poorest he that is in England hath a life to live, as the greatest he...every man that is to live under a government ought first by his own consent to put himself under that government; and I do think that the poorest man in England is not at all bound in a strict sense to that government that he hath not had a voice to put himself under...

COLONEL RAINBOROUGH in the Putney debates 1647

Characterizations of the opposing parties

If any were grieved at the dishonour of the kingdom, or the griping of the poor, or the unjust oppressions of the subject...he was a Puritan; if any, out of mere morality and civil honesty, discountenanced the abominations of those days, he was a Puritan...in short, all that crossed the views of the needy courtiers, the proud encroaching priests, the thievish projectors, the lewd nobility and gentry – whoever was zealous for God's glory or worship, could not endure blasphemous oaths, ribald conversation, profane scoffs, Sabbath-breaking, derision of the word of God, and the like...all these were Puritans; and if Puritans, then enemies to the king and his government, seditious, factious hypocrites, ambitious disturbers of the public peace, and finally, the pest of the kingdom. Such false logic did the children of darkness use to argue with against the hated children of light.

MRS LUCY HUTCHINSON *Memoirs of Col. Hutchinson*

And abundance of the ignorant sort of the country, who were civil, did flock into the parliament, and filled up their armies afterward, merely because they heard men *swear* for the Common Prayer and bishops, and heard others *pray* that were against them; and because they heard the king's soldiers with horrid oaths abuse the name of God, and saw them live in debauchery, and the parliament's soldiers flock to sermons and talking of religion, and praying and singing psalms together on their guards. And all the sober men that I was acquainted with, who were against the parliament, were wont to say, 'the king hath the better cause, but the parliament hath the better men'.

RICHARD BAXTER *Autobiography* 1696

Amongst these excellent tempers, amongst this goodly wheat, whilst men slept, the enemy came and sowed tares, there sprang up of later years a sort of people sour, sullen, suspicious, querulous, peevish, envious, reserved, narrow-hearted, close-fisted, self-conceited, ignorant, stiff-necked, Children of Belial...ever prone to despise dominion, to speak evil of dignities, to gainsay order, rule, and authority; who have accounted it their honour to contend with kings and governors, and to disquiet the peace of kingdoms;... breathing nothing but sedition and calumnies against the established government, aspiring without measure, railing without reason, and making their own wild fancies the square and rule of their consciences.

EDWARD CHAMBERLAYNE *Angliae notitia* 1669

Cromwell in the civil war

I can say this of Naseby, that when I saw the enemy draw up and march in gallant order towards us, and we a company of poor ignorant men, to seek how to order our battle...I could not...but smile out to God in praises, in assurance of victory, because God would, by things that are not, bring to naught things that are. Of which I had great assurance; and God did it.

Letter from Cromwell to an MP 1645

Further reading General histories. The best introductory accounts are C. Hill *The century of revolution* 1961; I. Roots *The great rebellion* 1966. See also C. V. Wedgwood *The king's peace* 1955 and *The king's war* 1958; J. P. Kenyon *The Stuarts* illustrated 1956. P. Zagorin *History of political thought in the English revolution* 1954 is clear and useful.

Collections of documents. J. P. Kenyon *The Stuart constitution* 1966 is very well annotated; C. Hill and E. Dell *The good old cause* 2nd ed 1969 is polemical and lively. P. A. M. Taylor ed *The origins of the English civil war* Boston 1960 is a kind of printed seminar.

Contemporary works. The most important contemporary account is Clarendon's *History of the rebellion and civil wars* ed W. D. Macray 6 vols 1888; there is a handy abridgement by G. Huehns 1955. Hobbes *Behemoth* ed F. Tonnies 1889, though also royalist, gives a quite different version. Lucy Hutchinson *Memoirs of the life of Colonel Hutchinson* ed C. Firth 1906 gives the view of an Independent. For political thought see Hobbes *Leviathan*; James I *Political works* ed

C. H. McIlwain 1918; Filmer *Patriarcha* ed P. Laslett 1949. A. S. P.
Woodhouse *Puritanism and liberty* 1938 is a collection of Leveller
debates and manifestoes.

Milton and church reform 1641–4, 1659

The difficulties of the Anglican church dated from the Reformation,
but they came to a head in the 1630s with the activities of Archbishop
Laud. There were three main parties in the church at this time: the
high Anglicans (or Laudians), moderate Anglicans, and Puritans (or
Presbyterians). Outside the Anglican church were the Catholics, the
Independents, and various sects.

The Puritans opposed the Laudians in two ways: they wanted to
purify church government and ritual on the model of the continental
Protestant churches (this included abolishing the bishops and substi-
tuting presbyters); and they were opposed to the spread of Arminianism
(belief in free will) among the high Anglicans, because it conflicted
with their Calvinist belief in predestination.

Laud was anxious to enforce his own view of church discipline,
which included a strong emphasis on ceremonial and the idea of 'the
beauty of holiness'. To his antagonists this was popery. In addition to
this doctrinal and ecclesiastical opposition, there was much secular,
political hostility to the bishops' interference in state affairs (Laud was
virtually prime minister). Laud attempted to silence Puritan opposition by strict censorship of press and pulpit. Many Puritans were
driven out of the church into separatism, and there were large
migrations to the Netherlands and America. Perhaps the majority
would have been content with moderate church reform and moderate
limitations on the power of bishops, but Laud's extremism made this
impossible. The Long Parliament struck back at him; amid a barrage
of pamphleteering and petitioning the bishops were removed from
power; eventually Laud was executed and episcopacy (the rule of
bishops in the church) abolished.

The Westminster Assembly (consisting mostly of Presbyterians)
was set up to decide the question of church government and doctrine.
It proved impossible to do this to everyone's satisfaction. The
Presbyterians wanted to imitate the Scottish model; this would have
meant a theocratic system tolerating no dissent. There was strong
opposition from the Independents and the smaller sects over the issue
of toleration; for these groups, Presbyterianism rapidly replaced
episcopacy as the enemy: 'New presbyter is but old priest writ large',

46

said Milton *On the new forcers of conscience*. Some were in favour of complete disestablishment of the church from the state and toleration for private conscience (though few were prepared to tolerate Catholics).

After the second civil war (1648) the Presbyterians moved into opposition; they were appalled at the execution of the king. The establishment of the commonwealth did not settle the church problem, however. Cromwell at first favoured disestablishment, and under the commonwealth and protectorate there was in practice a good deal of toleration for those groups that were not considered politically subversive. But the Church of England continued to muddle along, controlled by various committees; its position was not resolved until its drastic reconstitution at the Restoration.

Milton was the grandson of a Catholic and the son of an Anglican; though he was destined for the church, Laud's disciplinary measures made him a Puritan. In 1640 he was Presbyterian in his sympathies. When a group of Presbyterian ministers writing under the name of Smectymnuus (made up from their initials) engaged in pamphlet warfare with Bishop Hall, Milton came to their help in five pamphlets published in 1641–2: *Of reformation touching church discipline in England, Of prelatical episcopacy, Animadversions upon the remonstrant's defence against Smectymnuus, The reason of church government urged against prelaty* (the first to which he put his name), and *An apology against a pamphlet called 'A modest confutation'*. Relying on scripture and trying to discredit his opponents' use of early church history, Milton urged the abolition of bishops and the substitution of presbyters; he argued that until this was done the Reformation in England would not be complete. He put forward his view of the true minister, and prayed passionately for a reformed England. But though he was defending the official Presbyterian position, his future break with Presbyterianism was implied in his hostility not simply to bishops but to all hired priests.

The break came (though Milton never officially acknowledged it) as a result of attacks on his divorce pamphlets. Parliament's printing ordinance seemed a revival of Laudian censorship, and Milton immediately joined the toleration controversy. Religious liberty now became his overriding interest. In *Areopagitica* (1644) he argued that the licensing of the press inhibits the spread of Christian truth; the proliferation of sects, which the Presbyterians regarded with horror, seemed to Milton a sign of health, an essential means of testing truth. He moved into attack on the Presbyterian clergy for their support of

47

the king; they are savagely lashed in the *The tenure of kings* and in the posthumously published *Character of the Long Parliament*.

Milton lost all interest in external church reform in the 1650s and hoped instead for complete disestablishment: he envisaged ministers being elected and voluntarily supported by their congregations. At first he pinned his hopes on Cromwell, who made no move in this direction; in *A treatise of civil power in exclesiastical causes* and *Considerations touching the likeliest means to remove hirelings out of the church* (1659) he addressed his plea for toleration and disestablishment to Richard Cromwell's parliament and the Rump. The far more important religious work of these years was the formulation of his own system of theology in *Christian doctrine* (see the section on his religious opinions below).

The episcopal controversy

A particular of the manifold evils, pressures, and grievances caused, practised and occasioned by the prelates and their dependents... 2) The faintheartedness of ministers to preach the truth of God.... 4) The restraint of many godly and able men from the ministry... 6) The great increase of idle, lewd and dissolute, ignorant and erroneous men in the ministry, which swarm like the locusts of Egypt over the whole kingdom... 9) The hindering of godly books to be printed... 11) The growth of popery and increase of papists, priests and Jesuits... 14) The great conformity and likeness both continued and increased of our church to the church of Rome...
The root and branch petition 1640

They that would pull down the bishops and erect a new way of government, do as he that pulls down an old house, and builds another of another fashion. There's a great deal ado, and a great deal of trouble; the old rubbish must be carried away, and new materials must be brought; workmen must be provided; and perhaps the old one would have served as well.
JOHN SELDEN *Table talk* first pub. 1689

Sectarian views of the church

Matters of religion and the ways of God's worship are not at all entrusted by us to any human power, because therein we cannot remit, or exceed, a tittle of what our consciences dictate to be the mind of God, without wilful sin.
The first agreement of the people 1647

But the black earthly spirit of the priests wounded my life; and when I heard the bell toll to call people together to the steeple-house, it struck at my life; for it was just like a market-bell, to gather people together that the priest might set forth his ware to sale. O! the vast sums of money that are gotten by the trade they make of selling the scriptures, and by their preaching, from the highest bishop to the lowest priest! What one trade else in the world is

48

comparable to it? notwithstanding the scriptures were given forth freely, and Christ commanded his ministers to preach freely...

GEORGE FOX *Journal* 1694 (Fox was the founder of the Quakers.)

Toleration under the protectorate

XXXVII That such as profess faith in God by Jesus Christ (though differing in judgement from the doctrine, worship, or discipline publicly held forth) shall not be restrained from, but shall be protected in, the profession of the faith and exercise of their religion; so as they abuse not this liberty to the civil injury of others and to the actual disturbance of the public peace on their parts: provided this liberty be not extended to popery nor prelacy, nor to such as, under the profession of Christ, hold forth and practise licentiousness.

The instrument of government 1653

Milton on church reform

What numbers of faithful and freeborn Englishmen and good Christians have been constrained to forsake their dearest home, their friends and kindred, whom nothing but the wide ocean, and the savage deserts of America could hide and shelter from the fury of the bishops.   *Of reformation* 1641

If the splendour of gold and silver begin to lord it once again in the church of England, we shall see Antichrist shortly wallow here, though his chief kennel be at Rome.   *Ibid.*

As for ordination, what is it, but the laying on of hands, an outward sign or symbol of admission? it creates nothing, it confers nothing; it is the inward calling of God that makes a minister, and his own painful study and diligence that manures and improves his ministerial gifts.   *Animadversions* 1641

Instead of the great harm therefore that these men fear upon the dissolving of prelates, what an ease and happiness will it be to us, when tempting rewards are taken away, that the cunningest and most dangerous mercenaries will cease of themselves to frequent the fold, whom otherwise scarce all the prayers of the faithful could have kept back from devouring the flock?

Ibid.

If the religion be pure, spiritual, simple, and lowly, as the gospel most truly is, such must the face of the ministry be. And in like manner if the form of the ministry be grounded in the worldly degrees of authority, honour, temporal jurisdiction, we see it with our eyes it will turn the inward power and purity of the gospel into the outward carnality of the law; evaporating and exhaling the internal worship into empty conformities, and gay shows.

Reason of church government 1642

Methinks I see in my mind a noble and puissant nation rousing herself like a strong man after sleep, and shaking her invincible locks: methinks I see her as an eagle mewing her mighty youth, and kindling her undazzled eyes at the full midday beam; purging and unscaling her long abused sight at the fountain itself of heavenly radiance; while the whole noise of timorous and flocking birds...flutter about, amazed at what she means, and in their envious gabble would prognosticate a year of sects and schisms.

Areopagitica 1644

Further reading Two detailed books on Milton's pamphleteering on the subject of church and state are D. M. Wolfe *M in the Puritan revolution* 1941 and A. Barker *M and the Puritan dilemma* Toronto 1942. The best accounts of Puritanism are by W. Haller in his scholarly but passionate *The rise of Puritanism* New York 1938 and *Liberty and reformation in the Puritan revolution* New York 1955. See also C. H. and K. George *The Protestant mind of the English Reformation* Princeton 1961 and C. Hill *Society and Puritanism in pre-revolutionary England* 1964. For contemporary works see p. 62 below. The best way to understand religious controversy is through experience. Attend Roman Catholic and Anglican services, and the meeting of a dissenting sect such as the Plymouth Brethren. Jonson's *Alchemist* and *Bartholomew Fair* contain caricatures of Puritans.

Milton as a public servant 1649–60

The execution of Charles I was among other things a great tactical error. Charles' conduct at his trial and the patent illegality of the proceedings did much to restore his popularity. From now on his victors had to face their lack of constitutional status; the fact that they had no positive programme did not help. Cromwell's essential problem was the narrowness of his support. With each more conservative step that he took he broke with important groups, first with the political radicals, the Levellers, then with the republicans, then with religious radicals like the fifth monarchists. Because he depended on army support he could not accept the crown and thus satisfy the constitutionalists. He could not govern effectively either with or without a parliament. Cromwell was a man of action and not a theorist; he relied on his strong religious sense to guide him. His great interest was not in political reform but in religious liberty. He regarded himself as God's instrument, and was fond of referring to the English as the apple of God's eye. His strength held the government together; at his death there was confusion. The army and the civilians were unable to agree; there was a widespread desire for settled forms of government which the revolutionaries could not satisfy.

After three years spent on private study Milton returned to public controversy in 1649 with an attack on the royalist-Presbyterian alliance, and a defence of the right to execute tyrants, in *The tenure of kings and magistrates*. He argued that the ruler derives his power from the people by contract, and they have the right to revoke power if it is abused. Grateful for this unsolicited testimonial, the council of state hired Milton as secretary for foreign tongues, a post which combined letter-writing with propaganda and censorship (an ironical position for the author of *Areopagitica*). Much of his time was spent in the daily routine of a civil servant; his more glamorous work was to defend the regime from its critics. Immediately after Charles' death a book called *Eikon basilike* (the king's image) began to circulate. Based on Charles' notes (expanded by Gauden his chaplain, though this was not known at the time), it fed the new cult of Charles the martyr. Milton answered it, not very effectively, in *Eikonoklastes* (image-breaker). But there was a new opponent to face. The French scholar Claude de Saumaise (Salmasius) was commissioned by Charles II to attack the commonwealth in *Defensio regia pro Carolo I* (royal defence). Salmasius was ignorant of constitutional monarchy and asserted that the king was above the law, but he made telling attacks on the illegality of the commonwealth, its reliance on military force, and its lack of popular support. Milton answered in *Defensio pro populo anglicano* (1st defence of the English people). He wriggled out of the problem by defining the people as the enlightened part of the nation. The *2nd defence* was written in answer to Pierre du Moulin's *Regii sanguinis clamor* (cry of the king's blood) published anonymously. Milton became embroiled in controversy with Alexander More whom he thought to be the author of the *Clamor*, and the tedious *3rd defence* consists largely of personal abuse.

In the *1st defence* Milton was defending the Rump; the *2nd defence* was written under the protectorate. Milton's argument shifts from concern with the people to the idea of virtuous leadership. Cromwell is exhorted to become the ideal leader, but Milton devotes a good deal of space to praising his opponents; he is clearly uncertain about the tendencies of the protectorate government. After Cromwell's death Milton turned against the idea of a single ruler; his answer to the confusion of the pre-Restoration period was a proposal in *The ready and easy way to establish a free commonwealth* for the Rump to perpetuate itself as a permanent grand council, a kind of dictatorship by enlightened aristocracy. It was already out of date when it was published.

Milton's political views run through changes that are common with revolutionaries. It is possible to be cynical about them. He seems to have seized on political theories that were appropriate to the problem in hand without really thinking them through. He adapted his ideas to suit the political situation. But this is not altogether a fault. The doctrinaire republicans who opposed Cromwell were unrealistic and incapable of forming a government themselves. Milton was not really interested in abstract political theory; he was antipathetic to authority and ancient forms, whether in church or state. The good old cause for him was a political system guided by a virtuous elite who would allow religious freedom to the individual conscience. But he came to feel that only a virtuous nation would know how to use such liberty; the Restoration was a just punishment on a people who had abused their opportunity.

Cromwell's view of events

The scriptures say, the Rod has a voice, and he will make himself known, and he will make himself known by the judgements which he executeth. And do we not think he will, and does, by the providences of mercy and kindness which he hath for his people, and for their just liberties, whom he loves as the apple of his eye? Doth he not by them manifest himself?... By this voice has God spoken very loud on the behalf of his people, by judging their enemies in the late war, and restoring them a liberty to worship with the freedom of their consciences.

CROMWELL'S dissolution speech to the 1st protectorate parliament 1655

Supposing that this cause or this business must be carried on, either it is of God, or of man. If it be of man, I would I had never touched it with a finger; if I had not had a hope fixed in me that this cause, and this business, is of God, I would many years ago have run from it. If it be of God, he will bear it up. If it be of man, it will tumble. *Ibid.*

Views of Cromwell

The soldiers and sectaries most highly magnified him till he began to seek the crown and the establishment of his family. And then there were so many that would be half-kings themselves that a king did seem intolerable to them. The royalists abhorred him as a most perfidious hypocrite, and the Presbyterians thought him little better in his management of public matters.

BAXTER *Autobiography*

His wife and children were setting up for principality, which suited no better with any of them than scarlet on the ape; only, to speak the truth of himself, he had much natural greatness, and well became the place he had usurped.

MRS HUTCHINSON *Memoirs of Col. Hutchinson*

52

To reduce three nations, which perfectly hated him, to an entire obedience to all his dictates; to awe and govern those nations by an army that was indevoted to him, and wished his ruin, was an instance of a very prodigious address. But his greatness at home was but a shadow of the glory he had abroad...In a word, as he had all the wickedness against which damnation is denounced, and for which hellfire is prepared, so he had some virtues which have caused the memory of some men in all ages to be celebrated; and he will be looked upon by posterity as a brave bad man.

CLARENDON *History of the Rebellion*

22 November 1658 [Cromwell's funeral]
[The protector] was carried from Somerset House in a velvet bed of state drawn by six horses housed with the same: the pall held up by his new lords: Oliver lying in effigy in royal robes, and crowned with a crown, sceptre, and mund, like a king...But it was the joyfullest funeral that ever I saw, for there was none that cried, but dogs.   JOHN EVELYN *Diary*

Milton's arguments on tyranny and liberty

No man who knows aught, can be so stupid to deny that all men naturally were born free, being the image and resemblance of God himself, and were by privilege above all the creatures, born to command and not to obey: and that they lived so. Till from the root of Adam's transgression, falling among themselves to do wrong and violence, and foreseeing that such courses must needs tend to the destruction of them all, they agreed by common league to bind each other from mutual injury, and jointly to defend themselves against any that gave disturbance or opposition to such agreement. Hence came cities, towns, and commonwealths.   *The tenure of kings* 1649

Since the king or magistrate holds his authority of the people, both originally and naturally, for their good in the first place, and not his own, then may the people, as oft as they shall judge it for the best, either choose him or reject him, retain him or depose him though no tyrant, merely by the liberty and right of freeborn men to be governed as seems to them best.   *Ibid.*

Go on therefore, Cromwell, in your wonted magnanimity; it fits you well. Your country's deliverer, the founder of our liberty, and at the same time its protector, you can assume no other character more dignified or more august; for your exploits have surpassed not merely those of kings, but even those which have been fabled of our heroes. Consider often, how precious a thing you hold deposited with you, and by a parent how dear – liberty, commended and entrusted to your care by your country!...Suffer not that liberty, which you have gained with so many hardships, so many dangers, to be violated by yourself, or in any wise impaired by others.   *2nd defence* 1654

[In a free commonwealth] they who are greatest are perpetual servants and drudges to the public at their own cost and charges; neglect their own affairs; yet are not elevated above their brethren; live soberly in their families, walk the streets as other men, may be spoken to as freely, familiarly, friendly,

53

without adoration. Whereas a king must be adored like a demigod, with a dissolute and haughty court about him, of vast expense and luxury, masques and revels, to the debauching of our prime gentry both male and female; not in their pastimes only, but in earnest, by the loose employments of court service, which will be then thought honourable.

Ready and easy way 1660

If we return to kingship, and soon repent, as undoubtedly we shall when we begin to find the old encroachments coming on by little and little upon our consciences, which must necessarily proceed from king and bishop united inseparably in one interest, we may be forced perhaps to fight over again all that we have fought, and spend over again all that we have spent, but are never like to attain thus far as we are now advanced to the recovery of our freedom, never to have it in possession as we now have it, never to be vouchsafed hereafter the like mercies and signal assistances from heaven in our cause, if by our ingrateful backsliding we make these fruitless.   *Ibid.*

Statements by Milton's political adversaries

The form of government which they [the English fanatics] have introduced is quite new and was unheard of in former times. It is not popular, nor kingly, nor aristocratic, but military. Will they deny this? If they do deny it, the fact itself refutes them...Whom, therefore, will they convince of that which they mouth, that the supreme sovereignty resides with the people, when the leaders of the army are exercising tyranny and are oppressing the people themselves in harsh and intolerable servitude?

SALMASIUS *Defensio regia* 1649

The relation between a master and his servants is...the same as that between a king and his subjects. If pious and faithful servants and subjects wish to do the will of Christ, they ought to submit to their master and their king, although they are impious and unfaithful.   *Ibid.*

[A member of the Rota gets up to say] That it is all windy foppery from the beginning to the end, written to the elevation of that rabble and meant to cheat the ignorant. That you fight always with the flat of your hand like a rhetorician, and never contract the logical fist. That you trade altogether in universals, the religion of deceits and fallacy, but never come so near particulars as to let us know which among diverse things of the same kind you would be at. For you admire commonwealths in general, and cry down kingship as much at large, without any regard to the particular constitutions which only make either the one or the other good or bad, vainly supposing all slavery to be in the government of a single person, and nothing but liberty in that of many, which is so false that some kingdoms have had the most perfect form of commonwealths as ours had, and some republics have proved the greatest tyrannies.

The censure of the Rota upon...'A ready and easy way' 1660. This is a satire purporting to be by the republican Harrington.

Further reading M. M. Ross *M's royalism* Ithaca 1943 is a highly critical account of M's aristocratic leanings. Among many biographies of Cromwell, C. Hill *God's Englishman* 1970 and R. S. Paul *The lord protector* 1955 are recommended. There were several attempts by Marvell, Dryden and Waller to interpret Cromwell's achievements in poems about him; compare them.

Milton at the Restoration 1660–74

Charles II came back in 1660 on a surge of royalist feeling, promising indemnity for past actions and religious toleration for the future, but the country was soon to be disillusioned. Charles' government was incompetent and extravagant, and the contrast with Cromwell was striking; whereas Cromwell had tried to make England godly and powerful, Charles' main concern was to keep his throne safe and to avoid parliamentary interference. The hope of religious toleration was soon squashed by a series of repressive acts of parliament which divided the Church of England rigidly from the nonconformists; the nonconformists, or dissenters, included many Presbyterians who had welcomed the Restoration, but they became subject to various penalties and disadvantages as second-class citizens. Charles' own attempts to secure toleration for Catholics (and hence for Protestant nonconformists) were prevented by anti-Catholic feeling which was largely political.

Two of Milton's anti-monarchical tracts were condemned at the Restoration, but apart from a short spell in prison (illegal, as he had not been named as excluded from the Act of Indemnity) he escaped further punishment. Since Milton was the most vehement defender of regicide there is a question as to why he escaped. One answer is that he was not important enough; another, more likely, is that powerful friends interceded. The Restoration meant the destruction of Milton's hopes for the political and religious reformation of England. He lost his position and his wealth; he retired to private life and to poetry. He returned only once to public controversy with a blast against Catholicism in *Of true religion* 1673; the last years of his life were spent on his major poems, and then, as he acquired a public, on revising and publishing his early works. But though his years of public service might have seemed wasted, his political disappointment was of crucial importance for the writing of his great poems, and for his understanding of such ideas as servitude, liberty, and paradise.

FIG 2 St Giles' Church, Cripplegate, in the City of London, where Milton and his father are buried. The district was burnt in 1666 and 1941–2. In Milton's time the walls of Roman London ran alongside the church but it is now enclosed by the Barbican civic redevelopment.

The Restoration and after

29 May 1660
This day came in his majesty Charles II to London after a sad, and long exile, and calamitous suffering both of the king and church: being 17 years: This was also his birthday, and with a triumph of above 20,000 horse and foot, brandishing their swords and shouting with unexpressable joy: The ways strawed with flowers, the bells ringing, the streets hung with tapestry, fountains running with wine...I stood in the Strand, and beheld it, and blessed God; And all this without one drop of blood, and by that very army, which rebelled against him: but it was the Lord's doing, *et mirabile in oculis nostris*: for such a restoration was never seen in the mention of any history, ancient or modern, since the return of the Babylonian captivity, nor so joyful a day, and so bright, ever seen in this nation: this happening when to expect or effect it, was past all human policy.   EVELYN *Diary*

[The people] had hardened themselves by persecuting the innocent, and were at this time crucifying the seed, Christ, both in themselves and others; till at last they fell a-biting and devouring one another, until they were consumed one of another; who had turned against and judged that which God had wrought in them, and showed unto them. So shortly after God overthrew them and turned them upside down, and brought the king over them.

FOX Journal

By God I have leaped over a wall; by God I have run through a troop; and by my God I will go through this death, and he will make it easy to me.

THOMAS HARRISON at his execution as a regicide 1660

30 January 1661
This day (O the stupendious, and inscrutable judgements of God) were the carcasses of that arch-rebel Cromwell, Bradshaw the judge who condemned his majesty, and Ireton, son-in-law to the usurper, dragged out of their superb tombs (in Westminster among the kings), to Tyburn, and hanged on the gallows there from 9 in the morning till 6 at night, and then buried under that fatal and ignominious monument, in a deep pit: Thousands of people (who had seen them in all their pride and pompous insults) being spectators: look back at November 22 1658, and be astonished.

EVELYN Diary

The tenderness of the bowels, which is the quintessence of justice and compassion, the very mention of good nature, was laughed at and looked upon as the mark and character of a fool; and a roughness of manners, or hardheartedness and cruelty was affected. In the place of generosity, a vile and sordid love of money was entertained as the truest wisdom, and anything lawful that would contribute towards being rich. There was a total decay, or rather a final expiration of all friendship.

CLARENDON Life, by himself first pub. 1759

12 July 1667
It is strange how everybody do nowadays reflect upon Oliver, and commend him, what brave things he did, and made all the neighbour princes fear him; while here a prince, come in with all the love and prayers and good liking of his people, who have given greater signs of loyalty and willingness to serve him with their estates than ever was done by any people, hath lost all so soon, that it is a miracle what way a man could devise to lose so much in so little time.

SAMUEL PEPYS Diary

J.M. was, and is, a man of great learning and sharpness of wit as any man. It was his misfortune, living in a tumultuous time, to be tossed on the wrong side, and he writ, *flagrante bello*, certain dangerous treatises...At His Majesty's happy return, J.M. did partake...of his regal clemency, and has ever since expiated himself in a retired silence.

ANDREW MARVELL The rehearsal transprosed II 1673

Further reading An excellent history is D. Ogg *England in the reign of Charles II* 2nd ed 1956. A recent and balanced biography of the king is M. Ashley *Charles II* 1971. A good introduction to life in the 1660s is through the diaries of Pepys and Evelyn.

Milton's character, appearance, and blindness

He had light brown hair, his complexion exceeding fair; he was so fair that they called him the lady of Christ's College. His eye a dark grey; oval face.

JOHN AUBREY 1681

Of a very cheerful humour. He was very healthy, and free from all diseases, and only towards his later end he was visited with the gout spring and fall; he would be cheerful even in his gout-fits, and sing. *Ibid.*

He was an early riser (...at 4 o'clock...), yea, after he lost his sight. He had a man read to him; the first thing he read was the Hebrew bible...then he contemplated. At 7 his man came to him again and then read to him and wrote till dinner; the writing was as much as the reading...After dinner he used to walk 3 or 4 hours at a time; he always had a garden where he lived. Went to bed about 9. Temperate, rarely drank between meals. Extreme pleasant in his conversation, and at dinner, supper etc.; but satirical. *Ibid.*

He had naturally a sharp wit, and steady judgement; which helps toward attaining learning he improved by an indefatigable attention to his study; and was supported in that by a temperance, always observed by him, but in his youth even with great nicety. Anonymous biographer

He was of a moderate stature, and well proportioned, of a ruddy complexion, light brown hair, and handsome features; save that his eyes were none of the quickest. But his blindness, which proceeded from a *gutta serena* [disease of the optic nerve], added no further blemish to them. His deportment was sweet and affable; and his gait erect and manly, bespeaking courage and undauntedness. *Ibid.*

He rendered his studies and various works more easy and pleasant by allotting them their several portions of the day. Of these the time friendly to the muses fell to his poetry; and he waking early (as is the use of temperate men) had commonly a good stock of verses ready against his amanuensis came; which if it happened to be later than ordinary, he would complain, saying he wanted to be milked. *Ibid.*

His vein never happily flowed, but from the autumnal equinoctial to the vernal, and...whatever he attempted [at other times] was never to his satisfaction, though he courted his fancy never so much; so that in all the years he was about this poem [*PL*] he may be said to have spent but half his time therein. EDWARD PHILLIPS 1694

[Milton began to notice the failure of his sight about 1644; he was almost blind in 1650 and totally blind in 1652.]

For his book that he wrote against the late king that you would have me read, you should have taken notice of God's judgement upon him who struck him with blindness...God has begun his judgement upon him here, his punishment will be hereafter in hell.

Letter from ANNE SADLEIR to Roger Williams 1653

It is ten years, I think, more or less, since I felt my sight getting weak and dull...In the morning, if I began, as usual, to read anything, I felt my eyes at once thoroughly pained, and shrinking from the act of reading, but refreshed after moderate bodily exercise. If I looked at a lit candle, a kind of iris seemed to snatch it from me. Not very long after, a darkness coming over the left part of my left eye (for that eye became clouded some years before the other) removed from my vision all objects situated on that side... The other eye also failing perceptibly and gradually through a period of three years, I observed, some months before my sight was wholly gone, that objects I looked at without myself moving seemed all to swim, now to the right, now to the left...Yet the darkness which is perpetually before me, by night as well as by day, seems always nearer to a whitish than to a blackish, and such that, when the eye rolls itself, there is admitted, as through a small chink, a certain little trifle of light...If, as is written, 'Man shall not live by bread alone, but by every word that proceedeth out of the mouth of God', what should prevent one from resting likewise in the belief that his eyesight lies not in his eyes alone, but enough for all purposes in God's leading and providence? Verily, while only he looks out for me and provides for me, as he doth, leading me and leading me forth as with his hand through my whole life, I shall willingly, since it has seemed good to him, have given my eyes their long holiday.   Latin letter to Leonard Philaras, a Greek friend 1654

To be blind is not miserable; not to be able to bear blindness, that is miserable...There is a way...through weakness to the greatest strength. May I be one of the weakest, provided only in my weakness that immortal and better vigour be put forth with greater effect; provided only in my darkness the light of the divine countenance does but the more brightly shine: for then I shall at once be the weakest and the most mighty; shall be at once blind, and of the most piercing sight. Thus, through this infirmity should I be consummated, perfected; thus, through this darkness should I be enrobed in light.   *2nd defence* 1654

Milton's religious opinions

Disputes in religion will never be ended, because there wants a measure by which the business should be decided. The Puritan would be judged by the word of God; if he would speak clearly, he means himself, but that he is ashamed to say so.   JOHN SELDEN *Table talk* 1689

As a preliminary to the writing of his great religious poems Milton compiled a Latin theological treatise, the longest of his prose works, called *De doctrina christiana* (Christian doctrine). He probably finished it by 1660, but he did not attempt to publish it in his lifetime, partly because of its heretical tendencies. He intended it to be published posthumously, but Daniel Skinner, to whom he left it for this purpose, was prevented from doing so for political reasons and the manuscript remained unpublished till 1825.

Following his disagreement with the Presbyterians Milton came to believe that each individual must work out his own religious opinions. The tools for this task are the Bible, and the private inner light or conscience. Since scripture as transmitted by human agency is sometimes fallible, conscience becomes the chief arbiter. It is not possible for a man interpreting scripture according to his conscience to be a heretic; on the contrary, heresy means relying on tradition and church practices without applying conscience. (This did not prevent Milton from using the church fathers when he agreed with them.) Milton's emphasis on the individual conscience was thus in complete contrast to Anglican concern with tradition, conformity, and ritual, though doctrinally he was in some respects closer to Anglican thought than to Calvinism. He was critical of the inconsistency in the Puritan position which, while basing doctrine on the Bible, also demanded adherence to a limited Calvinist creed (especially predestination), and to a particular form of church government. In his Arminianism (belief that man is a free agent and that salvation is open to all) Milton broke with the Calvinist emphasis on predestination and the elect. Milton's Christianity is more democratic, more like that of the Quakers, than traditional Protestantism. Among other 'heretical' opinions Milton thought Christ to be subordinate to God the Father; he opposed infant baptism; and believed that the soul dies with the body until the resurrection (mortalism). An important part of *Christian doctrine* is devoted to the idea of Christian liberty.

In his early days he was a favourer of those Protestants then opprobriously called by the name of Puritans; in his middle years he was best pleased with the Independents and Anabaptists, as allowing of more liberty than others, and coming nearest in his opinion to the primitive practice; but in the latter part of his life, he was not a professed member of any particular sect among Christians, he frequented none of their assemblies, nor made use of their peculiar rites in his family.   JOHN TOLAND 1698

On the truth of scripture

The very essence of truth is plainness and brightness; the darkness and crookedness is our own. The wisdom of God created understanding, fit and proportionable to truth, the object and end of it, as the eye to the thing visible. If our understanding have a film of ignorance over it, or be blear with gazing on other false glisterings, what is that to truth? If we will but purge with sovereign eye-salve that intellectual ray which God hath planted in us, then we would believe the scriptures protesting their own plainness and perspicuity, calling to them to be instructed not only the wise and learned but the simple, the poor, the babes, foretelling an extraordinary effusion of God's spirit upon every age and sex, attributing to all men, and requiring from them, the ability of searching, trying, examining all things, and by the spirit discerning that which is good... *Of reformation* 1641

Every believer has a right to interpret the scriptures for himself, inasmuch as he has the Spirit for his guide, and the mind of Christ is in him.
Christian doctine late 1650s

Under the gospel we possess, as it were, a twofold scripture: one external, which is the written word; and the other internal, which is the Holy Spirit, written in the hearts of believers. *Ibid.*

On heresy

A man may be a heretic in the truth; and if he believe things only because his pastor says so, or the assembly so determines, without knowing other reason, though his belief be true yet the very truth he holds becomes his heresy. *Areopagitica* 1644

Heresy...is a religion taken up and believed from the traditions of men and additions to the word of God. Whence also it follows clearly, that of all known sects or pretended religions at this day in Christendom, popery is the only or the greatest heresy. *Of true religion* 1673

On the fall

It was from out the rind of one apple tasted that the knowledge of good and evil as two twins cleaving together leapt forth into the world. And perhaps this is that doom which Adam fell into of knowing good and evil, that is to say of knowing good by evil. As therefore the state of man now is, what wisdom can there be to choose, what continence to forbear, without the knowledge of evil? He that can apprehend and consider vice with all her baits and seeming pleasures, and yet abstain, and yet distinguish, and yet prefer that which is truly better, he is the true warfaring Christian. I cannot praise a fugitive and cloistered virtue, unexercised and unbreathed, that never sallies out and sees her adversary, but slinks out of the race where that immortal garland is to be run for, not without dust and heat. Assuredly we bring not innocence into the world, we bring impurity much rather; that which purifies us is trial and trial is by what is contrary.
Areopagitica 1644

No works whatever were required of Adam; a particular act only was forbidden. It was necessary that something should be forbidden or commanded as a test of fidelity, and that an act in its own nature indifferent, in order that man's obedience might be thereby manifested.
Christian doctrine late 1650s

What sin can be named, which was not included in this one act? It comprehended at once distrust in the divine veracity, and a proportionate credulity
in the assurances of Satan; unbelief; ingratitude; disobedience; gluttony; in
the man excessive uxuriousness, in the woman a want of proper regard for
her husband, in both an insensibility to the welfare of their offspring, and
that offspring the whole human race; parricide, theft, invasion of the rights
of others, sacrilege, deceit, presumption in aspiring to divine attributes, fraud
in the means employed to attain the object, pride, and arrogance.   *Ibid.*

On regeneration and Christian liberty

Regeneration is that change operated by the word and the Spirit whereby,
the old man being destroyed, the inward man is regenerated by God after his
own image, in all the faculties of his mind, insomuch that he becomes as it
were a new creature, and the whole man is sanctified both in body and soul
for the service of God and the performance of good works.   *Ibid.*

Christian liberty is that whereby we are loosed, as it were by enfranchisement,
through Christ our deliverer, from the bondage of sin, and consequently from
the rule of the law and of man; to the intent that being made sons instead of
servants, and perfect men instead of children, we may serve God in love
through the guidance of the Spirit of truth.   *Ibid.*

Further reading   The best introduction to religious thought is
through contemporary writers. The Anglican view of the world was
set out by Richard Hooker in the late 16th century in *Of the laws of
ecclesiastical polity* (Everyman). Sir Thomas Browne *Religio medici*
(Everyman) is an example of the Anglican mind at its best. See also
the sermons of Donne, Lancelot Andrews, Jeremy Taylor. C. A.
Patrides has edited *The Cambridge platonists* 1969. A classic of
Puritan literature is John Bunyan *Pilgrim's progress* (Oxford standard
authors). Spiritual autobiography is an important Puritan form; see
Richard Baxter *Autobiography*, George Fox *Journal* and Bunyan *Grace
abounding* (all in Everyman). St Paul's *Epistle to the Romans* was one
of the more important biblical texts for Puritans.

Milton's reputation in his lifetime

Recorded contemporary reactions to Milton are disappointing for the
modern reader. He first became widely known in England through his
divorce pamphlets, with an unenviable reputation as a 'divorcer'. His
attacks on the bishops made little mark, and his *Poems* of 1645 went
unnoticed, except by poets like Benlowes and Marvell whose own

poems show signs of close reading of Milton. After 1651 he became notorious in Europe as the defender of regicide; the *Defences* were more widely read abroad than in England. In 1660 he brought himself back into public notice with his defence of the good old cause. At the Restoration his political reputation may have hindered acceptance of his poems. *Paradise lost* made its way slowly with the public; 1,300 copies were sold in the first two years, followed by reprints and a second edition, and there was a market for Milton's early non-polemical works. Dryden did a good deal to advance Milton's reputation. After 1688 his political ideas seemed more acceptable, and from the same date his reputation as one of England's great poets began to be established.

It is like he spent his youth in loitering, bezelling and harlotting. Thus being grown to an impostume in the breast of the university, he was at length vomited out into a suburb sink about London...Where his morning haunts are I wist not; but he that would find him after dinner must search the playhouses or the bordelli, for there I have traced him.

?JOSEPH HALL *A modest confutation...of 'Animadversions'* 1642

A libertine that thinketh his wife a manacle, and his very garters to be shackles and fetters to him; one that, after the Independent fashion, will be tied by no obligation to God or man...

CLEMENT WALKER *History of Independency* II 1649

[Salmasius] is greatly delighted with the news that Milton's book has been publicly burnt by the hangman at Paris. There is no need for me to intrude my judgement about that book; but this I know, that it is generally good books whose fate it is to perish or be endangered in this way. Men come under the executioner's hand for the most part for their crimes and depravity, but books for their worth and excellence.

Latin letter from VOSSIUS to Heinsius 1651

[On the polemics of Salmasius and Milton] They are very good Latin both, and hardly to be judged which is better; and both very ill reasoning, hardly to be judged which is worse.   HOBBES *Behemoth* 1679

He was visited much by learned, more than he did desire. He was mightily importuned to go into France and Italy. Foreigners came much to see him, and much admired him, and offered him great preferments to come over to them, and the only inducement of several foreigners that came over into England, was chiefly to see Oliver Protector and Mr John Milton...He was much more admired abroad than at home.   AUBREY 1681

Milton as a reader

Ordinary Englishmen 300 years ago lived in an oral culture, that is to say one where most transactions went on by word of mouth; yet they belonged to a society whose politics were run in writing...It is evident that tradesmen had more occasions to use written and printed material than landowners did, and the tradition of radicalism among these trades, especially the cobblers, reveals at once the possible association between literacy and thinking for yourself politically...What has now to be done is to recognise what it means to observe only the literate activity of a society most of whose life was oral, above all to try to get the feel of how the attitude of the illiterate mass affected the literate few, and so was allowed for, taken into account, in the social process as a whole and particularly in the process of politics...It would seem that in the largely illiterate society of England in early Stuart times there may have been for a generation or so too many highly educated people, and in particular too many university trained clergymen for the number of livings available to support them...This paradox has its parallel in Africa and India in the 1960s...'Alienated intellectuals' is the phrase which has been applied to the unwanted graduate priests of Charles I's reign but in assessing their possible significance we must once again bear in mind the fact that such a surplus is exactly what might be expected to appear from time to time. There is no necessary connection between the presence of professional men without a proper livelihood and a general raising of educational standards except in so far as they took to teaching the poor their letters as a means of keeping alive.   PETER LASLETT *The world we have lost* 1965

Marriage and divorce

Marriage was ordained by God, instituted in paradise, was the relief of a natural necessity, and the first blessing from the Lord: he gave to man not a friend but a wife, that is, a friend and a wife too; for a good woman is in her soul the same that a man is, and she is a woman only in her body, that she may have the excellency of the one and the usefulness of the other and become amiable in both...The dominion of a man over his wife is no other than as the soul rules the body, for which it takes a mighty care and uses it with a delicate tenderness and watches to keep it from all evils and studies to make for it fair provision...and yet even the very government itself is divided, for man and wife in the family are as the sun and moon in the firmament of heaven.

> JEREMY TAYLOR *XX Sermons* 1653 (the son of a barber, Taylor became chaplain to Archbishop Laud and Charles I; after being captured by the parliamentarians, he retired to Golden Grove in Carmarthenshire; see Hopkins' poem 'Margaret, are you grieving over Goldengrove unleaving?')

> Here lies a she-sun, and a he-moon here:
> She gives the best light to his sphere,

Or each is both, and all, and so
They unto one another nothing owe.

DONNE *Epithalamion on the Lady Elizabeth* [*James I's daughter*] *and
Count Palatine being married on St Valentine's Day* 1613

It is clear from the passion of Milton's arguments that concern with
divorce is part of a concern with love and marriage. The Puritans
especially respected marriage, and married sexuality; and were inclined to offer the wife a more equal part. The erotic poetry and drama
of the period is well known. See also W. Haller 'Hail wedded love'
English literary history XIII 1946; J. B. Broadbent *Poetic love* 1964;
Alan Macfarlane *The family life of Ralph Josselin a 17c clergyman: an
essay in historical anthropology* 1970; C. L. Powell *English domestic
relations 1487–1653* 1917; G. Rattray Taylor *Sex in history* 1953 rev
ed 1959; Denis de Rougement *L'amour et l'occident* trans as *Passion
and society* 1940 rev 1956; H. M. Richmond *The school of love:
the evolution of the Stuart love lyric* 1964; and Lawrence Stone
has relevant chapters in *The crisis of the aristocracy*.

In the sex, is all the difference; which is but only in the body. For she hath
the same reasonable soul and, in that, there is neither *he*s nor *she*s; neither
excellence nor superiority; she hath the same soul, the same mind, the same
understanding; and tends to the same end of eternal salvation that he doth.

WILLIAM AUSTIN *Haec homo, wherein the excellency of the creation of
women is described by way of an essay* 1637

Araphil   If on my skin the noisome scar
       I should of the leprosy or canker wear,
    Or if the sulphurous breath of war
       Should blast my youth: should I not be thy fear?
Castara   In flesh may sickness horror move,
       But heavenly zeal will be by it refined:
    For then we'd like two angels love,
       Without a sense, embrace each other's mind.
Araphil   Were it not impious to repine
       'Gainst rigid fate, I should direct my breath
    That two must be, whom heaven did join
       In such a happy one, disjoined by death.
Castara   That's no divorce: then shall we see
       The rites in life were types of the marriage state;
    Our souls on earth contracted be
       But they in heaven their nuptials consummate.

WILLIAM HABINGTON (a Roman catholic) *Dialogue between Araphil and
Castara* 1634 (Castara was Lucy Herbert, whom he married)

65

Kingship

On M's varying attitude to kingship, especially in relation to Satan and Cromwell, see pp. 38–9, 131, 139 and 140–1 in *PL I–II* in this series; and the arguments about kingship and secular power in *PL* xii and *PR* iv. The biblical authorities are important, e.g. the Jews' false desire for a king *I Samuel* viii; bad kings – Rehoboam *I Kings* xiii–xiv, Ahab xvi, Jeroboam *II Kings* xiv, Ahaz xvi; good kings – Hezekiah *II Kings* xviii, *Josiah* xxii; Elijah's attitude to kings *II Kings* either side of xvi; obedience to kings *Romans* xiii (the classic text for the 17th century), *I Peter* ii.

Generalized, the problem can be seen like this: from the late 16th century to *c.* 1625 (death of James I, accession of Charles I), the following factors intensify: absolutism; density of regal imagery in poetry, painting, drama; importance and extravagance of court; patronage. But during the same period the following opposing factors also intensify: relativism; perversion of regal imagery to personal use; supremacy of individual experience. So the idea or role of kingship began to separate from the actual person-king; this separation ended with the separating of Charles I's head (crowned) from his body (human). Cf. 'Consciousness iii starts with self' (Charles Reich *The greening of America* 1970). The most economical literary symptoms of the change are Shakespeare's tragedies of kingship (including *Richard II* and *Henry IV*, each of which pre-enacts deposition, in Richard's case literally, and then execution; in Henry's mockingly when Falstaff pretends to be his father in the inn); Donne's relativism in his two *Anniversaries* ('Prince, subject, father, son are things forgot'); and his arrogation of kingship, and all its attributes (sun, honour, long life), to the bed in his (quite separate) love poem *The anniversary*:

> All kings, and all their favourites,
> All glory of honours, beauties, wits,
> The sun itself, which makes times, as they pass,
> Is elder by a year, now, than it was
> When thou and I first one another saw –
> All other things to their destruction draw.
>
> .   .   .   .
>
> Alas, as well as other princes, we
> (Who prince enough in one another be)
> Must leave at last, in death, these eyes and ears,
> Oft fed with true oaths, and with sweet salt tears
>
> .   .   .   .

Here upon earth, we're kings, and none but we
Can be such kings, nor of such subjects be.
Who is so safe as we? where none can do
Treason to us, except one of us two.
    True and false fears let us refrain;
Let us love nobly, and live, and add again
Years and years until years till we attain
To write threescore. This is the second of our reign.

Much can be learned also from which royal portraits (they were abundant at this time) seem to emphasize the heroic or divine king, or the person, or the role (in terms of regalia). See Rubens, Van Dyck, Lely and the engravers.

There was a helpful feature on Cromwell in the *Observer* colour supplement of 30 August 1970. The two poems by Waller printed below, on Cromwell and Charles II, ask for analysis of the psychology of their attitude to authority.

I see not then how the children of Adam, or of any man else, can be free from subjection to their parents. And this subordination of children is the fountain of all regal authority, by the ordination of God himself. From whence it follows, that civil power not only in general is by divine institution, but even the assigning of it specifically to the eldest parent. Which quite takes away that new and common distinction which refers only power universal or absolute to God... This lordship which Adam by creation had over the whole world, and by right descending from him the patriarchs did enjoy, was as large and absolute as the absolutest dominion of any monarch which hath been since the creation.   ROBERT FILMER *Patriarcha*

Every king is an image of God; a representation on earth of the divine majesty. But, Thou shalt not make unto thee any graven image... In Locke royalty is reduced to mere effigy and show; revolutionary republicanism seeks to abolish effigy and show... The old idea was that man must be governed by effigy and show; the new idea is – modern representative government. An end to idolatry is not so easy.

            NORMAN O. BROWN 'Representative' in his *Love's body* 1966

I confess it is not easy for me to contend with those many horrors of death wherewith God suffers me to be tempted; which are equally horrid either in the suddenness of a barbarous assassination, or in those greater formalities whereby my enemies (being more solemnly cruel) will, it may be, seek to add (as those did who crucified Christ) the mockery of justice to the cruelty of malice. That I may be destroyed, as with greater pomp and artifice so with less pity, it will be but a necessary policy to make my death appear as an act of justice done by subjects upon their sovereign; who know that no law

67

of God or man invests them with any power of judicature without me, much less against me; and who, being sworn and bound by all that is sacred before God and man to endeavour my preservation, must pretend justice to cover their perjury...The prayers and patience of my friends and loving subjects will contribute much to the sweetening of this bitter cup, which I doubt not but I shall more cheerfully take and drink as from God's hand (if it must be so), than they that give it to me, whose hands are unjustly and barbarously lifted up against me.   CHARLES I AND J. GAUDEN *Eikon basilike*

from *A panegyric to the Lord Protector [Cromwell]: of the present greatness, and joint interest, of His Highness and this nation c.* 1655

> While with a strong and yet a gentle hand
> You bridle faction and our hearts command,
> Protect us from ourselves and from the foe,
> Make us unite and make us conquer too:
>
> Let partial spirits still aloud complain,
> Think themselves injured that they cannot reign
> And own no liberty but where they may
> Without control upon their fellows prey.
>
> .   .   .   .   .   .
>
> Your drooping country, torn with civil hate,
> Restored by you is made a glorious state,
> The seat of empire, where the Irish come,
> And the unwilling Scotch, to fetch their doom;
>
> The sea's our own, and now all nations greet
> With bending sails each vessel of our fleet;
> Your power extends as far as winds can blow
> Or swelling sails upon the globe may go...

EDMUND WALLER MP 1606–87

from *To the King, upon His Majesty's happy return* 1660

> The rising sun complies with our weak sight –
> First gilds the clouds, then shows his globe of light
> At such a distance from our eyes as though
> He knew what harm his hasty beams would do.
>   But your full majesty at once breaks forth
> In the meridian of your reign. Your worth,
> Your youth, and all the splendour of your state
> (Wrapped up till now in clouds of adverse fate)
> With such a flood of light invade our eyes,
> And our spread hearts with so great joy surprise,
> That if Your Grace inclines that we should live,
> You must not, Sir, too hastily forgive!
> Our guilt preserves us from the excess of joy,
> Which scatters spirits and would life destroy...

EDMUND WALLER

Pamphleteering

Your conscience is scorched by the flames of adultery and rape, and of those perjuries by the help of which you debauched an unsuspecting girl, to whom you promised marriage and then abandoned to despair. You are writhing under the flames of that mercenary passion which impelled you, though covered with crimes, to lust after the functions of the priesthood, and to pollute the consecrated elements with your incestuous touch.   *Second defence*

Religion

For Milton's brand of puritanism, consider the imagery and tone of the excerpts from his prose on pp. 144 of *PL I–II* and 78–9 of *PL: introduction* in this series. Similarly for his attitude to bishops consider this from *Of reformation*:

He that, enabled with gifts from God, and the lawful and primitive choice of the church assembled in convenient numbers, faithfully from that time forward feeds his parochial flock, has his coequal and compresbyterial power to ordain ministers and deacons by public prayer, and vote of Christ's congregation, in like sort as he himself was ordained, and is a true apostolic bishop. But when he steps up into the chair of pontifical pride, and changes a moderate and exemplary house for a misgoverned and haughty palace, spiritual dignity for carnal precedence, and secular high office and employment for the high negotiations of his heavenly embassage, then he degrades, then he unbishops himself; he that makes him bishop makes him no bishop.

Note his insistence (cf. *Lycidas*) on bishop = pastor.

Surely there is not any prince in Christendom who, hearing this rare sophistry, can choose but smile? And if we be not blind at home, we may as well perceive that this worthy motto, 'No bishop no king', is of the same batch, and infanted out of the same fears – a mere ague-cake, coagulated of a certain fever they have, presaging their time to be short; and now, like those that are sinking, they catch round of that which is likeliest to hold them up; and would persuade regal power that, if they dive, he must after. But what greater debasement can there be to royal dignity, whose towering and steadfast height rests upon the unmovable foundations of justice and heroic virtue, than to chain it in a dependence of subsisting, or ruining, to the painted battlements and gaudy rottenness of prelatry, which want but one puff of the king's to blow them down like a pasteboard house built of court-cards?

from *Bartholomew Fair* 1614

Dan Jordan Knockem [a man of the turf]. Sir, I will take your counsel, and
   cut my hair, and leave vapours: I see that tobacco, and bottle-ale, and

pig, and Whit [Capt. Whit, a pimp], and very Ursla herself [a pig-woman], is all vanity.

Zeal-of-the-land Busy. Only pig was not comprehended in my admonition, the rest were. For long hair, it is an ensign of pride, a banner, and the world is full of those banners, very full of banners. And bottle-ale is a drink of Satan's, a diet-drink of Satan's, devized to puff us up, and make us swell in this latter age of vanity; as the smoke of tobacco to keep us in mist and error. But the fleshly woman, which you call Ursla, is above all to be avoided, having the marks upon her of the three enemies of man: the world, as being in the fair; the devil, as being in the fire; and the flesh, as being herself.

Mrs Purecraft. Brother Zeal-of-the-land! What shall we do? My daughter Win-the-fight is fallen into her fit of longing again!

Zeal-of-the-land Busy. For more pig? There is no more, is there?

Mrs Purecraft. To see some sights in the fair.

Zeal-of-the-land Busy. Sister, let her fly the impurity of the place swiftly, lest she partake of the pitch thereof. Thou art the seat of the beast, O Smithfield! and I will leave thee: idolatry peepeth out on every side of thee!

Dan Jordan Knockem. An excellent right hypocrite! Now his belly is full, he falls a-railing and kicking, the jade! A very good vapour! I'll in, and joy Ursla with telling how her pig works: two-and-a-half he ate to his share, and he has drunk a pailful. He eats with his eyes as well as his teeth...

BEN JONSON (III i)

For another view, see the section on Vanity Fair in Bunyan's *Pilgrim's progress* 1678.

from *Satire III*

       but, unmovèd, thou
Of force must one and, forced, but one, allow;
And the right. Ask thy father which is she;
Let him ask his: though truth and falsehood be
Near twins, yet truth a little elder is;
Be busy to seek her; believe me this,
He's not of none, nor worst, that seeks the best.
To adore, or scorn, an image, or protest,
May all be bad. Doubt wisely. In strange way,
To stand inquiring right is not to stray.

. . . .

Keep the truth which thou hast found. Men do not stand
In so ill case here that God hath with his hand
Signed kings blank charters to kill whom they hate;
Nor are they vicars, but hangmen to fate.
Fool and wretch, wilt thou let thy soul be tied
To man's laws, by which she shall not be tried
At the last day? O will it then boot thee

To say a Philip or a Gregory,
A Harry or a Martin taught thee this?
Is not this excuse for mere contraries
Equally strong? cannot both sides say so?
That thou may'st rightly obey power, her bounds know;
That passed, her nature and name is changed: to be
Then humble to her is idolatry...   JOHN DONNE 1572–1631

See also his *Holy Sonnet XVIII* 'Show me, dear Christ, thy spouse, so bright and clear'.

The British Church

I joy, dear mother, when I view
Thy perfect lineaments and hue
          Both sweet and bright.
Beauty in thee takes up her place
And dates her letters from thy face
          When she doth write.

A fine aspéct in fit array,
Neither too mean nor yet too gay,
          Shows who is best.
Outlandish looks may not compare
For all they either painted are
          Or else undressed.

She on the hills, which wantonly
Allureth all in hope to be
          By her preferred,
Hath kissed so long her painted shrines
That even her face by kissing shines
          For her reward.

She in the valley is so shy
Of dressing that her hair doth lie
          About her ears,
While she avoids her neighbour's pride,
She wholly goes on the other side,
          And nothing wears.

But, dearest mother, what those miss,
The mean, thy praise and glory is,
          And long may be.
Blessed be God, whose love it was
To double-moat thee with his grace,
          And none but thee.

                    GEORGE HERBERT 1593–1633

from *To all angels and saints*

> O glorious spirits, who after all your bands
> See the smooth face of God without a frown
>   Or strict commands;
> Where everyone is king and hath his crown,
> If not upon his head, yet in his hands:
>
> Not out of envy or maliciousness
> Do I forbear to crave your special aid.
>   I would address
> My vows to thee most gladly, blessed Maid
> And mother of my God, in my distress.
>
> .   .   .   .
>
> But now, alas! I dare not, for our king
> Whom we do all jointly adore and praise
>   Bids no such thing;
> And where his pleasure no injunction lays
> ('Tis your own case) ye never move a wing.
>
> All worship is prerogative, and a flower
> Of his rich crown from whom lies no appeal
>   At the last hour;
> Therefore we dare not from his garland steal
> To make a posy for inferior power...   GEORGE HERBERT

from *An elegy upon old Freeman, used hardly by the committee for lying in the cathedral and in church porches praying the common prayer by heart, etc.*

> Here in this homely cabinet
> Resteth a poor old anchorite.
> Upon the ground he laid all weathers,
> Not as most men, gooselike on feathers:
> For so indeed it came to pass,
> The Lord of lords his landlord was.
> He lived, instead of wainscot rooms,
> Like the possessed, among the tombs,
> As by some spirit thither led
> To be acquainted with the dead.
> Each morning from his bed so hallowed
> He rose, took up his cross and followed;
> To every porch he did repair
> To vent himself in common prayer
> Wherein he was alone devout
> When preaching jostled praying out.
> In such procession through the city,
> Maugre the devil and committee,
> He daily went; for which he fell
> Nor into Jacob's but Bridewell...

MATTHEW STEVENSON *Occasion's offspring* 1654

from *A poem in defence of the decent ornaments of Christ Church, Oxon.,
occasioned by a Banbury Brother, who called them idolatries*

Beauty in worship

You that profane our windows with a tongue
Set like some clock on purpose to go wrong;
Who, when you were at service, sighed because
You heard the organ's music, not the daw's:
Pitying our solemn state, shaking the head
To see no ruins from the floor to the lead;
To whose pure nose our cedar gave offence,
Crying it smelt of papists' frankincense;
Who, walking on our marbles, scoffing said,
'Whose bodies are under these tombstones laid?'
Counting our tapers works of darkness; and
Choosing to see priests in blue aprons stand
Rather than in rich copes which show the art
Of Sisera's prey embroidered in each part;
Then when you saw the altar's basin said,
'Why's not the ewer on the cupboard's head?'
Thinking our very Bibles too profane,
'Cause you ne'er bought such covers in Duck Lane;
Loathing all decency, as if you'd have
Altars as foul and homely as a grave.
Had you one spark of reason, you would find
Yourselves like idols, to have eyes, yet blind.
'Tis only some base niggard heresy
To think religion loves deformity.
Glory did never yet make God the less,
Neither can beauty defile holiness.
What's more magnificent than heaven? yet where
Is there more love and piety than there?
My heart doth wish (were't possible) to see
Paul's built with precious stones and porphyry;
To have our halls and galleries outshine
Altars in beauty, is to deck our swine
With orient pearl, whilst the deserving choir
Of God and angels wallow in the mire.
Our decent copes only distinction keep
That you may know the shepherd from the sheep,
As gaudy letters in the rubric show
How you may holidays from lay-days know.
Remember Aaron's robes and you will say
Ladies at masques are not so rich as they:
Then are the priest's words like thunderclaps when he
Is lightning-like rayed round with majesty.
May every temple shine like those of Nile
And still be free from rat or crocodile.
But you will urge both priest and church should be

73

The solemn patterns of humility.
Do not some boast of rags? Cynics deride
The pomp of kings, but with a greater pride;
Meekness consists not in the clothes, but heart;
Nature may be vainglorious well as art;
We may as lowly before God appear
Dressed with a glorious pearl as with a tear...

ABRAHAM WRIGHT ed Parnassus biceps 1656

To Mr John Milton of London, a youth eminent from his country and his virtues...In whose memory the whole world is treasured...Who with astronomy for his conductor hears the music of the spheres; with philosophy for his teacher deciphers the handwriting of God in those wonders of creation which proclaim His greatness; and with the most unwearied literary industry for his associate examines, restores, penetrates with ease the obscurities of antiquity, the desolations of ages and the labyrinths of learning...

this tribute is paid by CARLO DATI
A Patrician Florentine 1645

ISABEL RIVERS

The making of
a 17th-century poet

Milton's education

Milton came to regard all his activities, moral and intellectual, private and public, as training for his plan to write a great poem and hence, as a great poet, to act as a guide to his country. The subject of his education is thus not a question simply of how he spent his years at school and university, nor how the work that he did there and the habits of mind that he developed shaped his poetry. For many years he followed a programme of study in which he was essentially educating himself to be an educator.

This plan itself evolved out of an earlier, different one. Though he began writing poems at an early age Milton did not originally envisage poetry as a career (few did in the early 17th century). He was intended for the Anglican priesthood. In *The reason of church government* he justifies his involvement in controversy over 'the difficult labours of the church, to whose service by the intentions of my parents and friends I was destined of a child, and in mine own resolutions'. The reasons why Milton never took the step of ordination are complex, though in this passage he tells us succinctly that he was 'church-outed by the prelates'. But the fact that there were political and religious obstacles to his joining the Anglican ministry does not mean there was opposition in Milton's mind between the roles of priest and poet; the one led into the other. His father and his friends had some difficulty in understanding this; Milton was aware that his own consciously slow self-preparation for his future great task might appear to them simply as dilettantism, as reluctance to assume the responsibility of a career. In about 1632, the year that his Cambridge career came to an end, Milton wrote an

75

answer to a critical friend, enclosing the sonnet that begins 'How soon hath time the subtle thief of youth'. The argument of both letter and poem is that what seems to the observer idleness and lack of activity is a search for maturity, a period of self-denial dedicated to activity in the future. Milton illustrates his argument by reference to the parables of the talents and the labourers in the vineyard (*Matthew* xx, xxv). Here is part of the letter:

I...think myself bound though unasked, to give you account, as oft as occasion is, of this my tardy moving; according to the precept of my conscience, which I firmly trust is not without God...But if you think, as you said, that too much love of learning is in fault, and that I have given up myself to dream away my years in the arms of studious retirement like Endymion with the moon as the tale of Latmus goes, yet consider that if it were no more but the mere love of learning, whether it proceed from a principle bad, good, or natural it could not have held out thus long against so strong opposition on the other side of every kind, for if it be bad why should not all the fond hopes that forward youth and vanity are fledge with together with gain, pride, and ambition call me forward more powerfully, than a poor regardless and unprofitable sin of curiosity should be able to withhold me, whereby a man cuts himself off from all action and becomes the most helpless, pusillanimous and unweaponed creature in the world...If the love of learning as it is be the pursuit of something good, it would sooner follow the more excellent and supreme good known and presented and so be quickly diverted from the empty and fantastic chase of shadows and notions to the solid good flowing from due and timely obedience to that command in the gospel set out by the terrible seizing of him that hid the talent. It is more probable therefore that not the endless delight of speculation but this very consideration of that great commandment does not press forward as soon as may be to undergo but keeps off with a sacred reverence, and religious advisement how best to undergo, not taking thought of being late so it give advantage to be more fit, for those that were latest lost nothing when the master of the vineyard came to give each one his hire.

Though Milton at this stage was not sure how he would use his talent, yet he was sure that there was no inconsistency in his hesitation. The fact that he felt himself unfitted for the priesthood (or perhaps rather the priesthood unfitted for him) and uncertain of his immediate vocation did not mean that the years of his early education were wasted. In so far as his education was religious and ethical, its assumptions fed his image of the poet just as much as of the priest; in so far as it was literary, the disciplines imposed on the young Milton to a large extent determined the shape of the later writing.

What then were the stages of Milton's education? He provided a brief account in his *2nd defence of the English people*, a defence of both the establishment of the commonwealth and his own academic integrity against a hostile Europe:

My father destined me from a child for the pursuits of polite learning, which I prosecuted with such eagerness, that after I was twelve years old, I rarely retired to bed from my lucubrations till midnight...But as all this could not abate my instinctive ardour for learning, he provided me, in addition to the ordinary instructions of the grammar school, masters to give me daily lessons at home. Being thus instructed in various languages, and having got no slight taste of the sweetness of philosophy, he sent me to Cambridge, one of our two national colleges. There, aloof from all profligate conduct, and with the approbation of all good men, I studied seven years, according to the usual course of discipline and of scientific instruction – till I obtained, and with applause, the degree of master...At my father's country house, to which he had retired to pass the remainder of his days, being perfectly at my ease, I gave myself up entirely to reading the Greek and Latin writers; exchanging, however, sometimes, the country for the town, either for the purchase of books, or to learn something new in mathematics, or in music, which at that time furnished the sources of my amusement. After passing five years in this way, I had the curiosity, after the death of my mother, to see foreign countries.

There are thus three main stages of Milton's education to consider: his years at grammar school (St Paul's); at Cambridge; and in private study at home (at Hammersmith and Horton). We must bear in mind that during the period of formal education his interests ranged far outside the usual curriculum. This period of formal and self-imposed education lasted until he was thirty, when he embarked on his continental tour (itself a vital part of any educational scheme in his opinion). But even when he returned to England and began to engage in public controversy in 1641 with his tracts against the bishops, he felt he was being forced to write, as he says, 'out of mine own season, when I have [not] yet completed to my mind the full circle of my private studies'. Only the onset of blindness, making him dependent on readers, interfered with a lifetime's plan.

There have been few poets who have consciously set out to educate themselves as rigorously as Milton did. (One might give as a modern example Ezra Pound, who resolved early in his career to know more about poetry at the age of thirty than any man living.) But Milton relied heavily on the conventional education of his day, in spite of his criticisms of it and his plans for himself which went beyond its scope. What was the content of this conventional education?

At St Paul's School, founded in the early 16th century by John Colet, the friend of Erasmus, Milton underwent the typical humanist education of his day. Humanism was an educational movement which began in 14th-century Italy and reached England in the 16th century; it attempted both to recover the pattern of classical life as a moral framework, and to imitate the language and style of the classics as a means to that end. In the narrowest sense a humanist was a Latin teacher, but the term derives ultimately from the Latin *humanitas*, itself a translation of the Greek *paideia* in its meaning of culture or liberal education. (Compare the modern term 'humanities', which refers to studies that are literary, historical, and social as opposed to technical and scientific.) Humanist education was concerned with two main subjects: eloquence, or the style of what was read; and ethics, or its content. In practice eloquence was emphasized at the expense of ethics, though in theory humanist education was concerned with preparing men for public life (unlike medieval education which was concerned with the training of the priestly profession, the clerks). Because of the concern with eloquence and expression, the content was almost entirely literary. In medieval times the framework of preparatory education had been the seven liberal arts, consisting of the trivium (grammar, rhetoric, logic) and the quadrivium (arithmetic, geometry, music, astronomy). The trivium now became dominant. The languages studied were Latin, some Greek, and a smattering of Hebrew. A boy who went through the curriculum of St Paul's would have a good knowledge of the Roman poets, including Virgil, Horace, and especially Ovid, the historians, including Caesar and Sallust, and the oratory of Cicero; among Greek writers he would have read Homer, some tragedy, and the orator Isocrates; in addition he would know the Greek of the New Testament and some Hebrew grammar. English literature was not a subject for study in schools until the 20th century, but Milton's schoolmaster Alexander Gill was an enthusiastic reader of contemporary English poetry.

The way in which classical authors were taught permanently marked Milton's mature work. The schoolboy spent his time imitating his set authors in prose and verse, paraphrasing them, and translating from English into Latin and Greek. Conversation was carried on in Latin, and the really able boy would become as fluent in Latin as in English (an important accomplishment when Latin was the diplomatic language of Europe). The elements of this educational scheme were standard in England until at least 1914. At its best it provided a widespread and profound knowledge of Greek and

Latin literature such as few of us can now hope to attain; at its worst it degenerated into a mechanical application of specific techniques which left the schoolboy without any sense that the writings he tinkered with were works of art.

There was an important difference, however, between humanist education of the 16th and 17th centuries, and the classical education that developed from it in the 18th and 19th. The exercises that Milton performed were as often oral as written. Roman education had been centred on rhetoric, on the training of men for careers in public life; the arts of argument and persuasion were taught. Following this example English schoolboys were taught to speak in public, to debate either side of a proposition, however absurd. This aspect of his training was particularly important during Milton's Cambridge years and bore fruit years later in his polemical prose.

We must not forget that in addition to the regular school curriculum Milton carried his study of Latin, Greek and Hebrew further, and also learned French and Italian. He owed these opportunities to his father, as he reminds him in the Latin poem *Ad patrem*; this is a defence of time spent on poetry, perhaps written not long after the 'Letter to a friend' or as an apology for the writing of *Comus*:

Best of fathers, when at your expense the eloquence of Romulus' tongue was opened to me, and the beauties of Latin, and the proud words of the magniloquent Greeks, words that fitted the great mouth of Jove, you persuaded me to add the flowers of which Gaul boasts [i.e. French], and the language that the modern Italian pours from his degenerate mouth (giving proof by his speech of barbarian invasions), and also the mysteries that the Palestinian prophet utters. Thanks to you, if I wish to do so I can know everything there is in the sky, or on mother earth beneath the sky, or in the air flowing between them, or covered by the waves and the moving marble of the sea.

When Milton went up to Cambridge at the age of sixteen he was more than well prepared for his university career, and he was clearly disappointed at what was offered him. The Cambridge curriculum was much further from the humanist ideal than that of St Paul's. It was out of touch with contemporary thought, and attacks on it by men like Bacon and Hobbes who were associated with the new science were common. The curriculum still depended heavily on scholasticism, an intellectual discipline which had reached its high point in the 13th century. The term 'scholastic' refers both to a method and a range of study. The technique was that of logical disputation; the subjects were philosophy (based largely on Aristotle) and theology.

Scholastic education was much more 'academic' than the seven liberal arts of medieval preparatory education, and than the humanism which was now challenging it. Thus the subjects studied at Cambridge in Milton's day were mainly logic, ethics, physics, and metaphysics (theology). Milton drew heavily on this learning when he came to write *Paradise lost*, but he seems to have found it restrictive. However he had ample time for private reading; he continued with his studies in Greek and Hebrew, and also in mathematics. We can gather part of Milton's attitude to his official Cambridge education from his third *Prolusion*, one of the public academic performances he was obliged to give, in which he spoke against scholastic philosophy. Allowing for the artificial nature of such exercises, and for the fact that the disputant did not necessarily believe in the proposition he was advancing, we can nevertheless detect Milton's sympathies. He speaks on behalf of the humanist subjects, poetry, rhetoric, history, even geography, against the scholastic emphasis on logic and philosophy. His view of education is social and moral rather than intellectual; its purpose is not to sharpen a man's mind but to make him a useful member of society. But in spite of these reservations Milton carried away with him from the years of his formal education two important intellectual habits, of imitation and of disputation.

Milton left Cambridge apparently unsure about becoming a priest, but certain that he must prepare himself for a great task. For five more years he trained himself in retirement for the role which emerged as that of poet. From his surviving commonplace book we can deduce the programme Milton set himself. He worked through the early history of the church (work which stood him in good stead in his attacks of the bishops), and the ancient and modern political history of Europe. He indexed the notes in the commonplace book under the headings of ethics, economics (i.e. domestic matters) and politics. After he had returned from his travels and gained some experience as a teacher in London, he found time during his other polemical writing to publish the short tract *Of education*, which is one of the classics of humanist educational theory. In it Milton sets out his plan for a private academy, showing how far he thought the university education of his day fell short of its proper function. His belief is that education that proceeds without constant reference to its purpose is worthless. He gives two general definitions of education, the first of which places man in relation to God, the second in relation to society. This is the first:

The end then of learning is to repair the ruins of our first parents by regaining to know God aright, and out of that knowledge to love him, to imitate him, to be like him, as we may the nearest by possessing our souls of true virtue, which being united to the heavenly grace of faith makes up the highest perfection.

The second definition makes clear what is meant by the emphasis on virtue in the first:

I call therefore a complete and generous education that which fits a man to perform justly, skilfully and magnanimously all the offices both private and public of peace and war.

It is this large design that Milton had in mind for himself during his years of preparation. If it seems to us a curiously ambitious plan for a poet, that is because our view of poetry is more restricted than Milton's. Though he had to defend his years of apparent inaction, the career of poet to Milton was essentially an active one, implying direct involvement in public affairs. All his early training, the sense of self-importance nurtured by his father, contributed to his conviction that the poet was a teacher, an orator, a statesman, a prophet.

Poetic theory

Before we consider further the view of the poet that Milton evolved, and his idea of the kind of audience he hoped to address, we must ask how original his position was, and what he owed to classical and renaissance theories of the function of poetry. Perhaps the most crucial distinction between renaissance and modern critical theory is that, in the former, poetry was considered in terms of its purpose. The renaissance critic spoke of the intention of poetry and its power to move, while in recent years critical interest in the writer's intention and the work's effect has been diagnosed as 'the intentional fallacy' and 'the affective fallacy'. There are of course other critical positions, but few would now choose the renaissance critic's terminology, however many valuable ideas might be found to lie behind it.

The chief classical sources for renaissance critical theory were Aristotle, Horace, Cicero, and Quintilian; the influence of Plato was less direct. The first two are concerned with the nature of poetry, Aristotle in the *Poetics* more with theory, Horace in the *Art of poetry* more with the craft of writing. However Cicero and Quintilian deal not with poetic but with rhetoric. Renaissance critics seem to have drawn more on the rhetoricians than on theorists of poetry, partly because they found in the rhetoricians clear statements of the function of rhetoric and the nature of the orator, such as were not given for poetry. Aristotle's *Poetics* was certainly a very influential book in the renaissance: while the humanists degraded Aristotle the philosopher of the scholastics, they elevated Aristotle the critic, rhetorician, and political theorist. The important concept of poetry as imitation derives from him, but there were too many questions that he left unanswered or uncertain. It is still not clear, for example, whether Aristotle thought he was describing tragedy as it ought to be or tragedy as it was. There were no such problems with the Roman rhetoricians. In their writings on rhetoric Cicero (orator, politician and moralist of the 1st century BC) and Quintilian (teacher of rhetoric of the 1st century AD, who added to and systematized many of Cicero's ideas) were concerned with the kind of man the orator should be, the training he should receive, and the public and social purpose of oratory. The chief function of oratory was seen as persuasion. This did not mean (as it frequently became in practice in Roman schools) mere debating skill, but persuasion to a good end. Cicero defined the function of the orator as winning over, teaching, and moving men's minds (*De oratore* II 121). Following on from this definition of the orator's function, Quintilian emphasized the importance of the character and learning of the man who was to have such an effect on society. The way in which renaissance critics adapted Roman definitions of the orator to their own idea of the poet can be illustrated with reference to the writings of Ben Jonson.

Like many of his contemporaries (indeed like Milton), Jonson kept a commonplace book in which he noted interesting passages from his reading. He drew heavily on this material in the composition of his plays and poems, and it was published after his death under the title *Discoveries*. Many of these notes deal with the function of poetry and its style. In one of these he gives an account of the nature and influence of the poet, which is partly a translation from Quintilian's *Institutio oratoria*, with the exception that where Quintilian writes of the orator Jonson substitutes the poet:

I could never think the study of wisdom confined only to the philosopher; or of piety to the divine; or of state to the politic [i.e. politician]. But that he which can feign a commonwealth (which is the poet), can govern it with counsels, strengthen it with laws, correct it with judgements, inform it with religion and morals, is all these. We do not require in him mere elocution or an excellent faculty in verse, but the exact knowledge of all virtues and their contraries; with ability to render the one loved, the other hated, by his proper embattling them [i.e. setting them out].

82

The good poet must be a good as well as a learned man, and he must achieve good social effects. Poetry is thus to be judged with reference to the character of the poet, and his influence on his audience.

The best known renaissance definition of the poet as teacher is given by Sidney in his *Apology for poetry*. Like Jonson after him (and like Aristotle before) Sidney is concerned to show that poetry is superior to history and even to philosophy; indeed he calls the poet 'the right popular philosopher'. The poet is a better teacher than the philosopher because he moves the reader by his examples:

> [The poet] beginneth not with obscure definitions, which must blur the margent with interpretations and load the memory with doubtfulness; but he cometh to you with words set in delightful proportion, either accompanied with or prepared for the well-enchanting skill of music; and with a tale forsooth he cometh unto you, with a tale which holdeth children from play and old men from the chimney-corner. And, pretending no more, doth intend the winning of the mind from wickedness to virtue: even as the child is often brought to take most wholesome things by hiding them in such other as have a pleasant taste; which, if one should begin to tell them the nature of aloes or rhubarb they should receive, would sooner take their physic at their ears than at their mouth.

Put briefly, by offering the pleasures of verse, music, and story, the poet deceives the reader into swallowing down moral truths at the same time; the philosopher, who offers his truths undisguised, has no such success.

This sugared-pill theory of poetry seems simpleminded, and we must ask what Sidney meant by it. From one point of view the account was disingenuous: Sidney was answering Puritan attacks on the immorality of poetry, and he was anxious to argue that it had a useful moral function. But the argument is more complex than this. During the course of the *Apology* Sidney shifts his ground several times, and offers several different views of the nature of poetry. The sugared-pill version is perhaps intended as the most easily accessible one; more interesting is the proposition that Sidney puts forward that the poet is not so much a teacher or a craftsman (the latter aspect most interested other Elizabethan critics such as Gascoigne and Puttenham) as a creator. The poet is truly a maker (the proper translation of the Greek *poietes*); other arts and sciences work with existing nature, but the poet creates another nature:

> Only the poet, disdaining to be tied to any such subjection, lifted up with the vigour of his own invention, doth grow in effect into another nature, in making things either better than nature bringeth forth, or quite anew, forms

such as never were in nature...Nature never set forth the earth in so rich tapestry as divers poets have done; neither with pleasant rivers, fruitful trees, sweet-smelling flowers, nor whatsoever else may make the too-much-loved earth more lovely. Her world is brazen, the poets only deliver a golden... Neither let it be deemed too saucy a comparison to balance the highest point of man's wit with the efficacy of nature; but rather give right honour to the heavenly Maker of that maker, who having made man to his own likeness, set him beyond and over all the works of that second nature; which in nothing he showeth so much as in poetry, when with the force of a divine breath he bringeth things forth far surpassing her doings, with no small argument to the incredulous of that first accursed fall of Adam: since our erected wit maketh us know what perfection is, and yet our infected will keepeth us from reaching unto it.

Sidney is here using Platonism against Plato. Plato in attacking poets had argued that they were at two removes from reality, since they imitated (i.e. simply copied) the visible world which is itself only a copy of ideal form (*Republic* Book x). But Sidney argues that far from copying nature the poet transcends nature and apprehends true reality, the ideal form behind the deceptive appearance. Where nature is brazen, the poet creates a golden world. Sidney implies in fact that the barrier between art and nature is insurmountable. Though the poet puts before us a pattern of perfection, which our 'erected wit' can understand, our 'infected will', our fallen nature, prevents us from modelling ourselves on it.

This concept of the golden world is of the greatest importance in renaissance art. It helps us to understand that much of what seems to us in some renaissance works (or in the ritual elements of renaissance court life) to be flattery, or hypocrisy, or escapism, is not. Where we may now tend to see truth in irony, or exposure, or in imitative naturalism, renaissance critics and poets often saw truth in the ideal; the crude 'reality' of everyday life was a falling away from the ideal, a distortion of truth. Underlying this view of art, and Sidney's expression of it, is Christian theology.

A tension between the aims of art and its possible achievement is thus understood. On the one hand the poet is seen as a teacher, and the poem as a form of persuasion to right action, which does in fact influence men morally; on the other hand the poet provides us with an apprehension of the pattern underlying life which life itself has betrayed, and which, human nature being what it is, we cannot ever hope to fulfil. The writing of poetry becomes a perpetual struggle to close the gap between life as it is and life as it might be. This tension seems to be implied in Book VI of *The Fairy Queen*, when Spenser's

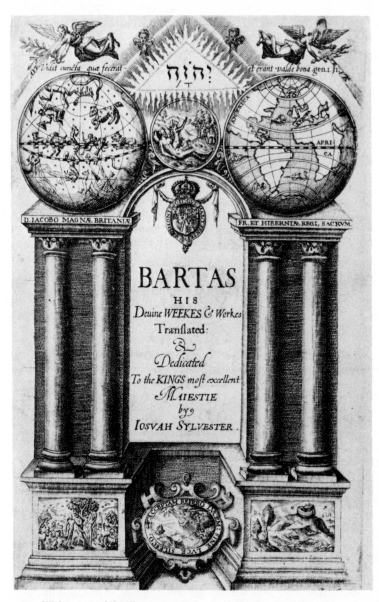

FIG 3   Title page of Guillaume de Saluste du Bartas *Divine weeks and works* trans Joshua Sylvester, engraved by Renold Elstrack 1621. Along with figs 4 and 7, this is reproduced in Arthur M. Hind *Engraving in England in the 16th and 17th centuries* 3 parts 1955, one of the most valuable sources for a swift sense of the period.

Sir Calidore, the Knight of Courtesy, by accident comes across the shepherd Colin Clout (Spenser's name for himself) piping and surrounded by dancing Graces; when Calidore presses forward to know more of them, they vanish, and Colin breaks his pipe in sorrow.

We are now in a better position to assess Milton's idea of the poet and his prophecies of his own future importance. He fully agrees with Jonson's view that only the good man can be a good poet; in the *Apology for Smectymnuus* he writes that in the course of his reading he was

confirmed in this opinion, that he who would not be frustrate of his hope to write well hereafter in laudable things, ought himself to be a true poem, that is, a composition, and pattern of the best and honourablest things; not presuming to sing high praises of heroic men, or famous cities, unless he have in himself the experience and the practice of all that which is praiseworthy.

In *The reason of church government* Milton reveals a theory of poetry drawing on all the sources available to him. In the following passage he uses the ideas that poetry can be made a delicious coating for truth, and that the poet combines the roles of teacher, orator, priest and especially the Hebrew prophet:

These abilities, wheresoever they be found, are the inspired gift of God rarely bestowed, but yet to some (though most abuse) in every nation; and are of power, beside the office of a pulpit, to inbreed and cherish in a great people the seeds of virtue and public civility, to allay the perturbations of the mind, and set the affections in right tune, to celebrate in glorious and lofty hymns the throne and equipage of God's almightiness, and what he works, and what he suffers to be wrought with high providence in his church, to sing the victorious agonies of martyrs and saints, the deeds and triumphs of just and pious nations doing valiantly through faith against the enemies of Christ, to deplore the general relapse of kingdoms and states from justice and God's true worship... Teaching over the whole book of sanctity and virtue through all the instances of example with such delight to those especially of soft and delicious temper who will not so much as look upon truth herself unless they see her elegantly dressed: that whereas the paths of honesty and good life appear now rugged and difficult, though they be indeed easy and pleasant, they would then appear to all men both easy and pleasant though they were rugged and difficult indeed. And what a benefit this would be to our youth and gentry may be soon guessed by what we know of the corruption and bane which they suck in daily from the writings and interludes of libidinous and ignorant poetasters, who having scarce ever heard of that which is the main consistence of a true poem, the choice of such persons as they ought to introduce, and what is moral and decent to each one, do for the most part lap up vicious principles in sweet pills to be swallowed down, and make the taste of virtuous documents harsh and sour.

In contrast to these nefarious modern practices Milton pledges himself to write a true poem:

Neither do I think it shame to covenant with any knowing reader, that for some few years yet I may go on trust with him toward the payment of what I am now indebted, as being a work not to be raised from the heat of youth, or the vapours of wine, like that which flows at waste from the pen of some vulgar amorist, or the trencher fury of a rhyming parasite, nor to be obtained by the invocation of Dame Memory and her siren daughters, but by devout prayer to that eternal Spirit who can enrich with all utterance and knowledge, and sends out his seraphim with the hallowed fire of his altar to touch and purify the lips of whom he pleases. To this must be added industrious and select reading, steady observation, insight into all seemly and generous arts and affairs.

Milton's statements of poetic theory and self-explanation are frequently unsystematic, and appear in what might seem at first glance the most unlikely places. Their tone is a peculiar combination of defensiveness and optimism. Although he is working within a tradition of received ideas about the social function of the poet, Milton writes as though he were the first person to view poetry in this particular light. There are various explanations for this paradox. One of them is the inevitable gap between theory and practice. Milton is careful to dissociate himself from those contemporary practitioners whom he categorizes as libidinous and ignorant poetasters, vulgar amorists, rhyming parasites. Whether or not his theory is to a certain extent conventional, in Milton's opinion there is no adequate contemporary realization of this theory. His defensiveness can partly be accounted for because he is searching for the truly national audience that exists only in his imagination, and to whom the categories of contemporary poetry that he despises are not directed. His optimism about reaching this audience is characteristic only of a short period of his life. Later, largely for political reasons, his concern changed to finding a 'fit' audience rather than a national one. The aspect of his theory which is most original to him, however, and which does provide the basis of his portrait of the poet in *Paradise lost*, is the idea of inspiration. The poet as inspired prophet gradually comes to overshadow the other components of Milton's idea.

The problem of the poet's role

In spite of the agreement in humanist theory about the role of the poet in relation to society, there were differing attitudes to the social status of poet and the writing of poetry as a career. Most poetry at

this time was aristocratic in outlook, but the term allows for conflicting attitudes. At one extreme the poet is seen as a kind of public
servant, the educator of the prince, the inculcator of moral values
which permeate society from the court; at the other, poetry is seen as
one of the courtier's own accomplishments, but it is peripheral to his
main business of making a place for himself at court, and he would not
dream of publishing his work, certainly not under his own name.
There is in other words a conflict between the professional and
amateur views of the poet's career; this was not to be resolved until
the end of the 17th century.

The poet as educator

Spenser is the chief Elizabethan practitioner of the view of poetry put
forward by Sidney. Milton referred in *Areopagitica* to 'our sage and
serious poet Spenser, whom I dare be known to think a better teacher
than Scotus or Aquinas'. Spenser's own claim, in the letter to
Raleigh prefacing *The Fairy Queen*, is explicit: he writes that the
object of the poem is 'to fashion a gentleman or noble person in
virtuous and gentle discipline'. Spenser was in fact excluded from the
position at court that he coveted, and spent most of his time in
Ireland. This isolation probably helped him to develop his nationalist,
rather than simply aristocratic, view of poetry. He used the materials
of British history and legend to create a symbolic fairyland that
operated on many levels, as an idealization of Elizabethan political
life, and a savage criticism of it; as a model of the courtier's search for
glory, and the Christian's search for the holy life; as an image of
Sidney's golden world, and as an admission of the inevitable flux and
imperfection of brazen reality. Two passages from his autobiographical
poem *Colin Clout's come home again* illustrate Spenser's technique.
The shepherd Colin is describing to his friends his journey from
Ireland to England; he gives two contradictory portraits of the court.
Spenser leaves it to the reader to work out the relationship between
them. First Colin gives the idealized view:

> Both heaven and heavenly graces do much more
> (Quoth he) abound in that same land than this:
> For there all happy peace and plenteous store
> Conspire in one to make contented bliss;
> No wailing there nor wretchedness is heard,
> No bloody issues nor no leprosies,
> No grisly famine nor no raging sword,

No nightly bodrags nor no hue and cries;
The shepherds there abroad may safely lie
On hills and downs withouten dread or danger;
No ravenous wolves the good man's hope destroy
Nor outlaws fell affray the forest ranger;
There learnèd arts do flourish in great honour
And poets' wits are had in peerless price;
Religion hath lay power to rest upon her,
Advancing virtue and suppressing vice.

Later he criticizes the courtiers for their abuse of their position,
particularly for their indulgence in what is seen as artificial love-
poetry:

And is Love then (said Corylas) once known
In court, and his sweet lore professèd there?
I weenèd sure he was our god alone,
And only woned in fields and forest here.
  Not so (quoth he), love most aboundeth there:
For all the walls and windows there are writ
All full of love, and love, and love my dear,
And all their talk and study is of it.
Ne any there doth brave or valiant seem
Unless that some gay mistress' badge he bears;
Ne any one himself doth ought esteem
Unless he swim in love up to the ears.
But they of Love and of his sacred lere
(As it should be) all otherwise devise
Than we poor shepherds are accustomed here,
And him do sue and serve all otherwise:
For with lewd speeches and licentious deeds
His mighty mysteries they do profane,
And use his idle name to other needs,
But as a compliment for courting vain.

In spite of the lip service paid to the idea of the patriotic epic
throughout Europe at this time (and it remained an ambition for poets
in England until the time of Pope), there was no real national audience
for heroic poetry in the early 17th century, as Drayton found to his
cost. Drayton, a prolific writer of many kinds of verse, sonnet, satire,
ode, elegy, and historical epistle, saw the function of his historical
poetry as the arousing of the idle nobility to action through the
example of the glorious past. Hence in the preface to the first part of
Polyolbion, a poetic tour of England's scenery and history, Drayton
attacks chamber poets for their refusal to publish, their reluctance to
adopt a serious role. But Drayton's epic was not well received; he had
difficulty in getting the second part published. The great disappoint-

ment of Drayton's career was this failure to find an appropriate audience; among his most interesting poems are the late elegies addressed to a small group of friends in which he advocates withdrawing from public concerns and relying on the judgement of posterity. This passage from the elegy *To Mr George Sandys* epitomizes Drayton's attitude to poetry and his sense of failure:

This very time wherein we two now live
Shall in the compass wound the Muses more
Than all the old English ignorance before;
Base balladry is so beloved and sought,
And those brave numbers are put by for naught
Which, rarely read, were able to awake
Bodies from graves, and to the ground to shake
The wandering clouds, and to our men at arms
'Gainst pikes and muskets were most powerful charms:
That, but I know, ensuing ages shall
Raise her again who now is in her fall,
And out of dust reduce our scattered rhymes,
The rejected jewels of these slothful times.

[Edmund Spenser 1552–99, friend of Sidney, civil servant in Ireland: *The fairy queen* 1590 and 1596, *Colin Clout, Amoretti, Epithalamion* 1595, *Four hymns* 1596. Michael Drayton 1563–1631, professional writer and friend of poets, published *Polyolbion* in 1612 and 1622, and his elegies in 1627.]

The poet as social figure

Drayton's difficulty was that he tried to find a public not centred on the court. Ben Jonson, whose view of poetry was as public and perhaps more professional than that of Spenser, created a form of poetry which was more courtly and aristocratic, less national, but which was socially and ethically directed none the less. The majority of Jonson's poems are addressed to specific members of the courts of James I and Charles I; they are gifts, adjuncts to social conversation. These poems depend on a particular relationship between the poet and the recipient of the poem. The poet is concerned to make the social relationship of poet and aristocratic patron into a moral one, to transform personality into symbol. The forms that Jonson uses are almost extensions of social ritual: the epistle, the elegy, the epitaph, poems in celebration of people, or recording important social events like marriages and deaths. It was Jonson who made the masque an important work of art. He set great store by his style; he avoided archaisms, obscurities, and eccentric wit, and aimed at simplicity and immediacy of language. In working out this style he partly modelled himself on Horace. Here is an extract from a long epistle *To Katherine, Lady Aubigny*, whose husband gave Jonson hospitality for five years:

'Tis grown almost a danger to speak true
Of any good mind, now: there are so few.
The bad, by number, are so fortified,
As what they have lost to expect, they dare deride.
So both the praised, and praisers suffer: yet,
For others' ill, ought none their good forget.
I, therefore, who profess myself in love
With every virtue, wheresoe'er it move
And howsoever; as I am at feud
With sin and vice, though with a throne endued;

. . . .

I, madam, am become your praiser. Where,
If it may stand with your soft blush to hear
Your self but told unto your self, and see
In my charácter, what your features be,
You will not from the paper slightly pass:
No lady but, at some time, loves her glass;
And this shall be no false one, but as much
Removed, as you from need to have it such.
Look then, and see yourself.

Jonson was as much interested in raising the status of the craft of letters as he was in moulding the aristocracy to his own image, and he had great influence on the rising generation of poets of the 1620s and 30s. But it must be admitted that many of Jonson's followers (who were sometimes known as Sons of Ben) imitated the surface qualities of his verse rather than his overriding professional and moral interests. Milton's contemporary at Cambridge, Thomas Randolph, is an example of a poet who modelled himself on Jonson in such a way; his volume of poems (published in the same year as *Lycidas*) is a patchwork of experimentation in Jonsonian modes: satires, elegies, epitaphs, Horatian imitations, odes.

[Ben Jonson 1572–1637, playwright, scholar, masque-writer, literary oracle, published his early *Works* in folio in 1616 (including his plays, an unprecedented step of self-assurance); the rest were published posthumously in 1640. His circle of friends was vast, including patrons like the Countess of Bedford, poets like Donne, scholars like Camden the antiquary.]

In his capacity as courtier poet, Thomas Carew followed not so much the professionalism of Jonson as the tradition of amateur gentlemen poets. It was a tradition that persisted for over a hundred years, from Wyatt to Rochester; Pope, securely professional and assured of his 18th-century reading public, caricatured them as the mob of gentlemen who wrote with ease. These amateurs were mostly courtiers who regarded the ability to write poetry as only one among many appropriate skills; they circulated their poems in manuscript but often disdained publication, and as a result a good deal of material has been lost or is hard to attribute. Love poetry was the predominating kind. For Carew this tradition was represented by the Donne of the *Songs and sonnets* (which only appeared in print posthumously in 1633 though they were widely known in manuscript before then); but his interest was rather in the way in which Donne broke with tradition.

The question of style: metaphysical poetry

So far we have been concerned with differentiating the various attitudes in the early 17th century to the poet's profession and his public; we have avoided categorizing poets stylistically, for example as 'metaphysicals'. We should distinguish two quite different ways of using the term 'metaphysical': one concerned with technique, the other with frame of mind. When Donne's contemporaries drew attention to the newness of his poetry it was chiefly with reference to the first category. But the search for poetic style and language in this period, for precision of expression, was always carried on in terms of existing poetic conventions, whether the poet chose to adopt the convention and make it his own, or rebut it and create a new style through defiance. We can see metaphysical poetry, in so far as it is a technique, partly as a process of turning convention upside down.

Carew's elegy on Donne's death lists the qualities he found original:

> The Muses' garden, with pedantic weeds
> O'erspread, was purged by thee; the lazy seeds
> Of servile imitation thrown away
> And fresh invention planted; thou didst pay
> The debts of our penurious bankrupt age:
> Licentious thefts that make poetic rage
> A mimic fury, when our souls must be
> Possessed or with Anacreon's ecstasy
> Or Pindar's, not their own; the subtle cheat

Of sly exchanges, and the juggling feat
Of two-edged words, or whatsoever wrong
By ours was done the Greek or Latin tongue,
Thou hast redeemed, and opened us a mine
Of rich and pregnant fancy, drawn a line
Of masculine expression...

Masculinity, intellectual agility, obscurity, roughness, 'strong lines', rejection of tradition, these are what contemporaries underlined. The extremes of the metaphysical style which Johnson was to deplore in his *Life of Cowley* can be illustrated from a very early poem by Dryden, *Upon the death of the Lord Hastings*, which shows him struggling to keep abreast of an intellectual fashion:

His body was an orb, his sublime soul
Did move on virtue's and on learning's pole:
Whose regular motions better to our view
Than Archimedes' sphere the heavens did show.

    .   .   .   .

Heaven's gifts, which do like falling stars appear
Scattered in others, all, as in their sphere,
Were fixed and conglobate in's soul: and thence
Shone through his body with sweet influence.

The metaphysical frame of mind

The metaphysical style was on its way out by 1660. But when we use 'metaphysical' to refer to a frame of mind, the term becomes more complex. There has been a great deal of confusing romanticism in the 20th century about the 'unified sensibility' that poets of the early 17th century were supposed to have possessed. While definitions of this kind seem mistaken (and would have been theologically impossible for men of the time), we can point out some characteristics of the metaphysical frame of mind, or more properly the allegorical frame of mind. This was not a 17th-century phenomenon but a traditional aspect of Christian thought, which began to die out towards the end of the 17th century. Put very briefly, it is a way of looking at the universe and of looking at history. In terms of the universe this means the ideas of correspondence between the several planes of existence, of the macrocosm and microcosm, of universal analogy, of *discordia concors* or unity in variety. The conceit, an analogy between things apparently unlike, is the poetic exemplification of these ideas. There is a widespread habit of seeing the universe itself as a metaphor, as hieroglyphics which must be deciphered, as God's handwriting. All objects are symbolic. In terms of history it is a similar habit of seeing events symbolically, which derives from the practice of reading the Old Testament in terms of the New, so that events or characters of the Old Testament are seen as prefigurations, shadows, or types of the life of Christ in the New Testament. This way of interpreting Christian history is known as typology.

It is this metaphysical or allegorical frame of mind that we associate with the religious poets of the 17th century. Before looking at them further we should distinguish two main traditions, the Anglo-Catholic, baroque line, which includes Southwell, Alabaster, Donne, Giles Fletcher, Herbert, Vaughan, and Crashaw; and the more puritan, moralistic, didactic line, which includes poets like Fulke Greville, Sylvester (in his translation of du Bartas' *Divine weeks*), and Quarles, and which culminates in Bunyan's prose allegories. These lines are meant as rough guides, and are not mutually exclusive.

Religious poetry: the baroque tradition

Among the characteristics of the Anglo-Catholic poets are their concern with the dramatic personal relationship between man and God; their habit of meditating on the events of Christ's life or the signs of the crucifixion; and their delight in the paradoxes of Christianity, for example the gap between divine love and human sin, or the mystery of the incarnation. One way that the relationship of man and God is defined is in terms of the experience of human love. A well-known example is Donne's *Holy Sonnet XIV*:

> Yet dearly I love you, and would be lovèd fain,
> But am betrothed unto your enemy:
> Divorce me, untie, or break that knot again,
> Take me to you, imprison me, for I
> Except you enthrall me, never shall be free,
> Nor ever chaste, except you ravish me.

This kind of definition of religious experience is part of an old Christian tradition: the habit of reading *The song of songs* as an allegory of Christ's union with the Church or God's with the soul is an example of it; but in late 16th- and 17th-century religious poetry it sometimes takes the form of 'sacred parody', a deliberate use of the techniques and materials of secular love poetry for religious ends. Thus two of Southwell's poems are reworkings of poems by the

94

courtier Dyer; and in *A child my choice* Southwell sets himself up as a new kind of love poet:

Let folly praise that fancy loves, I praise and love that child
Whose heart, no thought: whose tongue, no word: whose hand no deed
    defiled.

Several of the Anglo-Catholic devotional poets wrote sequences or groups of poems connected with the festivals of the church or the significant events of Christian history. Thus Alabaster wrote sonnets on 'the ensigns of Christ's crucifying', Southwell wrote sequences on the Virgin Mary, on the events of Christ's life, and on the stages of St Peter's experience; Donne wrote a sonnet sequence called *La corona*, 'a crown of prayer and praise', covering the events of Christ's life from annunciation to ascension; Herbert in *The temple* allegorized church architecture and incorporated features of the liturgy; Crashaw used the lives of saints – Theresa, Alexis, Mary Magdalen – as well as events like the nativity as a focus. These poets work with traditional materials, but they are always concerned with the paradox of expressing the inexpressible. Thus Giles Fletcher in *Christ's triumph after death* tries to describe a vision of God in the celestial city:

> A heavenly feast no hunger can consume,
> A light unseen, yet shines in every place,
> A sound no time can steal, a sweet perfúme
> No winds can scatter, an entire embrace
> That no satiety can e'er unlace.

Herbert in *The sacrifice* dramatizes the perpetual conflict between divine love and human ingratitude (the speaker is Christ on the cross):

> O all ye who pass by, behold and see:
> Man stole the fruit, but I must climb the tree,
> The tree of life to all but only me:
>   Was ever grief like mine?

Crashaw in *The holy nativity of our Lord God* (like Southwell in *The burning babe* or *New heaven, new war*) develops the paradox of God clothed in the flesh of a child:

> Welcome, all wonders in one sight!
> Eternity shut in a span.
> Summer in winter. Day in night.
> Heaven in earth, and God in man.

95

[Roman Catholics. Robert Southwell born 1561 was a Jesuit priest executed for his beliefs in 1595. William Alabaster 1568–1640, Catholic convert, wrote his divine sonnets in the late 1590s. Richard Crashaw 1613–49, Cambridge don and later Catholic convert who died in Italy, published *Steps to the temple* in 1646.

Anglicans. Giles Fletcher 1586–1623, Cambridge don and Anglican priest; *Christ's victory and triumph* 1610. Donne became Dean of St Paul's but was brought up as a Catholic; his religious poems probably date from *c.* 1617 but were published posthumously. George Herbert 1593–1633, Cambridge don, aspiring courtier, parish priest; *The temple* published at his death. Henry Vaughan 1622–95, Welsh doctor; *Silex scintillans* appeared in 1650 and 55.]

The problem of religious style

A further paradox that concerns several of the religious poets is that of the use of poetry as a means to devotion, of the proffering of a poem, an essentially secular and human object, as a gift to God. There is widespread concern with the moral problem raised by the writing of religious poetry, with the difficulty of finding an appropriate style. Marvell in *The coronet* and Herbert in *A wreath* approach the problem from different points of view. For Marvell the only true offering is an abandonment of poetry:

> And now when I have summed up all my store,
>   Thinking (so I myself deceive)
>   So rich a chaplet thence to weave
> As never yet the King of glory wore:
>   Alas! I find the serpent old
>   That twining in his speckled breast
>   About the flowers disguised does fold
>   With wreaths of fame and interest.
> Ah, foolish man, that would'st debase with them,
> And mortal glory, heaven's diadem!
> But thou who only could'st the serpent tame,
> Either his slippery knots at once untie
> And disentangle all his winding snare;
> Or shatter too with him my curious frame,
> And let these wither so that he may die,
> Though set with skill and chosen out with care:
> That they, while thou on both their spoils dost tread,
> May crown thy feet, that could not crown thy head.

In contrast Herbert parodies and then abandons 'art' for a simple style and way of life:

> A wreathèd garland of deservèd praise,
> Of praise deservèd, unto thee I give,

I give to thee, who knowest all my ways,
My crooked winding ways, wherein I live –
Wherein I die, not live: for life is straight,
Straight as a line, and ever tends to thee,
To thee, who art more far above deceit
Than deceit seems above simplicity.
Give me simplicity, that I may live,
So live and like, that I may know thy ways,
Know them, and practise them: then shall I give,
For this poor wreath, give thee a crown of praise.

Religious poetry: the didactic tradition

The best exemplar of the moralistic tradition in religious verse is
Quarles, whose *Emblems* were enormously popular as instructional
literature, and were to be reprinted many times in the 19th century.
An emblem is an allegorical picture accompanied by explanatory
verse; it has a clear connection with the conceit. The majority of
Quarles' emblems are moral reflections, concerned with the state of
the individual soul, rather than meditations on Christian symbols or
on the events of the Christian year. They are thus associated with the
Puritan emphasis on self-examination and moral reform, rather than
with the Anglican and Catholic interest in the personal relationship
with God. Emblem xiii of Book III shows a skeleton's hand reaching
for a sundial: the poem (one of Quarles' best; his usual standard is
more pedestrian) deals with the need for repentance before time runs
out. These are the last verses:

Behold these rags! am I a fitting guest
To taste the dainties of thy royal feast,
With hands and face unwashed, ungirt, unblest?

First, let the Jordan streams that find supplies
From the deep fountain of my heart, arise
And cleanse my spots and clear my leprous eyes.

I have a world of sins to be lamented:
I have a sea of tears that must be vented:
O spare till then; and then I die contented.

Others among the didactic poets are concerned with pointing
lessons from their observations of human failure. So Sylvester warns
in his bouncing couplets:

The world's a book in folio, printed all
With God's great works in letters capital:
Each creature is a page, and each effect

97

A fair chárácter, void of all defect.
But as young truants, toying in the schools
Instead of learning, learn to play the fools,
We gaze but on the babies and the cover,
The gaudy flowers and edges gilded over,
And never further for our lesson look
Within the volume of this various book:
Where learnèd nature rudest ones instructs
That by his wisdom God the world conducts.

[Joshua Sylvester 1563–1618, merchant and courtier, brought out his collected translation of the French Huguenot Du Bartas' *Divine weeks and works*
in 1605 and 1608. Francis Quarles 1592–1644, minor courtier, chronologer to
the city of London, published his *Divine poems* in 1630 and *Emblems* 1635.]

Poetic developments in the Interregnum and Restoration

The civil war, a decisive factor in Milton's poetic interests, had a
more general effect on the direction of poetry in his lifetime. The last
court masque, by Davenant, was performed in 1640; with the break-
up of the court the whole Jonsonian tradition of poetry, social,
aristocratic, depending on a particular relation between poet and
patron, suddenly ceased to exist. Similarly the overthrow of the
Anglican church meant that there was no longer any institutional
support for the tradition of devotional poetry, though poets like
Vaughan and Traherne continued the tradition in retirement. We
find in the 1650s various new interests reflected in poetry. The new
epics, Davenant's *Gondibert* and Cowley's *Davideis*, though making
use to a large extent of the old epic formulae, are also part of a movement to a more general, philosophical poetry of ideas. Cowley's
interest in science can be seen in his ode *To Mr Hobbes*, which
celebrates the defeat of Aristotelianism. Cowley tried to develop
poetry as a measured expression of thought, and at the same time
experimented with a style that would be properly lofty and dignified
for public and social themes. The extremes of his interests can be
illustrated from, first, a description of heaven in *Davideis* 1:

> For there no twilight of the sun's dull ray
> Glimmers upon the pure and native day;
> No pale-faced moon does in stol'n beams appear
> Or with dim taper scatters darkness there;
> On no smooth sphere the restless seasons slide,
> No circling motion doth swift time divide;
> Nothing is there to come, and nothing past,
> But an eternal now does always last.

And, second, his *Ode to the Royal Society*, where Cowley compares its members to 'Gideon's little band':

> Thus you prepared; and in the glorious fight
>   Their wondrous pattern too you take:
> Their old and empty pitchers first they brake,
> And with their hand they lifted up the light.
>   Io! Sound too the trumpets here!
> Already your victorious lights appear;
> New scenes of heaven already we espy,
> And crowds of golden worlds on high.

When with the Restoration of Charles II the court once more became a focus for poetry, the tone of such poetry, and the audience it was designed for, differed greatly from that of the earlier court. The difference between Jonson and Dryden is partly explicable in terms of the experience of the Interregnum years. Instead of an aristocratic and court-centred poetry we find in the 1650s a tendency to a more journalistic and specifically political kind of public poetry. There was, for example, no ready-made language for describing the achievement of Cromwell; a new set of terms had to be found. This is what Marvell attempted in *The first anniversary*:

> Hence oft I think, if in some happy hour
> High grace should meet in one with highest power,
> And then a seasonable people still
> Should bend to his, as he to heaven's will,
> What we might hope, what wonderful effect,
> From such a wished conjuncture might reflect.
> Sure, the mysterious work, where none withstand,
> Would forthwith finish under such a hand:
> Foreshortened time its useless course would stay,
> And soon precipitate the latest day.
> But a thick cloud about that morning lies
> And intercepts the beams of mortal eyes;
> That 'tis the most which we determine can:
> If these the times, then this must be the man.

At the Restoration Marvell turned his sharpened political awareness against the court, and established the techniques and the standard for the political satire which was to become the dominant poetic form of the period. Dryden, while inheriting many of the traditional assumptions about the social role of the poet on which Milton was brought up, strengthened his vague ambitions and magnificent symbols with the political sophistication brought about by years of social upheaval. Thus Dryden worked towards a high Virgilian style suitable for grand themes and public occasions, and at the same time developed the tools of satire to deal with the unpleasant realities of political life. In *Astraea redux* (a poem celebrating Charles' return) Dryden adopts the prophetic Virgilian stance:

> And now time's whiter series is begun
> Which in soft centuries shall smoothly run;
> Those clouds that overcast your morn shall fly
> Dispelled to farthest corners of the sky.
> Our nation with united interest blest,
> Not now content to poise, shall sway the rest.

Paradoxically Dryden took over the career of public poet that Milton was partly forced to abandon, but his work reflects the same tension between inherited conventions and the realities of the present.

[Abraham Cowley 1618–67, royalist agent, amateur scientist, essayist and man of letters, published his pindaric odes and *Davideis* 1656.

Andrew Marvell 1621–78, friend of Milton, MP, lyric poet, satirist, pamphleteer, was famous in his lifetime as a political figure; his early poems were not published till 1681. John Dryden 1631–1700, playwright, critic, Poet Laureate, Tory apologist, and translator, was the first truly professional writer of the period; his best-known satires, which draw heavily on the Bible and Milton, belong to the early 1680s.]

The development of Milton

The idiosyncrasy of Milton's political and religious views meant that his idea of the kind of poet he was able to become diverged sharply from the paths pursued by his contemporaries. The poetic world that Milton knew as a young man implied different views of the role of the poet, as socially responsible teacher or as gentleman amateur, and different social positions for him, as courtier, as semi-professional dependent on patronage, or as priest. We can now briefly look at the way in which Milton in his early poems drew on the poetic traditions of his day in his search for his own voice.

In the early stages of his search for a poetic identity Milton did not draw on English tradition. Apart from his youthful paraphrases of the *Psalms* the majority of the poems he wrote as a student are in Latin. It was Ovid, the Latin poet he had known best at school, who provided the tone and the style of these poems. In *Elegies V* and *VII*, belonging to the late 1620s, he tries his hand at heavily embroidered nature and love poetry, giving scope through its licensed artificiality for an effusion of personal feeling. But Milton soon found that the irresponsibility of the elegiac writers did not fit with his conception of the poet. Though he wrote his major Latin poetry in the 1630s after leaving Cambridge (partly in order to reach a European audience), he relied much less heavily on Ovid here than in the earlier poems. In the *Apology for Smectymnuus* Milton tells us how he abandoned his youthful passion for the elegiac poets and turned to Dante and Petrarch, as the celebrators of Beatrice and Laura, for they 'never write but honour of them to whom they devote their verse, displaying sublime and pure thoughts, without transgression'. In a series of Italian poems which we cannot date exactly, but which may belong to his Cambridge days, Milton adopts the role of the Petrarchan lover.

But for some reason the decision to write in English entailed the abandonment of the role of poetic lover, though Milton could have found in Spenser the model for a serious love poetry if he had wanted to. It was during the Cambridge years that he began to experiment with the traditions of English poetry. In the *Vacation exercise* of 1628 he expresses his preference for 'some graver subject' for his English theme, slighting in passing 'new fangled toys' and 'late fantastics', though it is not altogether clear whom he means to denigrate. In the early 1630s we find Milton experimenting with a variety of contemporary traditions, including devotional poetry, Jonsonian social poetry, and even 'strong lines'.

With the *Nativity ode* of 1629 Milton turned his hand to the rich tradition of devotional poetry, though he may not have been acquainted with the work of his contemporary practitioners. But he made important modifications of the tradition, and eventually, realizing its unsuitability for his own frame of mind, abandoned it. In the *Nativity ode*, for example, Milton uses the idea of sacred poetry as a gift, a consecration, but he avoids the Anglo-Catholic paradoxes of the divine in human shape, of the disparity between the giver of the poem and the giver of life, and concentrates instead on the working out of Christian history. Following his success with the *Nativity ode*, Milton clearly intended to write a sequence of poems on the events of Christ's life, but he only produced the unfinished poem on *The passion* and *The circumcision*. He attributed the failure of the first of these to the fact that it was 'above the years he had when he wrote it', but a more plausible reason might be that he tried to build the poem on a personal relation between man and God, a personal reaction to Christ's suffering, which was not his usual approach to Christianity; the whole poem is taken up with defining the stance he is to adopt. In

The circumcision, however, Milton returned to the theme of the *Nativity ode* (which was to be essentially the theme of *Paradise lost*), the problem of uniting human history to Christian history.

Interspersed among the religious poems of these years are various attempts to use contemporary witty styles. It has only recently come to be understood how much *Paradise lost* depends on structural wit, for example in the way that Satan's actions are constantly presented as a parody of God's, but it was only briefly that Milton was attracted to experimentation with verbal wit. The Hobson poems read like an academic exercise; they combine intellectual metaphysical jokes with Elizabethan delight in outrageous puns. Milton was a supreme exemplar of the metaphysical frame of mind, of the attempt to see unity in history, but he found metaphysical technique uncongenial. Having dabbled at it, in the period when he was prepared to test all poetic traditions and conventions, he moved on. This does not mean that Milton, having rejected a prevailing contemporary mode, abandoned technical innovation and lapsed into some pre-existing pattern. When we consider that the poetic movement of the time in formal terms was towards the antithetical balance of the closed rhyming couplet, with occasional escapes to the licensed irregularity of the ode on the side, Milton appears as the outstanding metrical innovator of the century. Jonson's or Cowley's experiments with the Pindaric ode, or Donne's deliberate forcing of the pentameter line, pale beside Milton's experiments with Italian and Greek forms (in *Lycidas* and *Samson agonistes* respectively) and with unrhymed verse. Milton did not so much adapt his own poetic personality to the conventions he used as recreate them to fit his needs.

It was during this early period of experiment, particularly just after he had left Cambridge and was rejecting the career of priest for that of poet, that Milton turned to the poetic forms and attitudes that Jonson had developed. The writing of poems like the *Epitaph on the Marchioness of Winchester* or the masques *Arcades* and *Comus* seems to imply that Milton was following both Jonson's social position, in trying to establish a circle of patrons, and his moral concerns, in using these patrons as symbols of moral worth and examples to society. At this stage of his career Milton was in no way challenging the social forms of his day; rather he was attempting to see how far the existing definition of the social role of the poet fitted his own developing conception. His use of Jonsonian attitudes correspondingly entailed the Jonsonian metrical simplicity, precision of expression, and definition of public moral themes that we find in *L'allegro* and *Il penseroso*.

But Milton clearly could not confine himself within the Jonsonian mould. It implied the poet as teacher, as craftsman, as public figure, but not as prophet or as priest. It was towards this conception that Milton was moving. His major poems in the 1630s are poems of self-definition. Milton constantly searches for a form or a convention that will fit him, but constantly finds himself breaking out of it because he does not yet know what he is looking for. The subject of these poems is the writing of poetry, the making of choices, the process of testing oneself, the adoption of an appropriate language and style of life for a particular role.

Thus *Comus* veers away from the masque tradition, which, as Jonson had developed it, though moral in intention, was essentially aristocratic, courtly, and social. Through his emphasis on chastity, on the Spenserian idea of the moral test, Milton's idea of virtue appears much more Platonic and personal that the public social idea of worth that Jonson tried to inculcate. For a time Milton was obsessed with the idea of chastity, though it is possible to exaggerate its importance, particularly in relation to his later work. This idea, as emerges from his account of his intellectual development in the *Apology for Smectymnuus*, was derived partly from Arthurian romance, partly from Plato, and partly from St Paul, so that to the humanist idea of the poet as teacher-orator Milton added the Christian knight, whose life was to be an active quest:

Only this my mind gave me that every free and gentle spirit without that oath ought to be born a knight, nor needed to expect the gilt spur, or the laying of a sword upon his shoulder to stir him up both by his counsel, and his arm to secure and protect the weakness of any attempted chastity.

Different definitions of the poet are tested in various poems. Thus in the Latin *Elegy VI*, addressed to his close friend Charles Diodati and written at about the same time as the *Nativity ode*, Milton compares the licentious life of the elegiac poet with the dedicated life of the epic poet, who is *vates* and *sacerdos*, seer and priest:

In addition the youth of such a poet must be chaste and free from crime, his conduct strict and his hand unstained. He must be like you, priest, when, shining in your sacred robe and washed with holy waters, you rise to go to face the angry gods...For the poet is sacred to the gods, priest of the gods; both his secret heart and his mouth tell of Jove.

Milton goes on to tell Diodati of his work on the *Nativity ode*; the connection between the idealized poet and himself is thus made explicit. Similarly in *L'allegro* and *Il penseroso* he weighs the choice between two different ways of life, two different kinds of poetry; the happy man chooses masque, comedy, and elegiac verse, while the thoughtful man prefers allegorical epic and tragedy. In *Ad patrem* he elaborates the lonely, retired, but elevated view of the poet of *Il penseroso*. In *Lycidas* he tries to resolve the problems of the relation of immaturity to self-dedication, of ambition to self-seeking and glory, of the career of priest to that of poet.

Milton wrote *Lycidas* not long before undertaking his continental tour. His successful reception in Italy helped him to clarify his ideas as to the kind of poet he wished to become and the subject matter for his poetry. His patriotic feelings were aroused, and he began to be convinced that his poem was to be a British epic. In *The reason of church government* he describes how he moved towards this decision:

If I were certain to write as men buy leases, for three lives and downward, there ought no regard be sooner had, than to God's glory by the honour and instruction of my country. For which cause, and not only for that I knew it would be hard to arrive at the second rank among the Latins, I applied myself to that resolution which Ariosto followed against the persuasions of Bembo, to fix all the industry and art I could unite to the adorning of my native tongue; not to make verbal curiosities the end, that were a toilsome vanity, but to be an interpreter and relater of the best and sagest things among mine own citizens throughout this island in the mother dialect.

In two Latin poems written on his return, *Mansus* (addressed to the one-time patron of Tasso), and *Epitaphium Damonis* (on the death of Diodati), he defined his subject as British, and particularly Arthurian, history. There are various reasons why this characteristic renaissance ambition (to be shared, similarly unfulfilled, by Dryden and Pope) remained only a dream. Milton's detailed readings in early British history (which bore fruit later in his *History of Britain*) convinced him that much of the material was mythical. The plans in the Trinity College MSS show that at the beginning of the 1640s Milton turned his attention away from patriotic epic and towards sacred drama, though he came to see eventually that in the pamphleteering and propagandizing activities that he carried on in the 1640s and 1650s he had fulfilled his patriotic aim. Arthurian history was discredited by the parliamentarian lawyers and scholars who sought in Saxon England for political ammunition against the royalists. But it was not so much this technical difficulty that shook Milton's faith in his newly found role. The political upheavals of the 1640s meant that the whole framework of his inherited assumptions about the poet and his material gave way. Spenser had Elizabeth, Jonson had James I and

Charles I, Dryden was to have Charles II, as focusing symbols of their ideas about society. Milton once more had to think out his role. Meanwhile he saw his opportunity in helping to shape the new England, though he felt himself to be writing only with his left hand, and he constantly reminded the readers of his prose of his poetic ambitions. *Areopagitica*, written in 1644, in which he adopts the style and tone of the ancient orator, marks the high point of his optimism about his ability to influence events.

In his Latin defences of the English people Milton believed that he had produced a work of epic stature. He saw in his involvement in political propaganda a resolution of the problem that had plagued him earlier, the demands of an active public life compared with the apparently passive and retired life of the poet. At the conclusion of the *Second defence* Milton regards himself as moulding history:

I have celebrated, as a testimony to them, I had almost said, a monument, which will not speedily perish, actions which were glorious, lofty, which were almost above all praise; and if I have done nothing else, I have assuredly discharged my trust....If, after achievements so magnanimous, ye basely fall off from your duty, if ye are guilty of anything unworthy of you, be assured, posterity will speak, and thus pronounce its judgement: The foundation was strongly laid, the beginning, more than the beginning, was excellent; but it will be inquired...who completed the fabric!...It will be seen that the harvest of glory was abundant; that there were materials for the greatest operations, but that men were not to be found for the work; yet, that there was not wanting one, who could give good counsel; who could exhort, encourage; who could adorn, and celebrate, in praises destined to endure forever, the transcendent deeds, and those who performed them.

The confused events of the last years of the Interregnum confirmed Milton in the pessimistic outlook implied here; men were found wanting to complete the work. After the Restoration Milton abstained almost entirely from interference in political events. But in spite of political disillusionment, he was able to define a new role for himself. The crucial physical debility that Milton suffered in the early 1650s in the course of his public activity, his blindness, came to assume a symbolic importance for him. In answer to the royalists who saw it as a divine infliction on the defender of regicides, Milton saw it as a sign of inner light, a mark that he was chosen. He found himself set apart from the rest of mankind in the company of blind bards and wise men like Homer and Tiresias. In his political activity he fulfilled his view of the poet as orator and statesman; the poet of *Paradise lost* is seer and prophet.

Suggestions for further reading

The standard accounts of M's education are by D. L. Clark *JM at St Paul's school* New York 1948 and H. F. Fletcher *The intellectual development of JM* 2 vols Urbana 1956, 1961 (not yet complete). Stimulating interpretations of M's youth are given by J. H. Hanford 'The youth of M' repr in *JM: poet and humanist* Cleveland 1966; W. Haller 'Church-outed by the prelates' in *The rise of puritanism* New York 1938; E. M. W. Tillyard *Milton* rev 1966.

Contemporary literary criticism is collected in G. C. Smith ed *Elizabethan critical essays* 2 vols 1904 and J. E. Spingarn ed *Critical essays of the 17c* 3 vols 1908–9. An excellent edition of Sidney's *Apology* is by G. Shepherd 1965.

Some useful anthologies of 17c poetry are *The Oxford book of 17c verse*; H. Gardner ed *Metaphysical poets* Penguin; H. Kenner ed *17c poetry: the schools of Donne and Jonson* New York 1964; M. K. Starkman ed *17c English poetry* 2 vols New York 1967; *Minor poets of the 17c* Everyman. The Muses' Library and Anchor Books publish convenient editions of some of the poets but Sylvester is available only in facsimile (Gainesville 1965) and Quarles is best read in 19th-century editions.

Critical works on the period are innumerable; a start can be made with P. Cruttwell *The Shakespearean moment* 1954; A. Alvarez *The school of Donne* 1961; W. Trimpi *Ben Jonson's poems* Stanford 1962; R. Nevo *The dial of virtue* Princeton 1963 (on political poetry); M. M. Ross *Poetry and dogma* New Brunswick 1954.

Some helpful books on background and special topics dealt with in this chapter are: R. Freeman *English emblem books* 1948; E. H. Miller *The professional writer in Elizabethan England* Cambridge Mass. 1959; B. Willey *The 17c background* 1934; H. N. Fairchild *Religious trends in English poetry* 1939; C. J. Friedrich *The age of the baroque 1610–1660* 1952; Lowry Nelson *Baroque lyric poetry* New Haven 1963; G. W. Whiting *M's literary milieu* Chapel Hill 1939.

English literature: an illustrated record ed R. Garnett and E. Gosse is a valuable and congenial introduction. The two introductory chapters to the *Pelican guide to English literature: 2 The age of Shakespeare* are good.

An interdisciplinary topic

Carew (1595–1639), author of the elegy on Donne quoted above, is one of several who might profitably be taken as a case study of the early 17th-century court poet who is not like Milton or Donne or Herbert or Jonson. Some independent work on him would be worth any amount of reading literary histories. His acquaintanceship was significant – Lord Herbert of Cherbury (Platonic poet, deist philosopher, ambassador to Paris), Ben Jonson, Aurelian Townshend, Sir William Davenant (who started the theatres again at the Restoration), Owen Feltham, Sir John Suckling, Van Dyck painted his portrait (1638, hangs at Windsor). His epitaph on Maria Wentworth who died 1633 at 18 is to be read on her magnificent tomb in St George's Church, Toddington, Beds. His masque for the Middle Temple, *Coelum britannicum*, had music by Lawes and scenery by Inigo Jones, as well as the participation of the Egerton children who acted in *Comus*. All these directions are worth following up; to be more ambitious, discover what he saw in Florence. Of his poems, some are primitivistic (*Rapture, Love's force*), some are in dialogue form, but most exhibit an obsession with glamorous decaying symbols and bright little fetishes. Ed by R. Dunlap and in the Everyman *Minor poets of the 17c*; see E. I. Selig *The flourishing wreath* 1958. Could well be conducted against the background of Don M. Wolfe *Milton and his England* illustrated Princeton 1971.

JOHN BROADBENT

Inside Milton

On page 80 of *PL: introduction* in this series I list some of the
recurrent themes in Milton's writing which may reveal his sub-
conscious preoccupations. Here I offer a few speculations about what
it felt like to be Milton. The speculations are affected by my own
anxieties, and may be misguided; but commentators who do *not*
speculate in this way are just as capable of being wrong, or subjective, or ambivalent:

We may be sure that John's childhood was as happy as a comfortable
environment and kindly, middle-class parents could make it.

W. R. PARKER *Milton: a biography* Oxford 1968

How happy is that? Again, Parker writes, 'That Milton loved Mary
Powell in 1642 (when he married her) few would question. That he
loved her after their reconciliation in 1645 is a belief of this biography, although many have doubted it.' But the question is, what
was loving for Milton?

Family

His great-grandfather and grandfather were Roman catholics; but his
father left home over a religious quarrel, and was a puritan Anglican.
Milton was a puritan but eventually of no church or sect; yet he
married, first, a girl of a royalist and possibly Catholic family. His
brother Christopher became a royalist and a Catholic. Why this
determination in each member of the family to individuate? We may
see it as a symptom of the family genius, or of England's virility then;
or we may see it as an assertion of self for fear of being submerged,
ignored. What had the women of this family failed to do, that the
men had so to inflate and define themselves? Or how had the men
denied the women's tenderness, and competed with each other?

c. 1600	Milton's parents married, father aged about 38, mother about 28.
1601	A chrisom child.
1602–7	Anne born. 1623 married Edward Phillips, a lawyer; he died 1631; soon after she married a friend, Thomas Agar, also a lawyer. Milton educated her sons Edward and John.
1608	Milton born.
1612	Sarah born, died in infancy.
1614	Tabitha born, died in infancy.
1615	Christopher born, became a lawyer; 1638 married.

Milton's father may have been difficult to compete with: well-known in his circle of successful businessmen, talented at music, strongly independent. News of his mother is thin: what does it mean when one parent is less talked of? She dressed Milton with extravagant elegance for his portrait at the age of ten – a portrait which coincided with his having his hair shorn at the behest of a puritan tutor, and with his parents setting him up as the genius of the family.

What was the matter with this family was not fanaticism, but the need for personal independence...As for our John Milton, he wrote verses which were considered marvellous when he was about ten years old, and he was henceforward brought up deliberately to be a man of genius. What colossal pride must have been latent in a family where such a thing was accepted as normal...His greatness was taken for granted, first of all by himself.

DENIS SAURAT Milton: man and thinker 1925 rev 1944

Again the demonic assertion: a family in which the eldest son has projected onto him the complete role of power-carrier, firebringer, father of the future – why? was it to appease the ancestors in some way, or to work out some unconscious bargain with, again, the family's women? What did power over words mean to them? Families do this kind of thing: what seems odd is that Milton accepted the role, and actually fulfilled it; successful men with high ambitions for their sons to live up to often incapacitate the sons. Perhaps Milton needed admiration so badly that he had to buy it. That would suggest that they had not given him some deeper, free gift – love, succour, the tender rough sensualities of mothering and fathering. Certainly those are absent, as felt experience, from his poetry: he can only write *about* them, as 'Relations dear, and all the charities Of father, son, and brother' (*PL* IV 756) – a supreme, and exclusively masculine, definition. At any rate, he paid a price. Immensely long hours of work; private tuition as well as St Paul's School; eyestrain and head-aches. These are sometimes recorded as admirable; and the weak eyes were probably inherited from his mother; but were they also an atoning for the sins of the family in some way? They remind one of the brutal training meted out to John Stuart Mill by his father (*Autobiography* ch. 1). Commentators agree on an inward blindness, a cut-offness from the actuality of things; perhaps that, perhaps even the physical blindness later, were psychosomatic wounds, self-inflicted to shield him from what was intolerable to experience, whatever it may have been.

Imagery and language

Observe [in the *Nativity ode*] the concretizing of the natural, the mechanical approach to the cosmos...Often a smooth and polished surface is suggested, a rounded and perhaps shining completion...The static and sculptural quality of Milton's nature-imagery [in *PL*], together with his mechanized cosmology, all constitute a rejection of the specifically vital ...The blindness so nobly treated in his poetry becomes a cruelly apt symbol of another opacity. The sun to him is 'dark' in more senses than one, and his great invocation to light takes on a new pathos from such a reading...[in Eden] you have excessive luxuriance side by side with a stony, carven immobility... Yet there is subtle variation in colour-perception. The mechanical and scientific imagery is often softly toned. There is little of the musty, the cob-webbed association, as in Webster; little of the harsh ordinary surfaces of daily affairs...But such subtlety of technique cannot of itself harmonize a wide chaos...Rhythmic and verbal modulation work to remedy a preliminary weakness in organization. This is how Milton becomes, in places, our most perfect 'technician' while failing as a 'maker' in the wider sense. He tries to do by art what art by itself cannot do.

G. WILSON KNIGHT *The burning oracle* 1939

What are the grounds of trying so hard to construct an ideal world? Critics repeatedly agree on the lack in his work of 'wholeness', as opposed to construction; but what is our prime experience of organic wholeness?

He exhibits a feeling *for* words rather than a capacity for feeling *through* words; we are often, in reading him, moved to comment that he is 'external' or that he works 'from the outside'...His strength is of the kind that we indicate when, distinguishing between intelligence and character, we lay the stress on the latter; it is a strength, that is, involving sad disabilities. He has 'character', moral grandeur, moral force; but he is, for the purposes of his undertaking [in *PL*], disastrously single-minded and simple-minded. He reveals everywhere a dominating sense of righteousness and a complete incapacity to question or explore its significance and conditions. This defect of intelligence is a defect of imagination. He offers as ultimate for our worship mere brute assertive will, though he condemns it unwittingly by his argument and by glimpses of his own finer human standard. His volume of moral passion owes its strength too much to innocence – a guileless unawareness of the subtleties of egotism – to be an apt agent for projecting an 'ordered whole of experience'.

F. R. LEAVIS Revaluation 1936

This comment owed some of its own fervour, I think, to a sense that Milton was being used as idol for a false social and educational system. During the 1920s the grip of classics, and with classics the public school ethos, weakened in England; new subjects, especially English and social sciences, were made available. But the change that might have come in the 20s, the change heralded by the marvellous years of *The waste land, Le cimetière marin, Ulysses,* was postponed for the doldrums of the 30s, and the second war. 1945 was another opportunity but there were more doldrums. At each stage the hindrances can be registered in Miltonic terms – stony structure, whether social or artistic; the word rather than the flesh; hierarchically wielded power; insistence on verbal knowledge; weightiness of the past. Milton of course for his own time wanted change too; but there is a paradox here that none of us can escape: to achieve change, we define a goal; but a defined goal is static; to defend it we must deny further change. Hence the conflict between first- and second-generation revolutionaries; Stalinism versus continuous revolution.

Another way of looking at it is anthropological:

The danger which is risked by boundary transgression is power. Those vulnerable margins and those attacking forces which threaten to destroy good order represent the powers inhering in the cosmos. Ritual which can harness these for good is harnessing power indeed.

MARY DOUGLAS Purity and danger: an analysis of concepts of pollution and taboo 1966

Milton harnessed that energy for us all when he ritualized Satan's transgression and defeat, even though he may have ritualized it for needs of his own unconscious, to do, I suppose, with some sense of 'what is wrong'.

So much for the aptness of the symbol itself. Now for the living situations to which it applies, and which are irremediably subject to paradox. The quest for purity is pursued by rejection. It follows that when purity is not a symbol but something lived it must be poor and barren. It is part of our condition that the purity for which we strive and sacrifice so much turns out to be hard and dead as a stone when we get it...Purity is the enemy of change, of ambiguity and compromise...the yearning for rigidity is in us all. It is part of our human condition to long for hard lines and clear concepts.　　*Ibid.*

III

Here are some of Milton's rituals of purity, clarifying, defining, purging:

settling in a skinny congealment of ease and sloth...their devotion most commonly comes to that queasy temper of lukewarmness that gives a vomit to God himself (*Of ref*).

they dare thus oil over and besmear so holy an unction [of kingship] with the corrupt and putrid ointment of their base flatteries (*RCG*).

terrifying plasters upon the rind and orifice of the sore (*RCG*).

a mere ague-cake, coagulated of a certain fever they have (*Of ref*).

an universal rottenness and gangrene in the whole function (*Of ref*).

the noisome and diseased tumour of prelacy (*Of ref*).

the drossy bullion of the people's sins (*Of ref*).

the very essence of truth is plainness and brightness: the darkness and crookedness is our own (*Of ref*).

He that cannot understand the sober, plain and unaffected style of the scriptures, will be ten times more puzzled with the knotty Africanisms, the pampered metaphors, the intricate and involved sentences of the fathers (*Of ref*).

with other deformed and fantastic dresses, in palls and mitres, gold, and gewgaws fetched from Aaron's old wardrobe, or the flamens' vestry (*Of ref*).

> Those pure immortal elements that know
> No gross, no unharmonious mixture foul,
> Eject him [man] tainted now, and purge him off
> As a distemper, gross to air as gross,
> And mortal food, as may dispose him best
> For dissolution wrought by sin, that first
> Distempered all things, and of incorrupt
> Corrupted.   God *PL* xi 50

The tangled thickets of the nymphs in *Nativity ode* and of the hair of Neæra in *Lycidas*, Dalila 'bedecked, ornate, and gay' with her 'circling wiles', her nets and trains, Sin with her snaky legs, 'the blind mazes of this tangled wood' in *Comus* (whose name means hairy) – all these intricate entrapping liquid formless unmargined, and usually female, things are Milton's symbols of *what is wrong* or dirty; and what is wrong and dirty has to be purged off, evacuated. The major evacuation is of 'painful superstition and blind zeal', along with everything ambiguous, false, fallacious, confused – 'Embryos and idiots, hermits and friars', suicides, the unintelligible builders of Babel, 'All the unaccomplished works of nature's hand, Abortive, monstrous or unkindly mixed' – in the Limbo of Fools. With a great fart they 'Fly o'er the backside of the world far off' (*PL* III 494). We may begin to see then that sin, wrong, may be defined as 'that which has to be expelled'; it turns out to be a mixture of the rotten, the over-decorated, the tangling, the puzzling, and the formless, what is unbounded. In *Paradise lost* it includes, apparently, our first parents. Or are they versions of the self that neither God nor Satan would permit to stay in Eden?

'You ask who this person in the dream can have been. It was *not* my mother.' We emend this: so it *was* his mother...the subject-matter of a repressed image or thought can make its way into consciousness on condition that it is *denied*. Negation is a way of taking account of what is repressed...The result is a kind of intellectual acceptance of what is repressed, though in all essentials the repression persists...To deny something in one's judgement is at bottom the same thing as to say: 'That is something I would rather repress.' A negative judgement is the intellectual substitute for repression... By the help of the symbol of negation, the thinking-process frees itself from the limitations of repression and enriches itself with the subject-matter without which it could not work efficiently.

The function of judgement is concerned ultimately with two sorts of decision. It may assert or deny that a thing has a particular property; or it may affirm or dispute that a particular image [*Vorstellung*] exists in reality. Originally the property to be decided about might be either 'good' or 'bad', 'useful' or 'harmful'. Expressed in the language of the oldest, that is, of the oral, instinctual impulses, the alternative runs thus: 'I should like to eat that, or I should like to spit it out'; or, carried a stage further, 'I should like to take this into me and keep that out of me'...Judging has been systematically developed out of what was in the first instance introduction into the ego or expulsion from the ego carried out according to the pleasure principle... Affirmation, as being a substitute for union, belongs to Eros; while negation, the derivative of expulsion, belongs to the instinct of destruction.

FREUD Negation 1925 in Collected papers v 1950

You can move further into this difficult area via Norman O. Brown *Life against death*; or track some of the literary cases of acceptance–negation, and other binary judgements, in your study of Milton's actual work.

What the poem [*PL*] is about is *punishment*...the attempt to justify the ways of God to men always means the punishing ways of God to Man, because it is not necessary to 'justify' the love of God. This justification is also a Hebraic compulsion...When we start to formulate our ideas about human nature and about man's place in the universe, we are predominantly liable to talk in fact about our own most primitive fears and passions, the shadows of which we dimly perceive and try to objectify. As a result, our theology, by whatever name we call it, reveals itself as still tied to the God of Wrath; patriarchal, aggressive, tense, aware of danger within and without, particularly aware of the danger of love, and deeply preoccupied with payment of a more or less material kind, which ranges from out-and-out simony to merely telling one's beads, or to the various neurotic compulsions.

Preoccupation with sin, one's own or other people's, also has the mechanical quality which subsumes it under payment in kind. For the belief in Original Sin is psychologically a tribute, a mechanical confession that we are incurable, and that therefore we must pay endlessly in order to be allowed to live...Milton's Latinism put a verbal veil between himself and contemporary, that was, living, reality. The result is literally monumental, static, relating more to the acoustical medium of stone than to the word becoming flesh, and to the past and dead rather than to the continuing present and future.

The characteristics of diction and imagery which I have mentioned spring directly from this attitude of abstraction and withdrawal...The fused metaphor...always appeals to living sense; and some dislike of living sense, with considerable implications about a too partial view of the world's intellectual structure, is what we may suspect when it is conspicuously absent, as it is with Milton and Eliot. In Milton the predominant image is the classical simile, which selects, intellectually, a common quality out of a host of dissimilarities. This is at best a purely denotative decoration, a kind of abstract illustration, with the maximum suppression or avoidance of associative overtones.   KATHLEEN NOTT *The emperor's clothes* 1953

Friendship

Milton's acquaintance with people of his own age and sort seems to have been slight. The records – mostly letters and verses – are all of relationships with tutors such as Alexander Gill, his headmaster at St Paul's (letter to him from Cambridge); Thomas Young, his extra private tutor, a puritan Scot (letter); the librarian of the Bodleian Library, Oxford (Latin poem about his poems); Charles Diodati whom he met at St Paul's (the friendship seems to have been based on study, and idealized by Milton); more than one might expect of poems for people he had met in Italy, as if it was there that he felt for the first time esteemed and identified – as an alien, master of an international culture, may feel on a visit. What is the nature of academic friendship?

Love

Josephine Miles lists the dominant words in Milton's early poems:

dark fair good great	*air day ear eye*	*bring come give*
high holy old sad	*God heaven height*	*go hear keep know*
sweet	*light night star*	*lie live make see*
	sun wind	*sing sit*

Eras and modes in English poetry 1957 rev 1964

Compared with others at the time, Milton's vocabulary is highly adjectival; rich in rather simple and often 'distant' natural items such as *star, wind, high, old*; among the verbs there is less activity than usual (*grow, die, move, take, stand* to cite a few from other poets); and there are no words whose prime value is erotic (*breast, kiss, love, beauty*...).

The first record of erotic feeling in Milton is a Latin poem to Diodati (*Elegy I*) in which he mentions watching 'the girls passing by like stars' outside the walls of the City when he was eighteen. All his erotic poetry is in a foreign language. The most passionate piece is *Elegy V* 'On the coming of spring', at the age of twenty – 'Lustful Faunus hunts some Oread to ravish and the nymph looks with trembling knees to hide herself...' It was about then, too (1627–8) that he admitted or pretended to a first love, in *Elegy VII*; but the girl he saw 'was borne away, never to return to my sight'. There is something of a habit in his life of falling for the fleeting, the distant or the impossible. A year later he met an Italian girl called Emilia and wrote sonnets to her, in Italian; but that is all we know of the incident. From then until his first marriage he spent, apparently, twelve years not only celibate but suppressing even his desires for love. He referred later to his Latin love poems as 'vain trophies of my profligacy' and said that with the academic work of his later twenties and thirties 'those flames were instantly extinguished, and from then on my heart has been frozen in thick-ribbed ice' (PS to Latin elegies in *Poems* 1645).

Milton said that he wanted to keep himself chaste so as to prepare himself for epic: 'he who tells of wars, and heaven under the maturity of Jove...his youth must be chaste and innocent of vice, his conduct strict, his hands unstained' (*Elegy VI* to Diodati). At the end of this study period, in 1637, his mother died. It was now that he tried to revive his schoolboy friendship with Diodati, as if they were Platonic lovers. Milton is 'imbued...with a mighty passion for Beauty' and finds in Diodati the Platonic 'Idea of Beauty, like some image of loveliness...that which the wisest men throughout the ages have approved'. Now aged 30, he went to Italy; and while he was there Diodati died. Milton's Latin elegy for him, *Epitaphium Damonis*, provided Diodati with a sexual heaven:

Because the blush of shame, and youth without a stain, were dear to you, because you did not taste the delights of the marriage-bed, lo! the trophies of virginity are laid up for you...

The whole stanza is the most erotic Milton ever wrote – for a young man, dead. In the lists of possible subjects for a tragedy or epic that Milton turned to making when he got home, adultery, sodomy and youthful death (Isaac sacrificed by his father, John the Baptist by Salome) figure most largely.

It was from this mood that his first anti-prelatical pamphlets sprang – the rage of actual purity.

Marriage

Then in 1642 he went suddenly into the royalist part of the country to Forest Hill, near Oxford, and visited the squire, Richard Powell, who owed his father (and failing him, himself) £500. He came back married to the 16-year-old Mary Powell. We do not know whether he went there to collect the money and came back with a wife instead; or whether, having lost his mother, and Diodati, and with a houseful of pupils to look after, and sexual needs to satisfy, he went deliberately for a wife. Either way, she was another case of the alienation of his erotic drive – distant, royalist, nearly twenty years younger, and she left him very shortly after the marriage which was either not consummated or consummated without spiritual intercourse. She sulked in the little academy; he found her stupid and dull. When she left, he wrote his pamphlets on divorce: splendid expressions of human love squeezed out of humiliation, despair, frustration. But the most splendid of all is an allegory in which Eros meets a false mate, and falls impotent to the ground like Samson shorn of his hair:

Fourthly, Marriage is a covenant, the very being whereof consists not in a forced cohabitation, and counterfeit performance of duties, but in unfeigned love and peace; and of matrimonial love, no doubt but that was chiefly meant which by the ancient sages was thus parabled: that Love, if he be not twin born, yet hath a brother wondrous like him, called Anteros; whom while he seeks all about, his chance is to meet with many false and feigning desires that wander singly up and down in his likeness; by them in their borrowed garb, Love, though not wholly blind, as poets wrong him, yet having but one eye, as being born an archer aiming, and that eye not the quickest in this dark region here below, which is not Love's proper sphere, partly out of the simplicity and credulity which is native to him, often deceived, embraces and consorts him with these obvious and suborned striplings, as if they were his mother's own sons; for so he thinks them, while they subtilly keep themselves most on his blind side. But after a while, as his manner is, when soaring up into the high tower of his Apogaeum, above the shadow of the earth, he darts out the direct rays of his then most piercing eyesight upon the impostures and trim disguises that were used with him, and discerns that this is not his genuine brother, as he imagined; he has no longer the power to hold fellowship with such a personated mate: for straight his arrows lose their golden heads, and shed their purple feathers, his silken braids untwine, and slip their knots, and that original and fiery virtue given him by fate all on a sudden goes out, and leaves him undeified and despoiled of all his force; till finding Anteros at last, he kindles and repairs the almost-faded ammunition of his deity by the reflection of a coequal and homogeneal fire. Thus mine author sung it to me: and by the leave of those who would be counted the only grave ones, this is no mere amatorious novel; (though to be wise and skilful in these matters, men heretofore of greatest name in virtue have esteemed it one of the highest arcs, that human contemplation circling up-wards can make from the globy sea whereon she stands;) but this is a deep and serious verity, shewing us that love in marriage cannot live nor subsist unless it be mutual; and where love cannot be, there can be left of wedlock nothing but the empty husk of an outside matrimony, as undelightful and unpleasing to God as any other kind of hypocrisy. So far is his command from tying men to the observance of duties which there is no help for, but they must be dissembled.

Repairs

As well as the divorce tracts, he calloused his wounds with drudgery – teaching more pupils (so the move to the larger, Barbican house); the tract on education, a Latin dictionary and grammar, a textbook of logic, editing his early poems, compiling the *History of Britain* and *De doctrina christiana*, paraphrasing the psalms; and all his political activity.

> Labour is blossoming or dancing where
> The body is not bruised to pleasure soul,
> Nor beauty born out of its own despair,
> Nor blear-eyed wisdom out of midnight oil.

Or can great deeds arise only out of pain? Three years after Mary had left him, the Powells had all their property sequestrated by parliament. A reunion was arranged, Mary to be found by Milton in a neighbour's house and beg his pardon. They all came to live with him in the Barbican house. Their first child was born next year, a handi-capped girl, Anne.

Middle age

During the later 1640s and the 1650s Milton's father and father-in-law died; his sight worsened, going altogether in 1652; in that year Mary Powell died; in 1656 he remarried but that wife and their first child died almost together; his nephew and pupil John Phillips published scurrilous satire against the Puritans and was fined for obscenity by the Council of State which included several friends of Milton; in 1660 the Commonwealth he had worked for fell to pieces and Charles II was restored. Milton's books were burnt, he was imprisoned, and expected to be executed. (He would have been half-hanged, taken down alive, castrated, his genitals stuffed in his mouth, his stomach slit open and his intestines taken out and burnt, and his carcase chopped into four quarters; the savagery of the unconscious is not all fantasy.)

Conclusions

Yet until the very last moment he had persisted in defending the good old cause in print, beseeching the people of England to defend their freedom against kings, bishops and censors. 'The egotism of such a man is a revelation of spirit' said Coleridge (*Table talk* 18 August 1833).

Let then the calumniators of the divine goodness cease to revile, or to make me the object of their superstitious imaginations. Let them consider...that I am not depressed by any sense of the divine displeasure; that, on the other hand, in the most momentous periods, I have had full experience of the favour and protection...in short I am unwilling to exchange my consciousness of rectitude with that of any other person...in proportion as I am weak, I shall be invincibly strong; and in proportion as I am blind, I shall more clearly see. O! that I may thus be perfected by feebleness, and irradiated by obscurity! And, indeed, in my blindness, I enjoy in no inconsiderable degree the favour of the Deity, who regards me with more tenderness and compassion in proportion as I am able to behold nothing but himself. Alas! for him who insults me, who maligns and merits public execration! For the divine law not only shields me from injury, but almost renders me too sacred to attack; not indeed so much from the privation of my sight, as from the overshadowing of those heavenly wings, which seem to have occasioned, he is wont to illuminate with an interior light, more precious and more pure.

2nd defence of the English people

Milton was neither harmonious nor triumphant, but a troubled, divided, and deeply ambivalent consciousness. For all the anguish and torment of the tragedies and bitter comedies, there is an inescapable quality of wholeness about Shakespeare...By comparison, Milton was a spoiled soul, one of the spiritually self-conscious and emotionally awkward...a measure of distortion, a failure of control, a deficiency in esthetic detachment, is not to be burked from the career. No matter how one manipulates them, there remains something strident and inflexible about many of Milton's ideas, something buried and beyond control about many of his feelings...Milton was never a man whose sense of life fitted easily into traditional vessels. He had to invent

his own version of an epic...as he invented his own version of a tragedy...
he had to invent an audience out of his own imagination to enjoy both
works...his great literary achievements, like those of Ibsen and Flaubert,
Euripides and Swift, end rather in a stalemate than in a fully resolved stasis.
The antinomy on which Milton's work centers undergoes a full exploration,
not a full resolution; we admire not the formal perfection with which a
conclusion is worked out, but the truth and energy with which a conflict is
explored down to its last grinding incompatibility.

ROBERT MARTIN ADAMS *Ikon: JM and the modern critics* Ithaca N.Y. 1955

there are places where he writes as though he were God, the coeternal Logos,
author of all concepts, who by uttering a word could call into being the
reality it named...To write omnifically, with such world- or word-creating
authority, is to assume a parental role. Milton's learned vocabulary, with its
demand for conscious construing, and his distant perspectives, represent the
authoritative unintelligibility of the parents' speech as heard by a child. (The
visual metaphors applied to Milton are often parental – gigantic loftiness,
stilts, spectacles.) But it is not enough to object that he assumes a parental
role; the question is, with what role do we respond?...[The adult response]
is difficult to define because you would have to be very sure of your own
identity as an adult for Milton's strongly parental writing to elicit it. Presumably one would be unflustered by the scale and noise and knowledge of his
language; one would recognise the game Milton is playing, the authoritarian
personality's need tó protect his own childish fears by grandiloquence, by
pretending to be the father whom he could not meet on equal terms; but one
would not judge; one might just walk away. One would react rather in the
way that the last two books of *Paradise lost* in general react to the tragedy of
human existence, with a slightly mournful down-to-earthness, a wary energy
and determination to go on living.

J. B. BROADBENT 'Milton's "mortal voice" and his "omnific word"'
Approaches to PL ed C. A. Patrides 1968

He, in a Word, was All Mind, an Intellectual Man.

JONATHAN RICHARDSON father and son *Explanatory notes and remarks on
PL* 1734 p. ciii

W. REAVLEY GAIR

Milton and science

Changes in knowledge

In Paradise Adam was endowed with the ability to have immediate and exact knowledge of all material things; when each creature was brought before him.

> I named them as they passed, and understood
> Their nature, with such knowledge God endued
> My sudden apprehension. *PL* VIII 352

In the world after the fall the purpose of learning is to 'repair the ruins of our first parents'; we may best do this 'by orderly conning over the visible and inferior creature', that is the natural world (*Of education*). God prohibits speculation into divine mysteries:

> heaven is for thee too high
> To know what passes there; be lowly wise:
> Think only what concerns thee and thy being. *PL* VIII 172

But he encourages the investigation of nature so that the resources of the created world may be utilized for the benefit of all men.

Milton used the word *science* to mean all knowledge, as well as in its modern sense. But, like most of his contemporaries, he did not share our scientific consciousness which demands precision of measurement, completeness of analysis, logical perfection of explanation and experimental proof of hypothesis in our knowledge of the material world. Natural science to Milton was not a number of distinct disciplines but simply a branch of philosophy.

Milton's lifetime, which spans the first three quarters of the 17th century, is rightly seen as a period of transition between the medieval and the modern. During it there occurred a change from a view of the world as an animate organism existing in its own right, to one in which the earth is part of a complex universal mechanism. This change took place primarily because of the astronomical discoveries that were made: astronomy was the most significant science for

Milton's generation. It is true that other fundamental discoveries were made, like William Harvey's (1578–1657) demonstration of the circulation of the blood, William Gilbert's (1540–1603) proof that the earth was a magnet, John Napier's (1550–1617) development of logarithms and the invention of an early form of calculating machine; but it is the astronomers, Copernicus, Brahe, Galileo, who made the greatest impact on the lives and imaginations of men. Their discoveries directly led to the work of Isaac Newton (1642–1727) on optics and on the infinitesimal calculus, and above all to his discovery of the laws of gravitation outlined first in 1684, ten years after Milton's death.

From his youth Milton regarded the study of the material world as an undertaking of profound importance, and he urged his contemporaries at Cambridge

to search out and examine the natures of all living creatures; and from them... turn to the study of the hidden virtues of stones and herbs... fly into the heavens and contemplate the manifold shapes of the clouds, the compacted power of the snow, and the source of the morning dews; then examine the chambers of the hail and the armouries of the thunderbolts. Let there be nothing secret from you about the purpose of either Jove or Nature when a dire tremendous comet threatens to set the skies on fire. Not even the tiniest stars should be hidden from you.   *Prolusion against scholastic philosophy*

This enthusiasm to investigate nature was shared by Francis Bacon (1561–1626), the most important philosopher of science in the English renaissance.

Scholasticism and empiricism: Milton and Bacon

Bacon and Milton share a common goal in that both advocate the study of the natural sciences in order to regain that command over all created things which Adam forfeited at the fall. Unlike Milton, however, Bacon feels it to be necessary to insulate science from religion, in order to advance the former; and he argues that between the knowledge available to man supernaturally, by faith and scripture, and the information available naturally, by sensory perception, there is a complete distinction. Milton and Bacon are in agreement that science cannot tell us anything directly about the nature of God but it must lead ultimately to him. But Bacon insists that teleological[1]

[1] Teleology is the doctrine of final causes: it asks the question, 'What purpose does it serve?' about things or events. It assumes that all things develop or move in accordance with an ultimate purpose that they are specifically designed to serve.

121

explanations must not be confused with the actual examination of objects; while Milton subordinates scientific fact to the truths of spiritual enlightenment.

In that same prolusion, *Against scholastic philosophy*, Milton attacks the logical methods of Aristotle as a barren discipline; Bacon made a similar accusation. The Middle Ages had developed Aristotle's thought into a rigid metaphysical system and in the 17th century scholars still tended only to ask the question 'why?' about events and never the question 'how?'. The medieval and renaissance scholar commonly looked upon the outside world in terms of the Aristotelian theory of hierarchical motion: according to it all objects possess special innate qualities which cause them to move towards a divinely predetermined place in creation. Any explanation about the physical world, therefore, had to square with this *a priori* presupposition: scholastic logic was, then, a process of deduction from general axiomatic principles which were based upon insufficient evidence. Bacon rejected this attitude of mind, not because he felt it to be invalid, but because it was sterile. Milton dismissed scholastic logic on the grounds that it could not reveal anything of importance: 'these studies which teach us nothing about things can give us no profit and no pleasure'. To both Bacon and Milton medieval natural philosophy had outlived its usefulness; it had degenerated into mere speculation about words divorced from experience.

Bacon recommends that an inductive method be substituted for the Aristotelian (or scholastic) deductive process; by this method, and the use of precise apparatus of measurement, he believes that most of the inaccuracies of the medieval assumptions will be eliminated. This systematic induction is a process whereby the evidence of all possible facts, all possible observations and experiments, is to be tabulated: simply as a result of this collection of data – so Bacon assumes – connections between different phenomena will become obvious, and thus general laws describing these relationships will automatically emerge. Unfortunately Bacon did not recognize the necessity for a working hypothesis before an experiment can be made. He himself made few practical experiments, though he is said to have died from bronchitis contracted in March 1626 when he got out of his coach to collect snow to stuff a chicken, in order to examine the effects of refrigeration.

The thinking of Bacon and Milton about man's knowledge of the physical world begins to diverge in proportion as Bacon's concern becomes more utilitarian and concerned with actual methods of research. Milton's major interest in the 17th-century developments in natural sciences was the increased awareness they afforded of the Creator's handiwork. He approved of much in the Baconian scientific philosophy but, for Bacon, since God was so remote in the natural world as to be present only in theoretical terms, he could for all practical purposes be ignored. The logical heir of Baconianism is material atheism; to Milton atheism was a philosophical absurdity.

Hobbes and materialism

> While in dark ignorance we lay afraid
> Of fancies, ghosts and every empty shade,
> Great Hobbes appeared, and by plain reason's light
> Put such fantastic thoughts to shameful flight.
>
> COWLEY On Mr Hobbes and his writings

Bacon's heir is Thomas Hobbes, who in *Leviathan* (1651), while paying lip-service to Christianity, expounds the first purely totalitarian materio-mechanistic philosophy. Hobbes is a *nominalist* as opposed to a *realist*: the fundamental difference between these two philosophical positions is that the *realist* recognizes an objective order in things in some sense pre-existing and prior to the conceptions in the human mind; whereas the *nominalist* insists that the human mind itself imposes order, coherence and pattern upon external phenomena. For Hobbes, concepts which assume the existence of a transcendental reality or heaven, like 'good' and 'evil', are, in fact, names and only names: they relate simply to ideas created by the human mind. Hobbes' basis for all knowledge is the material world, perceived through the senses. As the material world is the only thing that exists, if we describe it with sufficient detail we shall have described all that there is to describe and therefore know all that there is to know. Experiments with material objects are the source of 'truth'. Any concepts which assume that non-material things can exist, like 'soul', 'spirit', 'angel', 'God', are nonsense.

Concurrently with this atheism, Hobbes wholeheartedly commits himself to an extreme mechanical motion theory. This is an exhaustive explanation not merely of material objects, but of all facets of human experience: even 'thought' and 'perception' are the products of purely mechanical causes. Knowledge is the product of the active pressure of external material objects upon the sense organs; these pressures set up vibrations in the brain and nerves, which are 'ideas'. Human consciousness consists of these idea-vibrations in motion, either clear and swift, or in varying states of decay, depending upon the length of time that has passed since they were started. Man is simply a mechanism which acts in accordance with a complex chain of antecedent causes; he has no freedom of personal action. Hobbes is, then, a determinist.

Milton originally accepted the philosophy of determinism but in about 1644 with the publication of *Areopagitica*, advocating the freedom of the press and limited religious toleration, his philosophical position changed and he based all his subsequent major concepts upon the assumption that man's will is free. For Hobbes, however, man is merely a compound created by two forms of motion. These are the Vital, like breathing and the circulation of the blood (the latter concept was accepted by Milton but rejected by Bacon, although it was his personal physician, Harvey, who discovered it); and the Voluntary, like speaking and moving. Vital motion corresponds to our autonomic nervous system; voluntary to our behaviourism. Voluntary motion is energized by the imagination which creates 'endeavour' towards a pleasing sense-stimulation, and 'aversion' from a displeasing one. These impressions, set in motion by sense-stimulants, are distinct from the external material objects which cause them and an individual man has no means of determining whether the impressions he has acquired bear any significant relation to the impressions of any other individual, even when these impressions are stimulated by the same object: each individual exists in a private world of his own. Objects and our impressions of them are both merely patches of matter-in-motion and it is only through language that we can exchange information about them, in approximate and purely symbolic terms. If a motion results in a stimulus towards an object then that thing is desired and hence, to the person desiring, 'good'; if it is from an object, it is disliked and hence, to the person repelled, 'evil'. Moral values, being but names, remain relative to the individual and merely indicate his private love or hate.

According to Hobbes, man's basic and innate instinct is to preserve his own life, and he seeks to ensure this by gaining power over his environment and his fellow men. Man is a cautious, scheming, egotistical creature; as his entire existence is a form of motion, happiness cannot be a passive state but rather

a continual progress of the desire from one object to another; the attaining of the former being still but the way to the later.

Leviathan Everyman ed p. 49

FIG 4   Illustration engraved by Robert Vaughan to Elias Ashmole *Theatrum chemicum britannicum* 1652. God is dressed as a Stuart monarch.

125

So he lives in 'a perpetual and restless desire of power, that ceaseth only in death'.

The philosophy of Hobbes is a direct contradiction of the theological and philosophical convictions of Milton. It was, in some measure, as a protest against Hobbes' materialistic atheism that Milton wrote *Paradise lost*. In this poem it is fallen man who exists in a pit of darkness, subject to the agitation of nervous irritability and selfish preoccupation; and it is Satan who is accredited with the desire for power, the restless desire to assert what he believes to be his rightful inheritance. The Hobbian natural man exists in a state of perpetual war, competing with his fellow egoists for the power to ensure the preservation of his own life at the expense of theirs; Milton identifies war with disobedience, and war-mongering with Satan. In *Leviathan* Hobbes offers man a totalitarian form of government as a means of escape from his natural state of perpetual war; in *Paradise lost* Milton offers fallen man the doctrine of the Fortunate Fall: since man fell, it was necessary for Christ to offer himself as the Saviour, but through Christ man may rise to a place higher and more blessed than that from which Adam fell. It is not totalitarianism which man must accept to escape from his natural fallen condition – 'solitary, poor, nasty, brutish and short' as Hobbes describes it – but the offer of redemption in Christ through obedience to God.

Browne: science and faith

Before the publication of *Leviathan*, there had been others who had attempted to forestall the kind of thinking which it embodied by seeking to reassert the cause of religion in an age rapidly being dominated by scientific and material concerns. Sir Thomas Browne (1605–82), a Norwich doctor, antiquary and amateur archaeologist, defended religion from the attacks of science and yet remained a practising scientist. For Browne the natural world was a manifestation of God's permanently pervading presence and also of his absolute apartness from the limitations of material things. The world of nature is the art of God and our understanding of it is as an aspect of our adoration of him and his divine handiwork. For Browne, as for Milton, there is no conflict between the worlds of science and religion for they are merely different manifestations of the same thing; in consequence, the complement of scientific rationalism is faith. None of the observable facts of the world can ultimately conflict with scripture, for God is the author of both and he is without contradiction.

Like Bacon and Milton, Browne is not a pantheist, for he does not worship nature; and he is fearless in correcting what he can demonstrate to be inaccurately observed phenomena. In his *Pseudodoxia epidemica* or *Vulgar errors* (1646: a scientific treatise addressed to the learned world) Browne exposed a series of common misconceptions. He concerned himself with an extensive range of propositions, of which some are recognizably scientific – 'Of bodies electrical'; 'Of pygmies'; 'Of the pissing of toads'; others are quaint and apparently naive – 'That moles are blind'; 'That an elephant hath no joints' (and thus cannot get up if knocked down); 'That a badger hath the legs of one side shorter than of the other' (for running straight along hillsides); and still others we would classify as unnatural history – 'Of the unicorn's horn'; 'Of fairy stones'; 'That the root of mandrakes [a poisonous plant] resemble the shape of a man. That they naturally grow under gallows and places of execution. That the root gives a shriek upon eradication. That it is fatal or dangerous to dig them up'; 'Of the last and great promoter of false opinions... Satan'. This curious mixture is not an index to Browne's credulity but rather an indication of the serious lack of elementary scientific information among people in general; it also reflects the way in which all aspects of knowledge were blended together without distinction into categories.

Browne was responsible for formulating the pattern which scientific treatises still adopt: statement of proposition and the authority upon which it is based, description of experiment, results of this experiment, and the deductions to be made as a modification or confirmation of the original proposition. Browne's methodology is modern, but he believed in astrology, alchemy, magic, the Ptolemaic astronomy and in 1664 (when Milton was composing *Paradise lost*) he gave evidence against two women accused of witchcraft: they were hanged a week later.

Elements and humours

For Browne, as for Milton, it is man alone in whom the spiritual and material aspects of existence united: man is unique in that he shares a rational soul with the angels, and a body with the lower forms of animal life. The material world and the corruptible human body, subject to decay and death, were both composed of four primary *elements*. In the chaos which separates earth from heaven and hell, Milton describes matter still scattered into its elemental particles:

> For Hot, Cold, Moist and Dry, four champions fierce
> Strive here for mastery, and to battle bring
> Their embryon atoms. *PL* II 898

This reflects a simple form of atomic theory as expounded by Greek philosophers, and by Bacon; but the men of Milton's generation still tended to believe that all things were composed of earth, water, air and fire, which possessed the four primary qualities of dryness, moisture, cold and heat.

Since man was the link between earth and heaven, he represented within himself a world in miniature; he was the microcosm corresponding to the macrocosm of the universe. On the analogy of the four primary elements in the world, the human body contained four corresponding *humours*: blood, like air (hot and moist); phlegm, like water (cold and moist); choler, like fire (hot and dry); and melancholy, like earth (cold and dry). In a perfectly balanced personality these four humours would be distributed in exact amounts according to this sequence, but in descending order of abundance. Any man fortunate enough to possess a perfect distribution of elements would enjoy perfect health of body and mind; in practice this did not happen and each person's temperament varied from this ideal norm, in proportion to which humour was present to excess. In consequence there were four major categories into which human *temperaments* were divided; sanguine (blood), phlegmatic, choleric and melancholic. Of these the sanguine was considered the most desirable as blood was the most important material constituent of the body. The fundamental principle of 17th-century medicine was, therefore, to account for diseases by the over-abundance of one or other of the humours, and the treatment must aim to restore the correct balance – as, for example, by the letting of blood – for the particular temperament of the patient.

Doctors in the 17th century tended to believe that the more scourging the medicine, the more effective the treatment; their remedies were not gentle. Milton, speaking of the ultimate weapon of the church, excommunication, describes it in medical terms:

though it touch neither life nor limb, nor any worldly possession, yet has it such penetrating force, that swifter than any chemical sulphur, or that lightning which harms not the skin, and rifles the entrails, it scorches the inmost soul...a rough and vehement cleansing medicine, where the malady is obdurate, a mortifying to life, a kind of saving by undoing.

Reason of church government

This description may derive from the savage potions designed to cure people of the plague: doctors did not know how to cure specific diseases so they prescribed complex compounds of all kinds of drugs in the hope that something might work.

Body and soul

The body and the soul were linked together by 'spirit'. This is an emanation from the blood, which acts as an agent of the soul to perform essential bonding functions in the material body. There are three types of *spirit*; the natural (engendered from the liver), the vital (from the heart), and the animal (from the brain). They relate to the three aspects of the soul. With plants man shares the *vegetable soul*, whose property is growth; with animals he shares the *sensitive soul*, whose quality is sensory perception; and with the angels he shares the *rational soul*, which endows humanity with rational intellect. It is in practical application of this theory of human physiology that Satan first seeks to tempt Eve and is surprised by the angelic guard,

> Squat like a toad, close at the ear of Eve;
> Assaying by his devilish art to reach
> The organs of her fancy, and with them forge
> Illusions as he list, phantasms and dreams,
> Or if, inspiring venom, he might taint
> The animal spirits that from pure blood arise
> Like gentle breaths from rivers pure, thence raise
> At least distempered, discontented thoughts,
> Vain hopes, vain aims, inordinate desires
> Blown up with high conceits engendering pride.   *PL* iv 800

Satan is attempting to unbalance the perfect composition of humours in Eve by interfering with the linkage that ties her body to her soul; this distortion is designed to result in rebellion.

It is only the angels who can escape from the limitations of the mortal body, for they, being pure spirit,

> when they please
> Can either sex assume, or both; so soft
> And uncompounded is their essence pure,
> Not tied or manacled with joint or limb,
> Nor founded on the brittle strength of bones,
> Like cumbrous flesh.   *PL* i 423

In the human body, however, there is no such freedom from constraint; man's spiritual part, his divinely given intelligence, must always compete for mastery with his fleshly instincts. Similarly the extent to which any human body is distorted from its normal shape or function by a physical deformity is indicative of a proportional spiritual defect. This assumption is the primary reason why Milton is at such pains to explain to himself the reasons for his blindness. His argument is that a prophet is properly denied the distractions of mere physical vision in order that his spiritual insight might be proportionately increased; his blindness is an outer sign of an inner spiritual grace:

> that I may see and tell
> Of things invisible to mortal sight.   *PL* III 54

MACROCOSM (universe)		MICROCOSM (man)	
universal elements	*universal qualities*	*humours*	*temperament*
air	cold	blood (hot & moist)	sanguine
water	moisture	phlegm (cold & moist)	phlegmatic
fire	heat	choler (hot & dry)	choleric
earth	dryness	melancholy (cold & dry)	melancholic

form of life	*type of soul*	*property*	*human organ*
plants	vegetable	growth	liver
animals	animal	sensation	brain
angels	sensitive	intelligence	heart
	all three types of soul combine in man		

Melancholy

Renaissance physiology extended the functions of the brain and heart into spiritual states beyond those which modern medicine would recognize; but it did likewise share with modern psychology a conviction that many illnesses are psychosomatic: the interaction of soul or mind upon body was a recognized principle of 17th-century medicine. Milton illustrates this belief in his poetic analysis of two forms of the same mental state of melancholia. There were two major ways of assessing the melancholic type. On the one hand melancholia was

a degrading mental abnormality associated with fear and sorrow. It may be a morose, brooding morbidity of mind, it may be a sottish lethargy, or it may be an insanity accompanied by sorrowful and fearful delusions, often ridiculous.[1]

[1] L. Babb, *The Elizabethan malady* Michigan 1951.

There was also another form of it, quite distinct:

a condition which endows one with intellectual acumen and profundity, with artistic ability, sometimes with divine inspiration.

Milton composed his two early poems *L'allegro* and *Il penseroso* partly as a reflection of these contrasting interpretations: in the former, melancholy is 'loathed', and is born 'Mongst horrid shapes, and shrieks, and sights unholy'; whereas in the latter it is 'divine', a 'saint', a 'Goddess, sage and holy'; it is the former which he rejects and the latter which he welcomes. Milton is presenting his own personal ideas about the function and purpose of the poetic life in terms of the contemporary theories of melancholy with which his audience would already be familiar, so that he can more readily communicate with them: the theories of melancholia act as a carrier-wave upon which a personal modulation is superimposed. Milton displays an awareness of both the traditional elemental theory of life and the modern atomism of Bacon, but he makes no attempt to weigh their relative values and simply uses whichever is most appropriate to his poetic context. His attitude towards astronomy is the same.

Astronomy

In *Areopagitica* Milton recorded a visit he had made to Galileo in Florence, but spoke of the astronomer not as a scientist but as a symbol of the suffering created by bigotry:

There it was that I found and visited the famous Galileo grown old, a prisoner to the Inquisition, for thinking in astronomy otherwise than the Franciscan and Dominican licensers thought.

And later, in *Paradise lost*, he speaks of the moon

whose orb
Through optic glass the Tuscan artist views
At evening from the top of Fesolè.   I 287

While Milton appreciated the work of Galileo as a scientist, he admired him more as a martyr to the cause of truth: Milton does not, however, make any definite personal decision as to which current theory of celestial motion he prefers. Milton does not make any clear choice between the scholastic Aristotelian geocentric system and the Galileo–Copernicus heliocentric cosmos.

In the mid-17th century, three major astronomical theories were current. The oldest was the *Ptolemaic* (of Ptolemy of Alexandria *c.* 127–151 AD). According to this theory the earth was stationary at the centre of the heavenly arrangement and around it revolved a series of spheres which carried the sun, moon, the other planets and the fixed stars. All these heavenly bodies were kept in position and motion by being enclosed in the Empyrean Heaven which was the outermost sphere and where God and the saints dwelt. To this system was added the additional Christian gloss that each of the spheres was presided over by an angel and the music of the spheres was produced by the singing of these sirens. A vital notion involved in this theory was that, in the realm beneath the moon and including the earth, all things, as a result of the fall, were subject to change, decay and death; in the region beyond the moon's sphere all was eternal and stable. This cosmology had the merits of being approved by the oldest authorities, particularly the Bible and Aristotle, of fitting normal and uninformed human sensory observation and of appealing to common sense; it also lent support to the idea that man on earth was the focus of the cosmos.

The *Copernican* system (of Nicholas Koppernik 1473–1543, of Polish and German descent; Copernicus is the Latin form of his name) was heliocentric as opposed to geocentric, and it was developed during the latter part of the renaissance. According to it the earth revolved about the sun, as did the other planets; it also revolved about its own axis. If the earth is merely an obedient satellite of the sun, and both it and the planets are subject to movement and change, then man shares his mutable state with the rest of the cosmos. The disadvantage of this explanation for the public at large was that it contradicted common sense and could be properly assessed only by mathematical scientists: it is the same in our own time with the relativity theory of Einstein. In 1572 a supernova suddenly appeared in the constellation Cassiopeia and remained visible for two years. It was impossible to explain this phenomenon in Ptolemaic terms as occurring in the realm of change beneath the moon. From this time forward Copernican astronomy might be denied but could not be ignored.

There was, however, a third alternative. This was proposed by Tycho *Brahe* (1546–1603, of Copenhagen) who sought to retain the mathematical advantages of the Copernican system, while avoiding its most serious conflicts with traditional belief. According to Brahe the earth remained stationary and was the centre of the orbits of the sun, moon and fixed stars, all of which rotated about it once every twenty-four hours. The planets, however, orbited the sun, and the sun, in turn, orbited the earth with the planets in train. Tycho Brahe's system appealed to many who were aware of the mathematical inconsistencies of the Ptolemaic explanation and who were yet unwilling to wholeheartedly accept the Copernican alternative, which seemed to violate scriptural authority and common sense.

Milton frequently speaks of both the Ptolemaic and Copernican astronomy but makes no explicit reference to the Tychonic compromise. To Milton the poet, the old geocentric astronomy with its attendant hierarchy of spheres and spirits was a more suitable vehicle for conveying his message about God's purposes; to Milton the rationalist, the Copernican heliocentric pattern was a more plausible explanation: the Tychonic compromise was simply unnecessary. Milton always speaks of the universe as primarily a theocentric organism; and in practical terms, within limited mortal vision, it is physically geocentric. He emphasizes the immensity of the created cosmos and the consequent comparative minuteness of the earth:

> When I behold this goodly frame, this world
> Of heaven and earth consisting, and compute
> Their magnitudes, this earth a spot, a grain,
> An atom, with the firmament compared
> And all her numbered stars, that seem to roll
> Spaces incomprehensible.   PL VIII 15

Adam may have been the favoured of God, but post-lapsarian man must be constantly aware of his own insignificance. Milton's concern with astronomy is not that of the practising scientist but that of the moral teacher, who draws analogies from the observable rather than the theoretical nature of the heavens in order to illustrate his philosophical and theological statements.

Galileo used a variety of scientific instruments, including the compound microscope, and the thermometer, which he may have invented. In 1609 he first constructed a telescope but it was not until March 1610 that he announced that he had discovered with it the satellites of Jupiter. This observed detail amounted to experimental proof of the Copernican hypothesis for it confirmed that the Ptolemaic astronomy failed to take into account certain apparent facts of the planetary system. Milton, in *Paradise lost*, reveals his familiarity with discoveries made about the lunar surfaces with some form of 'optic glass'. Raphael ponders the questions raised by the new discoveries of the telescope; they may indicate that the moon is inhabited:

                    her spots thou seest
          As clouds, and clouds may rain, and rain produce
          Fruits in her softened soil, for some to eat
          Allotted there.   VIII 145

Similarly the angels on the seventh day of creation sang of

                          stars
          Numerous, and every star perhaps a world
          Of destined habitation.   VII 620

Milton's sense of cosmic perspective is expanded by Galileo's
discoveries, and his awareness of earthly man's insignificance is
increased. These new aids to observation could be used for good or
evil ends, for Milton ascribes to Satan in *Paradise regained* (IV 25) the
clever manipulation of the laws of optics, using the principles of
telescope and microscope, to create a panoramic X-ray mirage.

The cosmos

Milton's universe is based upon the hierarchical principle with God
as its centre and focus, Christ and the Holy Spirit as his agents, the
angels in their degrees, men in their stations, and all created things in
due order and proportion attendant upon him. The actual physical
arrangement of the cosmos is less significant than its teleological
meaning. In Book VIII of *Paradise lost* Adam enquires about the basis
of the heavenly economy, realizing that it is strange 'How nature wise
and frugal could commit Such disproportions' as to allow the whole
firmament to exist merely for the earth's benefit. In reply Raphael
points out that 'whether heaven move or earth Imports not' because
God has intentionally concealed the details of the heavenly arrangement from man's gaze, so that he should not waste time formulating
hypotheses to account for things which are of no concern to him.
God's heavenly plan is not to be explained. It is a source of divine
amusement that some men should be rash enough to try to uncover
the secrets of the cosmos:

          he [God] his fabric of the heavens
          Hath left to their disputes, perhaps to move
          His laughter at their quaint opinions wide
          Hereafter, when they come to model heaven
          And calculate the stars, how they will wield
          The mighty frame, how build, unbuild, contrive
          To save appearances.   76

After the fall the earth suffered a change in its climate: it became seasonal, either because God

> bid his angels turn askance
> The poles of earth twice ten degrees and more
> From the sun's axle   *PL* x 668

or because the course of the sun was changed:

> some say the sun
> Was bid turn reins from the equinoctial road.

The former explanation, that the change in climate was brought about by a shift in the inclination of the earth's axis to its present $23\frac{1}{2}°$, is the Copernican explanation; the latter is the Ptolemaic alternative. It is not 'how?' that finally matters, but 'why?'. And yet the more precise and detailed Milton's knowledge of the physical nature of the world is, the more plausible and consistent the divine world of his imagination becomes.

Providence and astrology

Milton's universe is providential and his God benevolent – there is nothing in life which cannot be accounted for.[1] Milton makes the scientific assumption that an ultimate consistency is part of the nature of things. For Milton it is reason which distinguishes man from the animals, and Christ embodied divine reason which man may share. Milton was bound, therefore, to challenge any assumption like astrology, which seemed to conflict with reasonableness and the idea of free will. Michael warns Adam, just before the expulsion from paradise,

> Let no man seek
> Henceforth to be foretold what shall befall
> Him or his children, evil he may be sure,
> Which neither his foreknowing can prevent,
> And he the future evil shall no less
> In apprehension than in substance feel
> Grievous to bear.   XI 770

[1] There is only one exception to this universal rule, a miracle: 'The extraordinary providence of God is that whereby God produces some effect out of the usual order of nature, or gives the power of producing the same effect to whomsoever he may appoint. This is what we call a miracle. Hence God alone is the primary author of miracles, as he only is able to invert that order of things which he has himself appointed.... The use of miracles is to manifest the divine power, and confirm our faith' (*Christian doctrine*). Satan, on the other hand, can only perform magic, which is merely a clever misuse of the laws of nature.

To assume that it is possible to predict the future is a denial of human freedom and, in any event, not desirable, because to know of misfortune before it occurs increases its terrors by anticipation. This declaration by Michael is an attack upon the assumptions of the astrologers and is in harmony with Milton's philosophical position. Milton does, however, use astrological assumptions elsewhere in his poem, as when he describes the tarnished image of the fallen Lucifer:

> As when the sun new risen
> Looks through the horizontal misty air
> Shorn of his beams, or from behind the moon
> In dim eclipse disastrous twilight sheds
> On half the nations, and with fear of change
> Perplexes monarchs. I 594

Meteors, comets, eclipses, earthquakes were all popularly believed to presage disasters, just as the epidemics of bubonic plague were explained as the visitations of the wrath of God upon an unregenerate and wicked people. Milton uses imagery derived from these sources as a poetic resource to convey other concepts, not to expound them as credible in themselves. There is a distinction to be made once again between Milton the poet and Milton the rationalist. The latter is aware of the contradictions and presumptions in the views of the astrologers; the former knows that the structure of his poems and the plausibility of their doctrine are largely dependent upon the emotional effect of the metaphorical way in which that message is conveyed. Since the Hebraic–Christian religion has very little mythology of its own, Milton borrowed the myths of classical antiquity to illustrate his Christian doctrine: he uses a pagan mythology as a vehicle to convey a Christian statement. He employs astrology in the same way, to add resonance to an abstract idea. As a rationalist Milton rejected astrology; as a poet he knew that it was still emotionally credible.

Alchemy

In the *General prologue to the Canterbury tales*, Chaucer describes the Doctor of Physic as 'grounded in astronomye', and

> He kepte his paciënt a ful greet deel
> In hourës by his magyk natureel.
> Wel koude he fortunen the áscendent
> Of his ymáges for his paciënt.
> He knew the cause of everich maladye,

> Were it of hoot, or coold, or moyste, or drye,
> And where they engendred, and of what humour. 415

He is an expert in restoring the proper balance of humours but was also expected to know the most propitious time for the administration of the remedy; to know when the planets were favourably disposed for treatment was an integral part of the successful practice of medicine. Chaucer's Doctor prefers, above all medicines, *aurum potabile*, liquified gold to be drunk:

> For gold in phisik is a cordial,
> Therefore he lovede gold in special.

He approves of 'potable gold' because he is naturally avaricious and has an arrangement with the apothecaries whereby he receives a share of the profit from the prescription of this costly remedy; but at the same time it was a recognized medieval medicine. Milton uses the metaphorical implications of the idea of this elixir, ascribing its creation as a virtue peculiar to the sun, so as to stress the purity of that heavenly body in contrast to the corruption of Satan:

> What wonder then if fields and regions here
> Breathe forth elixir pure, and rivers run
> Potable gold, when with one virtuous touch
> The arch-chemic sun so far from us remote
> Produces with terrestial humour mixed
> Here in the dark so many precious things
> Of colour glorious and effect so rare?   *PL* iii 606

The dream of the medieval alchemist was to discover the elixir which would cure all diseases and give everlasting life, and the stone which would enable one substance to be turned into another: Milton conflates these two ideas and ascribes these powers to the sun. Light itself is seen as an elixir, and the sun is credited with the engendering of precious stones in the earth, to contrast the more violently with the dark malevolence of Satan, who can only destroy. Light is the essence of God and of life as we know him and it. In the cosmos, sunlight is primary. The light of the moon and the stars is merely a reflection of the sun's light and without this central generating agency our faculty of seeing is inoperative. For Milton light is an all-pervading physical entity analogous to the spiritual omnipresence of God.

In his prose works, Milton speaks with contempt of the alchemists by identifying them with Roman Catholicism, which Milton automatically assumed that his audience despised, distrusted and feared. Speaking of bishops, he declares:

Their trade being, by the same alchemy that the Pope uses, to extract heaps
of gold and silver out of the drossy bullion of the people's sins.

Of reformation

They themselves are 'a distilled quintessence, a pure elixir of
mischief, pestilent alike to all' (*Reason of church government*).

Technology

William Camden, the most distinguished Elizabethan antiquary and
historian, in his *Remains of a greater work concerning Britain* (1605)
describes, at one point, certain frightening developments in the
science of war. He sees in the siege-engine the most appalling
prospects for civilization:

So violent is it in breaking, tearing, bruising, renting, razing, and ruinating
walls, towers, castles, ramparts and all that it encountereth, that it might
seem to have been invented by practice of the Devil, to the destruction of
mankind, as the only enemy of true valour and manful courageousness by
murdering afar off.

Milton ascribes to Satan the invention of the cannon and the first
making of gunpowder:

> sulphurous and nitrous foam
> They found, they mingled, and with subtle art,
> Concocted and adusted they reduced
> To blackest grain, and into store conveyed:
> Part hidden veins digged up (nor hath this earth
> Entrails unlike) of mineral and stone
> Whereof to found their engines and their balls
> Of missive ruin.
> PL VI 512

Milton pictures the rebel angels as miners who dig out the entrails of
the living animal Earth: they torture this great creature in the production of raw materials of war. By identifying the martial virtues with
Satan, Milton effectively condemns them and the science of war.
Satan is himself compared to a 'devilish engine' and, in the war in
heaven, he uses the stratagem of concealing his newly invented
weapons behind a phalanx of troops, who suddenly move aside for
the cannon to be discharged:

> Immediate in a flame,
> But soon obscured with smoke, all heaven appeared
> From those deep-throated engines belched, whose roar

> Embowelled with outrageous noise the air,
> And all her entrails tore, disgorging foul
> Their devilish glut, chained thunderbolts and hail
> Of iron globes, which on the victor host
> Levelled, with such impetuous fury smote,
> That whom they hit, none on their feet might stand,
> Though standing else as rocks, but down they fell
> By thousands, angel on archangel rolled.   VI 584

The hideous effects of gunfire are magnified when it is realized that this collapse of the opposing force is effected upon the army of Christ. The light of heaven is eclipsed by powder smoke, the very atmosphere is disembowelled by cannon shot – Milton's imagery is drawn from that most ghastly of 17th-century punishments, the 'drawing' of the entrails of the convicted traitor and the burning of them on a brazier at his side while he was still conscious. The massacre of the angelic host is equivalent to the slaughter of the common soldier in any war in any kingdom. Milton is less a pacifist than an active anti-militarist, for the military attitude is incompatible with his theological convictions. The only science which Milton condemns without reservation is that of war, for Satan is its originator: the only creative act which he performs is to invent more efficient ways of destruction.

Scientific education

In 1572 a proposal had been addressed to the Queen by Sir Humphrey Gilbert to found a school to be called Queen Elizabeth's Academy. Gilbert argued that this institution was necessary for the modern education of the sons of the gentry, for

> whereas in the universities men study only school [i.e. scholastic] learnings, in this academy they shall study matters of action meet for present practice both of peace and war. And if they will not dispose themselves to letters, yet they may learn languages or martial activities for the service of their country.
>   *Archaeologia* XXI 1827

This school was to have two professors of mathematics and one of engineering; the application of these disciplines to the sciences of navigation and fortification was to be particularly stressed.

Gilbert had a personal interest in the new sciences for he was an explorer and made two voyages to North America, on the second of which in 1583 he founded a colony in Newfoundland, but when venturing to sea in a small vessel called the *Squirrel*, of ten tons burthen only, he was on the 9th of September, at midnight, cast away, and together with the whole ship's company swallowed up.[1]

The explorers of the 17th century urgently needed the discovery of some accurate method of determining longitude, but this did not become possible until Newton's lunar theory allowed exact prediction of the moon's position, and until a naval chronometer was developed which would accurately keep Greenwich Mean Time (upon which standard point of reference all navigational calculations, and the world's time zones, are still based). It did not become possible to precisely determine longitude until late in the 18th century.

In his treatise *Of education* Milton gives a prominent place to practical scientific skills in his outline of those studies necessary for the education of the fully trained individual. He advocated that students should first study the principles of 'arithmetic, geometry, astronomy, and geography, with a general compact of physics'; and then

the instrumental science of trigonometry, and from thence to fortification, architecture, enginery, or navigation. And in natural philosophy they may proceed leisurely from the history of meteors, minerals, plants, and living creatures as far as anatomy.

This study is not to be undertaken in the abstract or in theory only, since he assumes that there will be utilized

the helpful experiences of hunters, fowlers, fishermen, shepherds, gardeners, apothecaries; and in the other sciences, architects, engineers, mariners, anatomists; who doubtless would be ready, some for reward and some to favour such a hopeful seminary. And this will give them such a real tincture of natural knowledge, as they shall never forget.

Milton's educational schemes are implausible because of the very demands they make upon the students; he makes the mistake of judging the intellectual capacity of others by his own. However, he was not alone in his concern for practical training in a variety of technological skills. As early as 1597 Gresham College had been

---

[1] Antony à Wood *Athenae Oxonienses* I 495. It was three years later on a voyage to Greenland and Iceland that there took place the first soccer international between the old world and the new: on 21 August 1586 Purser Henry Morgan tells how 'Divers times they [the Eskimos] did wave us on shore to play with them at the football, and some of our company went on shore to play with them, and our men did cast them down as soon as they did come to strike the ball'. The result is not known, but England should perhaps have been sent off. (R. Hakluyt *The English voyages* Everyman ed V 307.)

established in London to provide instruction in the sciences to both the scholarly, who were lectured to in the mornings in Latin, and the public at large, who were lectured to on the same subjects in the afternoons in English. This institution was founded mainly to supply the needs of craftsmen, merchants, navigators, mechanics who needed advanced scientific instruction both theoretical and practical if the country was to be developed.

Shortly before Milton's personal experiences as a teacher in London, which probably took place in 1639, another college with a technical bias had been established. In June 1636 Charles I granted a charter to Sir Francis Kynaston to establish, in Covent Garden, a school to be called the Museum Minervae. It was designed to attract the sons of the gentry and lesser nobility. Apart from languages, music and law, the students were to be instructed in physiology, anatomy, astronomy, optics, navigation, cosmography, arithmetic, geometry, algebra, fortification and architecture and the professors were expected to conduct research in their own fields. The professor of astronomy, a certain Nicholas Phiske, was required to

keep an exact diary of every of the celestial appearances and of the weather, that at last we may find the causes of our insulary varieties, and every month's observations shall be fairly written out, and given up to the library.
Constitutions 1636

The Museum Minervae did not uncover the secrets of the weather but Kynaston was successful in at least one experiment, for

by experience [he] falsified the alchemist's report, that a hen being fed for certain days with gold...should be converted into gold, and should lay golden eggs; but indeed became very fat.   WOOD *Athenae Oxonienses* III 39

These early scientific societies were to be eclipsed by an organization which first began as an informal club. The members met at Gresham College from about 1645 and, after the Restoration in 1660, their purpose was declared to be

to make faithful records of all the works of nature, or art which can come within their reach: that so the present age, and posterity, may be able to put a mark on the errors which have been strengthened by long prescription; to restore the truths that have lain neglected; to push on those which are already known, to more various uses; and to make the way more passable to what remains unrevealed.   SPRAT *History of the Royal Society* 1667

On 15 July 1662 they were incorporated by Charles II as the Royal Society. Their most distinguished member was Sir Isaac Newton, of whom Pope remarked 'God said, Let Newton be! and all was light.'

Science and morality

Modern science and technology operate upon the assumption that the universe is subject to mechanical laws which can be perceived and analysed: this applies both to natural and human phenomena. Both ourselves and our environment are subject to exact measurement, whether this be a process of objective analysis (about how things work), or a statistical survey (about what we are thinking), or a psychological analysis (about why we are thinking). This assumption tends to ignore the fact that the idea of the mechanical universe is a working hypothesis and not a proved conclusion. Dominating our consciousness of the material world, the idea of mechanism is so all-embracing that it either eliminates God altogether or removes him to so distant a function (as in the 'big bang' hypothesis in astronomy, about the origin of the universe) that no personal contact with him is feasible. Milton stands in conflict with this point of view: God is immediate and present in human existence and it is through him alone that life has meaning. Milton's philosophy denies the depersonalized concept of a deity become merely a synonym for an unknown mechanical cause.

Man must learn from the experiences of Adam in paradise that 'to obey is best'. The great Christian virtues of humility, temperance, fortitude, forgiveness, and the hope of resurrection must always be the ultimate goal of human endeavour:

> This having learned, thou hast attained the sum
> Of wisdom, hope no higher, though all the stars
> Thou knewest by name, and all the ethereal powers,
> All secrets of the deep, all nature's works. *PL* XII 575

For Milton the natural sciences of the material world have inescapable moral connotations: a basic scientific fact is that the earth's climate is subject to seasonal variations, but this was a consequence of the fall of man, 'else had the spring Perpetual smiled on earth with vernant flowers' (*PL* X 678).

Milton would have concurred with the eulogy of the Royal Society expressed by his fellow religious poet Abraham Cowley (1618–67), himself one of its members:

> Nature's great works no distance can obscure,
> No smallness her near objects can secure:
>> You've taught the curious sight to press
>> Into the privatest recess

Of her imperceptible littleness;
You've learned to read her smallest hand
And well begun her deepest sense to understand.

But science may have deceived both of them: while it opened up new horizons to the poet it challenged poetry, for the Royal Society resolved

to reject all the amplifications, digressions, and swellings of style; to return back to the primitive purity and shortness, when men delivered so many things almost in an equal number of words...[and they] exacted from their members a close, naked, natural way of speaking; positive expressions; clear senses; a native easiness; bringing all things as near the mathematical plainness, as they can.   SPRAT

Is the grand style in harmony with such precision?

Further reading

ASHLEY, M. *The golden century: Europe 1598–1715* 1969 ch. 10 on science and faith.
BABB, L. *The Elizabethan malady* Michigan 1951 on melancholy.
BERNAL, J. D. *Science in history* 2nd ed 1957.
BUSH, DOUGLAS *Science and English poetry* 1950.
BUSH, M. L. *Renaissance, reformation and the outer world* 1967.
DAMPIER, W. C. *A history of science* 1961.
JOHNSON, F. R. *Astronomical thought in renaissance England* Baltimore 1937.
JONES, R. F. *Ancients and moderns: a study of the rise of the scientific movement in 17c England* 1961.
NICOLSON, M. H. *The breaking of the circle* 1960 on new science and literature.
SVENDSEN, K. *Milton and science* Cambridge Mass. 1956.
WHITEHEAD, A. N. *Science and the modern world* Cambridge 1927.
WOLF, A. *A history of science, technology and philosophy in the 16th and 17th centuries* 1935.

Of contemporary works, see especially Bacon and Browne cited in the chapter; Jonson's *Alchemist*; James Winny ed. *The frame of order: an outline of Elizabethan belief taken from treatises of the late 16th century* 1957. The Roman scientist Lucretius influenced Milton: the latest translation of his work is *The way things are* by Rolfe Humphries (Indiana University Press paperback). For various superstitions and common bits of scientific lore see: Katharine M. Briggs *Pale Hecate's team* 1962; Alan Macfarlane *The family life of Ralph Josselin* Cambridge 1970; M. and C. H. B. Quennell *History of everyday things in England* vol. II for 1500–1732, 1933.

And now the lofty tube, the scale
With which they heaven itself assail,
Was mounted full against the moon,
And all stood ready to fall on,
Impatient who should have the honour
To plant an ensign first upon her;
When one, who for his deep belief
Was virtuoso-then-in-chief,
Approved the most profound and wise
To solve impossibilities,
Advancing gravely to apply
To the optic glass his judging eye,
Cried, 'Strange!'...

SAMUEL BUTLER *The elephant in the moon*

JOHN BROADBENT

The poets' bible

Texts

Milton could read the original Hebrew of the Old Testament and the
Greek of the New. The translation he chiefly used was a 1612 printing
of the Authorized Version, or King James Bible, of 1611. One of his
copies of it is in the British Museum. His third wife Elizabeth
Minshull used a Geneva Bible, of which a copy with her name in it
survives. The word *bible* derives from the Greek for book. The AV
was so called because it was the text authorized to be read in churches
by the king as head of the Church of England. Which text you used
was a matter of political significance because translation = interpretation. The AV was produced by a committee of 47 scholars and
divines whom James I had appointed to compromise between earlier
versions which had been 'high church' (e.g. Bishops' Bible) and 'low'
(e.g. Geneva Bible) in interpretation. The Bible had in any case only
recently become available in English, as a product of the reformation,
and also of the literacy which spread through the non-clerical classes
in the 16th century. Being able to read and interpret the Bible for
yourself had a significance similar to having the vote or the right to
secondary education.

Chief texts of the Old Testament established

in Hebrew	Pentateuch (*Genesis–Deuteronomy*)	5th century BC
in Greek	all *OT*	3rd century BC – the Septuagint
in Hebrew	all *OT*	10th century AD

Chief texts of the New Testament established

in Greek	all *NT*	4th century AD

Chief translation for western Europe

in Latin	whole Bible	405 AD by Jerome – the Vulgate

Language and poetry of the Bible

At 5,000 words, the Hebrew vocabulary of the *OT* is very small and therefore concrete. It lacks linking particles so it works in terse sentences without many subordinate clauses. A number of actual poems are contained in the *OT*, in addition to the psalms (temple hymn-book): they are based on two-line stanzas, the lines tending to repeat each other by parallel structure:

She put her hand to the nail, and her right hand to the workmen's hammer: and with the hammer she smote Sisera, she smote off his head, when she had pierced and stricken through his temples.

Judges v (song of Deborah and Barak)

The Greek of the *NT* was a much more elaborate language than the *OT* Hebrew, but also more demotic and cosmopolitan than the classical Greek of several centuries before. It was a vehicle for sophisticated philosophical concepts such as soul, spirit, righteousness, apocalypse.

In general, the two testaments gave sanctity to a body of literature and history, and a set of ideas, quite alien to England; and they gave an example also of poetry in the service of God. The best book on this subject is T. R. Henn *The Bible as literature* 1970. Here are some other materials:

The firſt dayes worke.   The ſeconde dayes worke.   The thirde dayes worke.

The fourth dayes worke.   The fifth dayes worke.   The ſixte dayes worke.

The firſt Chapter.

A
:ſd.ɛ.d
:li.18.a
t.40.b
b.41.a
l.44.c

IN ý begyn nynge God created hea uen ꞇ earth: and ý earth was voyde and emptie, and darck nes was v= pon the de= pe, ꞇ ý ſpre= te of God moued vpō the water.

And God ſayde: let there be light, ꞇ there was light. And God ſawe the light that it was good. Then God deuyded ý light from the darcknes, and called the light, Daye: and the darcknes, Night. Then of the euenynge and mornynge was made the firſt daye.

And God ſayde: let there be a firmament betwene the waters, and let it deuyde ý wa ters a ſunder. Then God made ý firmamēt, and parted the waters vnder the firmamēt, from the waters aboue the firmament: And ſo it came to paſſe. And God called ý firma ment, heauen. Then of the euenynge ꞇ mor nynge was made the ſeconde daye.

And God ſayde: let the waters vnder hea uen gather thē ſelues vnto one place, ý the dꝛye londe maye appeare. And ſo it came to paſſe. And God called ý dꝛye londe, Earth: and the gatheringe together of waters cal led he, ý See. And God ſawe ý it was good.

And God ſayde: let ý earth bringe forth grene graſſe and herbe, that beareth ſede: ꞇ frutefull trees, that maye beare fruce, euery one after his kynde, hauynge their owne ſe= de in them ſelues vpon the earth. And ſo it came to paſſe. And the earth brought forth grene graſſe and herbe, ý beareth ſede euery one after his kynde, ꞇ trees bearinge fruce, ꞇ

Iob 26.b
Pꝛo.8.c

B

a

FIG 5   First page of *Genesis* in Coverdale translation of the Bible. The wood-cut pictures, showing the six days of creation, and the initial, which derives from illuminated MSS, keep the printed word in touch with visual and hence with illiterate and oral modes of knowing and remembering.

MILTON from *Paradise regained*

>Or if I would delight my private hours
>With music or with poem, where so soon
>As in our native language can I find
>That solace? All our law and story strewed
>With hymns, our psalms with artful terms inscribed,
>Our Hebrew songs and harps in Babylon,
>That pleased so well our victors' ears, declare
>That rather Greece from us these arts derived;
>Ill-imitated, while they loudest sing
>The vices of their deities, and their own
>In fable, hymn, or song, so personating
>Their gods ridiculous, and themselves past shame... IV 331

D. H. LAWRENCE from *Hymns in a man's life*

I think it was good to be brought up a Protestant: and among Protestants, a Nonconformist, and among Nonconformists, a Congregationalist. Which sounds pharisaic. But I should have missed bitterly a direct knowledge of the Bible, and a direct relation to Galilee and Canaan, Moab and Kedron, those places that never existed on earth. And in the Church of England one would hardly have escaped those snobbish hierarchies of class, which spoil so much for a child. And the Primitive Methodists, when I was a boy, were always having 'revivals' and being 'saved', and I always had a horror of being saved.

So, altogether, I am grateful to my 'Congregational' upbringing. The Congregationalists are the oldest Nonconformists, descendents of the Oliver Cromwell Independents. They still had the Puritan tradition of no ritual. But they avoided the personal emotionalism which one found among the Methodists when I was a boy. *The evening news* 13 October 1928

CHRISTOPHER SMART from *Jubilate Agno* (Rejoice in the Lamb) XVI...XXV

For the letter ל which signifies GOD by himself is on the fibre of some leaf in every tree.
For ל is in the veins of all stones both precious and common.
For ל is upon every hair both of man and beast.
For ל is in the grain of wood.
For ל is in the ore of all metals.
For ל is on the scales of all fish.
For ל is on the petals of all flowers.
For ל is upon all shells.
For ל is in the constituent particles of air.

. . . .

For the Lord made a nosegay in the meadow with his disciples and preached upon the lily.

. . . .

For flowers are peculiarly the poetry of Christ.

. . . .

148

Let Ross, house of Ross rejoice with the great flabber-dabber-flat-clapping-fish with hands.
Vide Anson's voyage and Psalm 98th, ix.
Let Fisher, house of Fisher rejoice with Sandastros kind of burning stone with gold drops in the body of it. God be gracious to Fisher of Cambridge and to all of his name and kindred.

Composed during his confinement for psychiatric illness 1756–63. The Hebrew letter is *lamed*, twelfth in the alphabet, and component of *el* = God. Every verse of the twelfth strophe of *Psalm* cxix begins with it.

As the most distinctly poetic part of the Bible, the psalms were especially appealed to by poets and critics (e.g. Sidney in his *Apology for poetry*) as justifying art. Smart wrote a magnificent *Song to David* as the poet-king. See Wyatt's translation of the seven penitential psalms (vi, xxxii, xxxviii, li, cii, cxxx *De profundis*, cxliii) and Milton's paraphrases.

SMART from *A translation of the Psalms of David* CXIX Lamed

> O Lord of everlasting power,
> Whose throne immortal palms embower
>   Where cherubim are heard
> And angels kneel – thy glorious word
> For ever is in heaven preferred,
>   Exalted and ensphered.
>
> Thy truth from race to race consists
> And from eternities exists;
>   The far-extended sweep
> Of steadfast earth thou hast displayed
> And on the pillared arches laid
>   The waters of the deep.

JOHN DONNE from *Sermon II* preached at Lincoln's Inn
I acknowledge that my spiritual appetite carries me still upon the *Psalms* of David for a first course for the scriptures of the Old Testament; and upon the epistles of St Paul for a second course for the New...they are scriptures written in such forms as I have been most accustomed to: St Paul's being letters, and David's being poems; for God gives us not only that which is merely necessary but that which is convenient too; he does not only feed us, but 'feed us with marrow and with fatness'; he gives us our instruction in cheerful forms, not in a sour and sullen and angry and unacceptable way, but cheerfully, in psalms – which is also a limited and restrained form: not in an oration, not in prose, but in psalms; which is such a form as is both curious, and requires diligence in the making, and then when it is made can have nothing, 'no syllable taken from it, nor added to it'...

W. S. LANDOR from *Imaginary conversations* 1846
Who could imagine that Milton, who translated the Psalms worse than any man ever translated them before or since, should in this glorious hymn

[*PL* v 152ff] have made the 148th so much better than the original? But there is a wide difference between being bound to the wheels of a chariot and guiding it. He has ennobled that more noble one, 'O all ye works of the Lord...' But in:

> Ye mists and exhalations that now rise
> From hill or steaming lake, dusky or grey,
> Till the sun *paint* your fleecy skirts with *gold*...

Such a verse might well be ejected from any poem whatsoever: but here its prettiness is quite insufferable. Adam never knew anything either of paint or gold.

Authority and liberty

The next passages show how the two testaments were seen as hanging together and giving Christians a sense of location in a divinely ordered eternity; giving them also, however lowly, access to the majesty of God.

Attrib. ST PAUL from *Hebrews* xi

Now faith is the substance of things hoped for, the evidence of things not seen.

For by it the elders obtained a good report.

Through faith we understand that the worlds were framed by God, so that things which are seen were not made of things which do appear...

By faith they passed through the Red Sea as by dry land: which the Egyptians essaying to do were drowned.

By faith the walls of Jericho fell down, after they were compassed about seven days.

By faith the harlot Rahab perished not with them that believed not, when she had received the spies with peace.

And what more shall I say? for the time would fail me to tell of Gideon and of Barak and of Samson and of Jephthae, of David also and Samuel and of the prophets:

Who through faith subdued kingdoms, wrought righteousness, obtained promises, stopped the mouths of lions,

Quenched the violence of fire, escaped the edge of the sword, out of weakness were made strong, waxed valiant in fight, turned to flight the armies of the aliens.

Women received their dead raised to life again; and others were tortured, not accepting deliverance; that they might obtain a better resurrection...

MILTON from *De doctrina christiana*

Chapter XXX   Of the Holy Scriptures

The writings of the prophets, apostles and evangelists, composed under divine inspiration, are called THE HOLY SCRIPTURES. II Samuel xxiii 2 'the spirit of Jehovah spake by me, and his word was in my tongue'. Matthew xxii 43 'how then doth David'. . . ɪɪ Timothy iii 16 'all scripture is given by inspiration of God'. . . The Holy Scriptures were not written for occasional purposes only, as is the doctrine of the Papists, but for the use of the church throughout all ages, as well under the gospel as under the law. . . Deuteronomy xxx 8 'write it. . . that it may be for the time to come for ever and ever'. . . John v 39 'search the scriptures, for in them ye think ye have eternal life'. Romans xv 4 'whatsoever things were written aforetime were written for our learning, that we through patience and comfort of the scriptures might have hope'. ɪ Corinthians x 11 'they are written for our admonition, upon whom the ends of the world are come'.

Almost everything advanced in the New Testament is proved by citations from the Old. . . ɪɪ Timothy iii 15–17 'from a child thou hast known the holy scriptures, which are able to make thee wise unto salvation through faith which is in Christ Jesus: all scripture is given by inspiration of God, and is profitable for doctrine, for reproof, for correction, for instruction in righteousness'. It is true that the Scriptures which Timothy is here said to have 'known from a child' and which were of themselves 'able to make him wise unto salvation through faith in Christ' were probably those of the Old Testament alone, since no part of the New Testament appears to have existed during the infancy of Timothy. . .

The Scriptures, therefore, partly by reason of their own simplicity, and partly through the divine illumination, are plain and perspicuous in all things necessary to salvation, and adapted to the instruction even of the most unlearned, through the medium of diligent and constant reading: Psalm xix 7 'the law of Jehovah is perfect, converting the soul; the testimony of Jehovah is sure, making wise the simple'. . . Every believer has a right to interpret the Scriptures for himself, as he has the Spirit for his guide, and the mind of Christ is in him; nay, the expositions of the public interpreter can be of no use to him, except in so far as they are confirmed by his own conscience. . . Under the gospel we possess, as it were, a twofold Scripture: one external, which is the written word, and the other internal, which is the Holy Spirit, written in the hearts of believers, according to the promise of God. . .

JOHN BUNYAN from *The pilgrim's progress from this world to that which is to come: delivered under the similitude of a dream*
I dreamed, and behold, I saw a man clothed with rags, standing in a certain place, with his face from his own house, a Book in his hand, and a great burden upon his back [Isaiah lxiv 6; Luke xiv 33; Psalm xxxviii 4]. I looked, and saw him open the Book, and read therein; and as he read, he wept and trembled and not being able longer to contain, he brake out with a lamentable cry, saying, 'What shall I do?' [Acts ii 37]. . .

Pliable And do you think that the words of your Book are certainly true?
Christian Yes, verily; for it was made by Him that cannot lie. [Titus i 2]
Pliable Well said; what things are they?

[The Bible tells of joys to come]

Christian There is an endless kingdom to be inhabited, and everlasting life

151

*1.Cor.11.2.

*Or, Mannet, becauſe ſhe cō meth of man that is in Eli 1ſa, ſo maу, and I ſhal the woman.

Mat.19,5.
mar.10,7.
24.cor.6, 16.
epheſ 5,31.
p So that ma riage requi reth a greater duetie of vs towarde 1 wi ues, thē other wiſe we are bounde to ſhe we to our pa rents.

23 Then the man ſaid,* This now is bone of my bones, and fleſh of my fleſh. She ſhalbe called *woman, becauſe ſhe was ta ken out of man.

24 *Therefore ſhal man leaue p his father and his mother,and ſhal cleaue to his wife, and they ſhalbe one fleſh.

25 And they were bothe naked, the man & his wife,and were not q aſhamed.

q For before ſinne entred, all things we re honeſt and ſomely.

THE SITVACION OF THE GARDEN OF EDEN.

Becauſe mention is made in the tenth verſe of this ſeconde chapter of the riuer that watered the garden, we muſte note that Euphrates and Tygris called 11 : brewe, Perath and Hiddekel, were called but one riuer where they ioyned together,els they had ſure heades:that is ,two at their ſprings, & two where they fel into the Perſian ſea. In this countrey an i muſte plentiful land Adam dwelt,and this was called Paradiſe:that is ,a garden of pleaſure,becauſe of the frutefulnes and abundame thereof. And whereas it is ſaid that Piſhon compaſſeth the land of Hauilah,it is meant of Tygris,which in ſome place,as it paſſed by diuers pla ces,was called by ſundry names,as ſome time Diglitto,in other places Taſitygris,& of ſome Tuaſin or Ti ſhon. Likewiſe Euphrates towarde the countrey of Cuſh or Ethiopia,or Arabia was called Gihon. So that Tygris and Euphrates(which were but two riuers and ſome time when they ioyned together,were called after one name) were according to diuers places called by theſe foure names.ſ: that they might ſome to haue bene foure diuers riuers.

2.Cor.11.3.
d This is Sa taus chiefeſt ſubtiltie , to cauſe vs not to feare Gods threatnings.
e As though he ſhulde ſay, God doeth not forbid you to eat of the tre re,ſaue that he know eth that if you ſhulde eat thereof , you ſhulde be like to him.
Eccleſ.25, 33.
f Not ſo muv ſhe to pleaſe his wife , as bicion at her perſuaſion.
g They began to fele their miſetie , but they ſoght not to God for re medie.
*Ebr. things to gyrde aout the l bid their pruuitis.

CHAP. III.

The woman ſeduced by the ſerpēt. 6 Entiſeth her houſ bādt ſinne. 14 They thre are puniſhed. 15 Chriſt is promiſed. 19 Man is duſt. 22 Man is caſt out of paradiſe.

Wiſdo. 2,25.
a As Satan cā change him ſelfe into an Angel of light, ſo did he ab uſe the wiſdo me of the ſer pent to decea ue man.
b God ſuffe red Satan to make the ſer pent his inſtru ment and to ſpeake in him.
c In douting of Gods threatnig, ſhe yel ded to Satan.

N Ow *the ſerpent was more a ſubtil then anie beaſt of the field,which ỹ Lord God had made:and he b ſaid to the woman, Yea,hathe God in dede ſaid, Ye ſhal not eat of euerie tre of the garden?

2 And the woman ſaid vnto the ſerpēt, We eat of the frute of the trees of the garden,

3 But of the frute of the tre,which is in the middes of the garden, God hathe ſaid, Ye ſhal not eat of it,nether ſhal ye touche it, c leſt ye dye.

4 Then *the ſerpent ſaid to the woman, Ye ſhal n t d dye at all,

5 But God doeth knowe,that when ye ſhal eat thereof, your eyes ſhalbe opened,& ye ſhalbe as gods, e knowing good and euil.

6 So the woman (ſeing that the tre was good for meat,and that it was pleaſant to the eyes,& a tre to be deſired to get know ledge) toke of the frute thereof , and did * eat,and gaue alſo to her houſband with her,and he f did eat.

7 Then the eyes of them bothe were ope ned,& they s knewe that they were naked, and they ſewed figtre leaues together, and made them ſelues "breeches.

8 ¶Afterwarde they heard the voyce of

a.ii.

FIG 6　Page from the Geneva translation of the Bible, with verse that nick named it the Breeches Bible. The map shows the rivers in Iraq that define the area of Eden. This was the version owned by Milton's third wife, the blonde Elizabeth Minshull; she was 24 when they married in 1663.

to be given us; that we may inhabit that kingdom for ever. [Isaiah xlv 17; John x 27]

Pliable Well said; and what else?

Christian There are crowns of glory to be given us, and garments that will make us shine like the sun in the firmament of heaven. [II Timothy iv 8; Revelation iii 4; Matthew xiii 43]

Pliable This is very excellent; and what else?

Christian There shall be no more crying, nor sorrow: for He that is owner of the place will wipe all tears from our eyes. [Isaiah xxv 6; Revelation vii 16; xxi 4]

Pliable And what company shall we have there?

Christian There we shall be with seraphim and cherubim, creatures that will dazzle your eyes to look on them. [Isaiah vi 2] There also you shall meet with thousands and ten thousands that have gone before us to that place...

Mr Worldly Wiseman How camest thou by the burden at first?

Christian By reading this Book in my hand.

> [Worldly Wiseman does not like that men should be serious
> in reading the Bible]

Mr Worldly Wiseman I thought so; and it is happened unto thee as to other weak men, who, meddling with things too high for them, do suddenly fall into thy distractions; which distractions do not only unman men, as thine, I perceive, has done thee, but they run them upon desperate ventures, to obtain they know not what...

Authority and tyranny

FRIEDRICH NIETZSCHE from *Beyond good and evil* 1885

In the Jewish 'old testament', the book of divine justice, there are men and things and speeches in such a grand style that Greek and Indic literature has nothing to equal them. One stands in awe and reverence before these enormous remains of what man once had been, and one has sad thoughts about ancient Asia and its tiny promontory Europe...On the other hand: whoever is only a scrawny, tame, domestic animal...(like our 'cultured' men of today, including the Christians of cultured Christendom), has nothing to surprise nor distress him when he views these ruins. One's taste for the Old Testament is a touchstone as to 'great' and 'small'. Perhaps the cultured man of today will find the New Testament, the book of grace, much more in accordance with his heart. (It has much of the regular, tender-hearted, stuffy odour of the devotee and the small soul.) To have pasted this New Testament... together into one book with the Old Testament...is possibly the greatest recklessness and 'sin against the Holy Ghost' that literary Europe has on its conscience.

SAMUEL BUTLER from *The way of all flesh* 1903 (started 1872)

In those days [early 19th century] people believed with a simple down-rightness which I do not observe among educated men and women now. It had never so much as crossed Theobald's mind to doubt the literal accuracy of any syllable in the Bible. He had never seen any book in which this was disputed, nor met with anyone who doubted it. True, there was just a little scare about geology, but there was nothing in it. If it was said that God made the world in six days, why He did make it in six days, neither in more nor less; if it was said that He put Adam to sleep, took out one of his ribs and made a woman of it, why it was so as a matter of course. He, Adam, went to sleep as it might be himself, Theobald Pontifex, in a garden, as it might be the garden at Crampsford Rectory during the summer months when it was so pretty, only that it was larger, and had some tame wild animals in it. Then God came up to him, as it might be Mr Allaby or his father, dexterously took out one of his ribs without waking him, and miraculously healed the wound so that no trace of the operation remained.

See also Edmund Gosse *Father and son* 1907 (the father was a scientist but also a fundamentalist Plymouth Brother).

JAMES JOYCE from *A portrait of the artist as a young man* 1916

He sat again in the front bench of the chapel. The daylight without was already failing and, as it fell slowly through the dull red blinds, it seemed that the sun of the last day was going down and that all souls were being gathered for the judgement.

– *I am cast away from the sight of Thine eyes*: words taken, my dear little brothers in Christ, from the Book of Psalms, thirtieth chapter, twentythird verse, In the name of the Father and of the Son and of the Holy Ghost. Amen.

The preacher began to speak in a quiet friendly tone. His face was kind and he joined gently the fingers of each hand, forming a frail cage by the union of their tips.

– This morning we endeavoured, in our reflection upon hell, to make what our holy founder [St Francis Xavier] calls in his book of spiritual exercises, the composition of place. We endeavoured, that is, to imagine with the senses of the mind, in our imagination, the material character of that awful place and of the physical torments which all who are in hell endure. This evening we shall consider for a few moments the nature of the spiritual torments of hell...

Obscurities

Some of the tyranny is due to the sanctity which inheres in any writing, as a form of magic; one is not allowed to ask what it means, or consider that the text may be corrupt. Here is a set of poems from the *Song of Solomon*, or *Canticles*, printed in the language of the AV but in the form of Moffatt's *New translation of the Bible*, rev. ed. 1935, and annotated, to elucidate the difficulties. The title of the book is properly *The song of songs*; it has no connection with Solomon; its authorship is unknown; it was probably composed in the 3rd or

FIG 7 Title page of George Wither *Preparation to the Psalter* 1619, engraved by Francis Delaram. Wither started his literary career with satire and was twice gaoled for it. In the 1620s he turned to devotional writing, including a famous book of emblems. Unsuccessful royalist soldier. Died the year *PL* was published.

2nd century BC as a collection of love poems used in the week-long
marriage ceremonies of nomadic tribes. Jewish and Christian
authorities for many centuries interpreted it as an allegory of the
relationship between God and Israel, Christ and church and so on.
See S. Stewart *The enclosed garden: the tradition and the image in 17c
poetry* 1966.

> I am the rose of Sharon,[1]
> and the lily of the valleys.
>
> As the lily among thorns,
> so is the love among the daughters.[2]
>
> As the apple-tree among the trees of the wood,   5
> so is my beloved among the sons.
> I sat down under his shadow with great delight,
> and his fruit was sweet to my taste.
> He brought me to the banqueting-house,[3]
> and his banner over me was love.   10
> Stay me with flagons,[4]
> comfort me with apples;
> for I am sick of love.
> His left hand is under my head,
> and his right hand doth embrace me.   15
> I charge you,[5] O ye daughters of Jerusalem,
> by the roes and by the hinds of the field,
> that ye stir not up, nor awake my love,
> till he please.
>
> The voice of my beloved![6]   20
> behold, he cometh leaping upon the mountains,
> skipping upon the hills.
> My beloved is like a roe or a young hart:
> behold, he standeth behind our wall,
> he looketh forth at the windows,[7]   25
> showing himself through the lattice.
> My beloved spake, and said unto me,
> Rise up, my love, my fair one, and come away.
> For, lo, the winter is past,
> the rain is over and gone;   30
> The flowers appear on the earth;
> the time of the singing of birds is come,
> and the voice of the turtle[8] is heard in our land;

[1] Crocus of the plain and anemone of the valley. The bride is speaking; the groom
replies in 3–4.
[2] Among all women.
[3] Wine tent, advertised by a flag, used as metaphor for bed.
[4] Revive me with raisins – she is worn out.
[5] Cf. adjurations in 17th-century poetry to the sun not to rise.
[6] Another poem. The lover himself speaks 28–42.   [7] He is looking in.   [8] Dove.

The fig-tree putteth forth her green figs,
    and the vines with the tender grape give a good smell.   35
Arise, my love, my fair one, and come away.
O my dove, that art in the clefts of the rock,
    in the secret places of the stairs,
let me see thy countenance,
    let me hear thy voice;   40
for sweet is thy voice,
    and thy countenance is comely.

[Take us the foxes,
    the little foxes,
that spoil the vines: 45
    for our vines have tender grapes.][1]

My beloved is mine, and I am his:
    he feedeth among the lilies.[2]
Until the day break,
    and the shadows flee away,   50
turn, my beloved,
    and be thou like a roe or a young hart
    upon the mountains of Bether.[3]

EDWARD TAYLOR from *Meditation. Canticles i. 3. 'Thy good ointment'* 1682

How sweet a Lord is mine! If any should
    Guarded, engardened, nay embosomed be
In reeks of odours, gales of spices, folds
    Of aromatics, O how sweet was he!
    He would be sweet, and yet his sweetest wave,
    Compared to thee, my Lord, no sweet would have.

O box of ointments broke; sweetness most sweet;
    A surge of spices; odour's commonwealth;
A pillar of perfume; a steaming reek
    Of aromatic clouds; all-saving health.
    Sweetness itself thou art; and I presume
    In calling of thee sweet, who art perfume.

But woe is me, who have so quick a scent,
    To catch perfumes puffed out from pinks and roses
And other muscadels, as they get vent,
    Out of their mothers' wombs to bob our noses.
    And yet thy sweet perfume doth seldom latch,
    My Lord, within my mammulary catch.

[1] Intrusive fragment from a satire on marriage.
[2] My lilies; the bride is speaking. Cf. Marvell's *Nymph complaining*, when the fawn eats roses and lilies.
[3] Spicy slopes and crevices.

Am I denosed? or doth the world's ill scents
   Engarison my nostrils' narrow bore?
Or is my smell lost in these damps it vents?
   And shall I never find it any more?
   Or is it like the hawks' or hounds' whose breed
   Take stinking carrion for perfume indeed?

This is my case. All things smell sweet to me,
   Except they sweetness, Lord. Expel these damps;
Break up this garison; and let me see
   Thy aromatics pitching in these camps.
   O let the clouds of thy sweet vapours rise
   And both my mammularies circumcise.

Shall spirits thus my mammularies suck
   (As witches' elves their teats) and draw from thee,
My dear, dear Spirit, after fumes of muck?
   Be dunghill damps more sweet than graces be?
   Lord, clear these caves, these passes take and keep,
   And in these quarters lodge thy odours sweet....

Literary and religious use of the Bible

Here is a set of allusions to the Bible, to which you should add, for
Ezekiel, the Greek myths of Cadmus and the dragon's teeth, and
Midas and the whispering reeds, the 'whispering grass' song, the
kneebone–anklebone song, and the spiritual *Hear the word of the
Lord*; and, for *Ecclesiastes*, the invocation at *PL* VII and Henry James's
novel.

T. S. ELIOT from *The rock*
   A Cry from the North, from the West and from the South
   Whence thousands travel daily to the timekept City;
   Where My Word is unspoken,
   In the land of lobelias and tennis flannels
   The rabbit shall burrow and the thorn revisit,
   The nettle shall flourish on the gravel court,
   And the wind shall say: 'Here were decent godless people:
   Their only monument the asphalt road
   And a thousand lost golf balls.'

from *Ezekiel* xxxvii The vision of dry bones
   The hand of the LORD was upon me, and carried me out in the spirit of
the LORD, and set me down in the midst of the valley which was full of bones.
   And caused me to pass by them round about; and, behold, there were very
many in the open valley; and lo, they were very dry.

And he said unto me, 'Son of man, can these bones live?' And I answered, 'O Lord GOD, thou knowest.'

Again he said unto me, 'Prophesy upon these bones, and say unto them, "O ye dry bones, hear the word of the LORD.

Thus saith the Lord GOD unto these bones: Behold, I will cause breath to enter into you, and ye shall live;

And I will lay sinews upon you, and cover you with skin, and put breath in you, and ye shall live; and ye shall know that I am the LORD".'

So I prophesied as I was commanded; and as I prophesied, there was a noise, and behold a shaking, and the bones came together, bone to his bone.

And when I beheld, lo, the sinews and the flesh came up upon them, and the skin covered them above: but there was no breath in them.

Then he said unto me, 'Prophesy unto the wind, prophesy, son of man, and say to the wind, "Thus saith the Lord God: Come from the four winds, O breath, and breathe upon these slain, that they may live".'

So I prophesied as he commanded me, and the breath came into them, and they lived, and stood up upon their feet, an exceeding great army.

T. S. ELIOT from *Ash-Wednesday* II

> Lady, three white leopards sat under a juniper-tree
> In the cool of the day, having fed to satiety
> On my legs my heart my liver and that which had been contained
> In the hollow round of my skull. And God said
> Shall these bones live? shall these
> Bones live? And that which had been contained
> In the bones (which were already dry) said chirping
>
> .   .   .   .
>
>   And God said
> Prophesy to the wind, to the wind only for only
> The wind will listen. And the bones sang chirping
> With the burden of the grasshopper, saying...

from *Ecclesiastes* xii

Remember now thy Creator in the days of thy youth, while the evil days come not, nor the years draw nigh, when thou shalt say, 'I have no pleasure in them'...

Also when they shall be afraid of that which is high, and fears shall be in the way, and the almond tree shall flourish, and the grasshopper shall be a burden, and desire shall fail: because man goeth to his long home, and the mourners go about the streets;

Or ever the silver cord be loosed, or the golden bowl be broken, or the pitcher be broken at the fountain, or the wheel broken at the cistern.

Then shall the dust return to the earth as it was; and the spirit shall return unto God who gave it.

MILTON from *Paradise regained* II 16

> And the great Thisbite who on fiery wheels
> Rode up to heaven, yet once again to come.

DRYDEN from *MacFlecknoe*

> ...He said; but his last words were scarcely heard
> For Bruce and Longvil had a trap prepared
> And down they sent the yet declaiming bard:
> Sinking he left his drugget robe behind,
> Borne upwards by a subterranean wind;
> The mantle fell to the young prophet's part
> With double portion of his father's art.

R. S. THOMAS from *The cry of Elisha after Elijah* 1960

> The chariot of Israel came,
> And the bold, beautiful knights,
> To free from his close prison
> The friend who was my delight;
> Cold is my cry over the vast deep shaken,
> Bereft was I, for he was taken...

Milton and the Bible

See the general suggestions under Religion in the list of resources at the end of *PL: introduction* in this series; and construct projects from the biblical materials offered for specific works such as *Nativity ode, Lycidas, PL* I–III, IX–XII and *PR* (e.g. consider how *Psalm* lxv or *Ezekiel* xxxiv differs from *Lycidas*). A helpful start is the biblical section of L. P. Smith *Words and idioms: studies in the English language* 1925; for something strenuous try Kenneth Burke *The rhetoric of religion: studies in logology* Boston 1961 and E. R. Leach *Genesis as myth and other essays* 1969. It is difficult to keep up with Bible commentaries and so on (some are excellent) except by visiting shops; but go to specialized 'holy' shops, and educational booksellers; general bookshops are particularly feeble in their religious departments. The best just now is the *OT illustrations* volume, by Clifford M. Jones, of *The Cambridge Bible commentary on the New English Bible* ed P. R. Ackroyd *et al.* Cambridge 1971.

The questions to consider for Milton and the Bible are: What is my response to a biblical stimulus such as, say, Abraham, Jezebel, Moab, Corinth? What would Milton's have been? What is my equivalent of his sense of the continuity, or at least the parallelism, of British with Jewish history?

ROBERT LOWELL from *At a Bible house* in *Poems 1938–49* 1950

the redwood
Thrusting short awl-shaped leaves:
Three hundred feet of love
Where the Pacific heaves
The tap-root – wise above
Man's wisdom with the food
Squeezed from three thousand years'
Standing. It is all
A moment. The trees
Grow earthward: neither good
Nor evil, hopes nor fears,
Repulsion nor desire,
Earth, water, air or fire
Will serve to stay the fall.

HILARY CORKE from *Eden* 1961

Four waters out of Eden flow
Whose crystal is most cardinal:
Four angels stand upon the wall.
Within the wall two lovers stand
Beneath the passion-fruited bough,
Are hand in hand, are I and Thou.
The angels nod with kindly faces:
All songs are silent now.

J. B. TRAPP

Iconography

Images and myths: continuity and change

Iconography is the study of visual language – of artefacts, or parts of them, or accoutrements, which carry a message. But what can we say about iconography in relation to a poet who was at least indifferent if not hostile to man-made images? Milton nowhere mentions any identifiable idol in stone, bronze or pigment, seen at home or on the European travels by which he hoped to 'improve his conversation and enlarge his knowledge of men'. Unlike Spenser or Keats, he never made poetry or prose of a specific work of art. The palace of Pandemonium is described with epic vastness, not with exact detail; in this generalized visual mode Milton largely operated. His eye for the particular was not sensitive to the arts of design. Music, pure, controllable, accessible even in blindness, was the art he loved.

Nevertheless Milton's poems have attracted a great many illustrators, from John Baptist de Medina's twelve copper engravings for the lavish 1688 edition of *Paradise lost*. There is a separate chapter on Milton's illustrators in this volume. They had been trained in and were drawing on, often at several removes and even unknowingly, a rich and ancient tradition. Some of the figures, some of the compositional and expressive formulae used by the artists, have their origin in the art of the renaissance, some in medieval, some in early Christian art, some again in Greece and Rome, and a few in the earliest Near and Middle East. The springs of Milton's myths are to be found in Eastern creation legends, and in Greek and Roman literature: they reach him enriched or impoverished, but always changed in some way, by their passage through other cultures. Versions of the same myth, from different cultures, can go to form the compound that he presents. So, too, with the pictures. Our difficulty is often to control and select the reverberations set up by Milton's or the artist's use of them and by the knowledge that we ourselves bring to our experience.

Another problem is to decide whether visually expressive formulae

162

– the equivalent of literary *topoi* – carry a charge from one culture to another; and if so, how much. Answers will vary, but it is dangerous to abandon the varied and individual historical contexts in which specific works of art have been created, for the uniform sterility of archetypes. Continuity and change are in constant interplay in the transfer of visual motives from one place, one time, to another; and the transfer is often jerky, inconsequent and – almost – haphazard. Christian artists, from the 3rd century on, endlessly repeat a grouping for the temptation and fall of man: Adam on one side, Eve on the other, of the tree of knowledge, round which the serpent coils. We can find the same grouping in Mesopotamian art – two figures, one on each side of a date palm; two priests and a symbol of fertility. In the art of Greece the same formula – man, serpent-entwined tree, woman – is used to portray the contending of Poseidon and Athena for the role of protector of Athens. The tree is an olive; the serpent sacred. An artist, probably in the 16th century, altered a classical cameo showing this scene so that it should seem to illustrate the fall of man, perhaps simply in the attempt to turn all things to good. The point here is that the compound: man + (serpent)-tree + woman (man) means different things in different contexts. Because the tree is a fertility symbol in Mesopotamia and (perhaps) in Athens, it is not necessarily so in Christian art – or if it is, it is so in a different mode. Again, some of the earliest versions of the fall of man took as the basis of their composition the subject, common on sarcophagi and painted vases, of Hercules reaching across the dragon to take the golden apples from the Hesperian tree, while a nymph looks on; but this does not mean that Adam had anything Herculean about him in a Christian context. Artists trained, in pagan studios, to portray pagan subjects merely adapted their formulation to the demands of a Christian art. It is obvious that visual formulae such as these, which are used, in different cultures, to mean such radically different things, can carry little of their original significance from one culture to another. But they do form a constant. The visual language of which they are a part – for present purposes the classico-Christian European tradition – is remarkably strong and lasting. On the other hand, lesser formulae, such as gesture and attitude, though notoriously slippery to interpret, often survive the centuries with basic meaning unaltered. Within the classico-Christian cultural frame, continuity is naturally stronger. Both visual and verbal formulations, stabilized by the sacredness of the material, remain notably steady when they are dealing with the great truths of salvation. If they become too extravagant, the church is there to discipline them. Not even Milton could make it entirely new, but like all artists, he had to borrow and adapt.

How artists borrow can be plainly seen in the history of a single movement of hand and arm in a single scene: Adam's gesture of excuse when rebuked by the Lord. His right arm, bent across in front of his body, stabs with its right index finger at Eve: 'The woman whom thou gavest to be with me, she gave me of the tree and I did eat.' This exact gesture occurs again and again in Christian art, from the earliest to the latest. It is a clear and documentable case of cumulative borrowing, with a firm textual basis in the Bible.

A more complicated instance is the placing of Adam and Eve *vis-à-vis* each other. Whether they are set one on either side of the tree (as is usual), or both to one side of it, their relative positions are almost invariably the same. Adam, the male, superior being, is at Eve's right hand, on the male side, the side of honour. This could be coincidence or the result of poverty of choice. Adam can only be to one or other side of Eve, above or below her, in front or behind. Certainly, as more complex skills develop, more complex possibilities are evolved and used – Mannerist artists will place Adam slightly behind Eve's shoulder and slightly above her, so that to offer the apple she must turn and stretch. But it is behind Eve's right shoulder that Adam stands. If this were a random matter, one would expect an even split between right and left. It can be cautiously said that the formula reflects a primitive and long-lived belief in the primacy of the male and of the right side, and in some sort of relation between them (as Hippocrates indeed says).

St Mark's: creation and fall

Cut and dried answers in such matters are not possible. It is better to look at the specific traditions of Christian iconography. The best way to do this is to go to Venice and, entering the porch of the Basilica of St Mark, turn right and walk a few paces until you are under the southernmost of its domes. Look up, and you see laid out in concentric circles within the dome the Old Testament story of our beginnings (fig 8): the Days of Creation, Adam and Eve in Paradise, Temptation, Fall, Expulsion and Toil. Six-winged seraphs guard the edges. It is an unforgettable sight, like the continuation of the Old Testament story, as far as the Deliverance of the Children of Israel, in the mosaics of the walls and lunettes and spandrels and the other five cupolas of the atrium: Cain and Abel, Noah, Babel, Abraham,

FIG 8   The Creation in mosaic, before 1220, one of the cupolas
of the atrium (antechapel) of St Mark's, Venice.

Joseph and Moses, with figures of the Prophets. From this pre-history of salvation, we pass to the stupendous mosaic series chronicling its fulfilment in the New Testament, which covers the domes and upper walls of the church proper. Like the cathedral façades of France and Italy, indeed like any programme of biblical illustration, the mosaics inside St Mark's were intended to carry the beholder from the beginnings of his cosmos, his origins in Eden and his participation in the Old Adam, through the history of his spiritual ancestors to the story of the New Adam, his Redeemer and his Judge. They also represent a norm, a constant series which survives additions and contractions, combinations and re-combinations in the art of later centuries. One of the reasons for its resilience is that the cycle as we have it in St Mark's is an astonishingly close translation into mosaic of the illustrations in a literary and very early version – the Cotton *Genesis*. This is one of our earliest fully illustrated Old Testament manuscripts; a 5th- or 6th-century codex, perhaps made in Alexandria, it was almost completely destroyed by fire in the 18th century.

At St Mark's, the story of the first three chapters of *Genesis* begins with the Spirit of God, in the form of a dove (from the beginning the almost invariable form for representing the Holy Ghost, in whatever context), haloed, on a disk, moving above the waters. Next, the Logos-Creator, the Son, the Word of God, young, cross-nimbed, in classical robes, holding a cross-staff in his left hand while he gestures with his right, index finger extended, at two rayed disks, one light, one dark: the division of light and darkness. Above these disks is a winged female figure, arms outstretched, who is the personification of the first day and the emanation of the divine light, wisdom and goodness. She comes from two sources. As the angel of the day, she may have her ultimate origin in the companions of Ormuzd, the Mazdean (Persian) god of light; but her outward form is modelled on the Victory of Greco-Roman art. The next scene shows the same Logos creating the firmament and dividing the waters on the second day, the angel of the first day now joined by another. So the story passes through the days: dry land, grass, herbs, trees; lights in the firmament (a starry sphere with the sun and moon); birds and fishes; animals – the angels increasing by one with each day, the standing Creator with his gesture of might remaining unchanged (though sometimes not appearing at all).

On the sixth day, seated, he fashions an upright red homunculus from the dust of the earth in which his feet are still stuck, while the six angels look on adoring. On the seventh, the day of rest, the

Creator, enthroned and flanked by three angels on either side, blesses the kneeling seventh Day, placing his right hand on her head. Next comes the animation of Adam, with the Creator urging forward at Adam's breast, as if to make it enter, a tiny winged soul; this owes its form to the art of Greece and Rome. (In other versions, elsewhere, the Creator bends over to breathe life into Adam's face. One early 12th-century Roman manuscript shows the soul as a dove, flying to the first man along the line of his Creator's breath. In an early 15th-century French manuscript Christ blows down a kind of trumpet on Adam's face and we glimpse the legs of a homunculus-soul as the rest disappears head-first into Adam's mouth. Another 12th-century version shows the Creator cradling Adam in his arms; this version survived at least as far as the 14th century.) Next, at St Mark's, the Creator leads Adam through the *Porta Paradisi* into the walled garden of Eden, pointing out its trees and its four rivers, Pison, Gihon, Hiddekel and Euphrates, who loll in it in the form of Roman river-gods, flowing urns at their sides. Then comes the naming of the animals, again based visually on a Greco-Roman composition, Orpheus and the beasts (there is a 4th- or 5th-century ivory in Florence which may represent either of these two subjects). Then the Creator takes a rib from the sleeping Adam and, standing apart, fashions a fully formed, standing Eve (other versions of the scene show her struggling clear of Adam's side). The Creator then presents his new creature, naked and unashamed, to her awakened mate. Later this scene often shows the Lord joining the hands of the pair, which signifies the institution of the sacrament of matrimony and the marriage of Christ with his Church.

The pace of the narrative quickens to pass from the temptation of Eve by the Serpent (the 12th-century Bible already mentioned shows him kissing her lips), to the temptation of Adam, the fruit passing from hand to hand (perhaps here a fig); then the fall, the hiding of nakedness with figleaf aprons, the concealment in the garden, the rebuke from the enthroned Creator. Eve makes a despairing gesture with her right hand and Adam points his exculpating finger. The Creator sentences the Serpent and the pair as they kneel at either side of his throne; in his mercy he clothes them, at St Mark's in togas, not the more usual skins, and himself expels them through the gates of Paradise; the symbol of their redemption, the fiery Cross, glows in a bush behind them. Expelled, Adam delves with his mattock (sometimes elsewhere with a spade. Eve sits pregnant or nursing, and spins.

Other creations and falls to the 13th century

The St Mark's mosaics do not represent the whole tradition. There were already others, which intermingle with St Mark's and each other to form the later iconography of *Genesis*. It is useful to summarize here the other traditions available to artists before the execution of the St Mark's mosaics – i.e. before about 1220, when the tide of the 12th-century renaissance and the romanesque style was turning and 13th-century eclectic learning and the Gothic style were asserting themselves. The St Mark's mosaics are, indeed, retardataire and late-classical in character. A Byzantine tradition, which we know only from later Octateuch manuscripts of the 13th and 14th centuries, uses a different iconographic type for the Creator and for his creation. The bearded figure of God the Father, which was to become universal in the West from the 14th century, stands within the spheres of the empyrean and the fixed stars and behind the sphere of the sun, moon and planets, displaying, almost embracing, his creation. That is for the first day: on subsequent days there is only the Creator's hand, stretching out of the circle of the heavens with rays emanating from it, as the agent of creation. Darkness is a woman with a veil, light a man with a torch or fire-pots. The creation and animation of Adam are effected by rays, again streaming from the hand of God in heaven to a recumbent figure in the act of sitting up under their power. The Tempter is a curious beast, half camel, half serpent. Adam and Eve, clad in skins, are expelled by the cherub and another cherub's face appears on the gate (Roman Bibles and later manuscripts have a six-winged seraph in the same place). Outside the gates, they sit in attitudes of dejection while a yoke of oxen and a plough stand idly by. We shall see that many of these formulations seep into the common stock of Western illustration during the 12th century, often through Sicily, though we cannot always plot their exact course. It looks as if the Byzantine – or at least the Eastern – tradition is responsible for the bearded Creator and ultimately for his appearance as God the Father, the universal type from the 14th century on, in the West.

Another important pre-Cotton-*Genesis*-St Mark's group of monuments are the early Christian sarcophagi and the wall-paintings of the catacombs; these date from the late 2nd to the 5th century. (It is important to remember that no monument showing an Old or New Testament subject survives which is earlier than the 2nd century AD.) A few sarcophagi show the creation of man, the only creation scene for which there was a model ready to hand in pagan art: the creation of man by Prometheus. A famous example, of about 400, the so-called Dogma sarcophagus in Rome, may be either Christian or pagan, the creator God or Prometheus. If it is Christian, it shows the three persons of the Trinity about their task, with Adam prostrate on the ground and a little naked Eve before the throne.

Also before the mosaics of St Mark's in time are the manuscript cycles attached to the two Anglo-Saxon paraphrases of *Genesis*, *Exodus*, etc. – the 'Cædmon' manuscript in Oxford (*c.* 1025) and the manuscript of Ælfric's *Hexateuch* in the British Museum (*c.* 1050). Like Milton, they have at their beginning the fall of the angels. In the Ælfric manuscript it is a single miniature, followed at once by the second day of creation. In the 'Cædmon' manuscript a Creator in glory is followed by a creation of the angels. Then war in heaven, and the fall of the angels into the monstrous fish-mouth of hell, and so on. This manuscript is the first to show the agent of temptation as other than the speaking serpent (a subject of considerable speculation) or dragon of *Genesis*. A couple of centuries later, a single variation is introduced which is then almost invariable for two centuries. But here an emissary from Satan in hell, a naked spirit, flies up to tempt Eve in the garden as a serpent. Then Satan himself, as an angel of light, brings the apple to Eve, who eats, and to Adam who doubts (a gesture repeated, in varying forms, throughout the history of the scene); urges Eve to give Adam the apple; then changes to a winged devil, with horns and a tail, spitting venom as they grovel in consciousness of their deed, and to a serpent when cursed by God.

Creations and falls from the 13th century

We have now reached again the chronological point, having looked at the pre-St Mark's monuments, where Eastern and Western iconography have thoroughly permeated each other. In the 13th century, with the growth of affective piety, new iconographic types are freely coined as books of devotion increase in number and in richness of illustration and as the great cathedral façades and porches come more and more to be decorated with the whole scheme of salvation. One of the most majestic types is the enthroned Christ-Creator (bearded, young, echoing the Christ in Majesty to be seen on the 12th-century *Portail royal* at Chartres). We see him marking out the globe of the elements – earth, air, fire and water – with a pair of compasses. The most splendid appearances of this Creator with the compasses are in the frontispieces that preside over the immense French *Bibles moralisées*, a little later than the mosaics of St Mark's, with their vast series of medallions arranged in pairs to show biblical scenes and their moral applications. Perhaps William Blake knew and used this image, which he could also have known from its verbal source in *Proverbs* viii – 'When he set a compass upon the face of the earth' – for his so-called *Ancient of Days*, though for Blake the compasses were a symbol of abhorred limit and restriction, while for the 13th-century artist they would have expressed God's infinite care in his exact creation.

Michelangelo 1508 The great painted cycles of Michelangelo's Sistine ceiling and of the Vatican Logge, designed by Raphael and executed by his pupils, will have to serve as examples from the 16th century. They are the renaissance descendants of the St Mark's mosaics and the Bibles on the cathedral façades: in them the tradition culminates. Michelangelo, when he began work on his Sistine ceiling in 1508, found the walls already frescoed with parallel scenes from the lives of Moses and of Christ, and Perugino's *Coronation of the Virgin* (*c.* 1481) where his own stupendous *Last Judgment* was later to be, on the altar wall. His ceiling takes mankind's story from Creation to Noah, with the Prophets and Sibyls in the spandrels to remind us yet more strongly that these events are the preparation for the coming of Christ. The Creator is the Byzantine bearded Father, first shown separating, by main force, as a sort of Atlas, light from darkness. As, in the next scene, he creates by his double-handed majestic gesture the sun, moon and planets and sets the firmament in the midst of the waters, he is borne up in air, the *putti* round him more adoring than supporting. Earlier tradition has been translated, transformed into Michelangelo's own 'language of the gods', just as in the creation (and animation) of Adam, where the touch of the outstretched fingers seems to allow the divine current to pass from the hand of God to the recumbent but now vitalized first parent in a radically humanized version of the old Byzantine type. (There is a convenient plate in Potter *Preface to M.*) Who the young woman is in God's left arm, and who the child on whose shoulder his left hand rests, we do not know. For his creation of Eve, Michelangelo has again used an earlier type, not from the St Mark's-Cotton-*Genesis* tradition, which usually shows Eve free-standing. Here she steps out of the body of Adam and raises her hands in supplication to her Maker. For his fall and expulsion, Michelangelo has seated Eve on the ground in *contrap-*

FIG 9 Engraving by Léonard Gaultiez after Michelangelo *The last judgment* (fresco on the altar wall of the Sistine Chapel, Vatican, 1536–41). Bibliothèque des Arts Décoratifs, Paris.

posto, reaching up and back to take the fruit from the Tempter while Adam, already tainted, reaches greedily – and exceptionally – over her to snatch at more fruit for himself. Close by, as if to suggest the rapidity of their fall, they are expelled by the angel, flying down with fiery sword. Naked and desperate, they are without even leafy girdles, as they also originally were in Michelangelo's source, Masaccio's fresco (1426) in the Carmine in Florence, and more melancholy, ashamed and afflicted than in the earlier version, despite the anguish of their cries there.

Raphael 1519 Michelangelo was everywhere drawn upon. Raphael, or the assistants who painted in 1519 the fifty-two frescoes of the so-called 'Bible of Raphael' in the Vatican Logge, borrowed Michelangelo's figure of God flying through the sky for their separation of light and darkness, the creation of the firmament and creation of the sun and moon. Of their illustrations of creation, the most striking is the creation of the animals, with God the Father walking through a landscape peopled with wild beasts and birds in amity, across a terrain strewn with other beasts half-finished, as if struggling (as in Milton) to be free of the earth from which they come.

Iconography of Adam and Eve

Having seen the history of these cycles relatively near to Milton's day, and incidentally having watched the image of the Creator reach a form approximating Milton's powerful Father, let us look more closely at the Creator's masterpiece, mankind. We have already seen something of his creation and of the creation of Eve and we have seen how the mosaic artists of the early 13th century, in their attempts to construct two perfect human beings, do not shrink from full frontal nudity. The church sanctioned it on the ground that their nakedness symbolized the frailty of their human condition, and the bodily perfections of the pair are shown as surviving the fall.

The Limbourg Brothers c. 1415 To pass from earlier medieval versions to the miraculous full-page miniature of the temptation, fall and expulsion painted by the Brothers Limbourg for the *Très riches heures* of the Duke of Berry, in the second decade of the 15th century, is to pass into the dawn of an age where the antique canons of human perfection were being found again. The miniature, all delicacy and air, shows the walled garden of Paradise, high among far-away mountains, with an elaborate Gothic gateway and a Gothic covered well or fountain in its midst. Pubic shading on Eve's naked body emphasizes her freedom from shame. She is assailed by the Tempter in the shape of a serpent with a female torso – the standard portrayal of the period; the fruit which she plucks and offers to Adam is the standard north European apple. As she takes her mate by the shoulder from behind as he kneels, he raises his left arm as if to ward off temptation's stroke. Adam's naked body is constructed on something that approaches classical proportion, again with the unashamed realism of genitals. His attitude is also antique: it is borrowed from a classical statue-type known as the 'kneeling Persian' – the warrior crouching, his arm crooked and lifted as a protection against the blow about to fall on him. The rebuke of Adam and Eve, administered by a white-bearded Father to the pair who now know their nakedness, is deflected by Adam, with the same gesture that we saw in St Mark's, towards Eve, the weaker vessel. Expelled by the fiery angel, they clutch their fig-leaves to them.

Hildesheim cathedral c. 1015 The work of the Limbourgs is a beginning and a culmination: an attempt at Mediterranean perfection in a north European language. On the bronze doors of the cathedral at Hildesheim (*c.* 1015) we can see the transalpine ancestors of the Adam and Eve in the Duke of Berry's reminder of Paradise lost. The figures in the Hildesheim rebuke are convulsed with shame: Adam, pressing his fig-leaf to him with his left hand and sweeping his right arm across his body in desperate accusation, Eve stooping and looking up apprehensively as she transfers the blame to the dragon at her feet, spitting its venom back over its shoulder. The expulsion shows the sorrow and the loss: there is nothing to match it until Rembrandt's squinting Neanderthal Adam and Eve in his *Fall of man* six hundred years later. Adam seems to grope fearfully forward into his new condition; Eve turns back to look again, in an attitude of melancholy, head in hand, no less memorable for its conventionality. It is noticeable that Eve, in such scenes, is usually shown as the more sorrowful and regretful.

The body Between the Hildesheim doors and the Limbourg miniature in time stand a whole series of sculptural and manuscript representations of the fall and its protagonists: the ravishing Eve, lying on her side, from the 12th-century sculpture at Autun (whose ancestor may perhaps be found in the manuscript of Ælfric's paraphrase); the 13th-century Adam and Eve at Bamberg, the first medieval life-size free-standing nude figures, their proportions elongated in Gothic elegance, but beginning to approach classic form. About this time, a renewed interest in the human body is beginning to show itself, with new opportunities of depicting it. This interest goes along with a change of view about what the artists should portray as the culmination of history: the Last Judgment, not the apocalyptic vision. In the Last Judgment, souls, including those of Adam and Eve, were to be shown as naked bodies, raised in perfection. The 12th century tolerated Adam and Eve's nudity as the expression of their frailty: the 13th (Vincent of Beauvais, c. 1190–1264, is a convenient codifier) positively encouraged its portrayal. The dangers of this to the unlearned, for whom visual representations were a Bible, are clear. Not only can a skilled artist provoke too much veneration for the image he has made, but his naked creations can command 'Go thou and do likewise' in a sense repugnant to morals. The Protestant reformers saw both dangers and reacted against them with violence, though the number of images of Adam and Eve produced in Germany during the first half of the 16th century alone suggests that the lesson of the fall was more than enough to counter any suggestion of indecency in the portrayal. Not long after the Council of Trent (1545–63), when Pope Paul IV wished to destroy Michelangelo's *Last Judgment* because of its indecent exposures of the human body, Daniele (Ricciarelli) da Volterra had been commissioned to clothe the offending limbs. The Inquisition had been active but no formal proscription of human nudity and other improper and indecorous subjects in religious art was issued by the Church until the decree of Trent in 1563. If they wanted an opportunity to portray the nude body artists were thenceforth better advised to illustrate pagan mythology; in religious art, they turned more and more to illustrating doctrine.

Dürer 1504 This has taken us out of our chronological sequence, but it will suggest the process by which licence encourages skill and knowledge and *vice versa*. The Gothic interest in the human body finds its artistic expression where it is allowed: its Adams and Eves are the forerunners of the attempts of Lorenzo Ghiberti (1378–1455) in Florence to re-establish the classical canons. But the first to make a systematic attempt at doing so and to apply the attempt to our first parents was the German artist Albrecht Dürer (1471–1528), also the author of a book on human proportion. The ideal figures of the

174

Adam and Eve in his engraving of the fall (1504) are achieved by means of numerous measured studies of the human body, and application of the ancient canons. The more elongated, elegant, single figures of the pair of paintings (1507) now in the Prado Museum, Madrid, in supple, leaning poses and soft contours, carry the search as far as Dürer was able. They foreshadow the Northern Mannerist renderings of such artists as Bartholomaeus Spranger (1546–1611). In many ways, Spranger is closer in spirit to Lucas Cranach (1472–1553), whose many Adams and Eves, like his Venuses, slimmer, less solid, more delicate than Dürer's, carry a stronger erotic charge.

Venice: Titian and Tintoretto c. 1565 But it is to the great Venetians, Titian (c. 1487–1576) and Tintoretto (1518–1594), that we must go for the supreme picturings of the fall. Like Dürer's and Cranach's, Titian's picture is not part of a series or cycle, but a single free-standing reminder of what we are and why, and what we have forsaken. The canvas (c. 1560–70), now in the Prado Museum, shows Adam attempting to restrain Eve from plucking the fruit, in a gesture of tenderness and alarm, more studied and rhetorical than the homely one that Adam employs in many northern painters (in Cranach, he scratches his head in doubt). Tintoretto's picture (1550–1), now in the Accademia in Venice, is one of a series opening with creation and passing to the death of Abel. In a landscape all pale browns and greens behind the two bodies, Adam recoils from the calm, soft entreaty of Eve as she holds the apple out to him, almost as if he already sees the consequences of the proffered corruption – the expulsion, which the painter has placed in the background. These are the high points of Italian achievement in the pictorial tradition of the fall of man. The tragedy is there, but the beauty of its expression softens the blow.

Rembrandt 1638 To turn from these two to the culmination of the northern tradition in Rembrandt's etching of 1638 (fig 10) is to feel the full misery of the human condition. Rembrandt has nothing, either, of the sunniness and openness, none of the blond and ruddy Flemish beauty of Rubens (whose *Paradise*, with the fall, of about 1620, is now in the Mauritshuis at The Hague). There is nothing fortunate in Rembrandt's fall. What other artist would have dared to show our first parents like this: sinister creatures, mean, already corrupt almost; Adam's body's shadow darkening Eve's belly, his left hand reaching avidly for the apple while his right shows fear and

FIG 10   Rembrandt *Fall of man*, etched 1638.

apprehension? The tempest is gathering, nature's joints cracking and straining. If this fall took place, as was the received opinion, at high noon, the midday devil prompting to sloth and lust, it was a dark noon, an unnatural one, presided over by the piggish dragon-Tempter, grotesquely horrible, in the tree.

Other images

We have reached, simultaneously, Milton's lifetime and the end of the narrative of creation and fall as it is given in *Genesis*, but there are questions still. What do the artists tell us about the angels, good and bad; especially Satan, and the Tempter? What do they show about the look and nature of the tree, of its fruit, of the character of the first sin? Do they offer us solutions to the problems which vexed the biblical commentators, such as whether Adam and Eve had navels? (On the last point the answer is fairly clear: as Sir Thomas Browne testily complains in *Pseudodoxia epidemica* 1646, the artists give little guidance, though in general and in defiance of the truth, they persist in so equipping them.) What do painters and sculptors tell us about the life and death of Adam and Eve outside paradise? There are other larger and more complicated questions too: in particular, what appearances the two make in liturgical illustration, or in other art where the artist's first concern is to illustrate the truth of the New Testament or the tradition of the Church, rather than the shadow of the Old? (There is no space to go into their transformations in alchemical illustration, the most important of the pseudo-religious metaphoric modes in which they are employed.)

Angels Some of the answers have already been seen. The female angels of the St Mark's mosaics are the direct descendants of the female Victories of Greco-Roman art – though their ancestry goes back to Babylonia. The angels of early Christian art – catacomb paintings and sarcophagi – in biblical contexts at least are young, male and wingless (the type that Rembrandt, perhaps because he had read and interpreted the Bible itself, reverted to). Angels are not invariably winged until about the 9th century and until the later Middle Ages they are as frequently female as male. The renaissance often goes back to the classical putto-genius. In scenes of war in heaven the angels are naturally male. The seraphim, until the later Middle Ages, are given three folded pairs of wings (as at St Mark's), according to the description in *Isaiah* vi. Archangels are always young men, as beautiful, or in expulsion scenes as menacing too in their beauty, as artists can make them.

Fallen angels As early as the 11th century, fallen angels are shown as blackened and misshapen, naked and stripped of their shining garments; or as tailed devils, in human form. The 13th and 14th centuries have them as monstrous, bestial figures, often shaggy, horned and tailed, claw- or cloven-hoofed, bat-winged; sometimes with deformed and hideous human faces, rat-like heads, beaks, swinish snouts; sometimes with grinning masks at bellies, pubes, shoulders, knees.

Satan There are occasional medieval picturings of the devil, in another context, as a toad; but he does not so appear as tempter of Eve except in Milton's illustrators (Lucas van Leyden's curious creature is not quite a toad). No rendering of Satan's majesty in ruin – or, indeed, of the infernal council – is to be found anywhere (except in Milton illustration) before the Satan-hero, Romantic school of criticism, though Satan is often of giant size. The Tempter himself, or rather itself (for the biblical account mentions only a serpent and not the devil) appears throughout early Christian art in the West (though not, as we have seen, in Byzantium) as some sort of serpent. Occasionally in the 11th century he is a dragon (Hildesheim doors), or changes from fallen angel to serpent, to angel of light, to devil (the 'Cædmon' manuscript); or in the 12th a clawed, beaky devil emerging from the mouth of the serpent to hand the fruit to Eve. But about the end of the 12th century or the beginning of the 13th the type develops that is almost universal until biblical text and scientific knowledge combine to dismiss it. This is the Tempter with the body of a serpent and the head and torso of a human being, usually a woman and often the mirror-image of Eve. Probably plays dramatizing the temptation and fall played a part in the development of the type. At all events, it is another instance of the medieval habit of blaming things on woman; and it gives a plausible explanation of how the serpent was able to speak to Eve. Some versions were more elaborate than others: in the 14th century a winged and glittering creature; in the painting by Hugo van der Goes (*c.* 1465, Vienna, Kunsthistorisches Museum) a female-headed salamander, all beautiful colours and poisonous breath. Other 16th-century pictures have a young man; others of the same century and the preceding, a fully grown male devil with pointed beard and horns; or a serpent devil; Titian, a putto with horns; Lucas van Leyden (1494–1533) a squat figure, half-toad, half-human. Michelangelo and Raphael still use the female-headed hybrid, but during the 16th century the Tempter becomes more and more serpent. The end of the tradition is represented by such 18th-century productions as J. J. Scheuchzer's *Physica sacra* (1731–5) which lays out, in word and image, the Mesopotamian species of the genus serpent and discusses the likely culprit.

Tree and fruit   The forbidden tree in the West is usually a fig or, more commonly in northern Europe, an apple. The Eastern tradition and some apocryphal Jewish writings speak for the fig, perhaps by way of an easy conflation with the apron-tree; and in Mediterranean areas, where figs are common, they are frequently shown as the fruit of the fall. Another Eastern tradition is for the grape, which Cranach among others puts into some of his pictures: the inflammation of wine and the inflammation of sin could easily be compared. Others occur and it often looks as if artists merely selected a fruit that was as common as sin itself in the locality where they worked. But the most usual is the apple. As early as the 5th century the pun *malum*:evil *malum*: apple helped this identification, which is proverbial today. Titian has a peach – *Persicum malum* – perhaps in allusion to the site of paradise.

Sin   To consider for a moment the nature of the primal sin, before pursuing the iconography of the fruit, and its consequences and their remedy: how was one to show its essential nature? The typological manuals seem to suggest that it had at least a strong element of gluttony. But the simplest, and from the 15th century onwards the most usual, way was to take the sin as sexuality (though most commentators denied that there was copulation in Eden). The Flemish and German painters, especially, of the 16th century, show Adam and Eve entwined in a way that makes their immediate intentions obvious – Mabuse (*c.* 1478–1533/6), for example, shows Adam casually reaching into the tree to pluck the fruit, his right arm slung round Eve's neck, so that his hand rests on her breast (Palermo, National Gallery).

The sinful fruits might grow on less material trees. There is an iconographic tradition (12th to 15th centuries) which shows a Tree of Sin, Adam at its top and Pride at its base, often opposed to a Tree of Virtues, with Christ above and Humility nourishing its root. The branches are the other six deadly sins – lechery, gluttony, avarice, wrath, envy and sloth – and the leaves their subdivisions. These are attempts to convey something of the all-embracing nature of the first sin, according to St Augustine (and to Milton) the *massa perditionis*.

Death Augustinian subtleties of *actus* and *reatus*, psychological fact and forensic guilt, can hardly be illustrated, nor the opinion that Eve fell from pride and Adam from concupiscence (or in Scotus' opinion from excessive affection for Eve). But the Pauline notion of death by sin can; and this is what is increasingly shown, in various ways and in various contexts from the 14th century onwards, especially in northern Europe and commonly at the time of the Reformation. In the fourteenth book of the *City of God*, St Augustine expounds St Paul's doctrine of the fall and in the most splendid family of manuscripts of the French translation of Augustine's work there is, at this point, a full page of the fall, in a walled paradise. Outside it, St Paul leans gravely on the sword which is his attribute and confronts Death, a skinny skeletal figure with dart and glass (halfway to the image of Time sometimes illustrated in the 16th and 17th centuries in this context). Here, the tree has nothing remarkable about it. It is sin's consequences that are the matter in hand, as they are in the four menacing woodcuts which Hans Holbein prefixed to both his Dance of Death suite and his Old Testament illustrations of 1538. These images speak explicitly of Sin and Death. In the creation cut, the emphasis is on Eve, the initiator of the tragedy; in the fall the pair are surrounded by animal images of lust and sin, an ape at Eve's back while the serpent, as if with a triumphant cry, curls down the tree. In the expulsion, Death gambols on ahead with his fiddle, on which he will play the tune they have composed for themselves to dance to; in the toil (as already in the *Bible moralisée*) he aids Adam in the work that will shorten life, while Eve sits suckling the child she has brought forth in pain, her distaff ready to hand for when this task is done. The recently rediscovered panel by Hans Baldung Grien (1484–1545) shows Death actually laying hold of Eve.

Redemption Artists, especially German artists, contemporary with or earlier than Holbein and Hans Baldung Grien, use other images for driving the lesson home, often combining these with images of spiritual life. About 1481 Berthold Furtmeyer made a striking and beautiful page for a missal: a tree of life and death with the Virgin Mary on the one side handing down the eucharist, the bread of life, to men and women of good life from one side of the tree, which bears the crucified Christ in its branches; while the other side has Adam on the ground, the serpent, and Eve handing down the apples of death (a skull in the branches on that side) to evil-doers.

Furtmeyer's miniature combines several powerful images – 'Mary, second Eve', repairer through her son of the first fault; 'Christ, second Adam', and the cross as the tree of life. All are already pictured explicitly about the year 1000 and all are widely diffused throughout the art of the Middle Ages and the renaissance. In addition, the miniature is a reworking of a figure from the much-read 14th-century poem, Guillaume de Deguilleville's *Pèlerinage de l'âme*: the living and the dead tree, which is most strikingly embodied in a painting of the German renaissance, by Lucas Cranach the Elder, of 1529, now in Gotha. Cranach's altarpiece exists in several versions and was much copied in all media and in Protestant contexts throughout the 16th century. On one side, that of the dead tree, are the fall, the absolute depravity of sin, the law, the old covenant; on the other, the green and living side, are baptism, righteousness, grace and the new covenant, with texts from St Paul to speed the lesson on its way. One extraordinary Italian image of the 17th century, by Giacinto Calandrucci (1646–1707), based on a Flemish 16th-century prototype, shows Adam and Eve shouldering the Cross as they trudge from Eden, scourged by Death and threatened by the angel. They carry their redemption with them in the hour of their misfortune. The trudge is long: there is no redemption for Adam and Eve until Judgment Day, when Christ on the rainbow, with lily and sword (as in medieval art), or striding down to damn sinners (as in Michelangelo's Sistine Chapel) or beckoning up the just (as in Rubens' *Great Last Judgment* of 1616, in Munich) raises them to heaven from the crowds of humankind.

Conclusion Eve–Mary, Adam–Christ, the Tree and the Cross – a final equation, this time a Christian–pagan one: Eve–Pandora (*PL* IV 708). There is only one instance of this, surprisingly, in the history of art: the panel in the Louvre by Jean Cousin (1490–1560), *Eva prima Pandora*, painted about 1548 for an unknown purpose, in a humanist manner as elegant as the conception. That this syncretistic image should be so isolated emphasizes how closely sacred art holds to the prescriptions and proprieties of the Church that commissioned or controlled it. As a poet in no need of a commission, Milton moves more freely among the possibilities: he can evoke pagan images only to reject them: an artist cannot.

Samson

The iconographical tradition of Samson is far less rich and complicated than that of creation and fall. Incidents from *Judges* xiii ff. are fairly often illustrated in manuscript illumination (both Bibles and books of devotion) and in 12th-century sculpture, particularly on column capitals, during the Middle Ages. Almost no extant examples date from the early Christian period. During the 16th and 17th centuries the story of Samson came more and more to be used by the painters, reaching its high point in Dutch art and especially in the incomparable images of Rembrandt. Nineteenth-century painting again found the betrayal and agonies of Samson congenial subjects.

Samson is both the Christian Hercules and one of the Old Testament heroic types of Christ; he is also both the personification of fortitude and one of the most frequently represented figures in later medieval and renaissance series of the strong or wise man overcome by the wiles of woman – Adam's heir in this too. It is in his character as the Christian Hercules and/or the type of Christ that he most often appears in medieval art: his rending of the jaws of the lion is likened to Christ's rending of the mouth of hell, or his victory over the devil; his carrying away of the gates of Gaza symbolizes either the resurrection or the bearing of the cross (the gates sometimes have a cross on them to make the lesson plainer). The later Middle Ages and the renaissance show Samson much more frequently as Delilah's victim, his hair clipped, as he lies in her lap, by shears wielded by Delilah herself, as in Mantegna's (*c.* 1430–1506) late picture in the National Gallery and Rubens's in the Alte Pinakothek, Munich, *c.* 1615, or by the Philistine, as in Van Dyck's, of before 1620, in the Dulwich College Gallery.

In the enamel plates finished by Nicolas of Verdun in 1181 for the Klosterneuburg Altar, a typical 12th-century typological series can be seen. The annunciation to the wife of Manoah by the angel is set against the annunciation to Isaac and the annunciation to Mary, and uses their pictorial formula. Samson's nativity, Manoah in the hat which identifies him as a Jew looking on at mother and midwife with the child, corresponds to the nativity of Christ; his circumcision to that of Isaac and of Christ. Samson rending the jaws of the lion as he stands and faces it prefigures the harrowing of hell; the young Samson manfully mounting the slope as he carries off the gates of Gaza is made the type of the resurrection. In all these doings of his youth Samson is beardless, with flowing hair. In the most elaborate series of the *Bible moralisée*, with painted medallions in pairs, the binding of Samson is the scourging of Christ, Delilah cutting Samson's hair is a lesson against lechery and a figure of the spirit seduced by the flesh to despair and suicide, Samson at the mill is the spiritually blind sinner, Samson brought forth to the feast to be mocked prefigures the mocking of Christ.

During the 15th and 16th centuries the scene of Samson, overcome with wine, asleep in Delilah's lap for the better cropping of his hair is common as an example of the strong man putting himself at the mercy of woman. Perhaps Mantegna's painting is one of such a series; or it may be one of a series of Old Testament women. At all events, such subjects were popular and appear in suites of engravings, especially German, tapestries and elsewhere. Most frequently they include Aristotle bitted and bridled and ridden like a horse by Campaspe or Phyllis; Virgil exposed to public derision in a basket halfway up the tower by the king's daughter; Adam destroyed by his trust in Eve and other scenes. Throughout the history of art, the most popular scene remains the rending of the lion, for which a classical prototype, Hercules and the Nemean lion, existed and was often used. This is the scene *par excellence* in which Samson exemplifies the virtue of fortitude. Sometimes, Samson confronts the lion and forces its jaws apart; more usually he stands behind its head, sometimes kneeling on its back, to do the same. In the splendid Rubens in Stockholm (*c.* 1625) the contest is one of strain and tenseness: frequently, as in Dürer's woodcut of 1497/8, Samson's attitude is almost nonchalant. From the late 15th century, even here, in his boyhood, Samson is usually bushily bearded as well as flowing-locked: the fashion of the time has more effect than the biblical text.

If the scene of Samson and the lion is overall the most frequently shown in art, it is exceeded in popularity in 16th- and 17th-century painting by the scene of Delilah's betrayal. The most magnificent Samson series, as well as the most unusual in choice of subject, comprises the five paintings by Rembrandt, dating from 1628 to 1641 – the sacrifice of Manoah (1641), in Dresden; Samson's wedding to the daughter of the Philistines in Timrath and his riddle (1638), also in Dresden; Samson threatening his father-in-law (1635), in Berlin; Samson and Delilah (1628), also in Berlin; and the blinding (1636), in Frankfurt. These images use traditional formulae, but they transcend them. Manoah and his wife do not, as the Bible says they did, 'fall on their faces on the ground': the scene suggests the annunciation to the Virgin (as in Nicolas of Verdun). They kneel in reverence and peace: there is no hint of the terror with which earlier Dutch painters had invested the scene, nothing of the flame which made Manoah say 'because we have seen God, we shall surely die', though he averts his eyes. The angel, high at the left, ascending in an effusion of gentle light rather than a flash, is in human shape. Rembrandt's language of gesture was never more beautifully and subtly employed than in this latest in time of his Samson series. Three years earlier, he had painted the much more opulent and rhetorical Samson's wedding, with the bride seated statuesque in the middle of the picture and Samson counting out to the wondering guests, on his fingers, the points of his riddle. Yet earlier is the terrible scene of the blinding, with the wide-eyed, triumphant Delilah holding out his shorn locks like a scalp to the light which streams in, while black-armoured Philistines throw themselves on Samson to bind him and one of them thrusts forward with a halberd at his face. This is great rhetoric in a 17th-century Dutch mould. So is the unforgettable image of the swarthy young giant threatening, with clenched fist, the timid, petrified, skull-capped old father-in-law, anxiously keeping the window ledge between them. Earliest in time of execution of them all is the sinister scene of Delilah calling over her shoulder to the tip-toeing Philistine behind her.

These are the supreme statements in paint of the most dramatic moments in the life of Samson: their selection of incident and their rhetorical mode are not Milton's, but in their restrained humanity they are as moving as his poem.

Further reading

M. Brion and H. Heimann, *The Bible in art. Miniatures, paintings and sculptures inspired by the OT* 1956 is a splendid picture-book, with suggestive notes; but there is no satisfactory account of *OT* iconography in English. The best dictionaries are German and the best of the shorter dictionaries is E. Kirschbaum *et al. Lexikon der christlichen Ikonographie* Rome 1968–1972. Much fuller is L. Réau *L'iconographie de l'art chrétien* including the *OT*, Paris, 6 vols 1955–9. Gertrud Schiller *The iconography of Christian art* 3 vols so far published in German, 2 in English translation, London 1971, aims at completeness in many volumes. *The Oxford companion to art* ed H. Osborne Oxford 1970 is often useful.

On more specific topics, the first chapter of Samuel C. Chew *The pilgrimage of life* 1962 is stimulating. The essay by J. B. Trapp in *Approaches to PL* ed C. A. Patrides 1968 gives a longer account, with references and pictures, of the fall. Marcia R. Pointon *Milton and English art* Manchester 1970 is richly illustrated and interesting.

Betty Radice *Who's who in the ancient world* 1971 and H. Daniel *Encyclopaedia of themes and subjects in painting* 1971 with many illustrations are useful works to start exploring from. See also the Resources for further study in art and iconography at the end of *PL: introduction* in this series, and the next two chapters here.

---

from *Adam* and *Eve* (Viollet-le-Duc's figures on Notre Dame, Paris)
He, on the cathedral's steep ascent,
stands and stares near where the rose-window is,
as if awed by the apotheosis
which, when it had reached its full extent,
set him over these and these below.
And he towers and joys in his duration. . .

She, on the cathedral's vast ascent,
simply stands there near the window-rose,
with the apple in the apple-pose,
ever henceforth guilty-innocent
of the growingness she brought to birth
since that time she lovingly departed
from the old eternities and started
struggling like a young year through the Earth. . .

RAINER MARIA RILKE 1908 trans. J. B. Leishman 1964

ROY DANIELLS

Milton and renaissance art

Mannerism

In this chapter we shall be looking into the relation between Milton's poems and two comprehensive art forms known as Mannerism and Baroque. Mannerism is the name given to an artistic manifestation falling approximately between the years 1520 and 1600 and found, for the most part, in Italy. Its characteristics will appear as we consider certain definitive works, beginning with Raphael's picture of the Transfiguration of Christ.

Raphael Raphael, born in 1483, the son of a painter, perfected his art with great rapidity and after learning all he could in Florence, went to Rome. Here at the age of 26 he was executing on the walls of some apartments in the Pope's own palace, the Vatican, a series of pictures which are among the world's masterpieces. When he died in 1520, he was engaged on his *Transfiguration*. The figure of Christ, ascended a little from a hilltop, is attended by Moses and Elijah; below, on the earth, are Peter, James and John, in a state of amazement at the sight. In the foreground, quite separated from this scene, the remaining disciples are clustered to the left, while on the right about the same number of figures support the possessed child whose story, in the gospels, follows the account of the transfiguration. The two groups gesture wildly but cannot seem to communicate. In the immediate foreground is a kneeling woman turned *contrapposto*; she is the mother of the afflicted boy. Her beauty, elegance and display of attitude seem inconsistent with her concern for him. (*Contrapposto*, a device by which the parts of the body are turned asymmetrically but balanced one against another, was to become, in various forms, a hallmark of Mannerism.)

The impression we receive from Raphael's *Transfiguration* is that of interrupted flow. The uplifted Christ appears full of love and grace

FIG 11 *The transfiguration* by Raphael 1519–20. Vatican. Peter, James and John went up the mountain with Jesus; the figures on the left are the other apostles. See *Matthew* xvii. The original is 9 feet across.

but not even his most intimate disciples can quite look at him; the rest, down below, in spite of a few gestures, have no communication with what takes place above them; the boy's family and friends have still less and the mother herself is totally unaware of the hilltop vision.

Michelangelo In the Sistine Chapel, nearby, we find Michelangelo's *Last Judgment*, begun about fourteen years after Raphael's death. It too, but on a far more massive and comprehensive scale, deals with uncertainties. One would expect the figure of Christ to be unimpeachably majestic, his double gesture uplifting those on his right hand and rejecting those on his left. In actual fact he resembles an athlete in action; his left arm rejects the sinister side while his raised right hand menaces them. He is visibly wrathful. The Virgin, close beside him, who should according to tradition be turning a benign regard on the saved, looks hesitant, mournful and anxious. In spite of the enormous sense of power in the person of Christ, there is no soaring or plunging movement in the scene. The downward moving figures of the damned are merely turbulent; the upward moving saints seem weighted and encumbered. Nothing resolves itself. All this had been anticipated on the ceiling of the chapel. There Michelangelo had earlier given us Sibyls and Prophets arrested in a duality of intention. Traditionally the media of divine communication, they seem self-absorbed, deeply anxious, apprehensive and unwilling to give forth their message. In Michelangelo, as in Raphael, there is an ability to combine attitudes and gestures of great expressiveness, often refined into extreme grace and elegance, with the implications of inhibition and uncertainty we have discussed. In one drawing of Michelangelo's we find the flagellation of Christ – though it represents a victim who is bound and being beaten – given the grace and rhythm of dance. It is hard to explain why this peculiar elegance should appear in the arts at this time but there is no question as to its wide influence and persistence.

We turn now to a pair of Mannerist painters of a somewhat younger generation: Pontormo and Parmigianino.

Pontormo Jacopo Pontormo (1494–1556) was an odd, shy, secretive man, whose house contained a studio reached only by a ladder, which he could draw up after him. He was deeply religious and expressed his devotion in paintings full of graceful but strangely tense figures. Pontormo's masterpiece is his *Deposition* – a name given to any representation of the taking down of Christ's body from the cross. At first sight, this altarpiece seems decorative rather than thematic. The positioning of heads and arms creates a rising, oval spiral. The body of Christ is clearly substantial but the young angelic bearers seem ready to levitate. The colours, in addition to lighting a dark chapel, induce a state of mind. They have unexpected tonal values. Pink, red, yellow, blue, purple, green, beige, brown: they are all bright and luminous. We are already prepared for something extraordinary by the absence of the traditional rocky tomb and three crosses. These colours further predispose us to enter a world unrelated to space or time, where the body of Christ has become sacramental. The balance of sensibilities to be evoked and those to be avoided is extremely delicate. Grief at the Saviour's death is refined into wonder. The body, historically scourged, battered, pierced, becomes instead an immaculate presence. The deposition-burial theme, heavy with a sense of death, must suggest instead the life-giving power of the sacramental flesh and blood. At the same time, the image of Christ as triumphant in resurrection must on no account be anticipated. The scene must be timeless and unlocated because the resurgence of spirit which it offers to the faithful, though limited in scope and in need of perpetual renewal, is always accessible where two or three are gathered together. The mind lifts; it does not soar.

Pontormo's *Deposition*, like many other Mannerist works, reveals the inner state of mind of the artist, not an external event in its actual or traditional form. This subjective image or *disegno interno* is one of Mannerism's distinguishing traits.

Parmigianino Francesco Parmigianino (1503–40) was born in Parma, where much of his best work is still to be seen. He too was a strange and intense character. When young he was noted for his elegance and pleasant manners but toward the end of his short life he became interested in alchemy, appeared long-haired and unkempt, neglected his work, was imprisoned for failing to keep to a contract, and, when he died, was at his own request buried naked with a cross of cypress on his breast. He evokes both admiration and sympathy.

The best-known work of Parmigianino is his *Madonna of the long neck* in Florence. The Virgin has a grace and elegance which would seem voluptuous if they were not restrained by an extreme stylization. As its name implies, this picture relies on elongation of the figure to the point where, miraculously avoiding any suggestion of attenuation, emaciation or caricature, the Madonna and Child seem ready to levitate from the throne where she is seated. The right side of the composition carries the eye back, first to an ascetic prophet-like figure, small in the distance; then to a row of slender columns without capitals, complying with the convention of a classical ruin but resembling instead a colonnade of great elegance; and finally to a distant skyline. The left side, by contrast, is closely packed with eager spectators; they are angels, but more seductively beautiful and smooth-limbed than worshippers should be; one of them holds aloft a delicate oval vase, symbol of the womb of the Virgin, filled although sealed.

Far from displaying a clear contrast between pagan voluptuousness and Christian asceticism, this composition mingles them in ways suggestive of unexpected interrelation. A delicate equilibrium is achieved; no impulse is carried through, no emotion decidedly asserts itself. Everything seems poised in an uncertainty.

Mannerism in Milton's early poems These 16th-century Italian paintings invite comparison with Milton's pre-war compositions. It would be of interest to note how, in the *Nativity hymn*, pagan and Christian elements are unexpectedly balanced, and with what loving care Milton evokes the last enchantments of the pagan age. It is tempting to linger over *L'allegro* and *Il penseroso* and see that, although these figures objectify the desires of Milton as Puritan student, at no point is either of them a participant in the action described. *Comus* and *Lycidas*, however, claim our full attention.

The uniqueness of *Comus*, considered as drama, is that the characters never do connect with each other. The Brothers, having delivered two strangely unrelated sets of speeches, fail to arrest Comus and cannot release their sister. When Comus and the Lady encounter, their dialogue is from two irreconcilable viewpoints and its declamations seem to be delivered for the benefit of the audience; the Lady's utterance has a 'different pace' from that of her tempter. The Lady has not a word to say to her rescuers; the Brothers are almost as limited in their communication. In other respects, too, there is an odd lack of sweep or continuity in *Comus*. Each character has his own habitat and carries his own impenetrable aura with him as he moves about. Jove, we suppose, inhabits a classical Olympus; the Spirit, a Platonic world; Comus, the enchanted wood; the young Bridge-waters, a pastoral region adjacent to Ludlow; Sabrina, a submerged fairy world; Venus and Adonis, the Hesperides; the God whom Milton ultimately evokes, the heaven of Christian belief. In these and many other ways, *Comus* is characterized by discontinuity, limited releases of action, and unfulfilled moral implications. The reader finds refuge in the compelling beauty of the images, as Sabrina did among the water nymphs who 'held up their pearlèd wrists and took her in'.

Let us go on to *Lycidas* in the context of Mannerism. The central or thematic figure in a Mannerist painting is commonly, by any one of a variety of devices, rendered ambiguous or hard to locate. Why in *Lycidas*, we ask, is grief for Edward King so quickly disposed of? Why is the poet's concern for his own career, if that is in fact the central theme, so strangely contorted? (e.g. the revision of 'his goarie scalpe rowle down' into something milder, as though Milton were afraid of his own apprehensions?) Why is Christ, pervasive in the poem, specifically introduced only obliquely? Why do the Muses, old Damaetas, the nymphs, Camus, the sensuous Amaryllis and Neaera, all appear so fleetingly and leave so slight a mark, while St Peter holds the centre of the stage for about one-eighth of the poem? As Mannerist paintings often make their most telling impact by refusals to satisfy expectation, so, in *Lycidas*, Milton rises to an impassioned eloquence in passages that are, by his own admission, interpolations. There is a weighty pronouncement by Phoebus Apollo (whom we have seen in Milton's *Vacation exercise* representing Christ); and there is an outburst from Peter, the wrathful one among the apostles. After each tremendous intrusion, we are carefully returned to Fountain Arethuse or to the banks of Alpheus, but no one can pretend that the pattern of the pastoral lament has not been changed, the colour of its oratory made more vivid, its location in time and place wrenched, its focus shifted. The *disegno interno* of Milton's secret griefs, projected on to public affairs, has produced a succession of figures related to one another by little more than their capacity, stage by stage, to embody, with elegant if somewhat strained *contrapposto*, the exact state of Milton's mind. Even in its ostensible resolution, *Lycidas* betrays a hesitation or suspension between two polarities. We seem to see the lost friend entering heaven, but immediately it becomes apparent that he is washing his locks with nectar on the outskirts of a classical Elysium and that, far from being lost to this world, he returns as a classical genius of the local shore. This is a real interpenetration of opposing traditions, for these images do not translate themselves into easy Christian equivalents.

It has been shown that what in the arts might be called a Mannerist sensibility is found to correspond fairly well with changes in the relation of the artist to sources of power, particularly of absolute power. One would not wish to force a close parallel between the brief perfection of the high renaissance in Italy and in England – what has been likened to a *cresta sottile*, a wave's short-lived crest, the summit of a ridge; but if we consider the shift, after Spenser's death, from Elizabethan stability (however precarious) to Jacobean forebodings and Caroline realizations of acute conflict in church and state, and compare this to the troubles in Florence when the republic fell, and corresponding troubles in Rome, leading to the sack of 1527, the similarities are of interest. This was particularly so in the lives of creative artists who, without losing sight of Christian and Platonic ideals, found themselves disorientated from sources of absolute power – in hereditary monarch, Machiavellian prince, reigning pope, or Almighty God. Michelangelo speaks of an interview between himself and the Pontiff with a rope (literally or figuratively) about his neck. Milton, losing his loyalty to king and established church, but passionately devoted to the will of God, was early embarked on a course that would endanger his life and leave him with no ultimate resource but divine compassion.

One source of the strangeness of Mannerist sensibility is, then, a disturbed relation between the artist and his patron, or his prime source of beneficent power. This disturbance has usually some connection with the impermanence of high renaissance forms and ideals.

Baroque

The thirty years between *Lycidas* and *Paradise lost* brought a change in the concept of government in England, and a shift in European sensibility affecting both the arts and the sciences. From the suspensions and frustrations expressed in his earlier poems, Milton moved on into the experience of real and effective power: the impact of propaganda; the shock of Cromwell's cavalry charges; the defiance of authority by rebels; the resurgence of defeated forces and the Restoration of Charles II; the crushing afflictions in his personal life. In ways difficult to explain, Milton also acquired the devices of style that would serve to express his mature sensibility, so profoundly changed.

Long ago, critics noted the influence of Tuscan poets on the style of *Paradise lost*. The impact of Italian architecture, painting and statuary upon Milton, even during the months of his stay in Italy, is incapable of such assessment. It is known that Bernini and Milton were both present at an entertainment in the Palazzo Barberini, itself a fine example of Baroque design. Bernini was then at the height of his powers and during the previous decade had been occupied in imposing Baroque form on St Peter's and its environs.

Bernini Gianlorenzo Bernini (1598–1680) enjoyed a lifetime neatly encompassing Milton's. His father was a Tuscan sculptor, his mother a Neapolitan woman. A passionate man, of enormous vitality, he could be called the creator of Roman Baroque. Five popes employed his services. He largely determined how we look at St Peter's both from within and from without. His Triton's Fountain in Piazza Barberini, his Fountain of the Rivers in Piazza Navona, and his dramatic statuary in the Villa Borghese, are among Baroque's definitive works. He was a man of intense religious feeling, a friend of the Jesuits and willing servant of the papacy. Like Milton, he was pre-eminent in his own field and eager to devote his creative powers to the service of God.

The most striking faculty possessed by architects and other artists who created the Baroque style was that of projecting a concept of absolute and undivided power. This basic impulse is apparent even in armorial bearings and details of decoration – crossed keys for papal authority, the sun emblem for Louis XIV. In sacred architecture and adornment, the power of Christ, as ostensible subject, is easily shifted to the authority of the Church and the power of the pope. In secular building, the glory of kings and princes takes its place. In England, although the civil war put a damper on regal and ecclesiastical power (preventing, for example, the expansion of Whitehall into a grandiose palace), yet the impulse toward a supreme expression of Baroque was not denied: the architecture of Milton's cosmos in *Paradise lost* is the most impressive fulfilment in existence of the principles of Baroque design.

Before expanding this statement, we should look, however cursorily, at some definitive Baroque. A good place to begin is St Peter's Basilica in Vatican City. This vast edifice, reputedly erected over the apostle's grave, is the centre of the Roman Catholic world. Every visitor is impressed, if not overwhelmed, by Bernini's masterly handling of space in the approach to St Peter's. He may not be aware that Mussolini, by cutting an avenue – via della Conciliazione – straight up to the piazza, negated the element of surprise that was intended and has made impossible the sudden total impact of a sight long expected and at last superbly revealed. As Milton's Satan, after struggling through chaos, sees our universe in the distance and then,

FIG 12 Aerial view of the Vatican and St Peter's, Rome, the cathedral church of the Pope and the Roman Catholic Church. The piazza designed 1656–67 by Gian Lorenzo Bernini. (The dome is by Michelangelo.)

reaching the opening, 'Looks down with wonder at the sudden view Of all this world at once', so the 17th-century pilgrim to Rome, after finding his way through the narrow streets of the adjacent Borgo district, strove toward the domes (of which, from the Bridge of Angels that had carried him over the Tiber, he had already achieved a distant view) and came suddenly to a sight of the vast piazza with its cheerful fountains, and beyond them the columned facade of the Basilica, as uniquely impressive in its symbolic assertion of power as in the claim its apostle had to primacy.

There was a refinement which Bernini planned but could not execute because his patron died. In addition to the huge, curving, quadruple colonnades stretching like two arms to embrace the faithful gathered in the piazza, there was to be a third and much shorter colonnade standing a little back from the area between the ends of the larger ones. This area would thus have formed a kind of portico, from which the pilgrim, already sheltered, would have been able to view in one sweep the whole of the symbolic piazza into which he was advancing. Milton, with a similar design upon his readers, uses an analogous device. Through Satan's eyes we see our universe and all the stars, 'with wonder'; on Michael's mount of vision, Adam sees the earth from China to Peru; before the throne of God, not only do we sense total space but also past and future time, into eternity. In each instance there is a sense of mastery in the observer, as well as of comprehensiveness in what is seen.

The pilgrim, as he crosses the piazza, may pause at a particular marked paving stone and, from this focal point, be amazed to see the forest of columns in the colonnade lined up to present the appearance of a single row; he can now look out into the world and see with what ease all may come into the fold. Similarly, Milton invites every reader to come into the story of 'our woe' and of how Christ shall 'restore us'.

In the centre of the piazza stands the magnificent Egyptian obelisk (nearly twice as high as Cleopatra's Needle on the Thames Embankment), which cost so much forethought, ingenuity and labour to re-erect that the event has already become a legend. Crowned with a cross and bearing now the inscription CHRISTUS REGNAT, this obelisk exemplifies the Baroque desire to master even the most weighty and intractable symbols of power in the pre-Christian world and force them to acknowledge a new rule; so, on top of the column of Marcus Aurelius, St Paul has displaced the statue of the emperor, and on Trajan's Column St Peter has similarly triumphed. Milton's use of classical materials is on a par with this architectural practice: the fallen angels are equated to pagan gods; Athens and Rome, presented with the fullest appreciation of their beauty and strength, are nevertheless formally declared inferior to Jerusalem; the enchantments of classical myth are employed to point a moral or adorn a tale.

Power, it is said, tends to corrupt. The art of Milton and of Bernini, though more single-minded and explicitly concerned with triumph than that of Shakespeare or of Michelangelo, is in neither instance as great, as humane, as universal or as persuasive. The pilgrim entering St Peter's looks down the arching nave and sees, in the far distance and framed by the pillars of Bernini's *baldacchino*, the *cathedra*, above which, in the stained glass of the lofty window of the apse, the Dove is seen descending. It is true that there are two altars in this axial perspective of St Peter's but they are overshadowed by these symbols of papal authority. The *baldacchino*, standing directly under the dome, rears its huge, bronze corkscrew columns to support an equally monumental bronze canopy, thus perpetuating on an heroic scale the traditional canopy carried by four standard-bearers over the pope, in processions. The *cathedra*, an idealized bishop's throne in bronze, similarly monumental, represents the pope's seat of authority, an authority emphasized by the bronze supporting figures, on a grand scale, of two Greek and two Latin fathers of the Church who supported the Roman claim to primacy. It is the authority of the pope that is being urged with such overwhelming eloquence; it is not the saving power of Christ. St Peter's is less a place of worship than a proclamation.

A parallel insistence appears in Milton. The self-justifying God of *Paradise lost* III; the rejection of Athens in *Paradise regained*; Samson's slaughter of the Philistines: within the terms of the debate as Milton sets it up, these cannot be questioned, but they have the uneasy finality of a manifesto. The somewhat forced alliance of faith and reason that characterizes Baroque provokes a sense of wonder rather than of mystery and to that extent robs absolute power of its credibility. The rational autocrat is likely to appear, at least intermittently, a tyrant. That both Milton and Bernini sweep over and subdue these questionings does not entirely extinguish them.

Metamorphosis One remarkable parallel between Bernini and Milton is their interest in metamorphosis – the kind of sudden transformation that sums up a whole life by showing what has been, changing before one's eyes into what will be. The Son, mounting his chariot of vengeance; Eve eating the apple; Satan on his belly prone; these are moments filled with emotion in which we share, designed to impress on us the actuality of psychological crisis, laden with implications of past and future, which meet at these points of decision. Bernini's sculptures of *David, Pluto and Proserpina, Apollo and Daphne, St Teresa* and *Vision of Constantine* beautifully illustrate this preoccupation with metamorphosis. In Daphne we see a nymph who is becoming an olive tree with such rapidity that, though she still seems to be in flight, her toes are becoming rooted, bark is sheathing her body and her upflung hands are branching into foliage. Similarly, David is seen with his eyes fixed on Goliath and the stone on the point of whirling to leave the sling; from this point we know, and are reminded by Saul's armour lying unused, that David will never be the same again.

The Baroque handling of metamorphoses is an advance on the classical use, as in Ovid. When we consider Eve or Satan in *Paradise lost*, or David among others in the Borghese museum, or Constantine at the entrance of the Vatican, we find ourselves in the presence of symbolic or representative characters. Each is caught at a moment of personal crisis coinciding with a crisis of divine purpose; in each instance, the outcome, in addition to summing up the total experience of the individual, provides a node or punctuation in the vista of Christian history.

Allegory Baroque artists bend many traditional devices to their own ends. In addition to classical metamorphosis, they find medieval allegory a malleable form. It is not allowed to develop along medieval lines, on its own plane which must then be transposed to the plane of common experience. On the contrary, it is generally obliged to serve some urgent purpose. Bernini's figure of Truth, although it makes use of the conventions of allegorical expression, is an embodiment of the sculptor's personal dismay and hope, at a crisis in his life; he willed that it should be kept as a memorial in the perpetual custody of his family. Milton's Sin and Death, although so dramatically presented and given so close a relation to Satan, are nevertheless dismissed when they have served their allegorical turn. No decorative Dance of Death accompanies Adam and Eve from the Garden. Similarly, as we read we find that chaos is far more real as spatial experience than as allegorically enthroned in space. Milton and Bernini are intensely possessed by a feeling for actuality; allegory is not their natural mode of expression.

Borromini Bernini furnishes many analogues to Milton because his art took a conceptual turn. He wishes to record history, to express beliefs, to embody ideas. A more subtle set of parallels can be sought in the work of Borromini, an architect in whose mind formal considerations, hardly to be expressed as ideas, were uppermost. Francesco Borromini (1599–1667), although somewhat overshadowed by the fame and success of Bernini, possessed a more original, subtle and attractive genius. His influence upon the design of palaces and churches in Europe was widespread. The cathedral in Birmingham is clearly indebted to his buildings. Although Borromini is difficult to analyse, he is useful to us because he parallels, as Bernini does not, the mysterious inner light by which Milton composed. The cherubs for which Borromini is famous seem to have come straight from heaven, filled with perception and divine compassion. Like Milton, he had a capacity, which seems almost miraculous, to impart unity of effect to aggregations of diverse elements. His personal philosophy appears to have been that of the Stoics and it is believed that it was in a spirit of Stoicism and not of despair that he took his own life.

His church of San Carlo alle Quattro Fontane in Rome, begun in the year that *Lycidas* was published, creates a monumental effect of modulated but unrestricted space within a site so confined that – according to popular tradition – the ground-plan is no larger than the cross-section of a single main pillar in St Peter's. The interior of San Carlo advances its sixteen Corinthian columns, grouped to catch the eye, while the wall seems to retreat from them by continuously curving and by turning into niches, panels and frames suggestive of anything but solid backing. Vigorous and explicit assertion is thus complemented by a sense of fluid movement and unbounded recession. By innumerable subtleties Borromini persuades us to accept his volume of space as monumental and illimitable. The site is rectangular, the facade itself is curved. The dome is in origin renaissance; the renaissance circle, however, has become a Mannerist oval. The length of the nave suggests the form of a Latin cross; the handling of the apses connected by the shorter axis is, however, such as to create the illusion of a Greek cross, with equal arms. 'The spectator is stimulated to let his eye wander ceaselessly', said one of the ecclesiastics for whom Borromini designed the church. Light and space were, for Borromini, inseparable. His handling of clarity and obscurity had the effect of vitalizing forms by reducing their rigidity, by creating an interplay between solids and vacancies. He could even guide the course of light by reflecting it from stone.

How beautifully these elements in Borromini's work correspond to Milton's devices and effects in *Paradise lost* will be immediately apparent. The garden of Eden is walled but we never, from the inside, approach its boundaries. Adam looks up into a starry heaven but never sees, beyond the spheres, the containing shell. We are never able to conceive a plan for the garden; it is a place of various view. The acts of power and purpose in *Paradise lost* are realized against time-schemes that fade into world history or into eternity. As we move through chaos, we have no inclination to go right or left; the axis of will from God, inviting Adam and Eve upward and thrusting Satan downward, absorbs all sense of direction. Total space has from eternity been within the mind of an omnipresent God; from chaos he has effected a limited withdrawal of his ordering power; hell is scooped out from the lower levels of chaos; our universe, measured with golden compasses, is contained within its shell. Intercommunication among these spatial regions goes on all the time; even Raphael is seen in heaven, on earth, in passage, and in hell's environs. Light continually defines spatial relations: God is light and even Satan orients himself by this outpouring; Uriel comes and goes on a sunbeam; the cycle of life in Eden is not seasonal but diurnal, determined by light of sun and moon.

Later developments Bernini (1598–1680), Borromini (1599–1667), Poussin (1593/4–1665) and Rembrandt (1606–69) are men of the same generation as Milton (1608–74). As the 1660s proceed, they all adopt styles less freely flowing and ebullient, more contained and restrained than hitherto. Similarly, *Paradise regained* and *Samson agonistes* can easily be identified as Milton's on stylistic grounds, yet the reader feels a profound difference. The vast energies of Baroque are not, as in *Paradise lost*, released in great acts of creation, rebellion, or judgement. In *Paradise regained*, the Son of Man declines to act; his powers are totally reserved for his coming work of redemption. In *Samson*, the hero is incapable of action until his stored-up energies are released in one act of retribution and deliverance. A sense of cosmic equilibrium prevails.

Poussin In Poussin's *Apollo and Daphne*, a pastoral scene reveals a dozen of the Immortals, including Apollo, Mercury, Cupid, Daphne and Peneus, in a sweeping line of relaxed forms brought round into a stable oval by figures farther off and by a group of cattle. The childish Cupid has bent his bow, which no one takes much notice of except

FIG 13 *Inspiration of the epic poet* by Nicholas Poussin (1593/4–1665). Calliope, muse of epic poetry; Apollo, god of poetry; the poet. Louvre, Paris.

Daphne. He is about to pierce her heart with a leaden arrow as he has already pierced Apollo's with a golden one. Poussin, as a minute analysis of the picture has revealed, is portraying the tension between life and death, between heat and moisture, between fertility and virginity. Upon this balance, his philosophical studies told him, the harmony of the world depends.

Nicolas Poussin was born in Normandy. After working in Paris, he went to Rome in 1624. Though he returned to Paris in 1640, he stayed only eighteen months, then returned to Rome where he continued to paint until his death. His resemblances to Milton include a commitment to the expression of ethical and religious ideas, an intense seriousness of purpose in his art, a cosmic sense growing out of his beliefs. Poussin's friends regarded him as a painter-philosopher who worked from his head, as one of them put it. Like Milton, he was adept at combining forms derived from the ancient pagan world with Christian themes. His *Adoration of the golden calf*

(National Gallery, London) has in the foreground a group of revellers, Bacchanalian figures dancing before the idol. In the distance, Moses and Joshua are seen carrying the Tables of the Law down from Mount Sinai, and the gestures of Aaron and of a kneeling group on the right side are made to carry the eye diagonally across the composition, past the golden calf, to the pair who are bringing down the word of the true God. If, as Poussin would assume, we are well grounded in the text of the Old Testament, we foresee that judgement will fall on three thousand of these revellers. At the moment, positive and negative elements are suspended and in balance.

Poussin's paintings illustrate the 17th-century imagination in landscapes, episodes and symbolism elaborately deployed. Among the most useful and accessible paintings of this kind are his *Four seasons* in the Louvre. They present a world of natural beauty, of religious significance and of classical allusion. Like the episodes of *Paradise lost*, they have a literal sense and a number of deeper, interrelated significances. *Spring* shows us Adam and Eve in the garden, where, as we know, the season never changes. In their conjugal happiness, we see the sacrament of marriage. The sun is rising and may be taken as a reference to Apollo. *Summer* shows Boaz and Ruth in the foreground. Behind them and stretching into the distance is a fabulously opulent field of wheat which reapers are cutting and binding into enormous sheaves. It is noon and maidens are laying out loaves of bread, doubtless made from this same grain, which five horses are threshing out in the distance. The bread of the eucharist is clearly symbolized; Ruth on her knees and Boaz blessing her are ancestors of Christ as Man. The glow of noon suffuses this mellow scene of harvest and it takes little imagination to feel that Ceres herself is present among the sheaves. In *Autumn*, the spies sent by the Children of Israel in the land of Canaan are returning with an immense cluster of grapes, borne on a staff between them. These complete the symbolism of the eucharist. It is possible that other doctrinal meanings lie just below the surface: as Adam and Eve recall man in innocence, without law, and Ruth with Boaz the Church as the Bride of Christ, this scene may suggest the Promised Land and the theme of fulfilment. It is afternoon and autumnal grapes, together with apples being harvested, may remind us of Bacchus and of nature's abundance. *Winter* presents Noah's Flood, with great expanses of chilling water steadily rising. It prefigures the Last Judgment. Doomed humanity struggles with the rising tide, watched from the rocks by a great serpent, himself also doomed. The Christian

FIG 14 *A dance to the music of time* by Poussin. Wallace Collection, London. Apollo as sun-god, hence master of time, as well as god of poetry; Time playing the lyre. For comparison with Milton's imagination in pastoral settings such as the early poems and *PL* IV.

reference is clear and may extend to the sacrament of baptism, for the ark, seen in the distance, is safely buoyed up; a rainbow of hope arches over it as the declining sun breaks through clouds. We see the destiny of mankind, whether saved or lost. The snake suggests an underworld, of Satan or of Pluto.

Poussin, like Milton, is deliberately exploiting the riches of tradition, both Christian and classical. The stories are biblical; the figures are in attitudes made familiar by classical friezes and sarcophagi. The five horses galloping abreast have galloped off a Greek vase. The flood scene owes its terror to Michelangelo's Flood, in the Sistine Chapel. Amid these likenesses, it is instructive to sense differences: Poussin, even in the last of his four scenes, is insisting on the divinely ordered harmony of the universe, the cyclical round of life, the triumph of fertility and the certainty of salvation. Milton, in handling these same themes, brings in the power and necessity of will, the decisive acts of God, of men and of obedient or rebellious angels. Milton is demonstrative, where Poussin is allusive. Milton convinces, while Poussin persuades.

Rembrandt An opportunity for the exercise of critical discrimination presents itself if we consider, side by side, the life and works of Milton and those of Rembrandt van Ryn (1606–69). Born in Leyden, at the time when Holland was achieving freedom and independence, Rembrandt settled in Amsterdam in 1632. He showed, early in his career, a cast of mind and kind of vision that Milton would have understood: his *Scholar in a lofty room* (National Gallery) combines a theme of meditative seriousness with the accentuating power of well-handled light and shade. Like Milton, he helped to create a 'Protestant iconography' – a set of representations of sacred and moral subjects so compelling that the one always brings to mind the other. To think of Adam and Eve is to recall Milton's garden: to mention the Prodigal Son is to see Rembrandt's two figures inclining toward each other.

After the death of his first wife, Rembrandt, amid many trials and misfortunes, devoted himself increasingly to biblical subjects. In the Louvre we can find his *Supper at Emmaus* (1648), an example of his power to make the substance of this world reveal itself as fraught with supernatural significance; not only the bread broken by Christ, but the intensity of the whole situation makes this apparent. We recall Milton's repeated demonstrations of the divine origin and essential goodness of our material world.

Rembrandt excelled in portraits. *Bathsheba* (Louvre) portrays his second wife. His self-portraits, of which examples may be seen in Kenwood (Hampstead) and in the National Gallery, reveal the progressive stages of his life both physical and spiritual. A concern with the destiny, as well as with the appearance or character, of the person portrayed is Rembrandt's hallmark; again we are reminded of Milton, who could never write of himself except in a context of dedication and every one of whose created characters defines his role with reference to the will of God. What differentiates Rembrandt from Milton is his gradual withdrawal from the externals of Baroque design, into a shadowed world of deep and quiet implications. Milton's *Paradise regained* and *Samson*, though quieter and more meditative than *Paradise lost*, are still explicit in their grand statement of purpose and their marshalling of the forces of right reason.

Tintoretto The National Gallery possesses a splendid, glowing *St George and the Dragon* by Jacopo Robusti 'Tintoretto' (1518–94), one of the masters of Mannerist techniques. In the middle distance, St George flies at the fiery-tongued dragon at full gallop and with his lance pierces his open jaw. This tremendous pounce and thrust is curiously at variance with the prostrate body of a previous, unsuccessful attacker, with a background of fairy-tale castle walls and trees bordering the sea, and with the princess herself, whose position in the immediate foreground enables her to make a display of jewels, and of blue and crimson satin swirling out and quite immobilizing her, though she is, we suppose, fleeing. Overhead the same uncertainties appear, as a heavenly figure in a burst of brilliant rays is seen against storm-clouds still undispelled.

Rubens In London there can also be seen the last surviving ceiling painted by Peter Paul Rubens (1577–1640). It is an apotheosis of James I, in the Banqueting House at Whitehall, and shows the king rising with the willing aid of angels toward a triumphal wreath held out in readiness to crown him. It is pure Baroque, brilliant, lively and by its vigour saved from absurdity.

Wren Although no Baroque monuments could be erected in England during the period of the civil war and although the Puritans were naturally averse to shows of papal, ecclesiastical or royal power, a Baroque style in architecture can nevertheless be acknowledged in England. Sir Christopher Wren (1632–1723) rebuilt St Paul's after the Great Fire. Its emphasis, within, upon a central space, which he succeeded in unifying with the traditional nave and aisles, marks St Paul's as Baroque in conception, a judgement confirmed by the grandeur of its dome as seen from a distance and dominating the city of his day. The first stone of St Paul's was laid in the year following Milton's death. Wren's genius lay in his power to combine the architectural features his patrons wanted with influences borrowed from continental buildings into one magnificent impression of wholeness.

Milton It is helpful to see Milton's life and works as a transposition into English terms of issues and forms of expression common in Europe of the 16th and 17th centuries. The conflict in England between Anglican bishops and militant Puritans paralleled the far more bitter confrontations of the Reformation on the continent. The attempt of the Stuarts to perpetuate a conception of rule by divine right was similar in kind though not in degree to the claims made by emperors and popes abroad. Milton's own intransigent stance as a Puritan Independent was no more stubborn than the stand taken by Anabaptists in Germany.

Milton's architecture involves splendid gates and walls, huge vistas, an ascent from far by steps, a spacious park, great places of assembly, thrones and fortifications. These are similar to the works of Baroque architects but vaster and more sumptuous. The proclamations, audiences of state, weapons of war, journeys undertaken and purposes disclosed are similarly in the Baroque mode but of a scale unmatched.

Milton's Puritan temperament and sensibility make it inevitable that certain dominant themes in continental art should be transposed when used in *Paradise lost*. The theme of martyrdom becomes that of heroism. Abdiel is never in danger of his life; he is a faithful witness enduring hostile scorn. Similarly, the mystical ecstasy apparent in such a work as Bernini's St Teresa is not for Milton's sensibility; her expression of swooning rapture when pierced through by a dart in the hands of an angel is outside his range. His own equivalent is the calmness and confidence of the Son of Man when assaulted by temptation in *Paradise regained*. Devotional piety is a pervasive theme of Baroque painters; Milton substitutes a deliberate dedication of the will.

Baroque angels are especially notable. Bernini lined the balustrades of a bridge crossing the Tiber by St Peter's with angelic figures bearing nails, crown of thorns and other instruments of the crucifixion. Their faces express extremes of sorrow, dismay and compassion. Borromini's cherub heads are similarly filled with tenderness. Milton's angels, though compassionate, are primarily beings filled with power and purpose. Michael is both kind and understanding, but his demands on Adam are exacting and peremptory.

For the power of earthly rulers, whoever they are, Milton simply substitutes the power of God himself, undelegated. As a result, his characters show little of the humility which tradition attributes to the saints but rather an assumption of dignity, firmness and confidence, befitting one who feels that his will has been surrendered to a higher and divine will.

Further reading and looking

GOMBRICH, E. H. *The story of art* 1954.
  Symbolic images: studies in the art of the renaissance 1972.
HAUSER, A. *The social history of art* 1951.
PANOFSKY, E. *Studies in iconology* Oxford 1939.
PEVSNER, N. *Studies in art, architecture and design* vol 1 1968.
WIND, E. *Pagan mysteries in the renaissance* 1958 rev 1967.

CLARK, K. *A failure of nerve: Italian painting 1520–1535* Oxford 1967.
FREEDBERG, S. J. *Painting of the high renaissance in Rome and Florence* Cambridge Mass. 1961.
HALE, J. R. *England and the Italian renaissance* 1954.
HUYGHE, RENÉ ed *Larousse encyclopaedia of renaissance and Baroque art* 1964.
MURRAY, P. and L. *The art of the renaissance* 1963.
SYPHER, W. *Four stages of renaissance style: transformations in art and literature 1400–1700* 1955.
WITTKOWER, R. *Art and architecture in Italy 1600–1750* 1958.

HAUSER, A. *Mannerism* 1965.
SHEARMAN, J. *Mannerism* 1967.
WÜRTENGERGER, F. *Mannerism* 1963.

DOWNES, K. *English Baroque architecture* 1966.
FOKKER, T. H. *Roman Baroque art* 1938.
FRIEDRICH, C. J. *The age of the Baroque: 1610–1660* 1952.
International Congress of the History of Art *Acts* vol II Princeton 1963, especially articles by F. Hartt, W. Lotz, J. Shearman, and C. H. Smyth.
LEES-MILNE, J. *Baroque in Italy* 1959.
MOURGUES, O. DE *Metaphysical, Baroque and précieux poetry* Oxford 1953.
TAPIÉ, V. L. *The age of grandeur: Baroque and classicism in Europe* 1960.
WATERHOUSE, E. K. *Italian Baroque painting* 1963.
WITTKOWER, R. *Architectural principles in the age of humanism* 1952.

FREEDBERG, S. J. *Parmigianino: his works in painting* Cambridge Mass. 1950.
HARTT, F. *Michaelangelo* 1965.
  Giulio Romano New Haven 1958.

POPHAM, A. E. *The drawings of Parmigianino* 1953.
PORTOGHESI, P. *Borromini* 1968.
STOKES, A. *Michaelangelo* 1955.
TOLNAY, C. DE *The Medici chapel* part 3 of his *Michaelangelo* Princeton 1948.
WITTKOWER, R. *Bernini's bust of Louis XIV* Oxford 1951.

VASARI, G. *The lives of the painters, sculptors and architects.*

The new scientific world-view proceeded from Copernicus' discovery...
Man became a tiny, insignificant factor in the new disenchanted world. But
the most remarkable thing was that, out of this changed position, he developed
a new feeling of self-respect and pride. The consciousness of understanding
the great, overwhelmingly powerful universe, of which he himself was a mere
part, became the source of an unprecedented and boundless self-confidence...
The place of the earlier anthropocentric world-view was taken...by the
conception of an infinite continuity of interrelationships embracing man and
containing the ultimate ground of his existence...At the end of this development the fear of the judge of the universe is superseded...by the wonder at
the long unbroken breath which pervades the cosmos.

The whole of the art of the baroque is full of this shudder, full of the echo
of the infinite spaces and the interrelatedness of all being. The work of art in
its totality becomes the symbol of the universe.

ARNOLD HAUSER *The social history of art* vol II

Renaissance, mannerism and baroque 1951

Intellectually and theologically Milton holds the ideal of temperance; but
'poetically' the baroque image of Eve is so potent that his ethic and theology
seem almost irrelevant. If this particular dissociation does not appear in
other baroque artists, the reason for Milton's curious dilemma is not hard to
find: he was living in an era of baroque artistic vision, but he had a Puritan
(possibly a mannerist) distrust of the sensorium. *Paradise lost*, it happens, is
at the point at which his Counter-Reformation poetic imagination submerges
his *anti*-Counter-Reformation ethic. As poet he is the maker of resplendent
images; as Puritan he is a mighty image-breaker – *Eikonoklastes*...Donne is
always aware of the conflicts within him...Milton, on the contrary, is here
so enthralled by the wealth of his haptic imagination that he does not appear
to be fully awake to the contradictions between his baroque sensuousness and
his Puritanism. Thus occurs the discrepancy between Milton's pictorial and
conceptual thinking...An historical irony is implicit in Milton and all
baroque: while confidence in theological systems was being shaken during
the seventeenth century, confidence in the images of faith increased until the
image seemed capable of sustaining the faith: or, at the very least, to be self-
sustaining. Baroque religion projected its adoration into a worship of the
convincing image. WYLIE SYPHER *Four stages of renaissance style* 1955

JOHN DIXON HUNT

Milton's illustrators

Illustrations

No poet has attracted the visual artist quite like Milton. His poems
have provided the opportunity for many, often famous, artists to feed
their own visual imaginations upon his verbal art. Not surprisingly the
period of highest activity in Milton illustration coincided with and
continued from the period of the most prolific publishing of *Paradise
lost*. There were over a hundred publications of that poem in the 18th
century (compared with seven of *The fairy queen* and fifty editions of
Shakespeare's plays). Between 1769 and 1865 one hundred and
eighteen paintings based on *Paradise lost* alone were exhibited, in
addition to illustrated editions. When the decoration of the new
Houses of Parliament was mooted in the 1840s Milton, along with
Shakespeare, Spenser and British history, was designated as the
source from which entrants had to draw their subject matter: Milton
inspired 40 cartoons out of a total of 140 exhibited, with Shakespeare
(12) and Spenser (11) again far behind. In 1842 the octagonal room of
a small garden pavilion in the grounds of Buckingham Palace was
decorated with frescoes of scenes from *Comus*, Prince Albert having
been delighted by the masque at Covent Garden the previous year.[1]

Comus was selected for the royal garden pavilion because 'nothing
could be more beautifully adapted to the shades of a trim garden
devoted to the recreation of Our Lady Sovereign, than the chaste,
polished, yet picturesque elegance of the poem'. This explanation is
typical of some of the problems encountered in considering Milton
illustration: an (amusingly) inadequate account of the poem has sustained a pictorial representation that may, nevertheless, and perhaps by
devious ways, help us back to a fuller understanding of what the text
means to us. These problems and the possibilities of larger compre-
hension will be dealt with more fully in the second part of this essay.

[1] See John Steegman *Consort of taste 1830–70* 1950 pp. 202–4.

What is necessary first for a student of Milton is some guide to the illustrations; it is offered in the form of an annotated bibliography of the most important illustrations and any relevant discussions of them. By 'illustration' is meant any visual rendition of the poetry, whether published in an edition, intended for but never issued in one or offered, like a specific painting, separate and discrete.

Of general interest are two attempts to survey the field of Milton's illustrators: C. H. Collins-Baker 'Some illustrators of Milton's *PL* (1688–1850)', *The library* III 1948 pp. 1–21 and 101–19; and Marcia R. Pointon *Milton and English art* Manchester 1970. The first of these offers a detailed checklist of every illustrated edition, noting subjects, artists and engravers; it contains a useful index to the topics chosen for illustration. It is prefaced by some general observations on the technical and critical problems and briefly relates the history of Milton illustration to the development of British history painting. Marcia Pointon's study is more ambitious and is supported by over two hundred reproductions of items discussed, which makes it the best collection and annotation of visual material at present available. But her analysis is largely descriptive and while she occasionally makes some evaluation of the paintings and graphic works she is rarely concerned to assess their interpretative value, their significance as critical readings of the poetry.

Milton was first illustrated by Medina in an edition of *Paradise lost* of 1688 and this work has been discussed by Helen Gardner in an appendix to her *Reading of PL* Oxford 1965, where three of the plates are reproduced. One will be found in *PL: introduction* in this series. Medina is worth considering as the only contemporary illustrator of Milton; not only did he obviously read much of the poem carefully, but he demonstrates aptly the 17th-century notion of illustration as explication. The variety of styles that Medina used suggests the originality of Milton: sometimes, as with Book IX, he provides a visual narrative in the old-fashioned mode of a multi-episodic plate; on other occasions, as with Book I, he focuses upon one particular moment and banishes subsidiary events into the background in order to suggest the poem's richnesses. The especially Baroque effects of the plate for Book III should remind us that Medina shared with his poet a visual inheritance of European art; Milton's visit to Italy and especially to Rome, which was the centre of Italian baroque, must have conditioned his visual imagination;[1] with the result, to my mind

[1] Some account of Milton's Italian journey may be gathered from John Arthos, *Milton and the Italian cities* 1968, yet it only tantalizes us with passing references

at least, that some of the most remarkable illustrations of his poetry come from artists, like Medina, who shared these visual tastes or from those, like Fuseli, who had made them the object of special study.

Medina's designs continued to be used throughout the 18th century, even after a new illustrated edition was brought out by Tonson in 1720. The artists employed then were Sir James Thornhill and Louis Cheron; but their work tells us more about contemporary taste – a mixture of French classicism and rococo – than about their interpretation of Milton. Indeed, Cheron displays a fault that mars many of the lesser visual criticisms of Milton – a dependence on biblical sources rather than upon the text of the poetry. Thornhill might well have managed some English baroque visions of Milton, for his work at Greenwich suggests his abilities in that style; but he seems to have been less inspired by that potential in Milton than his son-in-law, William Hogarth, who attempted two illustrations of the heavenly and hellish councils.

Among the many illustrators of the late 18th century like Stothard, Westall, Lawrence, Burney, Barry and Romney (all discussed and illustrated in Pointon) two in particular distinguish themselves: Fuseli and Blake. Fuseli had studied in Rome[1] and the mannerist as well as baroque artists that succeeded Michelangelo there joined with Fuseli's dedication to romantic *Sturm und Drang* to determine his energetic and highly individual pictorial imagination. His major contribution to Milton illustration was the initiation in 1799 of his Milton Gallery, in direct emulation of Boydell's Shakespeare Gallery; these attempted to record in pictorial form the richness of those writers' work. Pointon lists the 47 subjects attempted by Fuseli and most of them are illustrated by Gert Schiff in *Johann Heinrich Füsslis Milton-Galerie* Zurich and Stuttgart 1963, the only thorough study of Fuseli's handling of Milton. F. Antal *Fuseli studies* London 1956 has some discussion of the same topic as well as a few illustrations. Fuseli discovered in Milton a world of emotion and fantasy,[2] where he could indulge his taste for the expression of intensity through outward gesture. As a result he succeeds in isolating the dramatic effects of

to what Milton must have seen in Rome; even speculations on the visual influences of that visit upon his poetry have still to be attempted. See previous chapter in this volume.

[1] See *Das Römische Skizzenbuch von J. H. Füssli* Zürich 1942, which illustrates some of Fuseli's Roman sketches and studies.

[2] One of his best known paintings – in the Tate Gallery – is *The shepherd's dream*, presumably illustrating *Paradise lost* 1 780ff. It would be interesting to discuss why Fuseli chose a simile in the text for his subject.

FIG 15 *Sin pursued by Death* (*PL* II 787) by John Henry Fuseli. One of a series of paintings and illustrations he made during the 1790s for his 'Milton Gallery' exhibition. This was an engraving published 1804. From the British Museum

Milton's poem – he was the first of numerous illustrators to choose the topic of Satan starting from Ithuriel's spear – and the more intense moments of inward conflict – Eve seeing her reflection, the obviously sexual undercurrents of the banished Adam and Eve. Engravings by Fuseli appear in the 1802 edition of *Paradise lost* and in *The poetical works* of 1805–8 (*The works of the British poets*) and 1806.

William Blake is undoubtedly the most important and the most original illustrator of Milton. His drawings of *Paradise lost* were begun in 1806 and at least two sets were tinted in water colour: that in the Boston Museum of Fine Arts is reproduced, along with other Milton designs, in Darrel Figgis *The paintings of William Blake* London 1925; that in the Huntington Library in their *Catalogue of William Blake's drawings and paintings* San Marino, California 1969. Three articles

FIG 16 *Satan starts at the touch of Ithuriel's spear* (*PL* IV 810), from an engraving by Fuseli for an edition published 1802. From the British Museum.

discuss his Milton work in some detail and provide useful reproductions: Morse Peckham's 'Blake, Milton and Edward Burney' *The Princeton University library chronicle* XI 1950 pp. 107–26; C. H. Collins-Baker 'William Blake, painter' *Huntington library bulletin* X 1936 pp. 135–48; E. J. Rose 'Blake's illustrations for *PL*, *L'allegro* and *Il penseroso:* a thematic reading' *Hartford Studies in literature* II 1970.

FIG 17 *Adam tempted by Eve* (*PL* IX 856), engraved by James Barry RA. Barry was professor of painting at the Academy; he died in squalor in 1806 but was buried in St Paul's. From the British Museum.

Blake is a master of gesture that is eloquent of spiritual life. In *Christ offers to redeem man* the figure of Christ springs lightly from the celestial clouds, his arms lifted in exultation, towards his Father who is bent and crouched like Blake's own Urizen. It is a supreme example of Blake's subtle manipulation of this poetry to his own ends (thus, God intimates the oppression and thraldom of arbitrary law, and Christ is the symbol of imaginative life from the prophetic book *Jerusalem*); nevertheless, the highly personal reading ensures a profound and arresting interpretation of Milton as well. The extraordinary gothic arch of Raphael's wings in *Raphael warns Adam and Eve* and the innocent animal world of Eden beyond are full of a spiritual language that is undoubtedly Blake's own; yet they are visions, too, of Milton that return us to fundamental truths in his poetry. Of this order is *Satan watches Adam and Eve*, where the inert and horizontal body of Satan is in grotesque contrast to the sublime and almost weightless presence of the human lovers, passionate yet innocent upon a bank of rich fruits. The serpent that entwines Satan's body further separates the world of constraint and law from the freedoms of a full and divine imagination. Blake evades the meaningless insistence upon mere bodily presence that Fuseli occasionally produced and which I discuss in the second part; yet his figures always retain a special and distinctly Blakean allusion to his admired Michelangelo and manage to contrive within their unique idiom memories of the contemporary baroque arts to which Milton's poetry is somehow indebted.

A friend and pupil of Blake's, Samuel Palmer (1805–81), illustrated the minor poems and his engravings are conveniently consulted in the 1889 edition of the *Shorter poems of John Milton*. The preface by Palmer's son reminds us how his father's nurse, a powerful influence upon his young imagination, was deeply versed in Milton and how as the artist grew up he found in the poetry a vast storehouse of imagery and suggestion. The Milton illustrations unite in a special degree the famous Palmer skill in visionary pastoral landscape with his attention to the moods of *L'allegro* and *Il penseroso*; with *Comus*, where he is forced to give much greater prominence to figures, his insights are far less rewarding.

Among 19th-century illustrators it is undoubtedly John Martin who deserves attention. Turner's endeavours with Milton are disappointing; his seven vignettes for the 1835 edition of *The poetical works* are obviously influenced by those of Martin, which had appeared in the 1825–7 edition of *Paradise lost* (large plates, also used in 1838)

FIG 18 From an oil painting by John Martin *c.* 1841 at the Tate Gallery, London, showing the fallen angels passing their time in the suburbs of hell while the peers consult in Pandemonium in the background (*PL* II). Martin married at 18. He was an expert on the London sewer system and his interest in urban technology – e.g. gaslighting – often appears in his work.

and that of 1826 (smaller plates). But Turner's designs lack the imaginative involvement with the poems that one might have expected from his own landscapes. The *Shipwreck of Lycidas*, in volume VI of the 1835 edition, is a poor echo of Turner's own dramatic seascapes, and the *Rising of the water nymphs* in *Comus*, in volume V, is a mere indulgence in a taste for Victorian nymphets. His favourite theme of vortex is best seen in *The fall of the rebel angels*, volume III, but a closer look at the rather inadequate handling of the figures detracts from the exciting conception of the huge dizziness of event which he certainly found in Milton. Otherwise the rather static vignettes have only a very general connection with the poetry.

John Martin's response, however, is undoubtedly magnificent. Like Turner he lacks any skill with figures nor has he what Collins Baker calls 'the special spiritual and religious understanding of Blake... Blake's unique integration of design with spiritual content'. But

FIG 19 *Sin and Death build a path from hell* (*PL* x 312),
engraved by Martin for an edition published 1825.

Martin's great contribution to our understanding of Milton was his
suggestion of the *scale* of the poetry, the invention of visible worlds –
infernal, paradisean or celestial – that matched the poetic creation.
Moreover, he achieved what at some stages it is vital to do with all
great art of the past, he annexed it to contemporary concerns and
circumstance; so that Satan's kingdom is lit with the new gaslamps of
Victorian cities (fig 18), the outer worlds of chaos and firmament
echo the engineering technology of tunnels, and the palaces of
Pandemonium are some feverish echo of the archeological and
anthropological zeal of the century – the dinosaur, for example, that
is glimpsed in the landscape of Martin's *Expulsion* being both a
brilliant prophecy of biological development and a celebration of the
scientific discoveries that have unravelled it. Martin achieves a terrific
emotional play with landscapes and natural phenomena: Adam and
Eve are dwarfed by the exotic intricacies of their paradise which has
no human scale (an interesting equivalent of Milton's scepticism of
its appropriateness for human life); or they are baffled by the sudden

216

bursts of light through the darkened jungles after the fall; or there is the tragic smallness of Satan before the prospect of

> the mole immense wrought on
> Over the foaming deep high arched, a bridge
> Of length prodigious joining to the wall
> Immovable of this now fenceless world. x 300

Above all it is Martin's skill with mezzotint engraving that ensures his brilliant effects of *chiaroscuro*. There is some attention to Martin's work by Kester Svendsen 'John Martin and the expulsion scene of *PL*' *Studies in English literature 1500–1900* I 1961 pp. 63–73 and by Merritt Y. Hughes 'Some illustrators of Milton: the expulsion from paradise' *Journ. of Eng. and Germanic philology* LX 1961.

It remains to add a note on Gustave Doré's illustrations for an edition of *Paradise lost* in 1882. Doré has recently enjoyed something of a vogue, but his elaborate and ornate designs for Milton are surely most unsatisfactory: his far too literal response to the text ensures only banalities: or the figures posture as in Victorian melodrama. It may well be that Doré is responsible for the dearth of Milton illustration since. The interpretative nature of the best visual criticism of Milton seems to have been lost by the 20th century and displaced by a merely decorative sense of 'illustration' (witness the Cresset Press *Paradise lost* of 1931 and that of the Golden Cockerel Press of 1937). The critical insistence of our times has been firmly upon the text: this explains, perhaps, the virtual neglect of any visual commentaries.

Interpretations

Such an active use of Milton by artists in England undoubtedly contributes much to our understanding of the history of the visual arts. But what should the literary student of Milton make of these many raids upon his territory by visual artists? Do they seem to pillage and despoil or at best leave the literary work quite undisturbed by their intrusion? Some answers to these questions will already have emerged from my account of the major illustrators; so also will some of the difficulties that a critical language encounters when it is forced to deal with visual material. Perhaps it is now worth discussing these problems explicitly.

The first and major opportunity afforded a reader by visual accounts of *Paradise lost* is to provoke and sharpen his response by the actual representation of elements of the poem (whether scenes or ideas). John Martin's sense of Miltonic space (discussed already) is perhaps the most dramatic example of how the illustrator can enlarge our awareness of the literary achievement; the increasing animalism in Medina's rendering of Satan during the poem may provide us with an immediate apprehension of one of Milton's less conspicuous devices.

Several issues are in question here. The most important and basic is that we should expect an artist to read the literary text well, though he would probably be attentive to elements in it that would suit his visual talents rather than the ones we, as literary critics, find easy to talk about. But he has first to show an understanding of what Milton says and then – a difficult adjudication, this – translate it into visual language. But what Milton 'says' to an illustrator may vary widely in importance. Medina is taken to task by one critic for neglecting to show Adam and Eve in skins at their expulsion from paradise: it's an error that signifies some inattention to details in the text, but is far less reprehensible than the images of Satan as satyr or popular devil that quite inappropriately decorate the pages of some early 18th-century editions.

What matters surely about visual representations of, say, the expulsion scene is how the artist handles the ambiguity of Milton's lines, how he 'reads' the text – a process we can only judge by ourselves reading the pictorial language used to interpret Milton. Fuseli's version delights mainly in naked mannerist gesture, so that we are reminded strongly of Eve's erotic impulses and of Adam's uxoriousness, neither particularly prominent in our minds at this point in the poem; meanwhile Michael disappears upwards, his relevance to Fuseli's image being again only a sub-Michelangelesque thrust of arm and calf.

Blake, on the other hand, no longer cares for a merely physical image. In the combined title page of the *Songs of innocence and experience* the figures of Adam and Eve are absorbed visually into the sweep of flames that drive them from Eden and symbolically into Blake's own vision of fallen humanity, supine and cringing in the snares of their own experience. In his actual design for Book XII of *Paradise lost* Blake continues to stylize, thus ensuring that we concentrate readily upon the meaning of the episode. Some details are exactly copied from the poem (Michael clasping their hands); some are neglected (the '*dreadful* Faces thronged and fiery arms' of the accompanying angels). But the overall effect is a magnificent affirmation in visual terms of Milton's ambiguity: the expulsion is not all evil – Michael's feet barely touching the serpent's head, the benign faces of the horsemen, the vigour of the flames that, as elsewhere in Blake, seem to burn and yet flourish like natural growth. Yet another expulsion scene, by John Martin, offers a different reading. We know that the painter's brother William, a convinced anti-Newtonist like Blake, believed that light was the mystic dwelling place of God.[1] So John banishes his Adam and Eve from a dazzling luminosity that bathes their figures in a final radiance before they enter the sombre landscape; the jagged streak of lightning also announces the wrath of God and the human tragedy. But as we grow used to the landscape a further source of light calls softly from the horizon and intimates the world before them and their Providential progress beyond Eden.

We expect, then, that an illustration will afford us insights into the poetry just as a critic does. Except that, while a critic usually expands the poetic meaning into explicit and extended commentary, the artist offers his 'criticism' in the imaginative shorthand of a visual language that is probably as compact as the poem's. But the value of illustrations – difficulties of a different medium apart – is precisely the value of any literary criticism of Milton: we look to the articulation of subtlety, to the explanations of the poem's structures and meanings, to any account of it that so transmutes it we are forced to see it anew. And inadequate visual, like inadequate verbal, criticism often forces us back into the text to identify what it is that Milton manages so well (the extraordinary achievement of his Satan, for example).

Visual criticism is, however, couched in a different language that needs as much skill sometimes to read as *Paradise lost* itself; and for all our dedication to a visual culture in modern society we are absurdly 'illiterate' in our understanding of art. It may be awkward learning about a poem from a picture, because of their different idiom. (Sometimes, though, the creative stature of certain Milton illustrators ensures insights denied to more pedestrian verbalizers!) Yet it is presumably important for the student of Milton who turns to illustrations for some critical commentary upon the poetry, to begin with some normative idea of it; he must have established some account of *Paradise lost* for himself before he can assess how another creative response to it, couched in visual gesture, will enlarge his understanding of the poem.

It may be worth enumerating a few of the special ways in which a visual language works in commenting upon Milton. It is above all

[1] Ruthven Todd *Tracks in the snow* 1946 p. 97.

immediate in its impact; we may take time finding our way around the crowded details of Blake's *Raphael warns Adam and Eve* or among the dark obscurities of the engraving of Turner's *Expulsion*, but they present themselves to the eye all together; in contrast, Milton's lines extend *in time* through our consciousness. This has led some illustrators – Medina, Turner even – to picture a variety of incidents on one plate, a frequent device in early painting but gradually abandoned after the renaissance. Alternatively, the slow accretion of our knowledge of the poem that comes only over extended periods of reading may be paralleled by Blake's richly symbolic accounts of Milton that themselves take time to comprehend, or by Martin's or Doré's extraordinary landscapes, where the figures of people and even angels are dwarfed by a topography that assumes the visual equivalence of Milton's colossal and extended exterprise in revealing God's infinite ways to a finite human vision.

There is also the need in visual image for explicitness, as Joshua Reynolds explained in his *Discourses*:

A great part of the beauty of the celebrated description of Eve in Milton's *Paradise lost* consists in using only general indistinct expressions, every reader making out the detail according to his own particular imagination – his own idea of beauty, grace, expression, dignity, or loveliness; but a painter, when he represents Eve on a canvas, is obliged to give a determined form, and his own idea of beauty distinctly expressed.

In surmounting these particular difficulties Blake is especially creative. While Fuseli's *Creation of Eve*,[1] for example, expresses his usual delight in the muscular mannerism of human form, Blake's Eve rises as if by divine levitation from a supine Adam. Beneath the crescent moon, with its allusion to the Woman Clothed with the Sun in *Revelation*, Blake's Eve is wholly ideal; since she speaks of matters of the spirit not of the body, the absence of corporeal detail is unremarked. Students particularly interested in Blake's response to Milton should consider his confident handling of visual equivalents for worlds of visionary understanding and seek to ask how he manages to evade the awkward translation of Milton's descriptions that troubles other illustrators. His handling of Sin, for example:

> Woman to the waist, and fair,
> But ended foul in many a scaly fold
> Voluminous and vast –

[1] Illustrated by Schiff; originally designed for Erasmus Darwin's *Temple of nature* 1803.

is characteristically indifferent to the anatomical anxieties that perplex other artists[1] and so manages to make his image function properly in the moral drama of the episode as 'a tragic figure, stamped with the horror of experience'.[2] Another instance to examine might be Blake's superb set of illustrations for *Paradise regained*,[3] which attend so readily to the strange spiritual realities of that poem without losing any sense of their human dimension: the Satan who tempts Christ to turn the stones into bread is plausible yet symbolically earthbound in his gestures.

It is for critical insights into Milton's poetry that one turns to his illustrators; with their different idiom, they may alert us to elements we had neglected in reading the poems. But there are two, less important, reasons of rather a different sort that might be urged. Any understanding of a poet like Milton depends to some extent upon our awareness of its context in the critical continuum. Illustrators allow us swift access to that historical perspective: the mannerist Milton's of Fuseli and Lawrence with their delight in anatomical gesture, the spiritual and symbolic poet of Blake, the prophet of the 'mechanical sublime' that Martin allows us, the emblematic or baroque language he speaks in Medina's illustrations – these, and many more, are all part of our understanding of Milton. There are literary equivalents, too, of this cultural stockpiling, but through the visual arts it is more quickly appreciated. And the (often unconscious) pressure of this critical continuum in which *our* opinions take their place is an important part of our response to the poetry.

Samuel Palmer's engravings for the minor poems, especially his rich and enclosed pastoral world in *The bellman* (*Il penseroso*) or the early morning agricultural glimpses of *The eastern gate* (*L'allegro*), cannot be divorced from our response to those poems. *The lonely tower* will always, once we have seen it,[4] insinuate its own redolent atmosphere into our reading of the lines in *Il penseroso*. Through Palmer's engravings we draw upon a peculiarly rich moment in English landscape taste to inform our reading of these minor poems.

[1] Satan's meeting with Sin and Death was a popular episode among artists. See fig. 15 for Fuseli; Blake's version is on the cover of *PL I–II* in this series; Hogarth's painting is in R. B. Beckett *Hogarth* 1949 plate 2; Gillray attempted several versions; another, engraved by Barry, is illustrated in *JWCL* XVII 1954 plate 55c.

[2] C. H. Collins-Baker in the article listed above.

[3] Recently seen in the Blake exhibition at the Fitzwilliam Museum and reproduced in the catalogue ed David Bindman, Cambridge 1970.

[4] Yeats is one poet who has testified to the impact of Palmer's engraving – see the second section of *Meditations in time of civil war* in *The tower*.

FIG 20 *The Lady from 'Comus'*, an oil painting by Joseph Wright of Derby, 1785. 'Was I deceived, or did a sable cloud Turn forth her silver lining on the night?' (220). Walker Art Gallery, Liverpool; his companion picture, *The Indian window*, is in the Derby Museum and Art Gallery. Wright was also an artist of technology: see F. D. Klingender *Art and the industrial revolution* 1947 rev 1968.

While it would be perfectly accurate to insist that Milton had nothing like Turner or Palmer in mind when he wrote

> Where the great sun begins his state
> Robed in flames, and amber light,
> The clouds in thousand liveries dight,

the visual memories of *The eastern gate* inevitably colour these lines and Milton's landscape once again is curiously prophetic of taste for over a hundred years after his death. His descriptions of Eden were precedent for many English landscape gardens of the 18th century[1] – a minor footnote to the history of his 'illustrations', but one which

---

[1] Horace Walpole notes particularly how Stourhead and Hagley seemed to be inspired by Milton: Isabel W. U. Chase *Horace Walpole: gardenist* Princeton 1943 pp. 15–16.

surely colours our reading of those sections of *Paradise lost*. And if Wright's *Lady from 'Comus'* (fig 20) does not seem too romantic a version of the episode, it is partly because its taste has in turn subtly reorganized our responses to the poem it illustrates, just as Palmer's special imagination fills out the generalized visual forms of Milton's

> Mountains on whose barren breast
> The labouring clouds do often rest

or the towers and battlements 'Bosomed high in tufted trees'.

Wright's magnificent picture makes another case for attention to Milton's illustrators; indeed, it exemplifies all the various critical experiences I have sketched in this essay. In the first place, it is arguably a fine visual interpretation of one of what a recent critic of the masque identifies as Milton's 'sequence of glimpses into the nature of grace'.[1] Joseph Wright takes the episode just before Comus appears to the virtuous Lady lost in the wood:

> Was I deceived, or did a sable cloud
> Turn forth her silver lining on the night?
> I did not err, there does a sable cloud
> Turn forth her silver lining on the night,
> And casts a gleam over this tufted grove.

The painter can interpret the Lady's fears and recovery of spirits in the newly developed landscape idiom of the late 18th century; but with his careful regard to gesture and the preternatural dazzle of light he also allows us to perceive 'the processes by which *grace* has come [in the masque] to mean both "charm, ease and refinement of movement" and "the divine influence which operates in men to regenerate and sanctify"'.[2] Secondly, and as a consequence of his very individual response to the literary work, Wright's picture returns us to the masque with a fresh sense of its meanings that thereafter colours them for us. Thirdly, by his unique and specifically historical response, Wright defines something about the attitudes of his own age.[3] For the various illustrations of Milton inform us of the varied popularity of different poems in succeeding periods; more specifically, they tell which episodes stood out and provided for a particular

[1] Philip Brockbank 'The measure of *Comus*', *Essays and studies* XXII 1968 p. 54.
[2] *Ibid* p. 61.
[3] In the case of such an illustrator as Doré we may perhaps see his failure to attend properly to Milton as a result of his conditioning by the age in which he worked – does anyone else recognize a Jules Verne fantasy in Doré's fabulous world of the Creation?

generation of readers an apt focus for their understanding of Milton. In this sense, the visual reactions of his illustrators at different historical moments to the common set of themes in Milton's poetry initiate his readers into some larger awareness of cultural history, of which the criticism of poems is part.

On each side an imperial city stood,
With towers and temples proudly elevate
On seven small hills, with palaces adorned,
Porches and theatres, baths, aqueducts,
Statues and trophies, and triumphal arcs,
Gardens and groves presented to his eyes,
Above the heighth of mountains interposed:
By what strange parallax or optic skill
Of vision multiplied through air, or glass
Of telescope, were curious to inquire.
And now the tempter thus his silence broke.
  The city which thou seest no other deem
Than great and glorious Rome, queen of the earth
So far renowned, and with the spoils enriched
Of nations; there the Capitol thou seest,
Above the rest lifting his stately head
On the Tarpeian rock, her citadel
Impregnable, and there Mount Palatine
The imperial palace, compass huge, and high
The structure, skill of noblest architects,
With gilded battlements, conspicuous far,
Turrets and terraces, and glittering spires.
Many a fair edifice besides, more like
Houses of gods (so well I have disposed
My airy microscope) thou mayst behold
Outside and inside both, pillars and roofs
Carved work, the hand of famed artificers
In cedar, marble, ivory, or gold.

.   .   .   .

To whom the Son of God unmoved replied.
Nor doth this grandeur and majestic show
Of luxury, though called magnificence,
More than of arms before, allure mine eye,
Much less my mind...   *PR* IV 33

The appropriateness of the material of *Paradise lost* to the genius and the limitations of Milton, is still more evident when we consider the visual imagery. I have already remarked, in a paper written some years ago, on Milton's weakness of visual observation...Mr Wilson Knight, who has devoted close study to recurrent imagery in poetry, has called attention to Milton's propensity towards images of engineering and mechanics; to me it seems that Milton is at his best in imagery suggestive of vast size, limitless space, abysmal depth, and light and darkness...We must, then, in reading *Paradise lost*, not expect to see clearly; our sense of sight must be blurred, so that our hearing may become more acute.   T. S. ELIOT

WINIFRED MAYNARD

Milton and music

Music in daily life

Who shall silence all the airs and madrigals, that whisper softness in chambers?

Milton was mocking at the futility of licensing laws in his plea for freedom of printing, *Areopagitica*; he was not consciously describing for us the musical background of his time, but he brings it to life in his ridicule:

> If we think to regulate printing, thereby to rectify manners, we must regulate all recreations and pastimes, all that is delightful to man. No music must be heard, no song be set or sung, but what is grave and doric. There must be licensing dancers, that no gesture, motion, or deportment be taught our youth but what by their allowance shall be thought honest;...It will ask more than the work of twenty licensers to examine all the lutes, the violins, and the guitars in every house; they must not be suffered to prattle as they do, but must be licensed what they may say...The villages also must have their visitors to enquire what lectures the bagpipe and the rebeck reads even to the balladry, and the gamut of every municipal fiddler, for these are the countryman's *Arcadias* and his *Monte Mayors*.[1]

This sarcastic flight of imagination depends for its whole effectiveness upon the amount and extent, far beyond what licensers could keep an ear on, of music-making in ordinary life. It would have no point unless it was true that young people learnt dancing, that many households possessed musical instruments, that lute-songs and madrigals were still being sung, and in the country, where the village fiddler still played for dancing, ballads were sung and the bagpipe and rebeck were played. It seems that music was present in all aspects of daily life, as it had been in Elizabethan times; in fact this could be a description of Elizabethan musical life, with its lute-songs and madrigals and

---

[1] That is, his equivalent to the romances (Sidney's *Arcadia* and Montemayor's *Diana*) read by more sophisticated people. See *The Oxford companion to music* for illustrations of the instruments mentioned in this passage, and information about them.

ballads, except that violins had then scarcely begun to replace viols. Yet it belongs to 1644, the time of the civil war; and so reminds us that the neat divisions we make, into reigns and periods, and the labels we pin on them, are often too tidy to be true. People did not suddenly cease to sing to the lute in their homes because the Elizabethan and the Jacobean ages were over, or because a protector ruled in place of a monarch. The great age of writing madrigals and airs ended while Milton was growing up, as in close succession the composers died – Campion, Dowland, Rosseter, Orlando Gibbons, Weelkes and others – but old songs and new were being sung, and making music at home went on being a favourite diversion in Commonwealth and Restoration times.

Pepys liked to have music wherever he was; he carried his flageolet in his pocket, and sometimes a song-book too, and he liked the newer style of music, which paid less attention to melody than to matching the speech-rhythms and intonations of the words in the accents and pitch of the music. This was the 'declamatory' style of song that Henry Lawes made for *Comus*, ten years before *Areopagitica*; naturally it was favoured by poets since it took such care to interpret their words, and all his contemporaries – Herrick, Waller, Carew, Cartwright and others – were eager for Lawes, who excelled in this style, to set their lyrics; his hand-written book of over three hundred of his own songs contains verse by them all.[1] And his songs were ideal for a man to sing by himself: one Sunday Pepys goes

after being trimmed, alone by water to Erith, all the way with my song-book singing of Mr Lawes's long recitative song in the beginning of his book.

His household must be musical too: the servants are chosen as much for musicianship as domestic usefulness; the boy must be able to take part in motets, the maids must sing. Only poor Mrs Pepys was hopelessly unmusical; and so at the Exchange

wife did a little business while Mercer [the maid] and I stayed in the coach; and in a quarter of an hour, I taught her the whole Lark's Song perfectly, so excellent an ear she hath.

Pepys himself played the flageolet, lute, treble viol, lyra and bass viols, and later the recorder; he took singing lessons, and kept a song-book into which he copied songs he liked; and he learnt enough of composition to write a few songs himself. He made music with his

[1] Thurston Dart has edited *Ten Ayres* by Henry Lawes (Stainer and Bell); non-singers can listen to *Songs for courtiers and cavaliers* side 2, songs by Lawes, L'Oiseau-Lyre OLS 142.

friends in taverns, and at the coffee house where he and Matthew Locke and Purcell's father sang Italian and Spanish songs one evening, and an eight-voice canon of Locke's own. He also enjoyed music in the open air, in his garden; after going to Deptford to see a spinet, he got home to find Pelham Humfrey, the gifted but conceited young composer just back from studying in France with Lully, in his garden with others, 'and there had most excellent music, late, in the dark, with great pleasure'. He enjoyed hearing and taking part in church music too, and he was quite alarmingly responsive to music in drama: the first time he saw Massinger and Dekker's play, *The virgin martyr*, in February 1661, he remarked only that it was 'a good but too sober a play for the company'. When it was revived in February 1668, it was embellished with music; and

that which did please me beyond anything in the whole world was the wind-music when the angel comes down, which is so sweet that it ravished me, and indeed, in a word, did wrap up my soul so that it made me really sick, just as I have formerly been when in love with my wife...

But his deepest and most constant pleasure was in having music in his own house; the first time his wife's new lady's maid, Mercer, has dinner with them he makes a revealing and characteristic entry:

After dinner, my wife and Mercer, and Tom and I, sat till eleven at night, singing and fiddling, and a great joy it is to see me master of so much pleasure in my house.

The other famous diarist of the age, John Evelyn, expressed himself with more reserve, but he too often mentions music in his accounts of both public and private occasions. He learnt some theory of music, and took lessons on the theorbo; he went to hear the outstanding instrumentalists and singers of the day; he received many musicians at his house and sometimes invited company to hear them; and when he was invited out to dinner, he mentions that music formed part of the entertainment.

Both Pepys and Evelyn were royalists, but many Puritans and their families were musical too: when the civil war drove men of the same family to take an unwilling stand on opposite sides, this outcome of their political views did not change their natural tastes and interests. There were of course extremist Puritans, for whom everything that did not directly advance the soul on its path to heaven was to be avoided; but it is remarkable how similar were the family lives and interests of men whom the war put in opposition. A striking example is provided by the lives of the Duke of Newcastle, a Cavalier, and of

Colonel Hutchinson, a Roundhead, both by their wives: and Mrs Hutchinson pays a sincere tribute to the Duke in her description of him, although he was a leader of the other side. *The Life of the Thrice Noble, High and Puissant Prince William Cavendish* was written in 1667, *by the Thrice Noble, Illustrious and Excellent Princess, Margaret, Duchess of Newcastle, His Wife,*[1] who is a joy to meet, both in her biography of her husband and in her earlier autobiography, breathlessly talkative (one of her sentences runs to over 3,400 words) and pleased with herself and her family. Writing of her husband, under the heading *His recreation and exercise*, she says:

His prime pastime and recreation hath always been the exercise of manage and weapons...The rest of his time he spends in music, poetry, architecture and the like.

His father had approved of his tastes for both music and sport in his youth:

One time it happened that a young gentleman, one of my lord's relations, had bought some land, at the same time when my lord had bought a singing-boy for 50 £, a horse for 50 £, and a dog for 2 £, which humour his father Sir Charles liked so well, that he was pleased to say, that if he should find his son to be so covetous, that he would buy land before he was 20 years of age, he would disinherit him.

Highly Cavalier actions and sentiments, we may think; but many Puritans were liberal in taste and manner of life too. Mrs Hutchinson herself did not care for music, or for anything but reading:

as for music and dancing I profited very little in them, and would never practise my lute or harpsichords but when my masters were with me; and for my needle I absolutely hated it.[2]

She admits she bossed other children and broke their dolls, and altogether she sounds unpleasantly priggish, but her husband was broader in his interests and attitudes. He loved music, was skilled in fencing, and delighted in landscape gardening. It was in fact through music that they met and married; after he left Peterhouse, he found life at home in Nottingham rather tame, and entered Lincoln's Inn, but found law uncongenial. His music-master, Colman, suggested he should go to stay in his house at Richmond, where Prince Charles's court was:

[1] Old editions of this may be found in libraries, and there is a facsimile reprint issued by Dawson 1970, and one forthcoming from Scolar.
[2] Lucy Hutchinson's *Life of Colonel Hutchinson* is available in the Everyman series.

He therefore went to Richmond, where he found a great deal of good young company, and many ingenuous persons, that by reason of the court, where the young princes were bred, entertained themselves in that place, and had frequent resort to the house where Mr Hutchinson tabled: the man being a skilful composer in music, the rest of the king's musicians often met at his house to practise new airs and prepare them for the king; and divers of the gentlemen and ladies that were affected with music, came thither to hear; others that were not, took that pretence, to entertain themselves with the company.

In the same house the young sister of Lucy Apsley was staying, to learn the lute while her mother was away with Lucy to arrange her marriage; Mr Hutchinson fell in love with what he heard about Lucy, and through hearing a song said to have been composed by her, and at the sight of books in Latin belonging to her – unendearing as this may seem. When she returned home, having refused the proposed marriage, they met and not long afterwards married. He was drawn into playing an active part in the civil war, and after the execution of the king was a member of the council of state that was formed. When after that he was in retirement in the country, he

pleased himself with music, and again fell to the practice of his viol, on which he played excellently well, and entertaining tutors for the diversion and education of his children in all sorts of music, he pleased himself in these innocent recreations during Oliver's mutable reign. As he had great delight, so he had great judgement, in music, and advanced his children's practice more than their tutors...He spared not any cost for the education of both his sons and daughters in languages, sciences, music, dancing, and all other qualities befitting their father's house.

It is not perhaps our mental picture of a Puritan at home, but it is not untypical. Many Puritans loved music, dancing, arts and sports, although it suited their opponents to spread tales to the contrary.

Cromwell himself 'loved a good voice and instrumental music well', according to the Oxford antiquarian Antony à Wood; when he entertained the Portuguese ambassador in 1653, he commanded a performance of Shirley's masque *Cupid and Death*, and in 1657 when one of his daughters was married, at the wedding feast at Whitehall, a contemporary letter relates

they had 48 violins, 50 trumpets and much mirth with frolics, besides mixed dancing (a thing heretofore accounted profane) till 5 of the clock yesterday morning.[1]

[1] Quoted by Scholes *The Puritans and music* p. 144.

The next week another daughter was married, and two pastoral songs specially written by Marvell were performed; in one, the bride and bridegroom played Cynthia and Endymion. His daughters had been taught to play the organ by Cromwell's organist, John Hingston, on the organ of Magdalen College which towards the end of the Commonwealth period was taken, apparently with the consent of the college, to Hampton Court for the use of Cromwell and his family; and he had quite a retinue of six or seven other musicians, and also two boy singers, whom he liked to hear singing Latin motets. This is not surprising; most Puritans had nothing against sacred music, as music: it was only as a part of religious services that they found it unacceptable, because they believed that worship should be simple and spontaneous. Similarly, they were not against music and dancing on suitable occasions – it was under Puritan rule, in 1651, that John Playford brought out his *English dancing master*. This collection of over a hundred ballad and other well-known tunes arranged to be used for country dances was so popular that new and larger editions continued to appear right down to 1728. Playford became the first full-time music publisher in England; year by year, he provided a rich variety of instrumental music, solo and part-songs, and convivial catches, for what must have been a receptive public, or he would have gone back to his book-selling business.

Music in education and upbringing

In Milton's own lifetime, then, as in his father's, music contributed much to social and family life; and it was mostly in the family circle and from private tutors that children learnt to sing and to play instruments: after the Reformation music had little or no place in most school curricula. Sometimes it was available as an 'extra' for the sons of gentlemen who wished them to have such accomplishments, but it was not part of the serious business of education. Milton's treatise *On education* reflects this view. In it he outlines a dauntingly thorough plan of teaching, to include grammar, Latin, Greek, mathematics, geography, natural philosophy, medicine, ethics, Scripture, theology, economics, politics, the acquiring of Italian 'at any odd hour', and Hebrew 'at a set hour', and preferably Chaldean and Syrian too; also Greek epic and drama, poetic theory, and logic: *then* the pupils can proceed to write and compose their own thoughts, which by now have some substance to draw on. After detailing all this, Milton turns to other aspects of their lives: 'Now will be worth the seeing what exercises and recreations may best agree, and become these studies.' They are to have an hour and a half off for exercise before lunch – more if they start really early in the morning – and a rest after it; and to learn swordsmanship and wrestling, and relax in hearing and making music:

The interim of unsweating themselves regularly, and convenient rest before meat, may both with profit and delight be taken up in recreating and composing their travailed spirits with the solemn and divine harmonies of music heard or learnt; either while the skilful organist plies his grave and fancied descant, in lofty fugues, or the whole symphony with artful and unimaginable touches adorn and grace the well-studied chords of some choice composer; sometimes the lute, or soft organ-stop waiting on elegant voices either to religious, martial or civil ditties; which if wise men and prophets be not extremely out, have a great power over dispositions and manners, to smooth and make them gentle from rustic harshness and distempered passions. The like also would not be unexpedient after meat to assist and cherish nature in her first concoction, and send their minds back to study in good tune and satisfaction. Where having followed it close under vigilant eyes till about two hours before supper, they are by a sudden alarm or watchword to be called out to their military motions.

Here music seems to be considered chiefly as a civilizing agent and an aid to digestion: but Milton does suggest it to provide not only profit, but delight. At the universities too, systematic teaching in practical music was not generally available, but some of the finest musicians and composers held college appointments as organists and choirmasters, and a musical undergraduate might arrange to have private tuition.

Although music was not an integral part of formal education, it was certainly widely valued in the 17th century as a social accomplishment and a source of domestic pleasure, and noblemen and gentlemen took care to provide it for their children, as many biographies and family records show. When Sir Ralph Verney, of Claydon House in Buckinghamshire, refused the Covenant at the end of 1643, he had to go into exile, and although his wife and two eldest children went with him, his wife returned to England three years later to try to regain possession of their home, which had been requisitioned as soldiers' quarters. Their descendant who compiled the *Memoirs of the Verney family* notes:

Amongst the scraps of manuscript that have come back from Blois to Claydon, and have so long outlasted the hands that traced their now faded characters, are many bits of verse, and songs sung to the guitar. More than one copy has been made of Henry Lawes's exquisite lines 'To his mistress going to sea'.

232

It is not surprising that this song of parting was often in the minds of Sir Ralph and Lady Mary during their enforced separation. In their letters they discuss the progress and upbringing of the children still in France with their father, Edmund ('Mun') and Peg. Sir Ralph writes (according to the *Memoirs* again):

Now if you like it...I would have André come every day to teach Munn the guitar and to sing to it, for the lute is so tedious a thing that I doubt (unless he made it his whole business) he would never play well; but this he may do, and not neglect his Latin, and also learn to sing with it.

Lady Mary approves this plan for Mun, then eleven years old, but she would like Peg to learn the lute as soon as she is old enough. Mun himself did not altogether escape the lute; six years later, when he was staying at the Hague with a Scots tutor, Dr Creighton, he was learning from various masters natural philosophy, Greek, lute-playing and drawing. His younger brother Jack was keenly musical; he wrote from school in Kensington, some time after his mother's death, to ask his father for the guitar that had been hers:

You did give it me when you went out of France, and then when I came over, you said I should not have it because it would be broken at school; that was a good reason, for we lay 18 in a chamber, but at this school we have but two to a chamber, and we keep our chamber door locked and therefore nobody comes in but them which we have a mind to let in... The viol hath put me in love with all sorts of music. My master doth see me proceed so much of the viol that he hath promised me to teach me for to play of the lute when the days grow longer; he hath also lent me one of his viols this Christmas for to practise on.

His interest in music outlasted his schooldays; in 1662 he took up a commercial post in Aleppo, and one of Edmund's parcels to him included a set of horse trappings and a crimson velvet saddle, and 'strings of all sorts for the lyra viol in 2 round black boxes to the value of 20 s., besides 5 bridges which cost ½ a crown'.

Music in Milton's early life

In a middle-class family such as Milton's, there was not the same social expectation of a little musical accomplishment as in families of high rank: social ambition may have prompted the cultivation of music in some households, but on the whole it depended on the genuine taste of the members. To Milton's father it was a passion, and as his nephew John Phillips relates, once his work as a scrivener and his dealings in property had brought him enough money to live on, perhaps naturally inclined rather to a retired life by his addiction to music (for his skill in which he stands registered among the composers of his time), he gave over his trade and went to live in the country.[1]

Phillips is not over-rating his place as a composer; he was a good enough one to have a madrigal included in the famous collection *The triumphs of Oriana* of 1601 (number 18, *Fair Oriana in the morn*), along with Morley, Wilbye and others, and to contribute motets to at least two collections of sacred music. One of these, *Tears or lamentations of a sorrowful soul*, consisted of penitential verses and rhymed paraphrases of psalms written by Sir William Leighton and set by himself and various composers including Byrd, Coperario, and Martin Peerson. The future poet was only six when it was published in 1614 but then and later he would hear these sacred songs sung in his home by his father's friends.[2] His father's settings of two psalm-tunes were used in Ravenscroft's *Whole book of Psalms* in 1621. Most psalm-tunes are of unknown composition; they are often ascribed to well-known composers who arranged them, and are found with various names. The tunes in Ravenscroft's book were all given the names of places where they were thought to have originated or where they were popular, mostly cathedral and university towns. The two arranged by Milton's father are 'Norwich' and 'York'; the latter had already appeared in a Scottish psalter as the 'Stilt Tune' – perhaps a joking reference to the awkward strides of the melody. His setting of it is still frequently sung, now with *Psalm* 122 from the Scottish Psalter of 1650, 'Pray that Jerusalem may have'.[3]

Since Milton's father took pleasure himself in arranging music for psalms, he was probably pleased that his son's first attempts at verse were metrical versions of *Psalms* 114 and 136. It was a natural way for Milton to start: the *Psalms* have always been deeply loved and closely woven into English life and worship and many people, not all of them poets, have tried their hand at arranging some. Sir Thomas Wyatt, Sir Philip Sidney and his sister Margaret, Sir Henry Wotton, Queen Elizabeth and James I all put some into verse; so did Bacon – he dedicated his to Herbert, who must have found them poetically somewhat indigestible. Herbert's own best known one is the twenty-third, 'The God of love my shepherd is'. Crashaw and Vaughan wrote some; so did Puritans such as Cromwell's captain Lord Fairfax,

[1] *The Life of Mr John Milton* by John Phillips in *Early lives* p. 18.
[2] Pearson's three anthems are available for singing, Edition Schott 10283, 10285, 10286.
[3] No. 826 in *Songs of praise*, no. 472 in *The English hymnal*.

and Wither, as well as Milton.[1] (And the line continues, with Burns, Cowper, Addison, Samuel Wesley, Isaac Watts; 'O God, our help in ages past' is Watts's version of *Psalm* 90.) For centuries people have read psalms, and also sung them, chanting Miles Coverdale's beautiful prose version which is still in the Prayer Book, or singing to hymn-like tunes the rather lame verses made by Thomas Sternhold, a Groom of the Robes to Henry VIII, John Hopkins and others. Their version was popular for many generations (it was bound together with the Prayer Book for about 600 editions, right into the 19th century), and when the thousands of people who gathered to hear open-air preaching at Paul's Cross in London stayed on to sing psalms, this would be the version they sang, in Queen Elizabeth's reign, in Charles I's time when Donne was holding crowds spell-bound, in Milton's day and long after.[2] Its last full-scale presentation was in Ravenscroft's Psalter; shortly afterwards Wither published his much better version, *The hymns and songs of the Church*, with sixteen tunes by Orlando Gibbons, and in 1638 came George Sandys' metrical psalms, set by Henry Lawes, for private devotional use. Milton did not use a psalm-tune metre for *Psalm* 114, so he would not intend it for singing, but his version of *Psalm* 136 is ideally suited; nearly everyone, reading the first verse

> Let us with a gladsome mind
> Praise the Lord, for he is kind
> For his mercies aye endure
> Ever faithful, ever sure.

will find himself inwardly singing it, not saying it (our tunes for it are later). Twenty-five years later he turned to versifying psalms again, in April 1648 – the first anniversary of his father's death, so Milton's rendering of *Psalms* 80–8 into common metre, suitable for singing, may have been intended as a memorial tribute.

His father taught Milton music, and thorough teaching it would be in that thoroughgoing family, with none of the dilettante approach preferred in some aristocratic families. Milton was an apt pupil. John Aubrey records: 'He had a delicate tunable voice and had good skill; his father instructed him; he had an organ in his house; he played on that most.' Perhaps Milton's organ was the one he first learnt on in his father's house. He may have been able to play the bass viol too:

[1] It would be well worth while to select a few psalms and collect and compare as many versions of them as possible. The article 'Psalter' in the fourth edition of Grove's *Dictionary of music and musicians*, vol IV, is inexhaustibly informative.

[2] See the *Oxford companion to music* plate 37 for a picture of preaching and singing at Paul's Cross.

Jonathan Richardson wrote his life of Milton in the following century, in 1734, but he knew people who had known the poet, and he records:

Music he loved extremely, and understood well. 'Tis said he composed, though nothing of that has been brought down to us. He diverted himself with performing, which they say he did well on the organ and bass viol; and this was a great relief to him after he had lost his sight.[1]

And his younger nephew, John Phillips, gives firsthand testimony that 'He had an excellent ear, and could bear a part both in vocal and instrumental music.' But it is the organ he is known to have loved hearing and playing. It would be a small chamber organ he learned on, but as a pupil at St Paul's School, which was then at the east end of St Paul's churchyard, he would attend services in the cathedral – not yet the one we know, but the Norman one that was destroyed in the Great Fire, but is surely preserved, with its organ, in *Penseroso*:

> But let my due feet never fail,
> To walk the studious cloisters pale,
> And love the high embowèd roof,
> With antique pillars massy proof,
> And storied windows richly dight,
> Casting a dim religious light,
> There let the pealing organ blow,
> To the full voiced choir below,
> In service high, and anthems clear
> As may with sweetness, through mine ear,
> Dissolve me into ecstasies,
> And bring all heaven before mine eyes.

Christ's College had an organ which he probably played during his residence there; and much later, he played on the Magdalen organ, whilst Cromwell had it at Hampton Court.[2]

Milton continued to study and enjoy music during the years he was living with his father at Horton, sometimes going up to London 'either for the purchase of books, or to learn something new in mathematics or in music, which at that time furnished the sources of my amusement' (*2nd defence*), and when, after that period of quiet study, he visited Italy, he sent back books on music from Venice, the last city in which he made a stay. His elder nephew, Edward Phillips, records that he

[1] *Explanatory notes and remarks* in *Early lives* p. 204.
[2] It was returned to Oxford after Cromwell's death. When in 1737 Magdalen installed a new organ, the old one went to Tewkesbury Abbey, where it is still to be seen and heard, although altered in tone and capacity by much renovation.

spent a month's time in viewing of that stately city, and shipped up a parcel of curious and rare books which he had picked up in his travels; particularly a chest or two of choice music books of the best masters flourishing about that time in Italy, namely, Luca Marenzio, Monte Verde, Horatio Vecchi, Cifa [Cifra], the prince of Venosa, and several others.

Monteverdi, Gesualdo prince of Venosa, Marenzio and Vecchi all composed splendid and striking madrigals. It is very probable that the fluid, freely variable rhythms of madrigal music, in which the melodic lines of the voices were shaped by the verbal phrases and were of no regular recurring length, provided part of the inspiration for the rhythmic variety of Milton's verse, and his avoidance of the monotony of end-stopped lines. Monteverdi, who had been Maestro di Cappella in Venice since 1613 and had published his first book of madrigals in the 1580s, had just published his eighth book in 1638. It presents works composed over a long span of time and includes some of his most marvellous and musically adventurous pieces: besides madrigals of love and of war, it contains several dramatic works, notably the operatic ballet, *Il ballo delle ingrate* (telling the fate of ladies who had hard-heartedly rejected their lovers' advances).[1] This is in the newly developed style of melodic recitative of which opera was born, and of which Monteverdi was one of the earliest exponents and the supreme master; his opera *Arianna*, which was performed again at Venice for the opening of the Teatro di San Moise in the autumn of 1639 – too late for Milton to see it – had been composed as early as 1608 and his *Orfeo* in 1607. Milton already had practical knowledge of this declamatory style of vocal writing through his collaborations with Henry Lawes in *Comus*, and probably in *Arcades* too; now he encountered it in the country where it had originated over half a century earlier. It had begun to be formulated in one of the academies – societies of cultured and artistic people – in Florence, and in another of them, the Academy of the Svogliati in which he was welcomed to membership, he would learn more of it. In Rome, he was personally greeted by Cardinal Barberini at a musical entertainment at his palace; and in that city there were many opportunities for hearing the new musical drama and for discussing the theories of ancient music that underlay it.

[1] Milton's discovery of Monteverdi is well worth sharing. Philips's set of five records, 6799 006, includes the whole of the eighth book; *Orfeo* is on DGG 2708 001 (two records). L'Oiseau-Lyre SOL 299 and HMV HQS 1102 both contain fine madrigals. A school madrigal group or small choir could sing *Il ballo* ed D. Stevens (pub Schott). D. Arnold's BBC Music Guide *Monteverdi madrigals* is a good introduction.

237

He probably heard the most famous organist of the day, Fresco-baldi; he certainly heard the famous singer Leonora Baroni. She both sang and played the theorbo (a bass lute), and during Milton's two stays in Rome, several of his new acquaintances in the academies would be writing the poems that were printed in honour of her in 1639. He too celebrated her enchanting singing, although his poems did not appear in the collection. In three Latin epigrams to Leonora singing in Rome, he compliments her in high-flown hyperbole: through her, God accustoms men to hear immortal sounds, he says in *Leonora i*: if the poet Torquato Tasso had lived in her day and gone mad for love of this Leonora, her music would have had power to restore him, says the second;[1] and the third declares that Parthenope is not dead by the shore of Naples: she lives and holds sway by the Tiber at Rome, she is Leonora.

Soon after his return from Italy, the wheel came full circle; Milton had had an extended and extensive education, now he took up the education of his nephews Edward and John Phillips. In doing so he took care to encourage in them, as his father had encouraged in him, love of music and some practical musicianship. 'He made his nephews songsters, and sing from the time they were with him', noted John Aubrey; and later records of their lives show that their interest in music, like Milton's own, was lasting.

The harmony of the spheres

From his early years, Milton was drawn not only to the music he heard and could make, but to music that no man can hear and only the whole universe could make. For the Greeks, music was associated in its composition and performance with poetry and dancing, and in its theory with mathematics and philosophy. Many ancient writers relate stories about the discoveries of Pythagoras: that hearing the same interval, or difference of pitch, produced again and again by the hammers of two blacksmiths beating hot iron, he had experiments made with hammers of other weights and recorded the numerical ratios of weights that produced harmonious intervals; and that he then made similar experiments with stringed instruments. Most often told of all, that he found by experiments with a monochord that when

---

[1] Tasso in fact lived in the previous century, 1544–95; his most famous poem, the epic (and romantic) story of a crusade, *Gerusalemme liberata*, had already twice been translated into English. Tasso had addressed love poems to the princesses Leonora and Lucrezia d'Este, sisters of the Duke of Ferrara, and legend attributed his later madness to love of that Leonora.

a string is 'stopped' so as to divide its length in certain ratios, intervals such as the octave, fourth, and fifth result, which are both mathematically and musically satisfying and pleasing.[1] Some of these experiments are clearly fictitious and invalid, but they show that it was generally believed that it was Pythagoras who discovered the connection between musical intervals and mathematical proportions.

This connection led to a belief, both mystical and factual, about the nature and structure of the universe. All order, all coherence, the orbits of the heavenly bodies, were seen as arising from and depending on 'number' and the 'harmony' of number: that is, on significant mathematical ratio. The universe was thought of as a system of spheres: at its centre was the earth, around it the seven spheres of the planets, and outermost of all, the celestial sphere, all but the earth moving in mathematical order – in harmony. It is not easy now, nor was it ever, to know how literally or figuratively to interpret that harmony. One thing is clear, and Pythagoras' monochord is a reminder of it: it is not harmony in the sense of hymn-like chords, and we must train our inner ears not to hear it that way. The Greek *harmoniai* were scales, and when we try to imagine the harmony of the spheres, we should be listening for a series of intervals such as make up an octave scale. The celestial sphere and the seven planetary spheres each produced one tone (some writers held that they produced only seven in all because Mercury and Venus, moving at the same speed, produced the same one); the earth, being motionless, in most accounts produced none, but in a version quoted by Morley, whose textbook of 1597, *A plain and easy introduction to practical music*, Milton would certainly know, it produced a tone an octave below that of the heavenly sphere. The production of sound was accounted for in various ways; by the friction of glassy spheres, by the vibration of metallic spheres, or, most picturesquely, in Plato's description in the *Republic* x:

The spindle turns on the knees of Necessity; and on the upper surface of each circle is a Siren, who goes round with them hymning a single sound and note. The eight together form one harmony, and round about, at equal intervals, there is another band, three in number, each sitting upon her throne; these are the Fates, daughters of Necessity...who accompany with their voices the harmony of the Sirens.

[1] Violin players make use of this discovery when they lightly stop a string halfway up, and higher, to produce 'harmonics' – notes an octave and more above the pitch of the open string. See the *Oxford companion to music* plates 70 and 101 for pictures of monochords.

How did Plato intend this picture? How literally were any of these accounts intended? It is rarely easy to know to what extent the world-pictures of other ages and nations were conscious inventions or creations, and what kind of truth they were framed to express. Often it is we who are naïve in assuming literal-mindedness in men of subtler races and ways of thought than our own. Probably the 'harmony' of the spheres referred primarily to the mathematical aspect of the planetary system, and the connection between music and mathematics made the word more than a simple metaphor: it corresponded with a truth about the universe, it was a given insight into the structure of things. The idea was nearer to being a myth than what we might today call a model: from classical times through the Middle Ages and on to Milton's day it seemed to men to say something highly significant about the nature of things that they could not express without such a figure or image; it was not until mid-17th-century writers adopted it as a merely outsize compliment, saying their ladies' voices excelled the music of the spheres, or that the spheres stood still to hear them sing, that its imaginative potency drained away and it came to seem a mere flight of fancy. Shakespeare knew how to have it both ways: it could stand for something to be desired but hardly more to be believed in than a blue moon:

> I bade you never speak of him again.
> But would you undertake another suit,
> I had rather hear you to solicit that
> Than music from the spheres.   *Twelfth night* III i

Or it could bear greater weight: Lorenzo says:

> Sit, Jessica. Look how the floor of heaven
> Is thick inlaid with patines of bright gold.
> There's not the smallest orb which thou beholdst
> But in his motion like an angel sings,
> Still quiring to the young-eyed cherubims.
> Such harmony is in immortal souls,
> But whilst this muddy vesture of decay
> Doth grossly close it in, we cannot hear it.   *Venice* V i

Milton himself used it in a courtly compliment to the Dowager Countess of Derby in the brief entertainment *Arcades*, together with a reference to man's inability to hear it, which is close both in its explanation and its expression to Lorenzo's: the genius of the wood speaks of

240

the heavenly tune, which none can hear
Of human mould with gross unpurgèd ear;
And yet such music worthiest were to blaze
The peerless height of her immortal praise,
Whose lustre leads us...

This follows a description of the sirens and the Fates so close to Plato's that it seems Milton's mind is so filled with his reading about the subject that it must pour out. The concept had already cast its spell on him early in his Cambridge years, as his choice of it for topic in *Prolusion II, De sphaerarum concentu*, makes clear. This essay was read to an assembly of undergraduates, and the quizzical, half-joking tone of its opening shows he is rather defensive about it: he does not wish to be thought wholly serious about matters that his hearers may dismiss as belonging solely to the realm of fancy. But as he considers what has been taught by Pythagoras, 'that god among philosophers', and Plato's description, and 'the fable of the Muses dancing day and night around about Jove's altars' (which appears in *Penseroso* 47–8), the concept exerts its potency over him, and he wonders, not whether there *is* a music of the spheres, but why it is inaudible to human ears.[1] In this discourse he keeps within the terms of classical legend, but there are hints of a line of thought that shortly would lead him to make the juxtaposition and contrast of pagan myth and Christian doctrine that is at the heart of the *Nativity ode*. The ode's distinctive presentation of the scheme of man's redemption, its whole way of seeing the incarnation, come from his reflection on these ideas.[2]

The human music

The mass of speculation and myth that survived from classical times to the Middle Ages was full of ideas that provoked Christian thought or invited assimilation to a Christian world-view. From the early 6th century to the 16th the best-known compilation of such information was the treatise by the Roman writer Boëthius *On music (De institutione musica)*. He made a threefold division of music into *musica mundana, musica humana,* and *musica instrumentalis*:

There are three kinds of music: and the first is the music of the universe (*Musica mundana*), the second the human music, the third that which is practised on certain instruments, e.g., the cithara, or the tibia, in short on all instruments on which one can play a melody.

[1] This prolusion provides the key to many of Milton's concepts. It would be a valuable study to read it and make a list of echoes of its ideas in his poems.
[2] See introduction and notes to *Nativity ode* in this series.

Under the first heading he discusses the music of the spheres; the last heading covers all actual music. The second category is an unfamiliar one and not easy to grasp, but it is a significant one. It is figurative: by the human music was meant a harmony of parts in the entire human being, a 'tempering' or tuning so that body and reason and instincts combined in right proportion and so echoed or copied the harmony of heaven. This whole concept, of a harmonious universal order providing both pattern and ideal for harmonious, well-ordered human life as well as a model for actual music, was one the medieval Christian mind could readily take over and link to thought-patterns of its own, which were still current in Milton's time. In the Christian world-picture, man stands in an equivocal position: created in the image and likeness of God, he shares in the divine nature, and the pattern for his life is in heaven. But man also shares with the animals a nature of instincts and passions, which is proper to them but too low a level of life for him, and the fatal choice of following its prompting led to the fall. Now the pull of his lower nature is strong, but man is offered grace and forgiveness through the redeeming love of Christ. He can choose afresh, as Adam could choose. He can stoop to the brute life that Comus has to offer, or he can look up and aspire, as in *At a solemn music*, to 'keep in tune with heaven'. In that poem, the terms of Boethius retain their own meaning, but are also infused with Christian content: the song heard in heaven is not only sphere-music but conscious praise,[1] and if man senses it as he listens to earthly music, he will answer it with the human music of a life that is ordered to give glory to God, as he did before sin broke the harmony of the whole of creation.

Music in Eden

That early, innocent life of man, before self-will and self-love came between him and God, is described in the life of Eden in *Paradise lost*. Adam's ears were then attuned to heavenly music; when Raphael has been instructing him he replies:

> Thy words
> Attentive, and with more delighted ear,
> Divine instructor, I have heard, than when
> Cherubic songs by night from neighbouring hills
> Aërial music send: V 544

[1] See *At a solemn music* in this series; and, e.g., *PL* III 365–415, VII 180–92 and 253–4, and especially 557–68 where the song is that of *Psalm 24*.

and when he himself was instructing Eve earlier, he described the
songs they both heard:

> Millions of spiritual creatures walk the earth
> Unseen, both when we wake, and when we sleep:
> All these with ceaseless praise his works behold
> Both day and night: how often from the steep
> Of echoing hill or thicket have we heard
> Celestial voices to the midnight air,
> Sole, or responsive each to other's note
> Singing their great Creator: oft in bands
> While they keep watch, or nightly rounding walk
> With heavenly touch of instrumental sounds
> In full harmonic number joined, their songs
> Divide the night, and lift our thoughts to heaven.   IV 677

In this harmony Adam and Eve take part by joining in praise with all
other created things and beings: Adam knows he is at one with sun,
moon and stars, the elements and all else, as he, most articulate of all
God's creation, raises his morning hymn of worship (V 153–209), with
biddings to praise like those of the Benedicite, a canticle for morning
prayer in the Prayer Book.

Books IV and V are full of the music of Eden and the music of
heaven heard in Eden, but the shadow of the fall is on IX. Song is
heard in it only twice, and the two occasions are starkly parallel. On
the morning of the fateful day, Adam and Eve as usual 'joined their
vocal worship to the choir Of creatures wanting voice'. Then Eve
parts from Adam, and goes her own way, meets the serpent, eats the
fruit of the tree, and says:

> O sovereign, virtuous, precious of all trees
> In paradise, of operation blest
> To sapience, hitherto obscured, infamed,
> And thy fair fruit let hang, as to no end
> Created; but henceforth my early care,
> Not without song, each morning, and due praise
> Shall tend thee...
>   So saying, from the tree her step she turned,
> But first low reverence done, as to the power
> That dwelt within...   IX 795...834

Her song of praise, her worship, she now offers to the tree. She can
still sing, but her song, like that of the rebel angels (II 546–55), is no
longer part of the universal praise of God.

Music in heaven: the dancing angels

The angels in *Paradise lost*, like the humans, are capable of choice: they offer praise or, like the rebels, withhold it. In having motive, they are unlike the spheres, but they are very like the spheres in their motion, and here Milton gains extra resonance, not found in biblical mentions, by drawing on the older mythology. Raphael tells how they responded to the Father's declaration of the begetting and anointing of the Son:

> That day, as other solemn days, they spent
> In song and dance about the sacred hill,
> Mystical dance, which yonder starry sphere
> Of planets and of fixed in all her wheels
> Resembles nearest, mazes intricate,
> Eccentric, intervolved, yet regular
> Then most, when most irregular they seem,
> And in their motions harmony divine
> So smoothes her charming tones, that God's own ear
> Listens delighted. v 618

In *Paradise regained* there is a similar response when God tells Gabriel that Jesus will triumph over the temptation he is about to undergo from Satan:

> So spake the Eternal Father, and all heaven
> Admiring stood a space, then into hymns
> Burst forth, and in celestial measures moved,
> Circling the throne and singing, while the hand
> Sung with the voice... i 168

'Mystical dance', 'celestial measures'. If we fully grasped the nature of these angels who dance as well as sing, we should glimpse the inmost mystery of poetic creation; they are among the most marvellous products of Milton's fusing, unifying imagination. But there are clues to the concepts that went to their making.

First, there are classical accounts that liken the movement of the spheres to a dance: Plato referred in *Timaeus* to

the figures of them moving as in a dance, and their meetings with one another, and the return of their orbits on themselves, and their approximations, and which of them in their conjunctions meet and which of them are in opposition, and how they get behind and before one another, and at what times they are severally eclipsed to our sight and again reappear.

He said it would be useless for him to describe their courses in detail without being able to point them out to his readers on a model or globe, but the likening of their intricate movements to dances brings the brief passage to life – almost literally, for it carries with it the association of a human activity. It is apt because dancing matches at so many points the movement of the heavenly bodies: rhythm, regularity, pattern, measured variation, are features basic to both. It is also capable of abstract application, as a description of scientific phenomena. There is a nicely poised use in *Paradise lost* when Raphael is answering Adam's questions about astral physics:

> What if the sun
> Be centre to the world, and other stars
> By his attractive virtue and their own
> Incited, dance about him various rounds? VIII 122

This holds in balance an image of dancing in homage, attracted by virtue, and the suggestion of magnetic fields, the 'dance' of iron filings in the vicinity of a magnet, the 'attraction' of a lodestone which is its peculiar property or 'virtue'. In the idea of involuntary motion which has a scientific cause, it is linked to the theory of the motion of the spheres. In its evocation of beings drawn to pay honour to a superior being it reminds us of another classical legacy, mentioned in *Prolusion II*, 'the fable of the Muses dancing day and night around about Jove's altars'.

The activity of the blessed who welcomed Lycidas to heaven seems modelled on that of the Muses:

> There entertain him all the saints above,
> In solemn troops, and sweet societies
> That sing, and singing in their glory move.

So does that of the angels who while other angels sleep,

> in their course
> Melodious hymns about the sovereign throne
> Alternate all night long... PL v 655

and the response of the angels in *Paradise regained* who hearing what shall be achieved by the Son

> in celestial measures moved
> Circling the throne and singing, while the hand
> Sung with the voice... I 170

In these actions they are the perfect exemplars of yet another Greek concept, *mousike*, for it meant something like 'poetry in musical performance'; music and poetry together, often with the added eloquence of dance. But whatever their classical inheritance and resemblance, these angels are beings of a new and Christian order. They do not move and make harmony everlastingly and involuntarily like the spheres: they 'Admiring stood a space, then into hymns burst forth' (*PR* I 169); their music is tribute, not mathematical consequence or scientific necessity. Music in Milton's heaven is acclamation and celebration, and his angels are intelligent beings giving worship to God.

Dancing on earth

It is clear that dancing was as potent an image or model for Milton as it was for the Greeks, although his emphasis is differently placed. For them, to represent the motion of the spheres as a dance signified the mathematical nature of the universe, and the connection between mathematics and music that was in some way a key to creation itself. For most men from the Middle Ages until a scientific world-view became dominant in the late 17th century, it typified order: the dance of the stars in their courses, the dance of the angels in heaven, the dance of the seas to the moon, all things in their appointed place and degree fulfilling their role in the cosmic plan. Sir John Davies pursued the idea throughout the 131 stanzas of *Orchestra or a poem of dancing* published in 1596. As Milton considered the variety and significance of earthly dancing he would have both conceptions in mind.

The celestial dance of the stars in their courses provides man with a pattern of the beauty of order, harmonious, ceremonious and sublime. Its perfection is unattainable on earth, but in so far as he takes it for his model his own life will take on those qualities: in Boethian terms, his human music will be in tune with the universal music, his whole being will attain its true human pitch and balance. In terms of the medieval Christian outlook, he will hold his rightful place in the chain of being, controlling the animal nature that drags him below it, and asserting his spiritual kinship with the angels and God; and divine grace will uphold that assertion. This is what the Lady does in *Comus*: in rejecting the blandishments of Comus her actions are in accord with her reason, she is holding fast to a high concept of human life; and supernatural help is added to her virtue. She does not need to express this herself in actual dance; the context of the masque, the whole dimension of which is symbolic dancing, expresses it for her. And the Attendant Spirit sums it up at the end as he returns to the upper air, that paradisal region cut off from man's sight just as the music of the spheres is cut off from his hearing:

> Mortals that would follow me,
> Love virtue, she alone is free,
> She can teach you how to climb
> Higher than the sphery chime;
> Or if virtue feeble were,
> Heaven itself would stoop to her.

He had restored the Lady and her Brothers to their parents after the adventure in a processional dance which would be one of grace and ceremony expressed in measured movement, complicated and intricate in its interweavings, perfectly patterned, a replica of the order of heaven. The impact of this, the main masque-dance, would be enhanced by its utter contrast with the dancing that had gone before: the spectacular anti-masque of Comus and his rout, the mere sound of which had made the Lady think of 'wanton dance'. For Milton there is added depravity in wanton dance precisely because of the higher associations – the dance of creation, of the stars, of the angels. To make ugliness out of beauty, lasciviousness out of grace: this is the shocking, disfiguring power of evil. Dancing, the symbol of order and measure, can become the incitement to and the enactment of unruly passion.[1]

Most human dancing touches neither of these extremes of sublimity and sensuality, for nor does most of human life. Most dancing expresses celebration: it may have an element of ceremony or symbolism as when it expresses concord in general, or the union of marriage in particular; or it may be a simple demonstration of pleasure and joy. This last kind of innocent merry-making naturally has a place in the life of *Allegro* (93–6) and in *Comus* too, in the country dancing.

Milton and Henry Lawes

The dances in *Comus* express the attitudes and emotions shared by a group – a rout of debased revellers, a junketing of rustics, a stately progress of nobles – and so dances already familiar and carrying associations and atmosphere for the hearers will be the most effective.[2] But the songs reveal the intentions or feelings of individuals; they are designed to increase the audience's knowledge or extend its insight,

---

[1] See *Nativity ode* 210, *PL* II 662, XI 618 and 714 for dancing associated with unholy rites or wantonness.

[2] Music for them would probably be selected from existing dance tunes. Sir Frederick Bridge's score for *Comus* (Novello 1908) provides dances and instrumental music mostly by William Lawes, Henry's brother.

not to call upon existing responses, and so their music is as carefully made for the immediate purpose as the words. It was made by Henry Lawes, Gentleman of the Chapel Royal, musician to the earl's family, music-master to his children, and a key figure in the preparing and presenting of the masque; and these songs are the only contemporary settings of words by Milton that are known to have survived. Very probably Lawes composed music for the songs in *Arcades* but it is lost. Later settings of *Comus* and of other poems and passages of Milton have other kinds of interest as they vividly display the succession of changes in musical taste and in style of performance, but only these five songs show the kind of music that Milton had in mind as he wrote.

It was a style that owed much to the theories and experiments of the group of poets, musicians and men of wide scholarly culture centred round Count Bardi in Florence in the 1580s, and known as the Camerata. They were aware that Plato had ranked the importance of the words above harmoniousness and rhythm in song, and they aimed at re-establishing that precedence in their own day and so creating something like the lost art of Greek music. Since even the Greek terms no longer yielded their original meaning, the concept that emerged was newly specific: Plato was taken to mean that the words, both in sense and rhythm, should govern vocal line and musical rhythm. So, writing for a single voice with string accompaniment, composers turned all their attention to interpreting the words they set and giving them added lyric or dramatic expressiveness in music that made no rival claims of its own. This is the kind of aim Lawes had in his songs for *Comus*: the songs are not set pieces, introduced like framed pictures into the middle of the action; they soar naturally from the surrounding dialogue and fall back into it. The music is simply a source of increased intensity, to heighten moments of emotion or strangeness or stress, and to reinforce the dramatic context.

The Lady's song, 'Sweet Echo', for instance, evolves naturally from the situation and from her rising fear; she is alone and lost and night is falling, she must try to make her brothers hear where she is, so 'Such noise as I can make to be heard farthest I'll venture' (226) and she appeals to Echo to give extra carrying-power to the sound. It is a beautiful and poignant song, fitted in every way to its purpose and context. It seems such a natural extension of the words that it is hard to read them in isolation once one knows them as song, which suggests both how aptly Milton has framed them for singing and how successfully Lawes has used what they offer. Lawes himself, as the Spirit, sings all the other songs; here he puts his pupil through her paces, in music at once taxing and rewarding to sing, for besides being the lady lost in the wood, she is the young Lady Alice singing before her parents and all their circle at this festivity in their honour. But not in any way that breaks or delays the story; her song is part of the action and carries it forward, because it is heard not by her brothers but by Comus and leads him to her, and by the Attendant Spirit whom it warns of her danger. The other songs, in which the Spirit makes his entry and exit, invokes Sabrina, breaks up the shepherds' dance and presents the children to their parents, are less musically memorable than the lady's song, but are similar in functional value and in fitness to the occasion.[1]

Milton was evidently pleased with the song-settings; he records on the title page of *Poems 1645* that the songs have been set by Lawes, and later pays tribute to his particular talents in a sonnet addressed to him:

> Harry whose tuneful and well-measured song
> First taught our English music how to span
> Words with just note and accent, not to scan
> With Midas' ears, committing short and long;
> Thy worth and skill exempts thee from the throng...

Some later settings of Milton

Comus was made for a special occasion, to be performed once only before the Earl of Bridgewater and his family and guests at Ludlow Castle, but just over a century later the masque was remade in the image and spirit of another age, and began a long and successful career on the public stage. The text was skilfully adapted by John Dalton and set by Thomas Arne,[2] and with Arne's sister Mrs Cibber, a famous actress and contralto singer, as the Lady, and his wife, an accomplished and acclaimed soprano, as Sabrina, the new piece made its début at Drury Lane Theatre on 4 March 1738. More songs were provided, some from Milton's text, some new and typically 18th-century drinking and love songs. Arne's settings and the extra dances

---

[1] For discussion of the songs, see the introduction to *Comus* in this series. The whole masque, with four of the five songs, is recorded on Argo PLP 1024/5.

[2] Arne was a versatile composer of songs, operas, masques, oratorios and instrumental music: some of the song-settings he wrote for revivals of Shakespeare's plays are still often sung. See *Oxford companion to music* plate 2 for a portrait and a caricature of him.

he provided (such as a Dance Tambourin for pastoral nymphs) are splendidly spirited: gay, languishing, enticing, solemn. The new version is no longer the moral masque Milton wrote; but it is a musical and spectacular entertainment of great charm, and a revival of it would probably be a great success today.[1]

The supremacy given to words over music in the Commonwealth period could probably only occur at a time when there was no really major composer. The musical inventiveness of a genius like Purcell, who began composing in the 1670s, could not be restricted to a style evolved largely from theories, and by the time of Handel, who settled in England in 1712, music was clearly the dominant partner. But in *Allegro* and *Penseroso* Handel recognized poetry that deserved respect; they were prepared for him by a librettist, Charles Jennens, whose arrangements of texts inspired some of his greatest works: *The Messiah, Saul,* and *Belshazzar*. To gain dramatic contrast, Jennens alternated passages from the two poems; their verbal parallels, the opening dismissals and invocations especially, invite this.[2] (The heightened contrast between the two ways of life that results gave scope for Jennens to add a piece of his own, *Il moderato*, also set by Handel.) Handel responded by recreating the landscapes and atmosphere in vivid and varied music, delicate, serene, robust, and rumbustious – it is no accident that Laughter is 'ho-ho-ho-holding both his sides', and with this Handel set off a long line of laughing-songs.

Perhaps it is a pity that Milton and Handel did not live in the same age, for opera and oratorio did not develop in England until after Milton's death, yet *Samson agonistes* reads almost as if planned for oratorio, and oratorio has very similar aims – to achieve dramatic intensity without costume or action. A librettist who had already arranged Dryden's *Alexander's feast* for Handel, Newburgh Hamilton, shortened *Samson* by more than half, and Handel provided some splendid duets and musical disputations; Act II ends with Dalila, her virgins and Harapha praising Dagon while Samson, the Israelites and Manoah praise Jehovah in resounding competition.[3]

[1] The complete music, without spoken dialogue, is recorded on L'Oiseau-Lyre OLS 140–1, and *Musica Britannica* III 1951, *Comus*, gives both words and music. Comparison of this version with that of Lawes and Milton reveals much about the attitudes to life, as well as to music, of both ages.
[2] It would be interesting to make one's own selection of contrasting passages and compare them with Jennens's. Novello publish a vocal score and there is a recording, L'Oiseau-Lyre SOL 60025–6.
[3] Harapha's air 'Honour and arms' is on Argo ZRG 504; Samson's moving lament 'Total eclipse' is on Classics for Pleasure CFP 111. Novello publish an

Haydn also set a text drawn from Milton, but drawn from afar. *The creation* uses a German translation of an English compilation, now lost, based on *Genesis*, paraphrases of psalms, and *Paradise lost*, particularly VII and VIII, the description of Eden in IV and the morning hymn in V. Probably it was the theme that inspired Haydn, as it did Milton, not the specific text, which is woefully un-Miltonic.

Several 18th-century cantatas and other compositions used parts of *Paradise lost*, and the shorter poems were more often drawn on; Purcell had set eight lines from *Allegro* as a duet, 'Let us wander, not unseen' and in the 18th century *Allegro* and *Arcades* provided songs for an operatic adaptation of *A midsummer night's dream* produced by Garrick in 1755; *May* was set in 1740 by Michael Festing, who led the band at Ranelagh pleasure-gardens, and in 1767 *Lycidas* was made into 'a musical entertainment' by William Jackson. The best known of 19th-century settings is Sir Hubert Parry's *Blest pair of sirens*, a rewarding piece to sing; he set *Allegro* and *Penseroso* too. This century, *May* has reappeared in Britten's *Spring symphony*, Alexander Goehr has made a choral setting of *Paradise lost* XI 779–805, and with Hugh Wood's *Scenes from Comus* for soprano and tenor with orchestra the wheel comes full circle, back to a work Milton wrote with a musical partnership in mind.

Further reading

BRENNECKE, E. *John Milton the Elder and his music* 1938.

DEAN, W. *Handel's dramatic oratorios and masques* 1959.

FINNEY, G. L. *Musical backgrounds for English literature: 1580–1650* New Jersey 1961.

HOLLANDER, J. *The untuning of the sky: ideas of music in English poetry, 1500–1700* New Jersey 1961.

HUTTON, J. 'Some English poems in praise of music' in *English miscellany* ed Praz, vol 2 Rome 1951.

MORRIS, B. '"Not without song": Milton and the composers' in *Approaches to PL* ed Patrides 1968.

MYERS, R. M. *Handel, Dryden and Milton* 1956.

OLLESON, E. 'The origin and libretto of Haydn's *Creation*' in *Haydn year book* IV Vienna 1968.

abridged vocal score. An alert reader of the text will notice lines and echoes from elsewhere in Milton – *Time, Passion, Ep. March. Winch., Nativity ode* and his psalms. His psalms were also used in a less successful venture, *The occasional oratorio*, concocted by the Rev. Thomas Morell for Handel to set to show his loyalty, as a naturalized Englishman, to the monarchy after the Jacobite revolution of 1745.

SPAETH, S. *Milton's knowledge of music* Ann Arbor 1963.
See also the sections on Music and dance in the list of resources at the ends of *PL: introduction* in this series, and *M's early poems: a general introduction* in this volume.

Upon Julia's voice

> So smooth, so sweet, so silver is thy voice
> As, could they hear, the damned would make no noise
> But listen to thee walking in thy chamber
> Melting melodious words to lutes of amber.

ROBERT HERRICK before 1648

from *Orchestra, or a poem on dancing*

> Concord's true picture shineth in this art,
> Where divers men and women rankèd be
> And every one doth dance a several part,
> Yet all as one in measure do agree,
> Observing perfect uniformity:
> All turn together, all together trace
> And all together honour and embrace.

SIR JOHN DAVIES 1596

from *The commendation of music*

> O lull me, lull me, charming air!
>   My senses rock with wonder sweet;
> Like snow on wool thy fallings are,
>   Soft as a spirit's are thy feet.
>   Grief who need fear
>   That hath an ear
>   Down let him lie
>   And slumbering die
> And change his soul for harmony.

WILLIAM STRODE before 1645

from *Music's duel* [between a female nightingale, and a man with a lute]

> This lesson too
> She gives him back: her supple breast thrills out
> Sharp airs, and staggers in a warbling doubt
> Of dallying sweetness, hovers o'er her skill,
> And folds in waved notes with a trembling bill
> The pliant series of her slippery song.
> Then starts she suddenly into a throng

252

Of short thick sobs, whose thundering volleys float
And roll themselves over her lubric throat
In panting murmurs, 'stilled out of her breast,
That ever-bubbling spring, the sugared nest
Of her delicious soul, that there does lie
Bathing in streams of liquid melody

.   .   .   .

Shame now and anger mixed a double stain
In the musician's face. Yet once again,
Mistress, I come: now reach a strain, my lute,
Above her mock, or be forever mute;
Or tune a song of victory to me,
Or to thyself sing thine own obsequy.
So said, his hands sprightly as fire he flings
And with a quavering coyness tastes the strings.
The sweet-lipped Sisters, musically frighted,
Singing their fears are fearfully delighted,
Trembling as when Apollo's golden hairs
Are fanned and frizzled in the wanton airs
Of his own breath, which married to his lyre
Doth tune the spheres, and make heaven's self look higher.
From this to that, from that to this he flies,
Feels music's pulse in all her arteries.
Caught in a net which Apollo spreads,
His fingers struggle with the vocal threads;
Following those little rills, he sinks into
A sea of Helicon; his hand does go
Those parts of sweetness which with nectar drop,
Softer than that which pants in Hebe's cup...

RICHARD CRASHAW before 1649

A song. Set by Mr Leveridge

> Jogging on from yonder green,
> O the pleasant sight I've seen!
> John and Dolly jog-jog-jogging,
> John and Dolly jogging on.
> Themselves cooling, Johnny was fooling,
> Cried she, 'Will you ne'er have done
> Jog-jog, jog-jog, jog-jog jogging on?
> The sun shines, make hay,
> Make hay, make hay, make hay good John.'
> 'Hey ho, hey ho, that I might do so
> Jog-jog, jog-jog, jogging,
> Jog-jog, jog-jogging on.'
>
> John to ease her of her pain
> Ended and begun again.
> He grew weary, jog-jog-jogging,
> She more cheery jogging on:

Cried, 'My deary, prithee tarry!
Sure you ha'nt already done
Jog-jog, jog-jog, jog-jog jogging on?
The sun's down, pray stay,
Pray stay, pray stay good John.'
'Hey ho that I might do so,
Jog-jog-jogging on.'   17th-century anthologies

Henry Purcell

The poet wishes well to the divine genius of Purcell and praises him that,
whereas other musicians have given utterance to the moods of man's mind,
he has, beyond that, uttered in notes the very make and species of man as
created both in him and in all men generally.

Have fair fallen, O fair, fair have fallen, so dear
To me, so arch-especial a spirit as heaves in Henry Purcell,
An age is now since passed, since parted; with the reversal
Of the outward sentence low lays him, listed to a heresy, here.
Not mood in him nor meaning proud fire or sacred fear,
Or love or pity or all that sweet notes not his might nursle:
It is the forged feature finds me; it is the rehearsal
Of own, of abrupt self there so thrusts on, so throngs the ear.

Let him oh! with his air of angels then lift me, lay me! only I'll
Have an eye for the sakes of him, quaint moonmark, to his pelted plumage
    under
Wings: so some great stormfowl, whenever he has walked his while

The thunder-purple seabeach plumèd purple-of-thunder,
If a wuthering of his palmy snow-pinions scatter a colossal smile
Off him, but meaning motion fans fresh our wits with wonder.

G. M. HOPKINS 1879

A song for St Cecilia's Day 1687

From harmony, from heavenly harmony
    This universal frame began.
    When nature underneath a heap
        Of jarring atoms lay
    And could not heave her head,
The tuneful voice was heard from high,
        'Arise, ye more than dead!'
Then cold and hot and moist and dry
    In order to their stations leap
    And music's power obey.
From harmony, from heavenly harmony
    This universal frame began:
    From harmony to harmony
Through all the compass of the notes it ran,
The diapason closing full in man.

What passion cannot music raise and quell?
   When Jubal struck the corded shell
His listening brethren stood around
And wondering on their faces fell
  To worship that celestial sound:
Less than a god they thought there could not dwell
   Within the hollow of that shell
   That spoke so sweetly and so well.
What passion cannot music raise and quell!

    The trumpet's loud clangour
      Excites us to arms
    With shrill notes of anger
      And mortal alarms.
   The double double double beat
     Of the thundering drum
     Cries, 'Hark, the foes come!
Charge! charge! 'tis too late to retreat.'

   The soft complaining flute
   In dying notes discovers
   The woes of hopeless lovers,
Whose dirge is whispered by the warbling lute.

Sharp violins proclaim
Their jealous pangs, and desperation,
Fury, frantic indignation,
Depth of pain and height of passion
   For the fair disdainful dame.

But O what art can teach,
  What human voice can reach
The sacred organ's praise?
Notes inspiring holy love,
Notes that wing their heavenly ways
  To mend the choirs above.

Orpheus could lead the savage race
And trees uprooted left their place,
  Sequacious of the lyre;
But bright Cecilia raised the wonder higher:
  When to her organ vocal breath was given
An angel heard, and straight appeared,
  Mistaking earth for heaven.

Grand chorus

As from the power of sacred lays
  The spheres began to move
And sung the great Creator's praise
  To all the blest above:
So when the last and dreadful hour

This crumbling pageant shall devour,
The trumpet shall be heard on high,
The dead shall live, the living die,
And music shall untune the sky.   JOHN DRYDEN

from *Song for St Cecilia's Day* (for Benjamin Britten)

...Restore our fallen day; O re-arrange.

O dear white children casual as birds,
Playing among the ruined languages,
So small beside your large confusion words,
So gay against the greater silences
Of dreadful things you did: O hang the head,
Impetuous child with the tremendous brain,
O weep, child, weep, O weep away the stain,
Lost innocence that wished your lover dead,
Weep for the lives your wishes never led.

O cry created as the bow of sin
Is drawn across our trembling violin.
O weep, child, weep, O weep away the stain.
O law drummed out by hearts against the still
Long winter of our intellectual will.
That what has been may never be again.
O flute that throbs with the thanksgiving breath
Of convalescents on the shores of death.
O bless the freedom that you never chose,
O trumpets that unguarded children blow
About the fortress of their inner foe.
O wear your tribulation like a rose.   W. H. AUDEN

from *The man with the blue guitar*

They said, 'You have a blue guitar,
You do not play things as they are.'

The man replied, 'Things as they are
Are changed upon the blue guitar.'

And they said then, 'But play, you must,
A tune beyond us, yet ourselves,

A tune upon the blue guitar
Of things exactly as they are.'

.   .   .   .   .   .

I sing a hero's head, large eye
And bearded bronze, but not a man,

Although I patch it as I can
And reach through him almost to man.

256

If to serenade almost to man
Is to miss, by that, things as they are,

Say that it is the serenade
Of a man that plays a blue guitar.

. . . . . .

Do not speak to us of the greatness of poetry,
Of the torches wisping in the underground,

Of the structure of vaults upon a point of light.
There are no shadows in our sun,

Day is desire and night is sleep.
There are no shadows anywhere.

The earth, for us, is flat and bare.
There are no shadows. Poetry

Exceeding music must take the place
Of empty heaven and its hymns,

Ourselves in music must take their place,
Even in the chattering of your guitar...

WALLACE STEVENS 1937

LORNA SAGE

Milton's early poems: a general introduction

An adjustment of perspective

Milton's 1645 *Poems of Mr John Milton, both English and Latin* (and Italian) included all his early major works – the *Nativity ode, Comus, Lycidas, L'allegro* and *Il penseroso. Comus* and *Lycidas* had been published before, but the collection was an important landmark in Milton's career: it announced unmistakably that he was a poet in whose development and range one ought to be interested. In collecting (and selecting) his work he was saying that he was not merely a man who happened to write poems, but a poet. Now, with so much retrospective knowledge, this hardly seems to need saying; at the time, however, this volume must have been a very private landmark, visible only to the poet himself and his acquaintance. None of these poems exerted any real pressure, attracted any articulate audience, until *Paradise lost*, twenty years later, reflected attention back on to his early work. When we realise this, Milton's tone in these poems – and the very act of issuing the volume – become more interesting and odd. The edition is arranged with great care, the poems seem consciously 'early poems' pointing to grander achievements to come. There is a kind of irony, which cannot have escaped Milton, in the contrast between his own sense of the importance of his work, and its apparent irrelevance to what was being talked about at the time.

The volume is not unlike T. S. Eliot's *Selected poems* of 1948 with *Lycidas* corresponding to *The waste land*, but its status couldn't have been more different. To illustrate: imagine a retrospective novel about upper middle-class life in the 1930s and 40s. It might plausibly introduce characters who were reading Eliot, perhaps with difficulty but nevertheless with the sense that his style and themes were a part of their world. But an historical novel about the 1630s and 40s would ring false if it portrayed literary circles talking in that way about Milton's poetry. It wouldn't have been Milton, but Abraham Cowley, George Herbert or John Cleveland who would have occupied that sort of position. They spoke a poetic dialect which was witty, current, demanding, giving the sense they knew 'where poetry was at' – not only in that century or that culture but that month, that week. You can imagine poets like these being able to measure each other's progress in ever more reflexive wit, more complete detachment from the old, idealistic Elizabethan style. Milton, in contrast, needed to be read in a wider context, European and classical, where change was slower, and less easily detected. In a way, again, he can be compared with Eliot whose links were also with Europe and a classical past. But Eliot was part of an articulate and forceful group of writers and critics who succeeded in broadening the taste of readers, whereas Milton was not.

It would be wrong to cast him in the role of 'romantically unknown genius' – personally he was in no way isolated. In the 1645 volume he printed a group of his friends' eulogies of himself in Italian and Latin, and in his preface to these he wrote (in Latin) that he 'sees a signal honour to himself in the favourable judgement of men of intellect reinforced by high distinction'. It is very hard for a modern reader to estimate rightly the importance of Latin as a common language in the 17th century, a cultural link between nations, times and places; but even allowing for the ease of educated Latin dialogue, there is a slight contradiction in prefacing the English poems, poems that must do their work in English if at all, with these learned encomia. The paradox of Milton's position is inescapable. In a Latin ode to the librarian of Oxford university, who had requested another copy of his poems (the first having been lost) some of the tension seems to emerge. There is rather more than the conventional scorn for the swinish multitude, and rather more than the conventional gesture towards posterity:

So, my labours, you have not been in vain, as it turns out: not in vain, the tricklings of my sluggish genius. Now at last I can tell you to look forward to peace and rest, all envy past, and to the happy home which kind Hermes, and Rouse with his expert guardianship, will provide: a home to which the insolent clamourings of the rabble will never penetrate, far away from the vulgar mob of readers. But perhaps the children of the future, in some distant and wiser age, will see things in a fairer light and with unprejudiced hearts. Then, when spite and malice are buried in the past, posterity with its balanced judgement will know – thanks to Rouse – what, if anything, I have deserved.

The tone is hard to decide about: Latin, of course, tends to de-
personalize, which is part of the reason why Milton used it. The
exaggeration seems both playful and strained – he protests too much
that he does not want to be read, or only by the initiate. The university library is an appropriate place to bury his book alive, but he's
impatient for the time when posterity will exhume it.

Milton's confidence, then, is an imposing construct. It is also,
possibly, precarious; his playful arrogance may function partly as
compensation. Whatever its motives, the tone of his wit is very
different from the wit of his contemporaries like Cowley:

> I thought, I'll swear, an handsome lie
> Had been no sin at all in poetry:
> But now I suffer an arrest,
> For words were spoke by me in jest.
> Dull, sottish god of love, and can it be
> Thou understand'st not raillery?
>
> 'Darts', and 'wounds', and 'flame', and 'heat',
> I named but for the rhyme, or the conceit;
> Nor meant my verse should raisèd be
> To this sad fame of prophecy;
> Truth gives a dull propriety to my style,
> And all the metaphors does spoil.

These lively stanzas from a poem called *The dissembler* show Cowley
having fun with the conventional 'props' of the love poet ('wounds'
and 'flame' etc.); his poems, like those of his most witty and self-
conscious contemporaries, mock at the poet's craft. At this period the
most 'modern' verse got its energy out of spinning ironic fantasies
round outdated styles.

In contrast one can note the essential and old-fashioned seriousness
of Milton even in *L'allegro*. Rather than seeming revolutionary, the
beginning of a career that was to change the direction of English
poetry, the *Poems of Mr John Milton* may well have seemed recog-
nizable and undisturbing.

His closest affinities, ironically, were with the courtier-poets who
carried on some aspects of the Elizabethan tradition in praise of the
Stuart kings. Masques, classical and pastoral imagery, became
symbols of the slightly hysterical gaiety of the life of the court. Here
is Thomas Carew (1595–1640) writing a poetical letter to his friend
Aurelian Townsend (1583–1651) who had suggested that Carew
should write an elegy on the part played in the Thirty Years' War by
the King of Sweden who died fighting for protestantism at the Battle
of Lützen in 1632:

> ...these are subjects proper to our clime,
> Tourneys, masques, theatres, better become
> Our halcyon days. What though the German drum
> Bellows for freedom and revenge, the noise
> Concerns not us, nor should divert our joys;
> Nor ought the thunder of their carabins
> Drown the sweet air of our tuned violins.
> Believe me, friend, if their prevailing powers
> Gain them a calm security like ours,
> They'll hang their arms up on the olive bough,
> And dance and revel then, as we do now.

Conformity in poetic tradition seemed to go along with conformity in religion and politics. Milton used the same genres, even some of the same props perhaps (*Comus* may well have been performed in costumes and disguises left over from one of Carew's court masques) but for very different ends. Thus he was in an oddly isolated position: he was using established modes in a new way, ultimately a subversive way. He belonged neither with witty sceptics like Cowley, nor deliberate conformists like Carew.

By the time he wrote *Lycidas* Milton was fully aware that what he was engaged on was a major rewriting of what had been passing for 'tradition': he was undoing the old symbolism, which associated pastoral imagery with the *status quo*, and reviving a more ancient association of pastoral with revolution. But despite the careful arrangement of the 1645 edition, he had not always been so certain of where he stood. He arrived at *Lycidas* by an idiosyncratic, sometimes untidy route which the 1645 volume seems to do its best to cover up. Any vulnerability, or sense of insecurity (such as his manoeuvres against the contemporary tide must have caused) is concealed in a masterly fashion. Milton has excluded muddle, failure, contingency, all the signs of the experiment he was continuously engaged in. The major exception to this, the unfinished poem *The passion*, only proves the rule. His note to this poem, 'This subject the author finding to be above the years he had, when he wrote it, and nothing satisfied with what was begun, left it unfinished', is an example of self-awareness, control, maturity. The fragment's very inclusion invites us to think of the poet as his own, very adequate, critic. He turns a nominal failure into an advertisement for his taste and judgement. Many pressures must have operated to make Milton present himself so determinedly as a finished product: isolation, I have suggested, was one. Another, and perhaps a greater, was his intention to make himself into a great poet: he wants this collection to appear as a controlled summary of a phase in his career, a career, of course, that was still to come. This may sound implausible, but psychologically it would make sense – having published what amounts to his 'early poems' he is then freed – and obliged – to write the 'major works' to follow. A modern comparison again may help here: James Joyce's *Portrait of the artist as a young man* (1916) ends (rather like *Lycidas*) with a gesture towards the as-yet unrealized future:

Welcome, O life! I go to encounter for the millionth time the reality of experience and to forge in the smithy of my soul the uncreated conscience of my race...Old father, old artificer, stand me now and ever in good stead.

The closer example of Joyce may serve to remind us that this kind of prophetic faith is anything but easy. We tend to under-rate the amount of creative energy certain artists – Milton and Joyce among them – put into shaping their lives in order to write their works. It is easy to be taken in by the illusion they project, and to treat them as distantly god-like figures in control of all the pressures and accidents of existence. But the future each of them refers to ('Tomorrow to fresh woods, and pastures new') is one he himself must painfully bring into being. We must resist, then, the temptation to look at Milton's 'early poems' entirely from the perspective of his later work, even though he himself has set about the task of excluding from our image of his career most of the symptoms of failure and uncertainty. He succeeds in this rather too thoroughly, I feel, for the reader's comfort – hence the rather off-putting impression of polish and limited perfection one gets at first. This was not what he meant when he said later that the poet should be 'himself a true poem'. The great danger is that the reader will be alienated by a poet who seems so self-sufficient and autonomous. It's this impression of Milton that has tempted many – notably Robert Graves in *Wife to Mr Milton* – to go rooting amongst Milton's laundry bills to prove that he was as inadequate, messy, and lacking in self-awareness as the rest of us.

Neither version – the godlike author of his own fate or Graves' arrogant prig – is really plausible. Milton is not defined by the myths of himself that have passed into literary tradition: the tension between product and process, finish and experiment, is at its liveliest in these poems. The gloss on the surface was a way of rationalizing, perhaps, the poet's isolation – he put the irony and the mess to one side in order to take himself – and poetry – seriously.

Idealism

Taking poetry seriously meant measuring himself against the highest demands that had been made of the arts; and for Milton, this meant getting involved with the vaguest and most 'inspiring' of renaissance philosophies – Neo-Platonism. In his earliest poems Milton is very literal-mindedly the high priest of this difficult poetic theology. Neo-Platonism was a tangle of mysticism and mathematics, magic and psychology, which derived from the merging, in the 15th and 16th centuries, of Christian faith with pagan myth and philosophy. Its forms were multiple, but were all based on the assumption (deriving from Plato) that there is not one 'world' but two: (i) the perceptible universe at the ends of our senses and (ii) an underlying pervasive 'paradigm' or idea (which might be called 'Harmony' or 'Beauty' or God). In a Latin letter to his friend Diodati in 1637 Milton declared himself an idealist in the most unambiguous terms:

Ceres in the fable did not search more laboriously for her daughter Proserpine, than I have sought, and still seek day and night, for this Idea of the beautiful – as though I am looking for a particular image of supreme beauty – through all the forms and appearances of things.

Arcades (?1632) had used a similar image for the artist, this time more elaborate and referring to the music of the spheres:

> ...in deep of night when drowsiness
> Hath locked up mortal sense, then listen I
> To the celestial sirens' harmony,
> That sit upon the nine enfolded spheres...
> And the low world in measured motion draw
> After the heavenly tune, which none can hear
> Of human mould with gross unpurgèd ear.

At a solemn music too, expounds the Platonist doctrine that all earthly music is an echo or copy of that heavenly music which is there all the time though 'gross unpurgèd' human ears cannot reach it. 'Music' becomes the favoured metaphor for all the arts, because it is the least 'gross', the least material and most evanescent, and there is a long tradition of the importance of music as a moral and religious force:

it was the opinion of very wise philosophers that the world is made up of music, that the heavens in their motion make harmony, and that even the human soul was formed on the same principle, and is therefore awakened and has its virtues brought to life, as it were, through music...I remember also having heard once that both Plato and Aristotle wish a man who is well constituted to be a musician; and with innumerable reasons they show that music's power over us is very great; and (for many reasons which would be too long to tell now) that music must of necessity be learned from childhood, not so much for the sake of that outward melody which is heard, but because of the power it has to induce a good new habit of mind and an inclination to virtue.   Castiglione *The courtier* 1528

By the time Milton was writing this sort of claim had become a well-worn commonplace. As Milton applied it, to begin with, in poetry it meant something like this: God first created the world, and man, as though he were composing music, by the harmonious interrelation of all their elements; 'disproportioned sin' as Milton calls it, distorted and fragmented the order of the creation, and now man can only re-achieve harmony through the arts, which imitate God's original 'harmony' and re-assemble the elements of the soul. (An image often used to explain how art affects people was the phenomenon of sympathetic vibration: if you have two lutes, tuned alike, and strike a note on one, the other will vibrate in sympathy. Similarly, if the poet achieves the right 'harmony' in his verse, his readers will find their feelings restored and harmonized.)

Assertions like these about the arts undoubtedly give them a central position, and sound inspiring: the artist does the jobs of psychologist, philosopher, teacher, doctor... But one's next reaction might be that, with all these grand claims, an essential fact about the artist is glossed over, or even missing altogether – the fact that he is someone who works in a particular medium, with particular problems. *How*, in terms of the poet's medium, language, is he to achieve this harmony? One of the reasons I quoted at length from Castiglione was to bring out the deliberate vagueness that is so characteristic of this mode of thought. Note the cultivation of mysteriousness. 'I remember... having heard once...with innumerable reasons...too long to tell'. Milton was excited and inspired by the power Platonism promised the poet, but how was he to achieve it, literally, in practice?

Poetry is particularly difficult to think about in Platonic terms, because the poet's medium is language, and words are so much and so obviously a part of the fallen everyday world of discord, controversy and utility. The meaning of words is fluid, ambiguous, determined by usage, and verbal rhetoric serves the purposes of lawyers and politicians as well as poets. Milton is painfully conscious at times that language is compromised by its involvement with what are to him superficial or alien elements in the culture. His initial response is to try to 'purify' it, to use it in as musical and unprosaic a way as possible. In two poems especially, the *Hymn on the morning of Christ's nativity* and *The passion*, we can see him battling with his medium, impatient of its inability to literally achieve the ideal order he wanted. One can imagine him, at this stage, tempted to turn away from language altogether in favour of formula and Idea. These poems represent, in a way, an early 'dead-end' for Milton, a path that led nowhere. But on the longer view he would probably never have got so much out of himself or his language if he had not started off asking the impossible. These dissatified 'paradigmatic' poems were a way of mapping out the possibilities and limits of words.

In the *Nativity ode* Milton seems to have tried to embed the meaning of the poem as much in pattern, metre, sound as in what is directly 'said'. He evades in this way our usual utilitarian desire to get quickly at the meaning of a statement, and makes us concentrate on its structure. A brief analysis of two stanzas will indicate something of the technique.

xiii   Ring out, ye crystal spheres,
      Once bless our human ears
       (If ye have power to touch our senses so),
      And let your silver chime
      Move in melodious time;
       And let the bass of heaven's deep organ blow,
      And with your ninefold harmony
      Make up full consort to the angelic symphony.

The stanza begins with a confident command, but the second line undercuts the confidence. It is clear now that this is a prayer: '*Once* bless' implies human ears have never heard the music, and perhaps never will. The parenthesis ('If...') confirms the doubt: 'our senses' are too dull and crude. The next two lines include both feelings, they sound confident but the rhyme ('time' and 'chime') is a cliché and thus suggests that human music can only mimic heaven's. ('Time' is a pun: it means musical time, but also reminds us that we live in a world dominated by time, and cannot grasp eternity.) The 'bass of heaven's deep organ' swells to a climax, where we seem to catch for a moment the richness of the eternal music, but the last two lines let it fade away. 'Harmony' and 'symphony' does the opposite of 'time' and 'chime' – that was an over-obvious rhyme, this is an under-stated almost inaudible one. The music fades away into *theory*, the idea of harmony, not the thing itself. Milton is here acting out, in his use of rhythm and rhyme, his sense of the inevitable distance between his earthly music and the full resonant harmony of heaven's. In the parts of the poem that are about the pagan 'gods' of earth, he uses effects of sound in a very different way.

xix   The oracles are dumb,
    No voice or hideous hum
      Runs through the archèd roof in words deceiving.
    Apollo from his shrine
    Can no more divine,
      With hollow shriek the steep of Delphos leaving.
    No nightly trance, or breathèd spell,
    Inspires the pale-eyed priest from the prophetic cell.

Here the rhythm is much less complex and hesitant: Milton doesn't have to make the distinction between two levels of harmony. The sound-effects suggest a primitive drum beat, or hectic pulse (anticipating Comus), and alliteration and feminine rhyme (deceiving–leaving) make the already heavy stresses even stronger. The stanza (like most of the stanzas about the fallen world) ends on a full rhyme. This earthly and discordant 'music' can be much more totally realized in words than can the music of the spheres, which lies on the very threshold of human perception.

The phrase 'words deceiving' in stanza xix may well indicate a real doubt here on Milton's part: words are much better, perhaps, at deceiving, than at telling the truth. Paganism can be fully, and kinetically embodied, whereas the positive Christian truth can only be indicated and suggested. But Milton went further than this in the *Hymn* to 'build-in' his Platonic convictions: he used the symbolism of numbers. The introduction has four 7-line stanzas, suggesting the seven days of the week, and the 28 days of the lunar month, i.e. the time-dominated world in which the poem begins. In the *Hymn* itself, the stanzas have 8 lines, indicating the poet's aspiration to get out of the seven-day week into the mystical 'eighth day' of eternity (they also refer to the musical octave, the basis of harmony). Modern scholars have rediscovered this elaborate number symbolism; one of them, Alastair Fowler, has called it aptly 'silent poetry'. Its use here is the most telling and extreme sign of Milton's desire to by-pass – he might have said transcend – the limits of language.

Number symbolism raises some basic questions about communication. The use of numerical formulae suggests an image of the poet-as-magician: if you build in the right numerical combinations, then the poem, rather like a spell or incantation, will have its desired effect. This of course is nonsense – we only respond to numbers through the medium of harmonies of sound and meaning. The *Nativity ode* is a great poem because of Milton's extraordinary craftsmanship in verse, because of its *poetic* logic. The number symbolism seems mainly interesting as a symptom of the (poetically) negative side of idealism: the logical end of a cult of 'silent poetry' is the epigram, or the anagram, or even an equation – if what matters is the formula, why art, why poetry at all? Milton was in danger of a subtle kind of alienation; it is only the isolated and inward-looking poet who will look for a magical formula to operate on his audience unawares. The *Hymn* escapes the final self-contradiction, though it has a rather self-conscious air of secret writing. In *The passion*, however, the inadequacy of his theoretical approach to poetry catches up with Milton; if he had treated the nativity as a divine rather than a human event, he treats Christ's suffering even more clearly as a theological paradox.

The passion is presented as a fragment, but it could never one suspects have been finished, because here Milton's alienation from his medium becomes nearly complete. The poem is set up in anti-poetic terms. The poet is obsessively aware of the paradox in the idea that God should die, and seems to regard the death as a fiction, or a play. He talks of the 'stage of air and earth'; Christ becomes 'most perfect *hero*' – his incarnation is merely a temporary role: 'O what a mask was there, what a disguise!' The underlying *idea* of God's sacrifice of himself in his Son has come so much into the foreground that the act itself becomes like acting – a kind of play God has produced to explain himself to man. The poet, not surprisingly, is moved less to pity than to intellectual excitement – he is less interested in Christ's pain, than in himself emulating God's ingenuity. He is writing about poetry, rather than writing it:

> Befriend me night...
> And work my flattered fancy to belief,
> That heaven and earth are coloured with my woe...
>
> ...on the softened quarry would I score
> My plaining verse as lively as before;
>   For sure so well instructed are my tears,
> That they would fitly fall in ordered characters.

He is consciously constructing fictions, with little faith in his own medium; just as he cannot believe in Christ really becoming human, so he cannot believe that his human verse can grasp God's meaning. The incongruity of the conceits ('The leaves should all be black whereon I write, And letters where my tears have washed a wannish white') is deliberate: the reader is *supposed* to register the gulf between the poem's language and its real meaning. We are not meant to be moved by any 'outer' harmony, but by the inner inexpressible truth; so, by a weird logic, the poem succeeds by failing: it cannot be finished, its fragmentary state seems to fit its 'message', that poetry cannot capture the ideal.

The passion is a self-defeated poem, but defeats are often more informative than victories. Milton's self-consciousness, his pre-occupation with the abstract and diagrammatic, had undermined his confidence in language; and without expression, any amount of heightened awareness is useless to anyone but the possessor. He might have maintained, as Cowley was to do later,

> Though no man hear it, no man it rehearse,
> Yet will there still be music in my verse.   *Davideis*

But, being Milton, he wanted to act on the world, not simply be right about it, so he had to come to a new working relationship with his language. His idealist questioning of the medium had given him a detailed understanding of sound and rhythm, which he could turn outwards as communication, having found little satisfaction in the loneliness of esoteric symbolism.

(A note on number symbolism: *Lycidas* is the last major poem in which Milton uses it extensively, and there it backs up a much more confident and flexible use of language. In *Comus* and *Paradise lost* Milton relegated the magic, the numbers, mainly to the use of the black magicians, Comus and Satan ('I under...well placed words... Wind me into the easy-hearted man And hug him into snares' – Comus). Comus' temptation speeches (665–89; 706–55) are 25 and 50 lines long, multiples of the five senses he hopes to entrap: Satan's speech to Eve has sinister properties too. Giving the numbers to the villains was a neat way of sloughing off this doubtful lore.)

Community

In his Latin poem *Ad patrem* (perhaps written as early as 1632) Milton recalled the original function of the poet in primitive heroic communities:

Songs were wont, in olden days, to adorn the rich feasts of kings, when luxury, and the limitless abyss of the bottomless gullet were yet unknown, and the banquet tables foamed only with modest wines. In those days, the bard, seated in accord with custom at the holiday feast, his unshorn locks bound with leaves from the oak-tree, used to sing of the achievements of heroes.

268

This 'bard' is not self-conscious or obscure: his presence is solid and confident, his place in the community assured, 'seated in accord with custom at the holiday feast'. In the early 1630s Milton put a lot of energy into immersing himself in the imagery and values of community. *Arcades, L'allegro, Il penseroso, Comus* (written between 1630 and 1634) are all public and communicative works. Milton seems, in them, to gain a fresh awareness that creativity is not confined to God and the artist: it is the world itself, in *L'allegro*, that produces, whether at work or at play, a spontaneous 'festival' of sound, song, dance, folk tale and pageant:

> the ploughman near at hand
> Whistles o'er the furrowed land,
> And the milkmaid singeth blithe,
> And the mower whets his scythe,
> And every shepherd tells his tale
> Under the hawthorn in the dale.
>
> Where throngs of knights and barons bold,
> In weeds of peace high triumphs hold,
> With store of ladies, whose bright eyes
> Rain influence, and judge the prize,
> Of wit, or arms, while both contend
> To win her grace, whom all commend.

Instead of looking through things to the ghostly paradigm 'beyond', Milton is here looking at them. The world of time no longer seems merely a blot on eternity: the gradations of light and shade, of dawn, noon, dusk and evening acquire a new vibrance. They're not merely scenery, a backcloth to heavenly revelation, but harmonious and valuable in themselves. His use of language changes too: it becomes relaxed and emphatic, and the words do their work without strain or distortion. The poet-figure in *L'allegro* seems to be letting the world speak, articulating the music nature and people make spontaneously. He can afford to be passive:

> And ever against eating cares,
> Lap me in soft Lydian airs,
> Married to immortal verse...

He's not a solitary 'maker' but himself part of the audience. The poet's dream merges into the dream of the whole community.

But *L'allegro* is, literally, only half the story. *Il penseroso*, its inseparable companion poem, reinstates the solitary behind the poet of society:

> Or let my lamp at midnight hour
> Be seen in some high lonely tower...

Outgoing interests have not distracted him from the ideal: the poet
has now a dual role – he is a hermit in the midst of a sunshine holiday,
a meditative presence set apart by his heightened awareness. The
relations between the two poems are inexhaustible. Each implies the
other, just as day follows night, and winter summer. Milton has
achieved a truce with the world. He becomes an accepted 'outsider';
he may lose himself in esoteric lore in his 'lonely tower' but he knows
his lamp will be 'seen'.

In these poems Milton employs myth in a new way: the *Nativity
ode* bristles with allusions to classical myth, like entries in a dictionary
of mythology, but here, though there are allusions to Orpheus, and to
classical deities, the overall effect is very different. Instead of a mosaic
of distinct references, the poems themselves compose one myth, a
radiant atmosphere of pastoral freshness. The whole society Milton
conjures up is a product of many imaginations: his milkmaid is a
glimpsed character from the collective consciousness of generations
of writers, folk singers, painters. This kind of myth is unspecific, not
the property of any one writer, or any one time: the pastoral image
changes constantly in its tone, even in its content, but retains always
the central sense of community. Each major poet gives the tradition
a new and particular stamp. Compare, for example, Yeats' version of
pastoral in *Under Ben Bulben* (1938):

> Sing the peasantry, and then
> Hard-riding country gentlemen,
> The holiness of monks, and after
> Porter-drinkers' randy laughter;
> Sing the lords and ladies gay
> That were beaten into the clay
> Through seven heroic centuries.

Yeats' community is aggressively masculine compared with Milton's,
but the underlying mythic shape is the same: hierarchy, interrelatedness, tradition and spontaneity are the values conveyed by
both.

Pastoral is 'a land too ripe for enigmas' (as the American poet
Wallace Stevens puts it). For Milton it perhaps served as a way of
humanizing the abstract intelligence, of exploring the traditions and
enduring norms at the base of human communities. But whatever
Milton's personal reasons for diverting his energies into this myth of
community, he coincided with what his society was asking of the poet.

For pastoral is not merely a literary convention: in the early 17th century pastoral pageants and masques were a way of enacting social solidarity, keeping an aristocratic society in touch with the clarity, order and serenity of a simpler pattern of existence.

Milton's *Arcades* (written for the Countess Dowager of Derby) and *Comus* (written for the Earl of Bridgewater) express not merely the poet's values, but his society's image of itself and its origins. In writing a masque the poet was absorbed into community in several ways: not only was he a purveyor of 'instant' myth for the aristocratic patrons who performed in the masque and were its audience, but he worked in co-operation with musicians and designers. When *Comus* was performed on 29 September 1634 in Ludlow Castle the focus of attention was not the verse, the music or the scenery as separate artistic achievements, but the occasion as a whole, and at the centre of it the noble 'actors', the children of the earl, Lady Alice Egerton (aged fifteen) and her two brothers John (eleven) and Thomas (nine), who played the major parts. The poet's role was subsumed in the social occasion; as the 'Genius of the Wood' had said in Milton's earlier masque *Arcades*, the artist in this context is a servant who 'with all helpful service will comply To further this night's glad solemnity'. In *Comus* the artists behind the masque were represented by the Attendant Spirit (Thyrsis) 'who to the service of this house belongs'. The parts Milton wrote for the young Egerton children were not meant to involve 'acting' in the professional sense (impersonating some other character than one's own). Rather, they were playing themselves, the poet was merely giving words to the beliefs and values they, perhaps unconsciously, held. Their youth is appropriate, for in the world of pastoral, wisdom is inherited (like rank) and the young have the balance and poise of 'heroic centuries' behind them. The surface texture of *Comus* provides a rich embodiment of the values of civilization; the Lady and her brothers have exactly the sense of responsibility, the implicit belief in the right order of things that one would expect. These orderly values are threatened by the encroachment of chaos and corruption in the person of Comus, and are saved by appealing to traditional purity and sanctity in Sabrina. Throughout the masque we are reminded of inherited ideals of harmony: the action which begins in the wild woods ends against a scene 'representing Ludlow Town and the President's castle' with country dances ('jigs and rural dance') succeeded by the 'court guise' of the Lady and her brothers (getting all the social strata in) and finally general dancing in which all the audience take part.

The composite artist-figure Thyrsis (played by the musician Henry Lawes, but representing all the artists concerned, including Milton) is the guide and guardian of the young people through the mazes of the wood. He supplies very much the kind of folk wisdom the poet wishes for in *Il penseroso*:

> And may at last my weary age
> Find out the peaceful hermitage,
> The hairy gown and mossy cell,
> Where I may sit and rightly spell
> Of every star that heaven doth shew,
> And every herb that sips the dew;
> Till old experience do attain
> To something like prophetic strain.

This kind of wisdom is certainly special, but it doesn't set the artist completely apart from the community, rather the reverse. Every community would have its hermit, or its 'Thyrsis' to supply traditional pastoral lore based on 'old experience'. On this view, the artist's role is as a repository of the knowledge built up collectively in his society. The only direct reference to Milton himself in *Comus* places him well inside the tradition. Thyrsis says:

> Care and utmost shifts
> How to secure the Lady from surprisal,
> Brought to my mind a certain shepherd lad
> Of small regard to see to, yet well skilled
> In every virtuous plant and healing herb
> That spreads her verdant leaf to the morning ray...

Milton is hidden away behind the action, referred to, but never seen.

So far it's possible to see in *Comus* a supremely decorous masque, with the poet entirely subservient to the social occasion. Milton seems to be articulating a myth which is not solely the product of his vision, but a collective ritual, a celebration of society's ties with a simpler past when every forest had its demon, and every river its nymph, like Sabrina:

> still she retains
> Her maiden gentleness, and oft at eve
> Visits the herds along the twilight meadows,
> Helping all urchin blasts, and ill-luck signs
> That the shrewd meddling elf delights to make,
> Which she with precious vialled liquors heals.
> For which the shepherds at their festivals
> Carol her goodness loud in rustic lays,
> And throw sweet garland wreaths into her stream
> Of pansies, pinks, and gaudy daffodils.

But this pastoral order, where all the meaning is immediate and displayed on the surface, is not the whole story. The structure of *Comus* goes beyond collective myth. Despite Milton's graceful reference to himself as 'a certain shepherd lad Of small regard to see to', he is in fact a dominant presence. *Comus* serves its society, but it also serves its author: the humility of the poet, if not exactly fake, is misleading. For the masque has not one, but two structural principles: in the one I've been exploring (call it the public or collective one) Sabrina is the answer to the threat represented by Comus, and the artists – Thyrsis and the 'shepherd lad' – are merely the means to articulating values inherent in human communities. In the other – which is allegorical – the answer to Comus is not Sabrina, but Thyrsis who, far from being a humble shepherd, is 'really' the Attendant Spirit, supplying the human characters with wisdom from *beyond the world*.[1]

Milton has contrived an extraordinary illusion in *Comus*: the illusion that the characters are free, are merely expressing their own sense of values, when at the same time they're acting out his own pre-determined purpose. Wallace Stevens in *Credences of summer* (1947) might well have been thinking of Milton's achievement when he explored the relationship between the pastoral poet and his characters:

> The personae of summer play the characters
> Of an inhuman author, who meditates
> With the gold bugs, in blue meadows, late at night.
> He does not hear his characters talk, he sees
> Them mottled, in the moodiest costumes,
>
> Of blue and yellow, sky and sun...
>   ...appropriate habit for
> The huge decorum, the manner of the time,
> Part of the mottled mood of summer's whole,
>
> In which the characters speak because they want
> To speak, the fat, the roseate characters,
> Free, for a moment, from malice and sudden cry,
> Complete in a completed scene, speaking
> Their parts as in a youthful happiness.

The last line recalls Milton's youthful characters in *Comus*, but we would hardly sum up the effect of the Lady's role as 'youthful happiness'. Milton has constrained his characters' youth into his mould; although the young Egertons had acted in masques before,

---

[1] These two structures might be set out in two different diagrams: in one Comus and Sabrina would appear as opposites, the corrupting and purifying forces of the natural world; in the other, they would *both* (as natural *forces*) be set over against, and below, the Spirit (whose power is from heaven).

the amount they had to learn for *Comus* must have taxed their powers. And not just the amount: the morality of the masque does not rely on the fact of their nobility, but demands that they work things out:

> Elder Bro. My sister is not so defenceless left
> As you imagine, she has a hidden strength
> Which you remember not.
>
> 2nd Bro. What hidden strength,
> Unless the strength of heaven, if you mean that?
>
> Elder Bro. I mean that too, but yet a hidden strength
> Which if heaven gave it, may be termed her own:
> 'Tis chastity, my brother, chastity;
> She that has that, is clad in cómplete steel...

In *Comus* it is not merely the artist-figures who are hermit-like: Milton has made the Lady, too, into someone who is not thoroughly at home in the world. The stress on chastity might be socially appropriate if it implied virginity before marriage, but as many commentators have noted, it seems in *Comus* to mean a permanent nunlike resolve to turn away from the world. The world of pastoral is very much a place for marriages ('There let Hymen oft appear', *L'allegro*); if you're thinking about people as members of a continuing community, then marriage is centrally important. But if, as Milton seems to be doing, you're thinking about people as individual pilgrims each working out their own relationship to God, the logical and central symbol is virginity. What Milton has done is make the myth of community a cover for an allegory of the individual's spiritual quest.

At this point it may be helpful to offer a tentative definition of 'allegory'. The word allegory originates in a compound of two Greek words, *allos* plus *agoreuein*; *agoreuein* means 'to speak openly, speak in the assembly'; *allos* means 'other'; so the compound means 'to do the reverse of speaking openly'. We have not really left behind the hint of 'secret writing' in the *Nativity ode* – allegory, like number symbolism, is a way of building in an underlying ideal meaning. It enables the poet to serve two purposes at once, to leave the imprint of his own world-view on public material. The 'inhuman author' Wallace Stevens humorously referred to is very much a presence in *Comus*, making the masque a statement about the artist's world and his powers, over and above the community occasion. Thus, despite Milton's foray into his society, we arrive back at the hard core of individuality that never quite gets absorbed into community values. The masques Lady Alice and her brothers had performed in at court had been spectacular and diffuse, their authors passively submitting to the occasion. *Comus* goes through the social ritual effectively enough, but it also does a lot more. Milton, it seems clear, could not find in the shared myth a full statement of all he meant, so that while serving the 'glad solemnity' of the evening at Ludlow, he also made his aristocratic 'actors' work something out for him. That 'something' is the allegory of *Comus* which, in its implications, moves a long way from the 'sunshine holiday' atmosphere of celebration. Milton's truce with his world was brief.

Allegory

If, in terms of the pastoral structure, Comus and Sabrina are opposing forces in nature, on the allegorical level they are both subject to a higher power – that represented by the Attendant Spirit. In the social myth the Spirit is a functionary, a sort of mythological admirable Crichton. Allegorically he is in a position much more like that of Shakespeare's Prospero in *The tempest*: an artist-god (or at least artist-wizard) who in some faintly sinister way is 'behind the whole thing'. It is he who introduces both Comus and Sabrina to the stage, and does it in a manner that draws attention to his own artistic and conjuring powers:

> And listen why, for I will tell ye now
> What never yet was heard in tale, or song
> From old, or modern bard in hall, or bower.   43
>
> I'll tell ye, 'tis not vain, or fabulous
> (Though so esteemed by shallow ignorance),
> What the sage poets taught by the heavenly Muse,
> Storied of old in high immortal verse
> Of dire chimeras and enchanted isles,
> And rifted rocks whose entrance leads to hell,
> For such there be, but unbelief is blind.   513
>
> Yet stay, be not disturbed, now I bethink me,
> Some other means I have that may be used,
> Which once of Meliboeus old I learnt
> The soothest shepherd that e'er piped on plains.   820
>   [Meliboeus is Spenser]

There's more than a suspicion that both Comus and Sabrina are conjured up by the Spirit; and in fact the whole landscape the young people travel through, like the island in *The tempest*, is subject to the powers of art, with sudden transformations and changes of atmosphere.

The Spirit surrounds the Lady and her brothers with a world which is peopled by emblematic objects and creatures representing moral choices.

The first of these is of course Comus himself. Milton shows himself a master of theatrical irony in the way he 'frames' Comus in the masque: for Comus believes himself in control of his world until, at the climax of his encounter with the Lady, he senses the presence of an over-riding will:

> She fables not, I feel that I do fear
> Her words set off by some superior power...   800

Even when he first enters (at line 93), in the very act of declaring his freedom from restraint, he is mimicking and parodying the earlier opening speech of the Spirit. Where the Spirit had regretted descending into 'this dim spot', Comus welcomes night, and exorcises day. The Spirit had disguised himself as a shepherd, and Comus, delighting in his own cunning, does so too. The 'message' of this is clear: Comus exists in an entirely determined world in which his actions, despite himself, serve the purposes of 'some superior power'. Evil, in *Comus*, would perhaps be more accurately defined as 'ungood', a perverse ignorance of reality and truth. To the Lady, when she enters, the wild wood is alien and disturbing – to Comus and his animal-headed followers it's 'home'. Allegorical images are always more complex and suggestive than the abstractions behind them; what Comus seems to represent is not merely animal sensuality but 'primitivism'. His temptation is subtly adapted to civilized and sophisticated people – high civilization can slip with frightening ease into decadence, when people feel they can now stop struggling and discovering, and rest at last. In his 'orient liquor' Comus offers the kind of peace to be got out of coming to terms with the primitive, the animal in oneself; his victims give up their journey through the wood, feeling that they have reached the apogee of human achievement:

> Soon as the potion works, their human countenance,
> The express resemblance of the gods, is changed
> Into some brutish form of wolf, or bear,
> Or ounce, or tiger, hog, or bearded goat,
> All other parts remaining as they were,
> And they, so perfect is their misery,
> Not once perceive their foul disfigurement,
> But boast themselves more comely than before
> And all their friends, and native home forget
> To roll with pleasure in a sensual sty.   68

Milton seems to be warning his society that, without the individual spirit of quest, civilization is in danger of rottenness, of losing sight of its true goal in another world.

The Lady and her brothers must find their way through a maze in which evil (at first) looks like good, and in which good wears a humble disguise (the Spirit always appears to them as their father's servant Thyrsis). One of the first things to be learnt is that their senses are dubious guides – the Lady, her eyes 'bleared' by Comus' magic dust, accepts him as a shepherd and follows him. It is at this point in the action that one of the most curious and characteristic effects of allegory makes itself felt: we are conscious of the urgency of the problem (the plight of the Lady) but there is a dream-like slowness in the reactions to it. The two Brothers spend lines 331–480 reconstructing their sister's predicament. Since action in *Comus* mirrors moral understanding, the brothers have to arrive at the right degree of awareness before the next thing can happen. Allegory is rather like the world Lewis Carroll's Alice discovers through the looking-glass, where, to get to your destination (the hill-top, for example, in front of you) you have to set out in the opposite direction. The Spirit, disguised as Thyrsis, explains this to the brothers. They cannot just rush off and gallantly rescue their sister from Comus,

> Far other arms, and other weapons must
> Be those that quell the might of hellish charms.

The 'other arms' he offers them are not arms at all, but a talisman, 'haemony':

> The leaf was darkish, and had prickles on it,
> But in another country, as he said,
> Bore a bright golden flower, but not in this soil:
> Unknown, and like esteemed, and the dull swain
> Treads on it daily with his clouted shoon,
> ...if you have this about you
> (As I will give you when we go) you may
> Boldly assault the necromancer's hall.   631

This 'small unsightly root But of divine effect' will enable them to see Comus for what he is. A lot of critical conjecture has centred on the precise meaning of 'haemony': did Milton intend it as a divine or a human gift? Are the brothers being granted divine insight, or are they gaining moral understanding? The question is complicated by the giver, who is the Spirit, but disguised as the human Thyrsis. It is as if Milton *wants* to blur the boundaries, so that divine grace and the

277

artist's wisdom, the Spirit and Thyrsis, become indistinguishable. Here he's taking advantage of allegory's indirectness to suggest more than he could say in some less ambiguous medium. He can imply that the artist is the unique source of spiritual truth, but without directly claiming it.[1]

In a sense, anyway, this scene with the Brothers is only a rehearsal for the one which follows between the Lady and Comus; the Brothers have been learning about the idea of Comus, the Lady faces the reality. Or does she? If *Comus* was a play this would certainly be its dramatic centre, but because it's a masque, and even more because it's an allegory, the conflict when it comes seems almost unreal. The Lady, without the aid of haemony, has come to see Comus in his true colours, as well as his 'oughly-headed monsters'. She brushes aside his offered cup in a stage direction. The Lady is taking up from where her brothers have left off: it's a symptom of her greater spiritual awareness – they have to grope towards understanding while she has, as it were, taken over their knowledge in a flash of intuition. Once this is accepted the scene does have a lot of power. It cannot be a true interaction of characters, because the Lady shuts her mind against Comus' arguments, and he cannot understand hers, but as a clash of rhetorics (Comus' lush imagery versus the Lady's vehemently pure abstractions) it generates a convincing violence:

> Thou hast nor ear, nor soul to apprehend
> The sublime notion, and high mystery
> That must be uttered to unfold the sage
> And serious doctrine of virginity,
> And thou art worthy that thou shouldst not know
> More happiness than this thy present lot.
> Enjoy your dear wit, and gay rhetoric,
> That hath so well been taught her dazzling fence,
> Thou art not fit to hear thyself convinced.   784

The very manner of the Lady's speech, its scornful purity and energetic loathing, conveys her inner certainty. Their argument may be 'about' temperance, but the Lady's impatient idealism takes her beyond the defence of 'proportion' to assert the positive value of abstinence. (We may recall that in her first speech in the wood she invoked Faith, Hope and Chastity, not Charity.) Her chastity

---

[1] Milton uses a very similar image in *Areopagitica* (1644); he talks of 'truth itself; whose first appearance to our eyes, bleared and dimmed with prejudice and custom, is more unsightly and unplausible than many errors, even as the person is of many a great man slight and contemptible to see to'. Comus blears the eyes of his victims, and the 'shepherd lad' is, we remember, 'of small regard to see to'.

becomes not something to be protected, but an aggressive force before which Comus quails.[1] His posture as 'tempter' ('I must dissemble And try her yet more strongly') is irrelevant, and almost absurd. The narcotic delights of his potion ('one sip of this Will bathe the drooping spirits in delight Beyond the bliss of dreams') cannot rival the strange joys she finds in purity. Once again, evil seems to be being portrayed as a feeble parody of virtue. The actual ignominy of Comus' retreat as the brothers rush in merely confirms what has already taken place psychologically. This sounds like a diagrammatic victory of virtue over vice; but the Lady remains 'In stony fetters fixed, and motionless' after Comus has been driven out. It is tempting to suppose that Milton means this as a way of saying that she has gone too far, and fallen into an excess of coldness, but this doesn't seem totally convincing. On the other hand, she's hardly 'fallen' to Comus' temptation. At this point an analogue may be helpful: in Book II of *The fairy queen* Spenser's Sir Guyon, champion of temperance, is tempted by Mammon with all the riches of the world. He resists completely, as the Lady does here, but on emerging from Mammon's cave he falls into a faint, his moral strength overcome by the very strain of exercising it. The Lady's state seems similar, a kind of trance induced not by yielding to Comus, but by resisting him. If this is the right reading, it means that Milton is less concerned at this point with the problems of those who yield to temptation (the Lady has made Comus' offerings and arguments seem futile) than with the inevitable human weakness of the good, the weakness that makes it impossible to always actively pursue virtue. To simplify – the Lady needs help,

[1] Comus, in likening the Lady's chastity to a 'neglected rose' is taking the predictable 'Cavalier' line (see Waller's famous lyric 'Go, lovely rose...') which portrays chastity as a passive and deprived state. But Milton's Lady is a militant virgin in the tradition of Spenser's Britomart, 'knight' of Chastity in *The fairy queen* III i 46:

> For she was full of amiable grace,
> And manly terror mixèd therewithall,
> That as the one stirred up affections base,
> So th'other did men's rash desires apall,
> And hold them back, that would in error fall;
> As he, that hath espied a vermeil rose,
> To which sharp thorns and briars the way forestall,
> Dare not for dread his hardy hand expose,
> But wishing it far off, his idle wish doth lose.

This bisexual image of woman, combining feminine beauty and purity with masculine aggression and strength, seems to have had a direct appeal for Puritan poets. It freed woman from her mythic impurity as Circe–Eve–Delilah, without the suggestions of idolatry involved in images like Crashaw's St Theresa.

not to ward off vice, but to achieve the full and free exercise of her
virtue. 'Haemony' was defensive, a talisman against moral blindness;
Sabrina, whom the Spirit invokes to free the Lady, is more positive –
the Faith, Hope and Chastity of the Lady's vision all in one. The
Lady has reached the (upper) limits of human virtue – inevitably
her restoration to her parents seems, from the point of view of
the allegory, an anticlimax. The insistently progressive logic of the
action demands some other ending – which it gets in the Spirit's
epilogue.

Before trying to assess the impact of the epilogue, it may be useful
briefly to look back at the content of the allegory. Milton is using the
basic Christian doctrine that divine providence works itself out in
individual destinies, but he gives the doctrine a peculiarly Puritan
and personal slant. The Lady and her brothers are only granted divine
aid when they have exerted their own strength to the utmost: crudely,
Milton's Spirit helps those that help themselves, and then the help is
indirect and happens through 'Thyrsis'. The Spirit isn't a *deus ex
machina*: he doesn't suddenly appear to the young people in his sky-
robes and perform a miracle, he is 'there' all the time, unrecognized.
This stress on the necessity for moral effort – rather than, for
example, on the more passive virtue of humility – seems distinctively
Puritan. Another ingredient in the structuring of the allegory, however, reveals Milton's concern with the role of the artist. The identification of Thyrsis with the Spirit is not just a cunning bit of dramatic
doubling, or a decorative metaphor; the Spirit intervenes in the action
through the artist Thyrsis, who mediates between heaven and earth.
Milton quite deliberately makes it impossible to tell whether it is
artist or angel who is shaping the experience of the young people
towards its final goal.

The Spirit's epilogue retains this ambiguity: he is again reminiscent
of Shakespeare's Prospero, as he comes forward to address the
audience at the end. Indeed, the end of *Comus* provides some very
interesting contrasts with the closing movements of *The tempest*:

> . . . these our actors,
> As I foretold you, were all spirits, and
> Are melted into air, into thin air:
> And, like the baseless fabric of this vision
> The cloud-capped towers, the gorgeous palaces,
> The solemn temples, the great globe itself,
> And all which it inherit, shall dissolve,
> And, like this insubstantial pageant faded,
> Leave not a wrack behind . . .

Prospero here (IV i) is conjuring away the last traces of the magical masque he produced to celebrate the betrothal of Ferdinand and Miranda; he foresees suddenly at this moment the end not only of the play, but of the theatre, the city, and dimly in the distance beyond, the end of our temporal world. The fading of the masque's illusion mirrors for Shakespeare the fate of all human art and civilization. The epilogue to *The tempest*, spoken by Prospero, picks up the same theme:

> Now my charms are all o'erthrown,
> And what strength I have's mine own,
> Which is most faint...
>   Now I want
> Spirits to enforce, art to enchant;
> And my ending is despair
> Unless I be relieved by prayer;
> Which pierces so, that it assaults
> Mercy itself, and frees all faults.
> As you from crimes would pardoned be,
> Let your indulgence set me free.

The rhythm, the painful desire of freedom, suggest *Comus*, but the tone is very different. Shakespeare's *magus* acknowledges his weakness, hands over the burden of his power to the audience – 'let your indulgence set me free'. He is no longer god-like, has no dignity but that of humanity. The epilogue of Milton's Spirit is so close, and yet so different in its implications, that it reads like a deliberate gesture against the tradition:

> To the ocean now I fly,
> And those happy climes that lie
> Where day never shuts his eye,
> Up in the broad fields of the sky...
>   Now my task is smoothly done
> I can fly, or I can run
> Quickly to the green earth's end,
> Where the bowed welkin slow doth bend,
> And from thence can soar as soon
> To the corners of the moon.
>   Mortals who would follow me,
> Love virtue, she alone is free,
> She can teach ye how to climb
> Higher than the sphery chime;
> Or if virtue feeble were,
> Heaven itself would stoop to her.

Milton's Spirit exults (more like Ariel than Prospero) in casting off the last vestiges of servitude, and his human disguise. Instead of restoring us to humanity, he invites us to follow him into the other-world of vision ('There eternal summer dwells'); a timeless 'entranced' region where 'Youth and Joy' are to be born from the union of the soul (Psyche) and Heavenly Love (celestial Cupid). This is the ending that makes sense of the Lady's praise of virginity. For Shakespeare the masque's trappings were a sad reminder of mortality; for Milton, the exercise of the artist's power in the masque acts as a sort of springboard into visions of eternal artifice. He doesn't want to return to the world where imagination has to start from scratch, 'the smoke and stir of this dim spot Which men call earth'. If one turns from the epilogue back to the Spirit's opening lines, it's clear how completely Milton has framed the masque, and 'placed' the world of time against the background of eternity.

In *Comus* Milton has reached a point where the world of the poet begins to jostle the world at large. The questing philosophy traceable in the allegory clashes with the dance-like ritual of the masque. In the final analysis Milton will not subsume his vision in the general life: the allegory stresses the achievement of individual autonomy – and that taken to its logical conclusion would mean not a celebration but a dissolution of community values. For the time he has managed to render these discontinuous meanings simultaneously, but one senses that allegory is only a temporary way of holding the conflicting priorities apart. In *Lycidas* (1637) there is no doubt of the alienation of the poet from the attitudes and institutions of his society. *Lycidas* makes society itself the 'outsider'.

'*Lycidas*'

In *Lycidas* Milton turns the tables, and takes over the collective medium of myth for a validation of individualism. He pursues the motifs of pastoral ('the homely slightly shepherd's trade') back to their origins, and discovers there an order which dwarfs and encloses 'society'. In *Lycidas* one sees clearly for the first time that distinctively Miltonic stance – he appeals to tradition, nature and Christianity *against* inherited attitudes and institutions. This is recognizably the Milton who, within three months of his unsuccessful marriage, published the first of four pamphlets on divorce, aligning a ponderous weight of authority on his side. This is not just the predictable protest of the individual against collective values; too often that sort of protest tacitly acknowledges the authority it attacks. Milton's protest takes the form of a determined *revision* of collective values in the light of personal experience. *Lycidas*, like *Comus*, sustains a lot of personal meaning, but unlike the masque it doesn't separate out meanings into layers or levels. In the interval between the two works Milton has acquired a new confidence – Edward King's death found him in an extraordinary state of readiness.

The major sign of unused energies in *Lycidas* is the way in which other voices break in on the 'uncouth swain'; the denunciatory violence of the 'dread voice' attacking corruption in the church ('Blind mouths! that scarce themselves know how to hold A sheep-hook...') reveals the power contained in the polished surface of the poem. This prophetic invective derives its assurance from Milton's conviction that there is a divine order in the world which will re-assert itself against chaos. This order, though, is not just asserted, but built into the poem in a rich web of metaphor and allusion. Almost any line leads one, through connotations and 'underground' links, into the centre of the poem's structure: for example, the Sicilian streams the shepherd-poet invokes, Arethuse (line 85) and Alpheus (line 132) are not merely there because they're appropriately pastoral. Two lines from *Arcades* provide the annotation which reveals their deeper and more specific relevance to the theme of *Lycidas*:

> Divine Alpheus, who by secret sluice
> Stole under seas to meet his Arethuse

– just as Lycidas 'sunk low, but mounted high', finding under the seas his union with the God he served. Milton doesn't here spell out this kind of allusion, but leaves it implicit. Submerged images create a fertile soil out of which the poem's larger meanings grow. This is very effective – he doesn't seem to be putting the meaning into your mind, but calling it up as a memory.

Edward King's death is the centre of the web of allusion; the poem moves out from this one individual loss to ponder the *repeated* obliteration of individual values in the natural world. This is a poem about the drowning and defeat of man's distinctness – human life, like the body of Orpheus, seems to be continuously defaced and dis-membered, all dignity of purpose lost. To take another, and more elaborate example of how local details work to widen the poem's scope: 'that sanguine flower inscribed with woe' (line 106) that grows by the river Cam, is the hyacinth. Milton's way of referring to it reminds us of the myth of the flower's origins. Hyacinthus was a beautiful youth loved by the sun-god Apollo; on his death Apollo metamorphosed him into the flower whose bloody ('sanguine') petals are marked with the Greek AI (alas) sign of Apollo's grief (the story is told in Ovid's *Metamorphoses*). Like Edward King, Hyacinthus died violently 'ere his prime', inexplicably and pointlessly as the early flowers (line 17) killed by frost. There's more to the allusion than this however, and the parallel story of Orpheus' fate (lines 58–63) suggests what it is. Orpheus too was a poet; he was killed and dismembered by the 'rout that made the hideous roar', the Bacchae, worshippers of Dionysus, god of wine, and of flowers and vegetation. The Bacchae sacrificed Orpheus to the dark, sensuous and irrational powers of earth, so that the crops might sprout, and the flowers return in the spring. These untimely deaths begin, dimly, at the back of one's mind, to assume a sinister pattern. The metamorphosis of Hyacinthus into a flower is not merely a pretty poetical fancy, but a reflection of pagan ritual. In the pagan past human sacrifice was used to perpetuate the natural cycle – the bodies and blood of the victims propitiated the dark gods, and were the source of new life. All man's individual, upward aspirations (symbolized perhaps by the service of the sun-god Apollo, patron of poetry) were thwarted in subjection to the insistent needs of nature. The world before Christ, Milton implies, was dominated by a seasonal, cyclic rhythm which demanded the continual reabsorption of man into nature. Christ's sacrifice freed humanity from this tragic loss of purpose and identity: his unique death broke the cycle.

Christian revelation promises a different metamorphosis – from earth to heaven. In the final perspective pagan magic is but a gruesome pre-figuration of this greater, all-encompassing truth. Edward King's death precipitated in Milton a major attempt to order and comprehend the human experience inherited as poetic myth. The shape he found in his materials was complex, but coherent: the repeated pattern of tragic sacrifice converted, through Christ, into a clear, linear path to individual immortality. By means of the kind of poetic shorthand I have indicated, *Lycidas* manages an encyclopedic range of reference in its 193 lines. There's another reason why this poem looms so large, however. The fluidity of its method of mythological allusion leads the reader outside the formal limits of the poem into many other poems written before, and since. Thus it gathers meaning from the work of other poets who have explored the same mythological territory in search of some order to accommodate death. To indicate some of the range of association, Spenser in Book III of *The fairy queen*:

> And all about grew every sort of flower,
> To which sad lovers were transformed of yore;

Fresh Hyacinthus, Phoebus' paramour,
And dearest love...

There wont fair Venus often to enjoy
Her dear Adonis' joyous company,
And reap sweet pleasure from the wanton boy;
There yet, some say, in secret he does lie,
Lappèd in flowers and precious spicery,
By her hid from the world, and from the skill
Of Stygian gods, which do her love envý;
But she herself, whenever that she will,
Possesseth him, and of his sweetness takes her fill.

And sooth it seems they say: for he may not
For ever die, and ever buried be
In baleful night where all things are forgot;
Albe he subject to mortality,
Yet is eterne in mutability,
And by succession made perpetual...   Canto vi

(Adonis, like Hyacinthus, was killed so that crops might grow, and
flowers return in the spring. In the passage above, Venus *reaps* sweet
pleasure from Adonis – his destruction is the source of fertility. In
the myth, Adonis was transformed into an anemone.) Spenser's use
of myth is more explicit than Milton's. Modern poets on the other
hand submerge their inherited symbolism, like Dylan Thomas:

Light breaks on secret lots,
On tips of thought where thoughts smell in the rain;
When logics die,
The secret of the soil grows through the eye,
And blood jumps in the sun...
                    Light breaks where no sun shines

Here the image of the dismembered body of the sacrificial hero is
vividly and directly associated with fertility – his thoughts are spring
shoots. Or the tone may be sardonic, as in the savagely funny query
of T. S. Eliot's speaker in *The waste land:*

'That corpse you planted last year in your garden,
Has it begun to sprout? Will it bloom this year?
Or has the sudden frost disturbed its bed?'

This associative game has a value in itself: it's certainly where poems
like these get a lot of their power from, echoing and re-echoing off
each other in our minds. But it would be wrong to give the impression
that *Lycidas* can be reduced to what it has in common with other
works. It's a very purposeful poem, with a strong sense of direction.
Part of the point of producing analogies from other poets is to high-

light the particular cast of Milton's mind. Spenser, for example, in the passage quoted above, sees Adonis' death in sexual terms: he is immortal through procreation, 'by succession made perpetual'. Milton's solution is very different. Lycidas' 'nuptial song' is sung in heaven – he is united, as the Spirit's epilogue promises in *Comus*, to God. Eliot's grotesque use of myth is part of an ironic perspective designed to humiliate himself and the reader: the Christian revelation has failed in *The waste land*, and there is no order, only fragments. But perhaps Dylan Thomas's lines provide the most revealing contrast with Milton. His vision, dwelling on the 'same' mythic material, neatly reverses the values Milton found there. Instead of Christianity superseding paganism, in Thomas, paganism takes over joyously from the other-worldliness of Christianity: only 'When logics die', when the individual loses his self-awareness and separate identity, can the imagination be alive and fertile. Compare the line 'blood jumps in the sun' with the shuddering description of Orpheus' 'gory visage' in *Lycidas*; for Milton the imagery of violent death is horrific, almost unthinkable. The result of contrasts like these is to emphasize Milton's individualism (which seems inseparable from his Christianity). Both Spenser and Dylan Thomas, however different in every other way, find imaginative satisfaction in a vision of cyclic decay and rebirth. Milton specifically interprets Christianity as a breaking of the pagan cycle which denies personal continuity. The pattern he wants to see is progressive, with an individual eternity at the end of it.

Milton sees in his inherited materials an order which confirms his own thinking; it's like the Rorschach inkblot test, where the subject sees in the random mass a reflection of his own preoccupations. But this is not really 'seeing' – it's more like a mixture of observation and projection. And that is what happens to the reader too; in reading *Lycidas* one seems to be supplying the meanings oneself, from other Milton poems, from other poems in the tradition, from the ragbag of mythological odds and ends general culture preserves. Milton has here perfected the art of suggestion or 'projection', rather than state-ment, as in the famous and terrifying lines of prophecy:

> Blind mouths! that scarce themselves know how to hold
> A sheep-hook, or have learned aught else the least
> That to the faithful herdsman's art belongs!
> What recks it them? What need they? They are sped;
> And when they list, their lean and flashy songs
> Grate on their scrannel pipes of wretched straw,

> The hungry sheep look up, and are not fed,
> But swoll'n with wind, and the rank mist they draw,
> Rot inwardly, and foul contagion spread:
> Besides what the grim wolf with privy paw
> Daily devours apace, and nothing said,
> But that two-handed engine at the door,
> Stands ready to smite once, and smite no more.

Even lines as violently explicit as these draw power from the tact and balance of the poet: the pastoral metaphor merges into colloquialism and proverbial-sounding wisdom ('the grim wolf...and nothing said'). This is not just surface noise, mouth-filling rhetoric. As John Ruskin pointed out in *Sesame and lilies* (1868), 'Blind mouths' has an underlying aptness backing up its impact:

> A 'Bishop' means 'a person who sees'.
> A 'Pastor' means 'a person who feeds'.
> The most unbishoply character a man can have is therefore to be blind.
> The most unpastoral is, instead of feeding, to want to be fed, to be a mouth.

Milton's learning is here translated directly into communicative force. The established church, professed upholder of 'tradition', is shown to be nothing of the sort, but a corrupt backwater breeding cynicism and sloth. Most important for the effect however is the strategic use Milton makes of vagueness: these lines are spoken by the 'pilot of the Galilean lake', who since he holds the keys and has 'mitred locks' is probably St Peter, but his anonymity allows for the possibility that this is Christ himself. Similarly the 'two-handed engine' suggests a range of meanings, from the two houses of parliament (who were to curb the bishops' power) to the fearful sword of the angel dividing the just from the unjust on the day of judgement. The image is so definite (and follows on from such clear references) that we can hardly avoid attaching reality to it: it becomes frighteningly urgent and immediate, partly because it cannot be tied down and comfortably pigeonholed. Obviously this is a technique that can't be used all the time without losing the reader in a maze of possibilities; but Milton roots it in direct reference and familiar idiom so that we're persuaded it follows, it will happen. As Milton rather smugly pointed out in his prefatory note to *Lycidas* ('And by occasion foretells the ruin of our corrupted clergy') events, by 1645, seemed to justify it.

There is no reason to doubt Milton's sincerity when, in the autobiographical passages in his prose, he implies that he made considerable sacrifices when he became actively involved in politics. But we can see in *Lycidas* at least traces of the reasons why he set poetry aside. In 1640 the 'civil commotions' in England created a fluid situation, full of potentiality for new structures in both church and state. The poet of *Lycidas* could hardly ignore the opportunity to translate the complex order he had found in poetic myth into actuality. The weight of learning and the organizational energy on display in *Lycidas* feed directly into Milton's prose. His use of imagery, for example, retains its coherence:

I trust hereby to make it manifest with what small willingness I endure to interrupt the pursuit of no less hopes than these, and leave a calm and pleasing solitariness...to embark on a troubled sea of noises and hoarse disputes. *The reason of church government* 1641

to be tossed and turmoiled with their unballasted wits in fathomless and unquiet deeps of controversy. *Of education* 1644

Truth is compared in Scripture to a streaming fountain; if her waters flow not in a perpetual progression, they sicken into a muddy pool of conformity and tradition. *Areopagitica* 1644

The imagery of sea, stream and pool sets out his commitment clearly: he fears the temporary chaos, but loathes more deeply the conformist alternative of passivity and corruption ('sicken into a muddy pool'). 'Perpetual progression' as in *Lycidas* is his ideal state. In *The reason of church government* the imagery of the kingdom of God ('There entertain him all the saints above, In solemn troops and sweet societies') is translated into a utopian social programme:

it were happy for the commonwealth, if our magistrates, as in those famous governments of old, would take into their care, not only the deciding contentious law-cases and brawls, but the managing of our public sports and festival pastimes [so that they] may civilize, adorn, and make discreet our minds by the learned and affable meeting of frequent academies and the procurement of wise and artful recitations, sweetened with eloquent and graceful enticements to the love and practice of justice, temperance and fortitude, instructing and bettering the nation at all opportunities, that the call of virtue and wisdom may be heard everywhere.

In the revolutionary context of the 1640s Milton saw a chance to reshape social and cultural life into something resembling the order, harmony and coherence of poetry. Instead of, as in *Comus*, being something of an accessory to social occasions, the poet might have a hand in directing the myth-making of his community. Milton might well have been reluctant to give up his 'calm and pleasing solitariness', but there was another and stronger pull towards translating the visions of his poetry into actuality.

It's often been pointed out that looking at society with an artist's

eye can be dangerous and naive; the case against the sort of programme Milton was engaged in has been put most strongly by
W. H. Auden:

All political theories which, like Plato's [and, one might add, Milton's] are
based on analogies drawn from artistic fabrication are bound, if put into
practice, to turn into tyrannies...A society which was really like a good
poem, embodying the aesthetic virtues of beauty, order, economy and subordination of detail to the whole, would be a nightmare of horror for, given
the historical reality of actual men, such a society could only come into being
through selective breeding, extermination of the physically and mentally
unfit, absolute obedience to its Director, and a large slave class kept out of
sight in the cellars.   *The dyer's hand* 1962

But the great difference here is that Milton, unlike Auden, thought
God had already created a community of individualists in the true
Christian communion. For Milton collective individualism, a
voluntary consensus based on active enquiry, was God's plan for the
world. The period of the Commonwealth didn't, however, see the
kind of 'creative' legislation Milton wanted, and his image of the
kingdom of God remained an image, becoming neither reality nor
nightmare. Instead the government confined itself to negative law-
making, demanding passive obedience, so that Milton's war with the
forces of conformity went on. Though his society had little appetite
for 'perpetual progression', he kept himself in a constant state of
evolution and development. The redefinition of his aims from poem to
poem didn't stop with *Lycidas*; the process went on through the years
of pamphleteering, growing if anything more compulsive. From one
angle, the 1645 volume, the 'early poems' look complete and satisfying. From another angle (as with everything of Milton's) the
volume is a springboard into the future.

Resources for further study

The list that follows does not include general works on Milton except
where they have a more than usually substantial and/or interesting
section on the early poems. For other aspects of Milton, especially
sources and early development, see other chapters in this volume, and
the list of resources in *PL: introduction* in this series. Places of
publication are London and/or New York unless specified.

Annotated editions	Art and iconography*
General on early poems	Speech
Ideas and topics in early poems	Music*
Illustrations	Milton's influence*

Literary history, Weltanschauung* History
Pastoral Reference
Anthologies Bibliography

* See also other chapters in this volume.

Annotated editions of the early poems

BROOKS, CLEANTH and HARDY, JOHN E. eds *Poems of Mr JM: the 1645 edition, with essays in analysis* 1951.

BULLOUGH, GEOFFREY and M. eds *M's dramatic poems* 1958.

HUGHES, MERRITT Y. ed *'Paradise regained', the minor poems and 'Samson agonistes'* 1937 *et seq.* (one vol. of *M: complete poems and major prose*).

MACCAFFREY, ISABEL G. ed *'Samson agonistes' and the shorter poems of JM* 1966.

PRINCE, F. T. ed *'Comus' and other poems of JM* Oxford 1968.

WARTON, THOMAS ed *Poems upon several occasions, English, Italian and Latin, with translations, by JM . . .with notes critical and explanatory, and other illustrations* 1785.

See also, for verse translations of Milton's Latin and Italian poems, WILLIAM COWPER *Latin and Italian poems of M translated into English verse* ed W. Hayley 1808, sometimes to be found in editions of Cowper's *Collected poems*.

General on early poems

There are a great many articles dealing with individual poems; for those see pages 18–23 in J. H. Hanford's Goldentree Bibliography of M 1966. There is surprisingly little criticism of the early poems as a group though – when not analysed separately, they tend to be treated briefly as a phase in the poet's development by writers really interested in arriving at the epic.

ALLEN, DON C. *The harmonious vision: studies in M's poetry* Baltimore 1954. Chs. on all the major early poems.

BROOKS, CLEANTH and HARDY, JOHN E. eds *Poems of Mr JM: the 1645 edition with essays in analysis* 1951. Detailed readings concentrating on the complex texture of imagery.

SUMMERS, JOSEPH H. ed *The lyric and dramatic M* 1965. Section one of this anthology is from the early Milton.

TUVE, ROSEMOND *Images and themes in five poems by M* Cambridge Mass. 1957.

Ideas and topics

BUTLER, CHRISTOPHER *Number symbolism* 1970. See ch. 6 'Number symbolism in England'.

DEMARAY, JOHN G. *M and the masque tradition* Cambridge Mass. 1968. Deals with the early poems up to *Comus*.

DIEKHOFF, JOHN S. ed *M on himself* Oxford 1939. Extracts from prose and verse anthologized to reveal Milton's version of himself, his problems and aims.

NELSON, LOWRY *Baroque lyric poetry* New Haven 1961.

PRINCE, F. T. *The Italian element in M's verse* Oxford 1954.

SAMUEL, IRENE *Plato and M* Ithaca New York 1947.

STARNES, D. T. and TALBERT, ERNEST W. 'M and the dictionaries' in their *Classical myth and legend in renaissance dictionaries* Chapel Hill 1955.

TILLYARD, E. M. W. *The Miltonic setting: past and present* 1938. Also relevant to discussion of Milton's influence (see Leavis *Revaluation*).

Illustrations

BLAKE, WILLIAM. There is no collection of Blake's illustrations to the early poems. See *L'allegro* with a note by W. P. Trent and *Il penseroso* with a note by C. B. Tinker, both published in New York (Limited Editions) 1954; *WB's illustrations of M's 'Comus'* reproduced by William Griggs 1890, and both series reprinted in colour in A. Fletcher *The transcendental masque* Ithaca, New York 1971; *Poems in English by JM, with illustrations by WB* ed H. C. Beeching and Geoffrey Keynes 2 vols (Nonesuch Press) 1926; '*On the morning of Christ's nativity': M's hymn with illustrations by WB* with a note by Geoffrey Keynes, Cambridge 1923. *The descent of peace* (watercolour) is in the Whitworth Art Gallery, Manchester.

FLAXMAN, J. *The Latin and Italian poems of M translated into English verse* (Cowper's translation) *illustrated by J. Flaxman* 1808.

PALMER, SAMUEL *The shorter poems of JM illustrated by S. Palmer* 1888. There is a lot of Samuel Palmer in the Victoria and Albert Museum: see, for example, the engraving of *The skylark*, and the watercolours *A towered city*, *The eastern gate* and *The brothers lingering under the vine*.

WRIGHT, JOSEPH *The lady in 'Comus'* (exhibited 1785) is in the Walker Art Gallery, Liverpool.

See MARCIA R. POINTON *M and English art* Manchester 1970, which has a great many reproductions.

Art and iconography

The best place to start is with *Studies in iconology* by ERWIN PANOFSKY or *Bellini's 'Feast of the gods'* by EDGAR WIND (especially pp. 45–55 'Comus, god of revelry'). Both of these explore and illustrate the close relationships between renaissance artists, and the ambiguous development of figures like Cupid or Comus.

CARRACCI (Annibale) 1560–1609. *Triumph of Bacchus* painted 1603–4 (Galleria Farnese Rome). Illusionist and proto-Baroque.

CORREGGIO 1494–1534. See the twin paintings *Allegory of pleasure* and *Allegory of virtue* (Louvre).

JONES, INIGO 1573–1652. Architect and enormously successful designer of court masques for James I and Charles I. See his designs for sets and costumes, e.g. those for *Salmacida spolia* (1640) at Chatsworth – not only in relation to *Comus*, but the semi-allegorical nature of M's landscapes in general. Reproductions in *Designs by Inigo Jones for masques and plays at court* ed Percy Simpson and C. F. Bell (Walpole and Malone Societies) 1924.

POUSSIN 1594–1665. In many ways the painter closest to Milton's early style, repays detailed comparison; explored structural parallels in pagan and Christian myth. For pastoral see *The kingdom of Flora* (Dresden), and on the important theme of metamorphosis *Echo and Narcissus* (Louvre), *Apollo and Daphne* (Munich) and *Pan and Syrinx* (Dresden). On allegory, see *Time saving Truth from Envy and Discord* (painted 1641, Louvre); and for parallelism of classical and Christian motifs compare the famous *Arcadian shepherds* (Louvre) with *The adoration of the shepherds* (Munich), and *Venus with the dead Adonis* (Caen) with the *Lamentation over the dead Christ* (Munich). For reproductions see Anthony Blunt *Nicholas Poussin. The A. W. Mellors lectures in the fine arts* (Phaidon Press) 1958.

RENI, GUIDO 1575–1642. Full Baroque splendour. See the procession of mythological and allegorical figures in *Aurora* painted 1613–14.

See also: JEAN R. HAGSTRUM *The sister arts: the tradition of literary pictorialism from Dryden to Gray* Chicago 1958, especially chs. 9, 10, 11, on Thomson, Collins and Gray. MARIO PRAZ 'M and Poussin' in *17c studies presented to Sir Herbert Grierson* Oxford 1938. EDGAR WIND *Pagan mysteries in the renaissance* 1958.

Speech

Shorter poems of JM read by William Devlin (with William Squire and Gary Watson) PLP 1016.

Comus read by Barbara Jefford, William Squire, Gary Watson, Patrick Garland, Ian Holm, Margaret Rawlings, Tony Church, Denis McCarthy. PLP 1024/5.

Music

The musical forms most clearly related to early Milton are songs ('airs'), madrigals and (later) opera. See MANFRED F. BUKOFZER *Music in the Baroque era* 1947, especially chs. 6 'English music during the Commonwealth and Restoration' and 10–12 on the form, theory and sociology of Baroque music.

GIBBONS, ORLANDO 1583–1625. *First set of madrigals and motets...for viols and voices* 1612.

HANDEL 1685–1759. Like Milton, full of 'quotations' from his predecessors. Most relevant are his Arcadian pastoral pieces: *Acis and Galatea* (1719); *L'allegro, il penseroso ed il moderato* (1740) adapted from Milton; and *Semele* (1744). For the characteristic Baroque interpenetration of words and music listen to his setting of Dryden's *Ode for St Cecilia's Day*, and for contrast the 'Newgate pastoral' of *The begger's opera* (1728) written by Gay.

LAWES, HENRY 1596–1662. Thyrsis/Attendant Spirit in *Comus*; wrote music for *Comus* and other masques. See Milton's 1646 sonnet to him, and his settings for five songs from *Comus* (ed H. J. Foss 1938) and *Airs and dialogues for one, two and three voices* 1653.

PURCELL, C. 1659–95. His *Dido and Aeneas* (1680) was probably the first continuous dramatic music heard in England. His series of celebratory odes for St Cecilia's Day was begun in 1683; besides those, listen to *The tempest* (1690) and *The fairy queen* (1692, adapted from *A midsummer night's dream*).

WILBYE, JOHN 1573–1638. Sets of madrigals, published in 1598 and 1609.

A poem like Crashaw's *Music's duel* in *Delights of the muses* 1646 will tell you a lot about the emotive, absolutist tendencies of Baroque music.

For further help see the following: GRETCHEN FINNEY *Musical backgrounds for English literature 1580–1650* New Brunswick 1962. JOHN HOLLANDER *The untuning of the sky. Ideas of music in English poetry* Princeton 1961. MERRITT Y. HUGHES 'Lydian airs' *Modern Language Notes* XL 1925 (cf. Butler *Number symbolism* ch. 5 'Aesthetic assumptions').

Milton's influence

HAVENS, RAYMOND D. *The influence of M on English poetry* Cambridge Mass. 1922. Still the most comprehensive study, assumes the goodness of M's influence.

LEAVIS, F. R. *Revaluation: tradition and development in English poetry* 1936. Not just the chapter on Milton, but note the use of 'Miltonic' throughout.

An independent investigation of Milton's influence could well be more free in its interpretation of 'influence' than Havens (above). For example, other 'Platonic' poems which might be compared with the *Nativity ode* are Spenser's *Four hymns*, Shelley's *To a skylark* and Browning's *Abt Vogler*. For pastoral, see below. The masque form has no immediate analogues, but Milton's Lady could usefully be compared with Richardson's Clarissa or Shaw's St Joan.

Literary history, Weltanschauung

BETHELL, S. L. *The cultural revolution of the 17c* 1951.

GRIERSON, H. J. C. *Cross-currents in English literature of the 17c* 1929.

LEISHMAN, J. B. '*L'allegro* and *Il penseroso* in relation to 17c poetry' *Essays and Studies* n.s. IV 1951 repr *M* ed Rudrum 1968.

NICOLSON, MARJORIE H. *The breaking of the circle* rev ed 1960.

SYPHER, WYLIE *Four stages of renaissance style: transformations in art and literature 1400–1700* 1955.

TILLYARD, E. M. W. *The metaphysicals and M* 1956.

WEDGWOOD, C. V. *Poetry and politics under the Stuarts* 1960.

Pastoral

Your own study of images and themes in the early poems could begin with an investigation of this genre. W. W. GREG *Pastoral poetry and pastoral drama* (1905) lays out the meaning of the convention, and see *Elizabethan poetry* (1952) by HALLETT SMITH, especially ch. 1 on pastoral, 'The vitality and versatility of a convention'. Look too at *Poly-olbion* by MICHAEL DRAYTON in vol IV of the tercentenary edition of his *Works* eds J. W. Hebel, K. Tillotson and B. A. Newdigate rev ed Oxford 1961. The following should help establish the solidity of the tradition, and the kind of problems pastoral deals with:

CHAMBERS, EDMUND K. ed *English pastorals* 1906. Anthology.

FRYE, NORTHROP. 'Varieties of literary utopia' and 'The revelation to Eve' in his *The stubborn structure* 1970.

KERMODE, FRANK ed *English pastoral poetry, from the beginnings to Marvell* 1952 (anthology with introduction) and introduction to Shakespeare's *Tempest* (Arden Edition) 1954 on nature, art and grace.

MADSEN, WILLIAM G. 'The idea of nature in M's poetry' in *Three studies in the renaissance: Sidney, Jonson, M* by Robert B. Young, W. Todd Furniss and Madsen. New Haven 1958.

WILLIAMS, RAYMOND 'Pastoral and counter-pastoral' *Critical Quarterly* x 1968; *The country and the city* 1973.

See also George Herbert's poem *Jordan I*, which parodies, briefly but tellingly, the language and assumptions of pastoral, and Andrew Marvell's *Upon Appleton House* and *The mower against gardens*. For detailed analysis of some of the techniques of pastoral look up WILLIAM EMPSON's analysis of a poem from Sidney's *Arcadia* in *Seven types of ambiguity* ch. 1 1930 and WINIFRED NOWOTTNY's continuation of the same line of enquiry in *The language poets use* 1962, ch. 6. The most exciting general study is *Some versions of pastoral* by EMPSON (1935); see especially chapters on *The beggar's opera* and Lewis Carroll's Alice books.

Milton had great impact on pastoral tradition: for straight Milton-influenced pastoral read some of James Thomson's *Seasons* (1730) or Mark Akenside's *The pleasures of the imagination* (1744). 19c reactions were sceptical and realistic; see Matthew Arnold's *Empedocles on Etna* (1852) where a young pastoral poet Callicles is counterpointed with the ironic reflections of philosophic Empedocles; or George Eliot's attack on pastoral fantasy and distancing in 'The natural history of German life' *Westminster Review* LXVI 1856. A fully fledged modern allegorical pastoral is *Mr Weston's good wine* (1927) by T. F. Powys.

Anthologies

BALD, R. C. ed *17c English poetry* 1959.

BROADBENT J. B. ed forthcoming anthologies of major and minor 17c poetry, with full suggestions for further study, for Signet Classics.

GRIERSON, H. J. C. and BULLOUGH, G. eds *The Oxford book of 17c verse* 1934.

HEBEL, J. W. and HUDSON, H. H. eds *Poetry of the English renaissance 1509–1660* 1932.

KERMODE, FRANK ed *English pastoral poetry, from the beginnings to Marvell* 1952.

ROLLINS, H. E. ed *Cavalier and Puritan: ballads of the great rebellion* 1923.

WHITE, HELEN C., RUTH WALLERSTEIN, RICARDO QUINTANA, A. B. CHAMBERS eds *17c verse and prose* vol I *1600–1660* rev ed 1971.

HONIGMAN E. A. J. ed *A book of masques in honour of Allardyce Nicoll* Cambridge 1967.

History

HILL, C. *The century of revolution 1603–1714* 1961.

PATRIDES, C. A. *The phoenix and the ladder: the rise and decline of the Christian view of history* Berkeley and Los Angeles 1964.

STEVENS, ALBERT K. 'M and Chartism' *Philological Quarterly* XII 1933.

STONE, LAWRENCE *The crisis of the aristocracy 1558–1641* 1965.

TAWNEY, R. H. *Religion and the rise of capitalism* 1926.

Reference

BRADSHAW, JOHN *A concordance to the poetical works of JM* 1894.

Brewer's dictionary of phrase and fable 1952 edition.

LE COMTE, EDWARD S. *A M dictionary* 1961.

OSGOOD, CHARLES G. *The classical mythology of M's English poems* 1900.

STEVENS, DAVID H. *A reference guide to M from 1800 to the present day* Chicago 1930.

The shorter Oxford English dictionary 2 vols third edition 1944, corrected 1959.

Bibliography

The most manageable kind of bibliography is one compiled yourself by following up footnotes, and thus arriving at a series of genuinely interrelated studies. Most annotated editions, and many books and articles contain fairly full bibliographies (e.g. Demaray *M and the masque tradition* Cambridge Mass. 1968). J. H. Hanford's *Milton Goldentree Bibliographies* 1966 is useful, and contains some notes on the items.

The tercentenary of Milton's birth: lines written in honour of the occasion
9 December 1608 : 9 December 1908

We need him now,
This latest Age in repetition cries:
For Belial, the adroit, is in our midst;
Mammon, more swoln to squeeze the slavish sweat
From hopeless toil: and overshadowingly
(Aggrandized, monstrous in his grinning mask
Of hypocritical Peace) inveterate Moloch
Remains the great example...   GEORGE MEREDITH

297

LORNA SAGE

Milton in literary history

In the hundred years after the publication of *Paradise lost* Milton's influence grew until it almost threatened to engulf the English poetic tradition. Since then it has declined and revived intermittently, but has never quite lost the aura of that unique acclaim. Tracing Milton's presence in literary history however, means looking beyond his rather inflexible image; although his poetry has been constantly a point of reference for English literature, it is a point of reference that has itself shifted and changed. Implicit in every official 'Milton' is a more unofficial version, which, like Blake's revolutionary heroes, comes to seem tyrannous and conventional in its turn.

Terms like 'influence' or 'reputation' hardly cover the kind of pressure Milton has exerted not only on poetry, but on the novel; not only on literature, but on painting, sculpture and architecture. During the 18th century Milton became not so much an object of attention, as a part of the very apparatus writers and readers used for perceiving and ordering their world. Often when artists claimed to be seeing merely what was there, they were using a Miltonic perspective; or when they projected the shape of the future it looked curiously like the (Miltonic) past. Both explicitly (in critical comment) and implicitly (in subliminal echoes and unexamined assumptions) Milton has stimulated and sustained many conflicting strands in the development of English literature. It is important to stress the element of conflict: 'Milton' has played many different roles in history, some conservative, some revolutionary. In fact, one could say that his only constant and unchanging function has been to generate divergence from the norms of the moment, and that is how his literary historical career began.

The late 17th century: Milton without a role

In the early 18th century Milton became, theoretically at least, the pillar of English classicism, but it took a labour of assimilation before he could be seen this way. Until the Restoration he was known as a polemicist rather than a poet, and even after the publication of *Paradise lost* his position in the literary world seemed difficult to tie down. The very ways in which his poem claimed classical status – the authority of its tone, the use of unrhymed verse, the golden age assurance of its diction – were at odds with the current ideal of the classical. Edmund Waller (1605–87) was a central influence in arriving at that current consensus, and a measure of how thoroughly Milton diverged from it. Waller (like Milton) had diagnosed a strain of uncertainty in English poets:

> ...who can hope his lines should long
> Last in a daily changing tongue?...
> When architects have done their part,
> The matter may betray their art;
> Time, if we use ill-chosen stone,
> Soon brings a well-built palace down.
> Poets that lasting marble seek
> Must carve in Latin or in Greek;
> We write in sand, our language grows,
> And like the tide, our work o'er flows.   *Of English verse*

Waller's use of rhyme here, his self-conscious 'Englishness', and his sense of the inevitable transience of modern vernacular poetry, had become a frequent refrain. Even Thomas Carew, celebrating Donne's achievement in 1633, had allowed into his verse that telling 'chime' of rhyme which symbolized the insecurity of modern poetry:

> Thou shalt yield no precédence, but of time,
> And the blind fate of language, whose tuned chime
> More charms the outward sense...
> *Elegy upon the death of the Dean of Paul's, Dr John Donne*

The language, at such moments, seems ephemeral. Rhyme was merely one symptom, though the most obvious and telling, of the difficulties of achieving an English classicism.

Waller's way out of this was to accept it. Rhyme for him (as for Dryden) when used with wit and sensitivity became a way of stressing the differentness of the modern writer. The ideal epic poet would turn

FIG 21 Title page of 1688 edition of *PL*, illustrated from designs by Medina (examples are reproduced in the volumes for *PL* I–II and IX–X in this series). This was a lavish, folio-size volume, published by subscription. The verses below the portrait are by Dryden.

his difficulties into advantages, would be consciously English, consciously contemporary, and write in couplets.[1] William Davenant's *Gondibert* came close to Waller's ideal:

> Now to thy matchless book,
> Wherein those few that can with judgement look
> May find old love in pure fresh language told,
> Like new-stamped coin made out of angel gold;
> Such truth in love as the antique world did know,
> In such a style as courts may boast of now;
> Which no bold tales of gods or monsters swell,
> But human passions, such as with us dwell.
> Man is thy theme; his virtue, or his rage,
> Drawn to the life in each elaborate page.
> Mars, nor Bellona, are not namèd here,
> But such a Gondibert as both might fear;
> Venus had here, and Hebë, been outshined
> By thy bright Bertha and thy Rhodalind.
> Such is thy happy skill, and such the odds
> Betwixt thy worthies and the Grecian gods!
> Whose deities in vain had here come down,
> Where mortal beauty wears the sovereign crown;
> Such as of flesh composed, by flesh and blood,
> Though not resisted, may be understood.

To Sir William Davenant, upon his first two books of 'Gondibert' 1653

Rhyme symbolized a whole complex of attitudes concerning the future of English poetry – for example, that the poet should aim at contemporaneity ('such a style as courts may boast of now') and at human personal and social life ('human passions, such as with us dwell', 'Such as...by flesh and blood...may be understood'). Against such a background Milton's prefatory remarks on the verse of *Paradise lost* stand out boldly:

The measure is English heroic verse without rhyme, as that of Homer in Greek, and of Virgil in Latin; rhyme being no necessary adjunct or true ornament of poem or good verse, in longer works especially, but the invention of a barbarous age, to set off wretched matter and lame metre; graced indeed since by the use of some famous modern poets, carried away by custom, but much to their own vexation, hindrance, and constraint to express many things otherwise, and for the most part worse than else they would have expressed them...This neglect then of rhyme so little is to be taken for a defect, though it may seem so perhaps to vulgar readers, that it is

---

[1] For further material on Milton's relationship to his contemporaries and near-contemporaries up to 1730 see the chapters on 'Epic' and 'The writing, publication and editing of *PL*' in the volume called *PL: introduction* in this series, and the first chapter of Broadbent *Some graver subject* 1960.

rather to be esteemed an example set, the first in English, of ancient liberty recovered to heroic poem from the troublesome and modern bondage of rhyming.

Couplets were fast, compact and convivial. Milton's blank verse seemed, in contrast, aloof and unsociable; it was hard to imagine him in any social role – certainly not a 'Milton in the streets'. Andrew Marvell recognized the significance of the choice of blank verse in his complimentary poem *On Mr Milton's 'Paradise lost'*:

> Well mightst thou scorn thy readers to allure
> With tinkling rhyme, of thy own sense secure;
> While the town Bays writes all the while and spells,
> And like a pack-horse tires without his bells;
> Their fancies like our bushy points appear,
> The poets tag them, we for fashion wear.
> I too transported by the mode offend,
> And while I meant to 'praise' thee must 'commend'.
> Thy verse created like thy theme, sublime,
> In number, weight, and measure, needs not rhyme.

Milton's verse, like his theme, is felt to be outside time altogether – it escapes the clownishness of fashionable taste, but at a cost. 'Sublime', ironically, seems to mean 'irrelevant'. Marvell's couplets, like Waller's, aim at something lower but more solid than sublimity: it is no accident that rhyme compels a witty Marvell to 'commend' Milton rather than 'praise' him – the gesture exactly catches the hesitancy of early reactions to *Paradise lost*. Milton had no obvious role in the complicated plot of contemporary poetic relationships, in which poets as violently politically opposed to each other as the Tory Waller and the Whig Marvell swapped satiric couplets. They had the intimate relationship of enemies who spoke the same (poetic) language; Milton, his pre-Restoration political activities covered by the Act of Oblivion, remained outside contemporary issues.[1]

Readers had to feel their way gradually to a direct response to the poem: the first illustrated edition was published in 1688, the first volume of annotation came out in 1695, but probably the most important trend took longer to develop. Before *Paradise lost* could become an active influence, Milton's version of classicism had to be

---

[1] In 1660 the returned royalists (soon to be christened 'Tories') took a very moderate line: less than thirty individuals were *not* covered by the general act of pardon. With the development of party politics in the 1670s and 80s protest and 'opposition' became to an extent institutionalized as part of a (relatively) stable political system. But this 'Whig' opposition was itself conservative compared with Milton's position; it absorbed some of the political ideas of the Interregnum, but others (like regicide) went underground until the late 18th century.

placed in some working relationship to current poetic idiom. What was required was rationalization and explanation, and it was the critic Addison who more than anyone provided it, and provided at the same time the first authoritative version of 'Milton'.

The early 18th century: epic mock epic

an ancient, but born two thousand years after his time

JONATHAN RICHARDSON 1734

Thought of as a 'modern', Milton lacked the saving graces of intimacy and argumentative relevance; approached as an 'ancient', his remoteness and assurance were virtues. This adjustment of perspective took place between 1690 and 1730, with Addison's essays in *The spectator* (1712) providing the most powerful statement of the new attitude.

Paradoxically, it was by becoming an ancient that Milton became relevant and modern; an important factor in establishing his claims to classicism was *On the sublime* by Longinus.[1] It was this late classical critic, rather than the more usual authorities Aristotle and Horace, who provided justification for placing Milton alongside Homer. Longinus praised rhetorical boldness and energy rather than correctness, and Addison wrote:

> I must also observe with Longinus, that the productions of a great genius, with many lapses and inadvertencies, are infinitely preferable to the works of an inferior kind of author, which are scrupulously exact and conformable to all the rules of correct writing.   *Spectator* no. 291

Addison lays particular stress on the fact that epic language was always, and should be, removed from current usage, and he praises precisely those aspects of the poem that set it above and apart. The stylistic faults he picks out can often be excused as the lapses of a 'great genius'; some, however, are the faults of a modern. Addison regrets Milton's excursions into wit, satire and contemporary usage; these 'failings' – Satan's punning, the satiric description of the Limbo of Fools (*PL* III), and what he labels 'idiomatic ways of speaking' in general – he sees as a deviation into the 'false refinements' and 'vicious taste' of 'modern writers'. 'Milton' for Addison was essentially 'sublime'.

[1] Nothing (not even his name) is known about the author of *On the sublime (peri hupsos)*; but it was for a long time attributed to 'Longinus', and is usually referred to that way. *On the sublime* was written in the 1st century AD and translated into English in the 17th.

Addison distanced Milton from the present, and in doing so made him easier to accommodate; he severed the more obvious links between the poet and his contemporaries in order to establish the original, epic status of *Paradise lost*:

Milton...by the choice of the noblest words and phrases which our tongue would afford him, has carried our language to a greater height than any of the English poets have ever done before or after him, and made the sublimity of his style equal to that of his sentiments. no. 285

In a way this is merely an extension of Marvell's line, 'Thy verse created like thy theme, sublime...' but the tone has changed to one of unqualified approval. 'This peculiar English', as Jonathan Richardson called it in his *Explanatory notes* on the poem in 1734, was enthroned as *the* language of epic. And by a natural if unexpected progression, 'Milton's English' became *the* style to mimic in mock-epic:

High on a gorgeous seat, that far outshone
Henley's gilt tub, or Flecknoe's Irish throne,
Or that where on her Curlls the public pours
All-bounteous, fragrant grains, and golden showers,
Great Theobald sat... ALEXANDER POPE *Dunciad variorum* II I

The relations between mock epic and 'straight' epic are always complicated. The relations between Milton and Pope are especially diverse and ambiguous, because 'Milton' for Pope is a two-faced figure: both Addison's classical genius, and a typically presumptuous modern radical.

To appreciate the subtlety with which Pope used Milton, it is necessary for a moment to look back at Dryden. He was a Tory, and became a Roman Catholic, and while he admired Milton, made little use of his achievement. For Dryden the symbolism of the fall held a very different message:

All that our monarch would for us ordain
Is but to enjoy the blessings of his reign.
Our land's an Eden, and the main's our fence,
While we preserve our state of innocence...
O! Let it be enough that once we fell,
And every heart conspire with every tongue
Still to have such a king, and this king long.
Prologue to *The unhappy favourite* by John Banks 1681

The state of innocence was the title of the couplet opera Dryden had made out of *Paradise lost* in 1674: stylistically, religiously, politically, he occupied the pole opposite to Milton. His sceptical and conservative rhetoric stresses the dangers of exploring the ways of kings, or of God:

For every man is building a several way; impotently conceited of his own model and his own materials: reason is always striving, and always at a loss; and of necessity it must so come to pass while 'tis exercised about that which is not its proper object. Let us be content at last to know God by his own methods; at least, so much of him as he is pleased to reveal to us in the sacred scriptures; to apprehend them to be the word of God is all our reason has to do; for all beyond it is the work of faith, which is the seal of heaven impressed upon our human understanding.   Preface to *Religio laici* 1682

Compare Milton's *Areopagitica* (1644): 'while the temple of the Lord was building...there must be many schisms and many dissections made in the quarry and in the timber...neither can every piece of the building be of one form'. With all the obvious scope for debate, Dryden does not directly take issue with Milton; instead he mocks later, lesser apostles of the sublime, like the 'Trew-Blew-Protestant Poet' Thomas Shadwell:

> The hoary prince in majesty appeared
> High on a throne of his own labours reared...
> His brows thick fogs, instead of glories, grace,
> And lambent dullness played around his face...
> *Mac Flecknoe* 106 (1684)

There is a pervasive allusion here to the style of *Paradise lost*, but Dryden, rather scornfully, keeps his distance; he does not pay Milton the compliment of specific quotation. It is at moments like this, however, that Dryden sets the pattern for Pope's cunningly contrived echoes of Milton. Pope's *Dunciad variorum* of 1729 attacks contemporary poets and poetasters for their bathetic pretensions to sublimity; like Dryden he contrasts them ('thick fogs, instead of glories') with the great classical writers they attempt to rival. Allusion to Milton in this context is nicely ambiguous, since Milton can be *both* an aspiring modern (like Dryden's 'Trew-Blew' hero), *and* an established classic.

Pope defines his own position and his own values very accurately, by using Milton as a point of reference. He makes Dryden's mock-epic technique harder-hitting by literal echoing of lines and phrases from Milton. His attitude to *Paradise lost* when he thought about it as a modern undertaking was intensely sceptical:

> Know then thyself, presume not God to scan;
> The proper study of mankind is man.   *Essay on man* II

This echoes Dryden, and further back, Waller; Pope's rhyme (scan/man) offers a handy emblem of the right bounds of human vision – bounds that Milton's claim to inspiration transcended. Four lines from Pope's *Imitations of Horace* (1737) encapsulate mockingly Milton's Satanic presumption:

> Milton's strong pinion now not heaven can bound,
> Now serpent-like, in prose he sweeps the ground,
> In quibbles, angel and archangel join,
> And God the Father turns a school-divine.   II i 99

(It should perhaps be mentioned here too that Dryden had supported Satan as the hero of *Paradise lost*.) Pope in these lines seems to share wholeheartedly Dryden's sense that any man – but especially a poet – should be constantly aware of his own limitations.

Elsewhere, though, Pope subscribes to Addison's image of Milton as sublime; this ambivalence leads him to use Milton's style in 'straight' as well as mock-epic contexts. The very lines about Satan's elevation he borrowed (and deflated) in the *Dunciad* are echoed by Pope, with serious appreciation, in his translation of Homer's *Iliad*: 'High on a throne, with stars of silver graced...' (XVIII 457). Even in his translation of Homer, however, Pope does not really *absorb* Milton's style. One sign of the high degree of awareness with which he borrowed from Milton, is the fact that he tends to use the same phrase or line not once, but several times, in different contexts. This suggests that he thought of his borrowings as quotations, a style quite distinct from his own, a separate element in his mosaic of allusions to other poets. This element he could use with a unique degree of precision, because, unlike Homer and Virgil, Milton can be quoted in English.

Milton's grand gestures are used to expose the pretensions of dwarfish moderns who set themselves up as poets and critics, but some of the irony almost invariably rubs off on Milton. For example Milton's distinctive line 'Smit with the love of sacred song' (*PL* III 29) becomes in the *Dunciad variorum* 'And smit with love of poesy and prate' (II 350). By echoing Milton's grand claim to inspiration Pope is able to belittle some faceless and anonymous contemporaries who think themselves equally 'inspired' (as they are – by the goddess Dulness). But the original claim itself, thus 'translated', begins to look not a little suspect; Pope invites his readers to think again about *any* poet who takes himself so seriously. Yet in the *Epistle to Mr Jervas* Pope echoes the same line ('Smit with the love of sister-arts...') apparently without irony; so he does in his Homer (*Iliad* I 354 'Smit with the love of honourable deeds').

Pope's 'Milton' then, shows sometimes one, sometimes the other of his faces, and sometimes both at once: the bathetic line in the

Dunciad II 271, 'In naked majesty great Dennis stands', evokes the
newly created splendour of Adam and Eve, in *PL* IV 290, who 'In
naked majesty seemed lords of all'. Here, as often, the allusion is
brief, but serves to sharpen our sense of the ludicrous ungainliness of
the modern 'great', by inviting comparison with the primitive
grandeur of Milton's figures (and of Milton). *Dunciad* II 301–2:

> Sudden, a burst of thunder shook the flood.
> Lo Smedley rose, in majesty of mud!

Pope, in a footnote, invites us to relate to *PL* II 266: 'And with the
majesty of darkness round Covers his throne.'

Together with (probably) Swift and Arbuthnot, Pope composed a
treatise of mock-advice for pretend-poets, *On the art of sinking in
poetry* (1727), a parody of Longinus' *On the sublime*. The quality Pope
finds in contemporary epic is not the Sublime, but the Profound, the
depths of bathos:

It must always be remembered that Darkness is an essential quality of the
Profound, or if there chance to be a glimmering, it must be as Milton
expresses it, 'No light, but rather darkness visible'. The chief figure of this
sort is 'The hyperbole, or impossible'.

In the same ironic vein he offers a 'receipt to make an epic poem',
again glancing, it would seem, at Milton:

For a battle. Pick a large quantity of images and descriptions from Homer's
Iliads, with a spice of two of Virgil, and if there remain any overplus, you
may lay them by for a skirmish. Season it well with similes, and it will make
an excellent battle.

It is the majestic, 'dark', sublime aspects of Milton's style that
both fascinate and repel Pope. Sublimity may be appropriate in
an ancient, but a modern, concerned with the all-too-human
rather than the superhuman, must evolve a more 'natural and easy'
style:

Milton's style, in his *Paradise lost*, is not natural; 'tis an exotic style. As his
subject lies a good deal out of our world, it has a particular propriety in those
parts of the poem: and, when he is on earth, wherever he is describing our
parents in paradise, you see he uses a more easy and natural way of writing.
Though his formal style may fit the higher parts of his own poem, it does
very ill for others who write on natural and pastoral subjects.

Pope reported in Spence's Anecdotes

The compliment he pays Milton in his poetic allusions is a real one,
but it has its dubious side. 'Milton' as quoted by Pope, is made to

seem naive, unironic, unselfconscious – unaware, for example, of the potential ridiculousness of the war in heaven. Sometimes, when he echoes Milton, Pope is parodying something that is *already* ironic in *Paradise lost*.

The most complex, and amusing example is Pope's use of epic 'machinery' in *The rape of the lock* (1714), which tells in inflated terms the story of how a belle, Belinda, loses (ambiguously) a lock of her hair (or her innocence) to a daring beau. Pope's 'sylphs' share the doubtful corporeality of Milton's angels, pointing the contrast between their whimsical triviality and the (supposed) high seriousness of Milton's spiritual battles. The Baron gets out his scissors to cut off the fatal lock:

> The peer now spreads the glittering forfex wide, ~
> To enclose the lock; now joins it, to divide;
> Even then, before the fatal engine closed,
> A wretched Sylph too fondly interposed;
> Fate urged the shears, and cut the Sylph in twain
> (But airy substance soon unites again):
> The meeting points the sacred hair dissever
> From the fair head, for ever and for ever!   III 147

Pope's note refers his readers to *Paradise lost* VI:

> the sword
> Of Michael from the armoury of God
> Was given him tempered so, that neither keen
> Nor solid might resist that edge: it met
> The sword of Satan with steep force to smite
> Descending, and in half cut sheer, nor stayed,
> But with swift wheel reverse, deep entering shared
> All his right side; then Satan first knew pain,
> And writhed him to and fro convolved; so sore
> The griding sword with discontinuous wound
> Passed through him, but the ethereal substance closed
> Not long divisible.   IV 320

Milton's angelic war echoes with grim irony renaissance romantic epics; Pope's very un-spiritual encounter parodies Milton with malicious delight. But perhaps the most far-reaching irony is that Milton has now been made to seem an embodiment of the very tradition he himself mocked:

> Not sedulous by nature to indite
> Wars, hitherto the only argument
> Heroic deemed, chief mastery to dissect

308

> With long and tedious havoc fabled knights
> In battles feigned...   *PL* IX 27

Epic mock epic mock epic...Pope has drawn Milton into the complex web of living and developing poetic relationships, and in every major critical battle over language or aims in poetry, Milton remains a vital participant. The role Pope cast him in, distinctive, majestic, inspired – and humourless – misses out, certainly, important features of the complete man, but it preserved the essential ingredient. That is, it has as much of the irritant as the classic about it. Poets who admired Milton far more whole-heartedly than Pope found themselves swamped by his influence, and instead of producing parody, and developing their own poetic identities, produced pastiche that deadened both their own and Milton's originality.

Mid to late 18th century: pastiche and pastoral

> I steal impatient from the sordid haunts
> Of strife and low ambition, to attend
> Thy sacred presence in the sylvan shade.
>   MARK AKENSIDE *Pleasures of imagination* 1744

Pastoral, traditionally, was the genre of the young poet. Before he attempted the major epic themes of civilization, he schooled himself in the more limited and intense imagery of the natural world. He had somehow to impress his own particular identity and purpose on the 'purling streams' and 'enchanted groves' of pastoral, symbols worn thin by generations of poets. In writing pastoral, Milton, or Pope, had felt themselves under pressure from the great poets of the past; the very limitation of the genre acted on them as a hot-house environment, in which they absorbed and transmuted the influence of their predecessors. But during the 18th century pastoral lost that sense of vital pressure and preparation, and became, for many poets, the only genre. In *L'allegro* and *Il penseroso* (and even more explicitly in *Lycidas*) Milton looked forward to his own future in poetry as well as back to Spenser and Shakespeare. The 'I' figures in these poems are consciously immature and developing:

> And when the sun begins to fling
> His flaring beams, me goddess bring
> To archèd walks of twilight groves,
> And shadows brown that Sylvan loves.   *Penseroso* 131

But 18th-century poets took on the stance of *il penseroso* without any sense of its limitations:

O! bear me then to vast embowering shades,
To twilight groves, and visionary vales,
To weeping grottoes, and prophetic glooms!

JAMES THOMSON Autumn first pub 1730

For Thomson (1700–48) *il penseroso* was a role he sustained throughout his life: poetry and pastoral were for him synonymous; to be a
poet was to be open always to the impressions of nature and the
influence of the past. The prevailing popular image of the poet in the
mid-century was not active and individualistic, but so receptive as to
be nearly anonymous. Akenside (1721–70) provided a telling description of the new stereotype: 'The ingenious youth, whom solitude
inspires'. The careers of these poets take a significantly different
shape from Milton's or Pope's. Their early poems – Thomson's
Seasons (1726–30), Akenside's *Pleasures of imagination* (1744) – are
their major works, tinkered with and rewritten over many years.
Whereas Pope drew Milton into the undignified farce of mock-epic
battles, Thomson and Akenside are passive under his influence:

His was the treasure of two thousand years,
Seldom indulged to man, a godlike mind,
Unlimited, and various, as his theme;
Astonishing as chaos; as the bloom
Of blowing Eden fair; soft as the talk
Of our grand parents, and as heaven sublime.

THOMSON Summer 1727

In their landscapes *Paradise lost* merges into Milton's early poems;
out of fragments from different contexts in Milton, they forge a whole
pastoral world, a region of the imagination at moments more solid
and real to them than any actual landscape:

I looked, and lo! the former scene was changed:
For verdant alleys and surrounding trees,
A solitary prospect, wide and wild,
Rushed on my senses. 'Twas a horrid pile
Of hills with many a shaggy forest mixed,
And many a sable cliff and glittering stream.
Aloft, recumbent o'er the hanging ridge,
The brown woods waved; while ever-trickling springs
Washed from the naked roots of oak and pine
The crumbling soil...

AKENSIDE Pleasures of imagination II 271

This is a poetry inspired by poetry, and fundamentally *about* poetry,
as much as nature. It is serious pastiche, an attempt to re-experience
and recreate poetic effects the writers find moving and impressive:

310

> These are the haunts of meditation, these
> The scenes where ancient bards the inspiring breath,
> Ecstatic, felt; and, from this world retired,
> Conversed with angels, and immortal forms,
> On gracious errands bent: to save the fall
> Of virtue struggling on the brink of vice;
> In waking whispers, and repeated dreams...
>
> THOMSON *Summer* revised version

Thomson here combines an echo of *Comus* (455–60) with a more generalized suggestion of Raphael's visit to Adam and Eve in *Paradise lost* v. Poetic creation is associated not with exploration and prophecy, but with memory:

> The balmy walks of May
> There breathe perennial sweets; the trembling chord
> Resounds for ever in the abstracted ear,
> Melodious...   AKENSIDE *Pleasures of imagination* III 368

A favourite illustration to Milton's works at this period showed the poet reclining, eyes raptly closed, in a 'solitary prospect, wide and wild', as the Muse whispered to him. Man, the point of growth and change that disrupted Milton's paradise, is absent, or plays only a minor picturesque part. As Swift noted, there is no significant action in Thomson's *Seasons*: 'I am not over fond of them, because they are all description, and nothing is doing, whereas Milton engages me in actions of the highest importance.' Their 'Milton', despite the apparent potency of his influence, is in the end a static figure; he is omnipresent but impersonal, fragmented, diffused and pastiched. They thought of Milton, as they thought of themselves, as passive in relation to his world.

The imaginations of the pastoral poets circle round the great poets of the past, endlessly appreciative and responsive, but the future is blank. The language of poetry tended to become fixed and narcissistic: to write, was to write about poetry. Milton had already written the poem of the universe:

> High on some cliff, to heaven up-piled,
> Of rude accéss, of prospect wild,
> Where, tangled round the jealous steep,
> Strange shades o'erbrow the valleys deep,
> And holy Genii guard the rock,
> Its glooms embrown, its springs unlock,
> While on its rich ambitious head
> An Eden, like his own, lies spread:
> I view that oak, the fancied glades among,

By which as Milton lay, his evening ear,
From many a cloud that dropped ethereal dew,
Nigh sphered in heaven, its native strains could hear;
On which that ancient trump he reached was hung:
   Thither oft, his glory greeting,
   From Waller's myrtle shades retreating,
With many a vow from Hope's aspiring tongue,
My trembling feet his guiding steps pursue;
   In vain! – Such bliss to one alone
   Of all the sons of soul was known;
   And Heaven and Fancy, kindred powers,
   Have now o'erturned the inspiring bowers,
Or curtained close such scene from every future view.

In these lines from his *Ode on the poetical character* William Collins reaches beyond pastiche: it is one of the few great poems on poetry, and in it he realizes, with painful sensitivity, the necessity of failure. Milton's paradise is lost forever; the poet cannot recapture it.

In other quarters the passive image of Milton came under more frank attack; not all Thomson's contemporaries shared his view of Milton as a dreamer. In 1730 Aaron Hill wrote to the novelist-to-be Samuel Richardson that he would 'be afraid of his *heart*, who, in the fame and popularity of Milton, could lose sight of his malice and wickedness'. Hill was voicing the attitudes that Richardson first made explicit in his novel *Pamela* (1740), the doubts of a newly articulate middle class, out of sympathy with the image of the 'great man'. The new bourgeois puritanism (very unlike Milton's), with its morality of self-restraint, and obsessive respect for order, propriety and property, detected a revolutionary boldness in Milton that the public eulogy ignored.[1] Dr Johnson, an admirer of Richardson's novels, struck the same note much later in his *Life* of Milton (1779):

Milton's republicanism was, I am afraid, founded in an envious hatred of greatness, and a sullen desire of independence; in petulance impatient of control, and pride disdainful of superiority. He hated monarchs in the state, and prelates in the church; for he hated all whom he was required to obey.

[1] The Puritan tradition had undergone far-reaching changes and splits by the mid-18th century: for Richardson (1689–1761) 'virtue' had come to mean a matter of verbal delicacy, class-consciousness and respectability, as much as a state of mind and soul. The rigid and feminine code of middle-class morality he embodied in his novels between 1740 and 1754 is the descendant of the kind of 'cloistered virtue' Milton dismissed in *Areopagitica* (1644) as superficial and corrupt. Ian Watt in *The rise of the novel* (1957) traces the development of the proto-Victorian, suburban taboos that characterized Richardson's morality. Milton's views on divorce, even without his revolutionary political position, would have sufficed to scandalize Richardson and many of his readers.

It is to be suspected, that his predominant desire was to destroy rather than establish, and that he felt not so much the love of liberty as repugnance to authority.

Johnson is here deliberately casting Milton in the role of his own Satan as an active and subversive Milton very different from the image of the poet put about by Thomson and Akenside. Johnson's irony neutralizes his apparent praise of Milton, as he restates the conventional tributes, giving them sinister Satanic undertones:

The appearances of nature, and the occurrence of life, did not satiate his appetite of greatness. To paint things as they are requires a minute attention, and employs the memory rather than the fancy. Milton's delight was to sport in the wide regions of possibility; reality was a scene too narrow for his mind. He sent his faculties out upon discovery, into worlds where only imagination can travel, and delighted to form new modes of existence, and furnish sentiment and action to superior beings, to trace the counsels of hell, or accompany the choirs of heaven.

This is the portrait of a poet of restless vision, not the poet's poet of memory.

Edward Young's *Conjectures on original composition* (1759) was symptomatic of the mix-up of attitudes towards Milton. He addressed the work to Richardson, the realist whose novels he admired, but he also invited poets to emulate Milton's brand of originality, not to pastiche blank verse but to *write* it, as a symbol of human potential: 'Blank is a term of diminution; what we mean by blank verse, is, verse unfallen, uncursed; verse reclaimed, reinthroned in the true language of the gods.' This prophetic note is not fulfilled in Young's own poetry; but gradually, in the late 18th century, 'Milton' comes to mean a style of thinking and feeling, more than a style of writing; his influence helped to undermine the passive literary orthodoxy established in his name.

The 19th century: 1 The romantic rewriting of 'Paradise lost'

that we may foresee and avoid
The terrors of creation, and redemption, and judgement
WILLIAM BLAKE *Jerusalem* 1804–20

In the romantic period Milton underwent the most thorough metamorphosis of his literary historical career. The solitary and preeminent bard of an inbred poetical establishment survived as an official image, but was largely an anachronism. The new Milton was hardly one figure at all; instead he was subsumed into the characters of his poetry, who took on a remarkable supraliterary life. Satan, Adam, Eve – and even Milton's God – became more vivid, three-dimensional and present to writers and readers, than the poem which had given them that distinctive shape. They appeared in contemporary literature, very recognizably Milton's characters (though with new names), but their new 'creators' refused to accept Milton's interpretation of their actions and relationships. Both poets and novelists felt that the plot of *Paradise lost* could (and should) have turned out differently. Illustrators of Milton, and painters inspired by him, parallel this trend – Fuseli, Blake and John Martin have none of the diffidence of earlier illustrators. They each see the poem from a new perspective: Fuseli, in the late 18th century, excludes Milton's God entirely from his universe; Blake (1757–1827) centres attention on the human pair; Martin, influenced by the new technology of the 19th century, is fascinated by the sheer engineering of the poem – especially the building of Pandemonium. Particular scenes and individual characters were abstracted from Milton and developed to what writers and painters felt to be their logically and imaginatively 'right' conclusions.

But these new conclusions have more the air of questions than answers. Writers scrutinized *Paradise lost*, as they scrutinized their own society, for the hidden oppressor. Satan was a tyrant, but did Milton's God make him one? Does goodness somehow 'cause' evil if, like the Lady in *Comus*, it substitutes chastity for charity, and refuses to mingle with the 'fallen'? They focused longingly on certain incidents – Satan standing 'stupidly good' or Comus ravished by the beauty of the Lady's song – as moments when it could have all gone otherwise. Numerous works explored these 'other' possibilities sparked off by the dramatic vitality of Milton's characters. The whole pattern of relationships in his poetry (between mankind and God, man and woman, good and evil) is shifted and recombined in romantic literature, as if in a kaleidoscope.

It is on the more experimental frontiers of romantic writing that this new approach to Milton begins. *Paradise lost* was especially useful as a source for novelists who wanted to import into prose fiction the boldness and scope of epic, to suggest that timeless events could happen *now* and in the future, not merely in the mythic past. While the realistic novel (in the tradition of Richardson and Jane Austen) was preoccupied with the minutiae of daily life, in the Gothic novel, prose infused with Miltonic overtones ceased to celebrate the normal and the reasonable. Gothic writers turned instead to the eccentric and the sublime, suggesting that man was too grand, too evil, or too good to be measured by the standards of 'propriety', 'manners' or even common sense. Fiction, whether in prose or in verse, developed a distinctive 'Miltonic' style that paid less attention to local verbal details than to large-scale melodramatic effects. It was, in a sense, debased coin, but it was a *lingua franca*, a shared language, that had a wide popular currency. Milton's characters, with their clear outlines and vivid energy, inspired writers and readers to think in images, and by leaps and bounds, rather than by logical progression.

Satan above all Milton's characters was an obsessive topic. He united, in one provoking image, the two types that preoccupied moral and political thought – the tyrant and the victim. The popular fictional image of Satan is first established in the novels of Ann Radcliffe (1764–1823); in her Satanic villains the tyrant is unequivocally uppermost. Characters like Montoni in her *Mysteries of Udolpho* (1794) are explicitly condemned (though there remains a residue of unexplained attraction):

He delighted in the energies of the passions; the difficulties and tempests of life, which wreck the happiness of others, roused and strengthened all the powers of his mind, and afforded him the highest enjoyments of which his nature was capable...He had...many and bitter enemies; but the rancour of their hatred proved the degree of his power; and as power was his chief aim, he gloried more in such hatred than it was possible he could in being esteemed...his eyes seemed almost to flash fire, and all the energies of his soul appeared to be roused for some great enterprise.

Here the reader is allowed to have it both ways – to explore the perverse daring of a character who defies the moral order, while comfortably labelling him evil and disowning him. The same formula – and recognizably the same style – is at work in Byron's verse tales:

> As if within that murkiness of mind
> Worked feelings fearful, and yet undefined.
> .   .   .   .
>
> He hated man too much to feel remorse,
> And thought the voice of wrath a sacred call,
> To pay the injuries of some on all.
> He knew himself a villain...   *The corsair* 1814
>
> There was in him a vital scorn of all:
> As if the worst had fallen which could befall,
> He stood a stranger in this breathing world,
> An erring spirit from another hurled...   *Lara* XVIII 1814

Here, however, one hears the note of 'might have been', the hints of past injuries which suggest that it could have been otherwise, and anticipate the later more fully developed sense of Satan as victim. Staunton, the hero-villain of Scott's *Heart of Midlothian* (1818), is similarly equivocal:

The fiery eye, the abrupt demeanour, the occasionally harsh, yet studiously subdued tone of voice, – the features, handsome, but now clouded with pride, now disturbed by suspicion, now inflamed with passion...those eyes that were now turbid with melancholy, now gleaming with scorn, and now sparkling with fury – was it the passions of a mere mortal they expressed, or the emotions of a fiend, who seeks, and seeks in vain, to conceal his fiendish designs under the borrowed mask of manly beauty? The whole partook of the mien, language, and port of the ruined archangel.

Later in the novel, Scott answers his rhetorical question in the negative: Staunton is not to be considered as human, and redeemable, but (symptom of his author's embarrassment) he is made the agent of his own destruction.

These authors circled round the problem of evil, but they had begun to redefine it. Evil they suggest is a state of tragic deprivation – the tyrant turns on others in a hopeless attempt to assuage some inner anguish. In Scott, the villain destroys himself; in *Frankenstein* (1817), however, Mary Shelley challenges the complacency of creators who disown their own creations. *Frankenstein* deliberately courts comparison with *Paradise lost*, not merely in terms of its presentation of evil, but in its questioning of 'good'. The hero of the title is a complex melodramatic character, who unites elements of Satan, Prometheus and Faust. Driven by an insatiable lust for knowledge and power, he usurps the role of God, and creates a living being which, as though to symbolize the perversity of its creator, appears a vile and misshapen monster. Frankenstein, haunted by the grotesque creature he loathes, becomes a lost spirit, wandering the earth (like Byron's heroes), destroying everything he touches:

Thus not the tenderness of friendship, nor the beauty of earth, nor of heaven, could redeem my soul from woe: the very accents of love were ineffectual. I was encompassed by a cloud which no beneficial influence could penetrate.

Frankenstein claims the reader's sympathy, but so too does the monster he created and cast off; from Frankenstein's point of view the monster is a devil, his inner spirit matching the ugliness of his body. But from the monster's point of view, Frankenstein is a god, who made him, and then left him to wander and sin in an alien and lonely world:

'Shall each man,' cried he, 'find a wife for his bosom, and each beast have his mate, and I be alone? I had feelings of affection, and they were requited by detestation and scorn. Man! you may hate; but beware!...Are you to be happy while I grovel in the intensity of my wretchedness? You can blast my other passions; but revenge remains – revenge, henceforth dearer than light or food!'

For the monster has learned to be evil: he began in childlike ignorance, loving and longing to be loved, but then, spurned, feared, and hated by 'good' and beautiful people:

Shall I not then hate them who abhor me? I will keep no terms with my enemies. I am miserable, and they shall share my wretchedness...The guilty are allowed, by human laws, bloody as they are, to speak in their own defence before they are condemned.

Mary Shelley puts into his mouth words that echo Satan in *Paradise lost* IV, but our attitude to them has been redirected. The monster, who in the beginning had appeared guilty, now seems innocent: in this paradoxical world, the 'innocent' who recoil from ugliness and evil are themselves guilty. The 'God' who set his creature free –

> Left him at large to his own dark designs,
> That with reiterated crimes he might
> Heap on himself damnation... *PL* I 213

– this creator is called in question. The book poses, with mind-teasing irony, the problem of ultimate responsibility.

Frankenstein shows something of the scope and power of the new 'translations' of *Paradise lost*. In Shelley's epic drama *Prometheus unbound*, Milton's version of the relationship between God and Satan is again questioned; Shelley's Prometheus begins, like Satan, by cursing and hating the god who has condemned him to eternal torment, but as the first act develops he begins to see that it is the god who inflicts suffering, rather than the victim, who is in real need of pity. And as soon as Prometheus stops thinking and feeling like a victim, Jupiter's power over him diminishes. Just as Mary Shelley argued that conscious goodness may cause evil, Shelley suggests that self-centred suffering can actually cause and perpetuate the repression under which it suffers. Blake's hellish *London* carries a similar message; there, the 'manacles' which bind the poor are 'mind-forged'.

For these writers *Paradise lost* has become a psychological allegory, a poetic fiction which reflects the collective, underlying, attitudes that shape societies and religions. For Shelley, Milton's god is the essence of the repressive myths humanity has perversely created and suffered under: Milton's epic, far from being a celebration of the divinely appointed order, is in Shelley's reading more like a diagnosis of conflicting aspects of human nature:

Milton has so far violated the popular creed (if this shall be judged to be a violation) as to have alleged no superiority of moral virtue to his god over his devil. And this bold neglect of a direct moral purpose is the most decisive proof of the supremacy of Milton's genius. He mingled as it were the elements of human nature as colours upon a single palette, and arranged them in the composition of his great picture according to the laws of epic truth, that is, according to the laws of that principle by which a series of actions of the external universe and of intelligent and ethical beings is calculated to excite the sympathy of succeeding generations of mankind.

A defence of poetry 1821

Shelley was openly scornful of the 18th century's passive Milton:

the sacred Milton was, let it ever be remembered, a republican, and a bold inquirer into morals and religion.   Preface to *Prometheus unbound* 1820

He saw himself as continuing Milton's enquiries, in re-applying his myth to the present: the poem, as he read it, *invited* questions and doubts.

For a radical writer to use 'the sacred Milton' as an ally was itself a snub to the literary establishment; and to rewrite Milton in popular fiction was a spectacular way of denying literary 'class distinction'. Balzac admired *Melmoth the wanderer* (1820) by Charles Robert Maturin (initially a priest and schoolteacher); it is a good example of the democratization of Milton (in this period everyone, even Mary Shelley's monster, read *Paradise lost*): the novel is full of verbal echoes of Milton, but Maturin is centrally interested, not in God and Satan, but in the brief relationship between Satan and Eve. His Satanic 'hero' Melmoth, doomed to eternal life and eternal damnation, wanders the earth until he arrives at an 'Indian isle' where 'flowers bloomed, and foliage thickened, without a hand to pluck, or a lip to taste them'. In this frankly paradisal setting he finds his destined victim:

The stranger approached, and the beautiful vision approached also, but not like a European female with low and graceful bendings, still less like an Indian girl with her low salaams, but like a young fawn, all animation, timidity, confidence, and cowardice, expressed in almost a single action. She sprung from the sands – ran to her favourite tree; – returned again with her guard of peacocks, who expanded their superb trains with a kind of instinctive motion, as if they felt the danger that menaced their protectress, and, clapping her hands with exultation, seemed to invite them to share in the delight she felt in gazing at the 'new flower that had grown in the sand'.

Immalee combines traits of Milton's Eve and Shakespeare's Miranda – she is touchingly innocent and seductively vulnerable. The confrontation with Melmoth, for the reader who recognizes the submerged archetypes, is surrounded with anticipatory irony: 'He experienced a sensation like that of his master when he visited paradise, – pity for the flowers he resolved to wither for ever.' At this point, however, as in *Frankenstein*, the expected fails to happen: instead of Melmoth infecting Immalee with his perverse and hopeless philosophy, she seduces him: 'In the logic of the schools he was well-versed, but in this logic of the heart and of nature, he was "ignorance itself".' Once more, the roles are reversed; it is the helpless villain who has to try to resist the temptation of innocence. He loves her, despite himself, and she returns his love: 'Her graduating attitudes beautifully, but painfully, expressed the submission of a female heart devoted to its object, to his frailties, his passions, and his very crimes.' This all-embracing love baffles the 'tempter'; her refusal to cast him off, to turn away in disgust, makes it impossible for him to destroy her (a comparison with the lady in *Comus* would be apt here). Instead, he denies his own evil: 'Let her be anything *but mine*!' The 'devil' is defeated by innocence and love.

The efficacy of works like *Melmoth* is admittedly limited – the style is redundant, over-stated, and heavily dependent on earlier literature. This relative crudity, however, is not entirely a limitation; in popularizing the complex moral themes it deals with, it generates the powerfully symbolic characters of major fiction. The 'Miltonic' figures that appear on the Gothic fringe of fiction in the early years of the century find their full fictional liberty in the novels of the Brontës, twenty years later. In *Jane Eyre* and *Wuthering Heights* (1847) the over-obvious reversals of attitude in earlier Gothic novels are embedded in freshly observed detail, though the distinctive pattern still emerges. In *Jane Eyre* the Satan–Eve relationship is a paradigm for working out the confrontation between the sexes. Rochester is certainly no Adam:

I am sure most people would have thought him an ugly man; yet there was so much unconscious pride in his port; so much ease in his demeanour; such a look of complete indifference to his own external appearance; so haughty a reliance on other qualities, intrinsic or adventitious, to atone for the lack of mere personal attractiveness, that in looking at him, one inevitably shared the indifference, and even in a blind, imperfect sense, put faith in the confidence.

Jane, however, is not so vulnerable as Eve: though she seems power-less – dependent, plain, innocent – she proves to have the strength to tame the devil in Rochester. His strength is undermined by his inner hell:

Pain, shame, ire – impatience, disgust, detestation – seemed momentarily to hold a quivering conflict in the large pupil dilating under his ebon eyebrow. Wild was the wrestle which should be paramount; but another feeling rose and triumphed: something hard and cynical; self-willed and resolute: it settled his passion and petrified his countenance.

Both of them have to overcome their own peculiar temptations alone – Rochester (as above) is tempted to accept that he is damned, to become calculatingly evil; Jane is tempted into a puritan 'paradise' of (for her) easy self-denial. Her 'Adam' would be the faultless St John Rivers:

I looked at his features, beautiful in their harmony, but strangely formidable in their still severity; at his brow, commanding, but not open; at his eyes, bright and deep and searching, but never soft; at his tall imposing figure; and fancied myself in idea *his wife*.

'Oh! It would never do!' – Jane, like Rochester, is a hybrid and passionate being: in their final reunion, Charlotte Brontë deliberately invokes *Samson agonistes*, to emphasize her conviction that it is only through evil and suffering that true bliss is achieved:

His form was of the same strong and stalwart contour as ever: his port was still erect, his hair was still raven black: nor were his features altered or sunk: not in one year's space, by any sorrow, could his athletic strength be quelled or his vigorous prime blighted. But in his countenance I saw a change: that looked desperate and brooding – that reminded me of some wronged and fettered wild beast or bird, dangerous to approach in his sullen woe. The caged eagle, whose gold-ringed eyes cruelty has extinguished, might look as looked that sightless Samson.
  And reader, do you think I feared him in his blind ferocity? – If you do, you little know me. A soft hope blent with my sorrow that soon I should dare to drop a kiss on that brow of rock.

The heroines of Ann Radcliffe or Scott would have recoiled with fear and incomprehension, saving their innocence, whereas Jane, 'ani-mating and piquant', has something of Dalilah about her. 'Woman' is no longer helplessly pure, 'man' is no longer the suspect villain: they still, though, retain the Miltonic overtones that give them spiritual, rather than social stature. They are compounded of warring passionate extremes, not of socially desirable (or undesirable) qualities.

In her preface to Emily's *Wuthering Heights*, Charlotte Brontë draws particular attention to the epic patterning of the novel; she compares the hero Heathcliffe to 'a magnate of the infernal world', and speaks of 'the decree which dooms him to carry hell with him wherever he wanders'. In the novel too the characters themselves think in terms of metaphysical polarities: 'If I were in heaven' says the first Catherine, 'I should be extremely miserable', and her daughter reiterates the theme, comparing her version of 'paradise' with that of her passionless Adam:

He wanted all to lie in an ecstasy of peace; I wanted all to sparkle and dance in a glorious jubilee. I said his paradise would be only half alive; and he said mine would be drunk.

The endless metamorphoses Miltonic images and characters undergo is a tribute to the vitality the poem had for its readers. The authors who rewrite him are inspired to bring his plot to a new conclusion by the concreteness and energy of his characters, who seemed to demand a life beyond the structure that contained them.

William Blake (1757–1827) came at the beginning of this period, but since he anticipated its central themes, he sums up perhaps better than anyone the universality of Milton and the Miltonic. As poet, painter and commentator Blake returned repeatedly to Milton as a source of inspiration; his illustrations of Milton are unique in their intensity and coherence – but like his Miltonic poems, they constitute a radical interpretation, not a passive following after. He rewrote *Paradise lost* many times, from many angles, in a fury of mingled inspiration and frustration:

Without contraries is no progression. Attraction and repulsion, reason and energy, love and hate, are necessary to human existence.
    From these contraries spring what the religious call good and evil. Good is the passive that obeys reason. Evil is the active springing from energy.
    Good is heaven. Evil is hell...

Those who restrain desire, do so because theirs is weak enough to be restrained; and the restrainer, or reason, usurps its place and governs the unwilling.
    And being restrained, it by degrees becomes passive, till it is only the shadow of desire.

The history of this is written in *Paradise lost*, and the governor or reason is called Messiah.

And the original archangel, or possessor of the command of the heavenly host, is called the Devil or Satan, and his children are called Sin and Death.

But in the book of *Job*, Milton's Messiah is called Satan.

For this history has been adopted by both parties.

. . . .

Note: The reason Milton wrote in fetters when he wrote of angels and God, and at liberty when of devils and hell, is because he was a true poet and of the Devil's party without knowing it.

The marriage of heaven and hell 1793

For Blake the theological system that enabled Milton to label God 'good' and Satan 'evil' was a weak and evasive rationalization. In seeking to end the essential struggle between 'contraries' an uninspired orthodoxy (which Milton here subscribed to) had cut Christianity off from its sources of so-called hellish energy (so-called by those whom Blake with bitter irony calls 'the religious'). Blake's attitude to Milton is obscured by this constant battle with names: Milton's God is Blake's version of the Devil, the eternal negation, 'a pretence of religion to destroy religion'; and Milton's Satan, in the opening books of the poem, is Blake's Messiah, though stained and distorted by Milton's failure of vision:

> And this is the manner of the Sons of Albion in their strength:
> They take the two contraries which are called qualities, with which
> Every Substance is clothed, they name them Good & Evil,
> From them they make an abstract, which is a negation...
> A murderer of its own body...   *Jerusalem* (1804–20) I 10

Milton's God, and the system of which he was the centre, was 'an abstract' in Blake's sense, pagan and materialistic:

in Milton, the Father is destiny, the Son a ratio of the five senses, and the Holy Ghost vacuum!   *Marriage of heaven and hell*

Despite himself, however, and despite the mask of order and restraint he wore, Milton had retained unawares the substance of his original inspiration: in Blake's reading the latent significance of *Paradise lost* was contrary to its surface direction. While its plot recorded the suppression of vitality, Milton's energy – expressed most clearly through Satan – refuted his moribund theology.

In *The marriage of heaven and hell*, *Jerusalem* and *Milton* (1804–8) Blake struggled to free Milton and his living characters – Satan, the angels, Adam and Eve – from the web of false judgements, compromise solutions, and misleading names in which they had become enmeshed. These extraordinary Prophetic Books do not have unifying plots like *Paradise lost*; instead incidents, characters and motifs are continuously reiterated and transmuted, so that an event like the fall can happen again and again, and characters shed one false identity after another. He pieces together vestiges and fragments of Milton's system, 'striving with systems to deliver individuals from those systems', using ironically the very terms and names he wants to banish. In *Milton* Blake resurrects Milton himself as the chief speaker in the poem; now, in eternity, Milton is seeking to rid himself of the weakness and resentment which dictated his negative conception of God:

> 'There is a negation, and there is a contrary:
> The negation must be destroyed to redeem the contraries.
> The negation is the spectre, the reasoning power in man:
> This is a false body, and encrustation over my immortal
> Spirit, a selfhood which must be put off and annihilated alway.
> To cleanse the face of my spirit by self-examination...
> I come...'   *Milton* II 47

'Milton' is now able to relive the composition of *Paradise lost* without inhibiting and falsifying his inspiration. The metre Blake uses here and in *Jerusalem* is symbolic of this greater freedom; parodying Milton's famous preface, he wrote:

When this verse was first dictated to me, I considered a monotonous cadence, like that used by Milton and Shakespeare and all writers of English blank verse, derived from the modern bondage of rhyming, to be a necessary and indispensable part of verse. But I soon found that in the mouth of a true orator such monotony was not only awkward, but as much a bondage as rhyme itself. I therefore have produced a variety in every line, both of cadences and number of syllables.   Preface to *Jerusalem*

The metre Blake arrived at was hypnotically irregular and incantatory; in *Milton* Milton the speaker has little of the personal voice of *Paradise lost*. He is stripped clean of the accidents (as Blake regarded them) of personality, opinion and prejudice. He realizes that the figure he worshipped as 'God' should truly be called Satan, and that the figure he originally called Satan was himself; in the following passage the names are, accordingly, redistributed:

> In the eastern porch of Satan's universe Milton stood and said:
> 'Satan! my spectre! I know my power thee to annihilate
> And be a greater in thy place and be thy tabernacle,

A covering for thee to do thy will, till one greater comes
And smites me as I smote thee and becomes my covering.
Such are the laws of thy false heavens; but laws of eternity
Are not such; know thou, I come to self annihilation.
Such are the laws of eternity, that each shall mutually
Annihilate himself for others' good, as I for thee.'   *Milton* ii 43

Something more complex than a reversal of roles is going on here, however: 'Milton' is casting off the impulse to rule and conquer, along with the need to explain and rationalize – the weaknesses that were expressed in his 'God'. Here a composite Milton–Satan recaptures his original messianic purpose, and God–Milton with his 'false heavens' recedes into mere illusion. The speaker's voice has lost all trace of the historical Milton. Blake has taken one element in Milton's style – the prophetic, apocalyptic strain – and developed it until Milton begins to merge with Jesus and the Old Testament prophets of the Millennium. This is Milton in his 'eternal lineaments', an embodiment of the perennial revolutionary, provoking always new visions, overturning even his own certainties.

In Blake Milton's presence is literal and forceful: but it would be misleading to talk of Milton's 'influence' on Blake, for the term implies something more automatic and passive than the reality. The same is true of the other writers of the Gothic-Romantic movement. It was the free play of Milton's characters, the feeling of potentiality aroused by his poems, not the monumental 'finish' of his achievement, that made him so central. Through Miltonic situations, characters and images writers struggled to recast the conventional universe. Error, ugliness, irregularity, 'evil', were not to be dismissed by the easy device of damnation, but resurrected to be loved, fought, and pitied. These writers were anti-realists, and their radicalism in ideas and emotions went with a bold neglect of form: 'morality and unity', said Blake, 'are secondary considerations, and belong to philosophy and not to poetry'. The Gothic 'Milton' inspired stylistic slackness, and over-easy appeals to stereotypes along with freedom from moral and social conventions. The rewritten *Paradise lost* was deliberately open-ended: whether written by Blake or Mary Shelley, it avoided the authoritarian tone of Milton's narrative voice. This is one of the reasons why the semi-underground appropriation of Milton between 1780 and 1850 coincided with the emergence of a new official 'placing' of Milton. There was a general reaction, eventually effective, against highly coloured theoretic gestures, whether in Milton or in contemporary novelists. The 'Milton' of prophetic writers was a Milton without a personal style; his formal power, the finesse of his verse-structure and diction had been by-passed. As Blake observed 'this history has been adopted by both parties', and it was not 'the Devil's party' but the deeply conservative Wordsworth who adopted the power of Milton's rhetoric. Words-worth used the voice of Milton, and Milton's God, against the prophets of change:

> Vain-glorious generation! what new powers
> On you have been conferred? what gifts, withheld
> From your progenitors, have ye received,
> Fit recompense of new desert? what claim
> Are ye prepared to urge, that my decrees
> For you should undergo a sudden change;
> And the weak functions of one busy day,
> Reclaiming and extirpating, perform
> What all the slowly-moving years of time,
> With their united force, have left undone?
> By nature's gradual processes be taught;
> By story be confounded! Ye aspire
> Rashly, to fall once more; and that false fruit,
> Which, to your overweening spirits, yields
> Hope of a flight celestial, will produce
> Misery and shame. But wisdom of her sons
> Shall not the less, though late, be justified.

The excursion (1814) IV 278

Wordsworth's 'Providence' (here speaking) has the same ponderous, unanswerable tone as Milton's God. The 'Milton' who speaks through Wordsworth is not Shelley's 'bold inquirer into morals and religion', but the representative of all that is stable and unchanging, of inherited sanctities and conscious purity.

Wordsworth's appeal to 'nature's gradual processes' was part of a move towards particularity and detail, both in prose and poetry. This trend was anti-heroic, consciously adapted to the actual scale of individual lives, and the limitations imposed on man by his nature. Milton was invoked (as above, by Wordsworth) to help set up this new perspective, but once set up it radically reduced his importance. The 'Milton' that emerged to be praised by the Victorians was a much less powerful presence than the 'Milton' loved and hated by Blake.

The 19th century: 2 The emergence of the Victorian Milton

I am not sure that the greatest man of his age, if ever that solitary super-lative existed, could escape these unfavourable reflections of himself in various small mirrors; and even Milton, looking for his portrait in a spoon, must submit to have the facial angle of a bumpkin.

GEORGE ELIOT Middlemarch 1872

Still the official figurehead of the central tradition in English poetry, the Victorian Milton was a more precarious figure than any of the earlier images. From the outside this new image appears hardly distinguishable from the Milton of the mid-18th century. But though he is still 'solitary', 'sublime' and 'unique', the expected epithets conceal a lack of substance: he was without the pervasive relevance of Thomson's 'bard' as well as the energetic contrariness of Blake's. Milton's absolute authority was delegated to Wordsworth and Keats almost imperceptibly; they did not effectively cast him off (though Keats consciously tried to); instead, in different ways, they absorbed, transmuted, and handed on to the next age what was most immediately usable in his achievement. This was a new treatment for Milton, and the long-term effect of it was a subtle erosion of his poetic identity. When people thought of him apart from Wordsworth and Keats, he was left with the qualities the age did not care for. William Morris summed them up at the end of the century: 'The union in his works of cold classicism with puritanism (the two things which I hate most in the world) repels me so that I *cannot* read him.'

Such frank dislike was, however, untypical of the century – most explicit comments are admiring. Perhaps the most famous tribute to Milton in English poetry is Wordsworth's resonant sonnet written in 1802:

> Milton! thou shouldst be living at this hour:
> England hath need of thee: she is a fen
> Of stagnant waters: altar, sword, and pen,
> Fireside, the heroic wealth of hall and bower,
> Have forfeited their ancient English dower
> Of inward happiness. We are selfish men;
> O! raise us up, return to us again;
> And give us manners, virtue, freedom, power.
> Thy soul was like a star, and dwelt apart;
> Thou hadst a voice whose sound was like the sea:
> Pure as the naked heavens, majestic, free,
> So didst thou travel on life's common way,
> In cheerful godliness; and yet thy heart
> The lowliest duties on herself did lay.

Though the poem has an air of voicing a collective attitude to Milton, certain phrases stand out as giving a new emphasis to the traditional picture – 'life's *common* way', 'the *lowliest* duties'. The high purpose implied in the Miltonic tone is also a humble one, implying the submission of the individual spirit to a larger, older, more inclusive order. This 'Milton' is a bulwark against anarchy – which Wordsworth feared would arise from the moral and social changes he deplored. He makes a deliberate effort to transpose the ritual sublimity of Milton's style into timeless, simple, homely contexts:

> For I must tread on shadowy ground, must sink
> Deep – and, aloft ascending, breathe in worlds
> To which the heaven of heavens is but a veil.
> All strength – all terror, single or in bands,
> That ever was put forth in personal form –
> Jehovah – with his thunder, and the choir
> Of shouting angels, and the empyreal thrones –
> I pass them unalarmed. Not Chaos, not
> The darkest pit of lowest Erebus,
> Nor aught of blinder vacancy, scooped out
> By help of dreams – can breed such fear and awe
> As fall upon us often when we look
> Into our Minds, into the Mind of Man –
> My haunt, and the main region of my song.   *The recluse* 1814

Wordsworth attaches rhetorical grandeur to 'substantial things'; his Miltonic cadences and diction are embedded in a simpler idiom, and the metaphysical scheme of *Paradise lost* is transferred to an immanent deity, hidden deep in the rhythms of the natural world, and the patterns of personal and domestic life. Miltonic polysyllables – 'gravitation', 'vicissitude', 'diurnal' – act for Wordsworth as an austere reminder of the ancient and regular rhythm of experience:

> A slumber did my spirit seal;
> I had no human fears;
> She seemed a thing that could not feel
> The touch of earthly years.
>
> No motion has she now, no force;
> She neither hears nor sees;
> Rolled round in earth's diurnal course,
> With rocks, and stones, and trees.

In this pared-down lyric, the one latinate epithet 'diurnal' carries an extraordinary force: and demonstrates how very thoroughly Wordsworth absorbed and redirected Miltonic mannerisms.

Some of the domestic, homely quality of Wordsworth rubbed off on Milton, though it co-existed rather uneasily with the facts of his life:

No one can rise from the perusal of this immortal poem without a deep sense of the grandeur and the purity of Milton's soul, or without feeling how susceptible of domestic enjoyments he really was, notwithstanding the discomforts which actually resulted from an apparently unhappy choice in marriage.

Coleridge's attempt here (in a lecture of 1818) to adapt Milton to a more local and personal angle of vision required some special pleading. The reader, tutored by Wordsworth, learned to find, like De Quincey, 'Paradise for his eye, in Miltonic beauty, lying outside his windows, paradise for his heart, in the perpetual happiness of his own fireside' (*William Wordsworth* 1839). Milton's own life, and those aspects of his work that most obviously reflected it, seemed alien and recalcitrant: 'repulsion was the law of his intellect' said De Quincey, 'he moved in solitary grandeur'.

Keats' influence, though in many ways opposed to Wordsworth, tended also to alienate poets and readers from Milton. His best-known comment on Milton is brief and telling – 'Life to him would be death to me.' This came in a letter of 1819, after he had abandoned unfinished his epic *Hyperion*. Keats' dissatisfaction with the poem focused on Milton's influence:

The *Paradise lost* though so fine in itself is a corruption of our language – it should be kept as it is unique – a curiosity – a beautiful and grand curiosity. The most remarkable production of the world. A northern dialect accommodating itself to Greek and Latin inversions and intonations.

The opening lines of *Hyperion* will demonstrate something of the extent of Milton's presence:

> Deep in the shady sadness of a vale
> Far sunken from the healthy breath of morn,
> Far from the fiery noon, and eve's one star,
> Sat grey-haired Saturn, quiet as a stone,
> Still as the silence round about his lair;
> Forest on forest hung about his head
> Like cloud on cloud.

The opening cadence, 'Deep in the shady sadness...Sat' is reminiscent of 'High on a throne of royal state...Satan exalted sat', the characteristic Miltonism Pope had parodied. But unlike Pope, Keats was attempting to make Milton's style his own. Keats' notes in his copy of *Paradise lost* indicate the particular feeling about Milton he was trying to capture: 'Milton has put vales in heaven and hell with the very utter affection and yearning of a great poet'. Keats, it seemed, wanted the atmosphere of Milton, without the metaphysical categories. The other echoes of Milton in the lines above – the fall of Mulciber, the lament of Samson – have the *feel* of 'fallenness' without the hard and fast theological implications. Keats' myth is very much a personal exploration of the poet's nature, and perhaps the Miltonic mode became oppressive because it threatened all the time to weigh down the exploratory impulse, to import irrelevant implications of fixity and certain knowledge. At any rate, the recast *Fall of Hyperion* is no less 'Miltonic' in local details, though it does capture more of 'the intense pleasure of not knowing' Keats felt in Milton's description of Pandemonium:

> Turning from these in awe, once more I raised
> My eyes to fathom the space every way;
> The embossed roof, the silent massy range
> Of columns north and south, ending in mist
> Of nothing... *The fall of Hyperion* 181–5

As in Wordsworth, there is still much of Milton, but it is a 'Milton' less metaphysical, less systematic, less insistent on 'fixities and definites'.

Both Wordsworth and Keats, though to very different ends, promoted an intense empiricism which was profoundly suspicious of plans, programmes, projected institutions – all things Milton himself had been energetically concerned in. What distinguishes them from Blake and Shelley (as far as Milton is concerned) is a positive distaste for plots for human betterment. They redirected attention on to the texture and feel of Milton's verse, and away from its issues and arguments. And this, gradually, produced a Milton mainly interesting in terms of technique. Many Victorian tributes to Milton are quietly damning while they praise – Tennyson's *Milton* (1863), written in 'alcaics', is a virtuoso example:

> O mighty-mouthed inventor of harmonies,
> O skilled to sing of Time or Eternity,
> God-gifted organ-voice of England,
>   Milton, a name to resound for ages;
> Whose Titan angels, Gabriel, Abdiel,
> Starred from Jehovah's gorgeous armouries,
> Tower, as the deep-domed empyrean
>   Rings to the roar of an angel onset –

>   Me rather all that bowery loneliness,
>   The brooks of Eden mazily murmuring,
>   And bloom profuse and cedar arches
>   Charm...

Tennyson gracefully refuses to find the war in heaven anything more than distantly picturesque. Blake had taken issue with Milton directly, but the Victorian reaction remained indirect; they left him on his pedestal while simply turning away.

George Eliot, in her novels and her criticism, sums up the convictions that edged Milton out from his central role. Casaubon in *Middlemarch* (1872), the worn scholar with the failing sight, seeking 'The Key to all Mythologies', is a dreadful indictment of all seekers for the absolute answer, the clue to the universe. Casaubon is not a literal portrait of Milton, but George Eliot several times invokes Milton to characterize him,[1] her heroine, Dorothea, marries Casaubon because of the power of the myth of the 'great man':

> She felt sure that she would have accepted the judicious Hooker if she had been born in time to save him from that wretched mistake he made in matrimony; or John Milton when his blindness had come on...The really delightful marriage must be that where your husband was a sort of father and could teach you even Hebrew if you wished it.

Casaubon is a pathetic and destructive figure, pitiful in his obsessive and useless scholarship, callous in his ignorance of the depth and complexity of human emotions. He searches eagerly in the dusty labyrinths of worn-out legends for a 'truth' that lies all around him in the texture of everyday experience. Casaubon is a judgement on Milton, by being a judgement on all those who show

> that impiety towards the present and the visible which flies for its motives, its sanctities, and its religion, to the remote, the vague, and the unknown.
>   GEORGE ELIOT Essay on Edward Young 1857

The 'archangelic tone', the 'telescopic view of human beings' seems to George Eliot merely 'egoism turned heavenwards', ignoring the constant and pressing need for human communication. Typically, these comments are directed against the 18th-century Miltonist Edward Young, rather than directly against Milton. But they would

---

[1] One of the living 'originals' George Eliot used for Casaubon is supposed to have been her friend the scholar Mark Pattison who published in 1879 a handbook on Milton in which heremarked that 'The appreciation of Milton is the last reward of consummated scholarship'.

cover Milton too; the earlier attempt by Wordsworth and Coleridge to invent an intimate and domestic 'Milton' in tune with the age had failed drastically.

George Meredith's *The egoist* (1879) pillories yet again the larger-than-life figure of the 'great man', in his self-deluded anti-hero Sir Willoughby Patterne:

> 'I tell you these things. I quite acknowledge they do not elevate me. They help to constitute my character. I tell you most humbly that I have in me much too much of the fallen archangel's pride.'
>
> Clara bowed her head over a sustained indrawn breath.
>
> 'It must be pride,' he said in a reverie superinduced by her thoughtfulness over the revelation and glorying in the black flames demoniacal wherewith he crowned himself.
>
> 'Can you not correct it?' said she.

Here the heroine's reaction can be profitably compared with that of the Gothic heroines of Maturin or the Brontës: she is unimpressed. The Satanic hero has become a 'tragic comedian', desperately trying to avoid seeing his real littleness. Clara's subdued mirth and exasperation make him seem like an actor strayed from some improbable melodrama. Meredith's sonnet *Lucifer in starlight* (1883), while allowing him more dignity, places him again in a universe where heroic postures are irrelevant:

> On a starred night Prince Lucifer uprose.
> Tired of his dark dominion swung the fiend
> Above the rolling ball in cloud part screened,
> Where sinners hugged their spectre of repose.
> Poor prey to his hot fit of pride were those.
> And now upon his western wing he leaned,
> Now his huge bulk o'er Afric's sands careened,
> Now the black planet shadowed Arctic snows.
> Soaring through wider zones that pricked his scars
> With memory of the old revolt from Awe,
> He reached a middle height, and at the stars,
> Which are the brain of heaven, he looked, and sank.
> Around the ancient track marched, rank on rank,
> The army of unalterable law.

This is a universe empty of personality – there is no opponent, and there can be no battle. Lucifer himself is but a star, his orbit fixed by an impersonal (neither lovable nor hateable) law. As in Tennyson's tribute the studied assurance of prosody and diction owes a lot to Milton, but the final effect is one of unreality.

It was perhaps impossible to take Milton seriously without

thoroughly disliking him. To appreciate Milton it became necessary to separate his poetry from his life and his ideas; Matthew Arnold's over-careful comments make this explicit:

The Milton of religious and political controversy, and perhaps of domestic life also, is not seldom disfigured by want of amenity, by acerbity. The Milton of poetry, on the other hand, is one of those great men 'who are modest'.

Milton 1888

The 'egoism' of the religious and political Milton, his confidence in his own integrity 'In darkness, and with dangers compassed round And solitude', was alien to the sophisticated and sensitive conservatism of the age, in all its forms. Gerard Manley Hopkins (1844–89), Catholic convert, Jesuit priest and poet, however opposed to the scepticism of Eliot or Meredith, shared their sense of the irrelevance of Milton's polemical stance. He is typical of the goodness and the narrowness of Victorian responses to Milton; theologically at an opposite pole, in stressing the sinfulness of the exercise of personal judgement, and the importance of ritual, Hopkins is not interested in taking issue with Milton. What does interest him is the detail of Milton's metrical technique. He notes in a letter of 1878 that 'Milton is the great standard in the use of counterpoint':

In *Paradise lost* and *Regained*, in the last more freely, it being an advance in his art, he employs counterpoint more or less everywhere, . . . but the choruses of *Samson agonistes* are in my judgement counterpointed throughout; that is, each line (or nearly so) has two different coexisting scansions.

His friend, and later editor, Robert Bridges in his book *Milton's prosody* (final ed 1921) amplified and clarified Hopkin's discovery:

and where the 'iambic' system seems entirely to disappear, it is maintained as a fictitious structure and scansion, not intended to be read but to be imagined as a time-beat on which the free rhythm is, so to speak, syncopated, as a melody.

The minute accuracy of these observations, compared with the wholesale 'borrowing' of Miltonic episodes and characters in early Romantic poetry and fiction, is a measure of the dissociation of form and content he had undergone during the 19th century. Hopkins' study of Milton led him to the conclusion that:

when you reach that point the secondary or 'mounted rhythm'...overpowers the original or conventional one and then this becomes superfluous and may be got rid of; by taking that last step you reach simple sprung rhythm. Milton must have known this but had reasons for not taking it.

Hopkins abandons the Miltonic superstructure, the 'original or conventional' scansion, just as Keats had done away with the metaphysical superstructure of Milton's images. What he arrived at was a texture of continuous, particular rhythms, without the abstract and schematic 'time-beat'; instead of counterpoint between regularity and variation, necessity and free will, there is a mingling and interaction of variations:

Let life, waned, ah let life, wind

Off her once skeined stained veined variety / upon, all on two spools; part,
pen, pack

Now her all in two flocks, two folds – black, white; / right, wrong; . . .

Spelt from Sibyl's leaves

His detailed study of Milton implies great praise, but it results in something entirely un- or even anti-Miltonic. A comment in a letter Hopkins wrote to Bridges in 1888 is a fitting epitaph on the Victorian Milton: 'The effect of studying masterpieces is to make me admire and do otherwise.' By default rather than by active criticism, the stage was set for a full-scale revaluation of Milton's position. As a result of fifty years of more or less faint praise and 'doing otherwise', his reputation seemed inflated. The poets and critics of the earlier 20th century – Ezra Pound, T. S. Eliot, F. R. Leavis – turned a general sense of Milton's irrelevance into an open attack on his traditional 'placing'. Stripped of his inherited aura, Milton was exposed to the kind of probing and irreverent attention reserved for fakes and forgeries. His reputation, though it had endured longer, had perhaps not much more validity than Waller's inflated 18th-century reputation.

Milton now

Milton's dislodgement, in the past decade, after his two centuries of predominance, was effected with remarkably little fuss.

F. R. LEAVIS *Revaluation* 1936

Leavis's ironic challenge caused (as no doubt it was meant to) a great deal of 'fuss'; there is no longer a secure consensus of admiration for Milton, but in its place a continuing debate about the importance and meaning of his achievement. Leavis's and Eliot's dismissive comments are still set as titles for essays:

although his work realises superbly one important element in poetry, he may still be considered as having done damage to the English language from which it has not wholly recovered.

T. S. ELIOT *A note on the verse of John Milton* 1936

333

the pattern, the stylized gesture and movement, has no particular expressive work to do, but functions by rote, of its own momentum, in the manner of a ritual. LEAVIS on Milton's verse *Revaluation*

The emphasis is on the sound, not the vision, upon the word, not the idea; and in the end it is the unique versification that is the most certain sign of Milton's intellectual mastership. ELIOT *Milton* 1947

The concentration on Milton's verse, however real the compliment, is inevitably, as with the Victorians, a slight to the man and his ideas. Both Eliot and Leavis found Milton the man impossible to like, or even to respect; there is a sense that he threatens them almost, that men like Milton are dangerous. This sorts oddly with their rather distant treatment of his poetry:

As a man he is antipathetic. Either from the moralist's point of view, or from the theologian's point of view, or from the psychologist's point of view, or from that of the political philosopher, or judging by the ordinary standards of likeableness in human beings, Milton is unsatisfactory.

Eliot here, in the opening of his 1936 essay, was making a lot of fuss; Leavis, while less absolute, was equally forceful: 'He has "character", moral grandeur, moral force; but he is, for the purpose of his undertaking, disastrously single-minded and simple-minded.' Robert Graves' *Wife to Mr Milton* (1943) explored this antipathy in domestic close-up, and found Milton, as George Eliot had found Casaubon, grossly inadequate. In his introduction Graves went further, suggesting why he found Milton not merely alien, but dangerous. He points out parallels between the 1640s and the 1940s:

The post-war Cromwellian solution of these political questions, which Milton endorsed, was drastic and unconstitutional – it would now be called 'undisguised Fascism'; and democratic journalists and politicians who quote with approval Wordsworth's 'Milton, thou should'st be living at this hour. England hath need of thee' should read, or re-read, Milton's life and works.

Curiously, this climax of denunciation, after nearly a century of hints and doubts, brought Milton much closer to his critics and readers: he had, as Leavis said, 'character'. *Paradise lost* was no longer, with Shakespeare and the Bible, an automatic part of every student's survival kit, and could now be read with curiosity (to see what happens) rather than with the weary expectation of 'sublimity'. What happened, and is still happening, is the sort of controversy Milton would have felt at home in, with personal libel, attacks on his morals, his learning and intelligence, his theology and his logic. The modern phase of Milton criticism looks like one of the pamphlet battles in which he engaged so energetically: even his defenders disagree violently about the sort of client they are defending.

The 'Milton' so disliked by Graves or Eliot was a man who chose 'perfection of the work' (in Yeats's terms) rather than 'perfection of the life', and the style he worked so hard to perfect seemed intolerably and irrelevantly 'grand'. Wallace Stevens in 1942 analysed the modern distaste for grandeur (which he calls 'nobility'):

It is hard to think of a thing more out of time than nobility. Looked at plainly it seems false and dead and ugly. To look at it at all makes us realise sharply that in our present, in the presence of our reality, the past looks false and is, therefore, dead and is, therefore, ugly; and we turn away from it as from something repulsive and particularly from the characteristic that it has a way of assuming: something that was noble in its day, grandeur that was, the rhetorical once. But as a wave is a force and not the water of which it is composed, which is never the same, so nobility is a force and not the manifestations of which it is composed, which are never the same. Possibly this description of it as a force will do more than anything else I can have said about it to reconcile you to it.   *The noble rider and the sound of words*

Stevens here goes a long way towards explaining both the difficulty of responding to Milton's kind of rhetoric, and its endless fascination. The 'force' he speaks of has come to be more and more distrusted, but also, indirectly, honoured. Milton's obsessive craftsmanship, his obstinate adherence to his vision, distorting language and character to get reality to 'fit' what he saw as God's logic – these are characteristics of the artist it is hard to discount. William Empson in *Milton's God* (1961) faces the problem squarely: Milton, he argues, tries hard to 'justify the ways of God', but succeeds in revealing the cruel absurdity of God's logic. On Satan's temptation of Eve he writes:

she feels the answer to this elaborate puzzle must be that God wants her to eat the apple, since what he is really testing is not her obedience but her courage, also whether her desire to get to Heaven is real enough to call all her courage out...As so often in human affairs, her problem is one of Inverse Probability. Thus a candidate in an Intelligence Test often has to think 'Which answer is the tester likely to have thought the intelligent one?', and this tends to make him irritated with the whole test. In this case, if God is good, that is, if he is the sort of teacher who wants to produce an independent-minded student, then he will love her for eating the apple.
                                        Milton's God rev ed 1965

Empson finds Milton's God all too human, and the celebrated 'order' of the poem's structure a desperate façade. His tone is deliberately 'disrespectful' and provocative, but his reading of the fall is thoroughly orthodox. The Jesuit Gerard Manley Hopkins explained the fall like this in a letter of 1883:

> Eve taking it as a challenge on God's part which it was the most subtle and refined morality in her to accept by an act of outward disobedience; Adam, not deceived about that but still deluded into thinking God would admire his generosity in sinning out of charity to his wife.

The point at issue here is not an academic one; the argument is about the limits of human freedom. C. S. Lewis (*A preface to PL* 1942), like Hopkins, regarded God's logic as a firm and reassuring framework which gave man a clear, though difficult duty:

> If conjugal love were the highest value in Adam's world, then of course his resolve would have been the correct one. But if there are things that have an even higher claim on a man, if the universe is imagined to be such that, when the pinch comes, a man ought to reject wife and mother and his own life also, then the case is altered, and then Adam can do no good to Eve...by becoming her accomplice.

The argument which justifies Milton's God, would justify Milton too for his God-like attitude to character and language.

This questioning and exploration of the ways of the artist who behaves like God is an urgent theme in modern fiction, as it was in Mary Shelley's *Frankenstein*. David Storey's *Radcliffe* (1963) is an example of the new Gothic, the sort of book that makes Milton's problems once more topical. His chronically introverted artist-hero commits a savage murder, and the book ends with him addressing the court at his trial:

> 'Oh, God!' he cried, shaking his fists at the court. 'I wanted something huge and *absolute*! I wanted an absolute! I wanted an ideal! I wanted an order for things!...I'm absolutely sure than men desire above all things a moral authority. And that it was from a will for moral authority that I acted, and with a sense of moral authority that *I* saw *everything*...This has been a trial before men when it should and could have been a trial before God.'

In the climate created by novels like this Milton's personality and his work are again very relevant. Is the man who seeks to impose his God, his vision on the world, insane, or has he a genuine spiritual insight into a universe wider, deeper, and more mysterious than that prosaically perceived by the realist? This century has seen (like the early 19th) a reaction against realism in the novel, and a movement back towards the epic's more schematic and metaphorical structure, where the artist is very conscious of the dangers of becoming an egoist.

The paradox that increasingly confronts writers is that the artist, the creator, turns so easily into the destroyer, excluding from 'his' world all untidiness, all disorder, and finally, all humanity: 'An artist with a murderer's hands; that was the ticket, the hieroglyphic of the times. For really it was Germany itself.' This is from Malcolm Lowry's *Under the volcano*, published in 1947, but set in 1939, where Fascism is diagnosed as the ultimate, literal expression of the desire for 'an absolute...an order for things'. Lowry's hero muses about the way in which man plays at being God, 'who sat as up in an organ loft somewhere playing, pulling out all the stops at random, and kingdoms divided and fell, and abominations dropped from the sky'. Lowry's novel shows how Milton's theme, and his handling of it, have become frighteningly relevant in modern fiction. God, Satan, Adam, Eve are roles each individual plays out, as Milton did in writing his poem, seeming sometimes guilty, sometimes innocent, sometimes in control, at others a mere puppet whose every action is predestined. We see Lowry's hero, early on in the book, using Milton's myth to try and work out his own position:

I've often wondered whether there isn't more in the old legend of the Garden of Eden, and so on, than meets the eye. What if Adam wasn't really banished from the place at all? That is, in the sense we used to understand it...What if his punishment really consisted...in his having to *go on living there*, alone, of course – suffering, unseen, cut off from God.

When 20th-century novelists and poets revisit Milton's paradise, they do so with conscious irony:

> Is there no change of death in paradise?
> Does ripe fruit never fall? Or do the boughs
> Hang always heavy in that perfect sky,
> Unchanging, yet so like our perishing earth,
> With rivers like our own that seek for seas
> They never find, the same receding shores
> That never touch with inarticulate pang?
> Why set the pear upon those river-banks
> Or spice the shores with odors of the plum?
> Alas, that they should wear our colours there,
> The silken weavings of our afternoons,
> And pick the strings of our insipid lutes!
>
> WALLACE STEVENS *Sunday morning*

Stevens' quietly insistent queries suggest that poets, not God, created paradise;[1] poets, Milton pre-eminently, have shaped our

---

[1] Cf. Yeats in *The tower* iii (1926): 'Death and life were not Till man made up the whole, Made lock, stock and barrel Out of his bitter soul.'

vision of the spiritual world, now perhaps, he suggests, fading, 'something that was noble in its day, the rhetorical once'. Its value, though, is changed rather than lost for Stevens. Instead of telling us about the universe outside us, the myth becomes a mirror in which we hope to discover ourselves. In Stevens' words, 'in the absence of a belief in God, the mind turns to its own creations and examines them'.

What it finds is, positively, the capacity to bring order out of chaos: again, a quotation from Stevens:

> Here I inhale profounder strength
> And as I am, I speak and move
>
> And things are as I think they are...

But this noble confidence, so easy to the poets of the past and to Milton, is constantly undermined; he cannot avoid seeing the other side of this magnificent figure:

> Like something on the stage, puffed out,
>
> His strutting studied through centuries.
>
> *The man with the blue guitar*

Stevens, like so many 20th-century writers, is constantly tempted to behave like Milton and to make an epic attempt to alter the world by the violence of imagination. Flann O'Brien's mock epic *At Swim-two-birds* (1939) was a (partly prophetic) exposé of this trend. He satirizes beautifully the self-indulgence of the Author-God; his novelist-hero spends all his day in bed, and even when he gets up takes care not to go near the windows (in case the reality 'out there' should clash with his version of it). Despite the farce, O'Brien's point is a very serious one, aimed directly at Milton and other 'moral' fictionalizers who, in separating the sheep from the goats, in punishing sin, are in danger of falling into the sadism and evil they condemn. O'Brien's novelist, like Frankenstein (or God) literally creates a character (Adam) made of flesh and blood, and O'Brien describes, in a scene that is both funny and horrific, what being created is like from 'Adam's' point of view:

He commenced to conduct an examination of the walls of the room he was in with a view to discovering which of them contained a door or other feasible means of egress. He had completed the examination of two of the walls when he experienced an unpleasant sensation embracing blindness, hysteria and a desire to vomit – the last a circumstance very complex and difficult of explanation, for in the course of his life he had never eaten. That this visitation was miraculous was soon evidenced by the appearance of a supernatural cloud or aura resembling steam in the vicinity of the fireplace. He dropped on one knee in his weakness and gazed at the long gauze-like wisps of vapour as they intermixed and thickened about the ceiling....A voice came from the interior of the cloud.

Are you there, Furriskey? it asked...

Yes sir, he answered.

The Author-God is both judge and jury: his creatures have no appeal against him. Furriskey is 'told' that he is a miserable sinner, predestined to damnation in his very conception (so that he feels the intoxicating effects of the fatal apple although he 'had never eaten'). This is an attack on Milton as well as Milton's God: O'Brien finds absurd and frightening the poet's power to evade and distort human reality, to seduce us into believing in, and acting on, his fictions.

Not that O'Brien, any more than Stevens, thinks that we can do without fictions, or that we can altogether avoid sometimes playing God, or the Devil: 'not only are we the heroes of our own life stories – we're the ones who conceive the story, and give other people the essences of minor characters'. This is John Barth in *The end of the road* (1958), an exploration of the destruction wrought by casting other people as 'minor characters', by refusing to see into their lives and allow them their independent existence. His 'hero' Jake uses a Miltonic role to evade responsibility for the seduction of his friend's wife:

I was The Unreason, or Not-Being and the two of us were fighting without quarter for possession of Rennie, like God and Satan for the soul of Man. This pretty ontological Manichaeism would certainly stand no close examination, but it had the triple virtue of excusing me from having to assign to Rennie any essence more specific than The Human Personality, further of allowing me to fornicate with a Mephistophelean relish, and finally of making it possible for me not to question my motives, since what I was doing was of the essence of my essence. Does one look for introspection from Satan?

Milton, like other great writers, has established some of the roles we play whether we mean to or not. In this century 'Milton' has been resented for this very reason, a kind of inverted tribute to his power. Attitudes to him seem to be divided into two main camps – the new Gothic or symbolist reworking of his themes by Lowry, Storey, Golding (*Free fall*);[1] and the satiric and mock-epic allusions reminiscent of Pope in O'Brien and Barth. What they all have in common is the feeling that

[1] Of which the heroine, Beatrice, is Dantesque; the novel is also an important commentary on Eliot. As we go to press, a possible third category, or reversion to the romantic re-writings, emerges in John Collier *M's PL: screenplay for cinema of the mind* New York 1973.

'Milton' is no longer a vague or unapproachable figure: writers feel that they are facing his problems; critics feel they can see through him, and round him:

> Adding a little human interest to the admittedly tricky client God, by emphasising his care to recover the reputation of his son...is about all that can be done to swing the jury when the facts of the case are so little in dispute. On the other hand, when he made the case as strong as he could for Satan, Eve and Adam, he somehow did not mind driving home the injustice of God, because God was not at that moment his client.
>
> EMPSON *Milton's God*

There is a new intimacy that goes with this new disrespect; John Barth's *The sot-weed factor* (1960) is set in the late 17th century; his hero is a would-be poet who sets out to 'out-epic' all previous epics (including Milton's). For him Milton's myth is a casual part of the business of growing up; he and his twin sister (whose initials reverse those of Adam and Eve)

> might spend an autumn morning playing at Adam and Eve out in the orchard...and when at dinner their father forbade them to return there, on account of the mud, Ebenezer would reply with a knowing nod, 'Mud's not the worst of't: I saw a snake as well.' And little Anna, when she had got her breath back, would declare, 'It didn't frighten *me*, but Eben's forehead has been sweating ever since,' and pass her brother the bread.

For novelists and poets, as for Eben and Anna here, Milton's poetry adds a symbolic undertone, that sometimes comes to the surface, but is never far away. 'Milton' now could be described as the 'fourth dimension' to much contemporary literature. His work provides a point of reference writers cannot afford to dispense with, especially since Milton forces on them the question of their own roles in the world. Even John Barth's improbable poet Ebenezer Cooke, cannot resist (any more than Barth) the temptation to emulate Milton:

> She wet his hand with tears...'I wish we two were the only folk on earth!'
> 'Eve and Adam?' The poet's face burned. 'So be it; but we must be God as well, and build a universe to hold our Garden.'

340

from *Little Gidding*

> If I think, again, of this place,
> And of people, not wholly commendable,
> Of no immediate kin or kindness,
> But some of peculiar genius,
> All touched by a common genius,
> United in the strife which divided them;
> If I think of a king at nightfall,
> Of three men, and more, on the scaffold
> And a few who died forgotten
> In other places, here and abroad,
> And of one who died blind and quiet,
> Why should we celebrate
> These dead men more than the dying?   T. S. ELIOT 1944

Index